The International Law of Human Rights in Africa

Basic Documents and Annotated Bibliography

Compiled by
M. HAMALENGWA, C. FLINTERMAN and E.V.O. DANKWA

Martinus Nijhoff Publishers
DORDRECHT / BOSTON / LONDON
United Nations Institute for Training and Research

Library of Congress Cataloging in Publication Data

The International law of human rights in Africa.

   Includes index.
   1. Human rights--Africa. 2. Human rights--Africa--
Bibliography. 3. Human rights. 4. Human rights--
Bibliography. I. Hamalengwa, M. II. Flinterman, C.,
1944-   . III. Dankwa, E. V. O.
LAW   342.6'085   87-20334
               346.0285

ISBN 90-247-3587-4

Published by Martinus Nijhoff Publishers,
P.O. Box 163, 3300 AD Dordrecht, The Netherlands

Sold and distributed in the U.S.A. and Canada
by Kluwer Academic Publishers,
101 Philip Drive, Norwell, MA 02061, U.S.A.

In all other countries, sold and distributed
by Kluwer Academic Publishers Group,
P.O. Box 322, 3300 AH Dordrecht, The Netherlands

All rights reserved
© 1988 by Kluwer Academic Publishers
Kluwer Academic Publishers incorporates the publishing programmes
of Martinus Nijhoff Publishers.
No part of the material protected by this copyright notice may be reproduced or utilized in any
form or by any means, electronic of mechanical, including photocopying, recording, or by any information storage and retrieval system, without written permission from the copright owners.

Printed in the Netherlands

MICHIGAN STATE UNIVERSITY LIBRARY
JUL 18 2025
WITHDRAWN

PLACE IN RETURN BOX to remove this checkout from your record.
TO AVOID FINES return on or before date due.

DATE DUE	DATE DUE	DATE DUE
JUN 1 3 1994	NOV 0 7 2008	MAR 0 8 2003
SEP 2 0 1995		
OCT 0 9 1996		
JUN 0 9 1998		
JAN 0 9 2006		

MSU Is An Affirmative Action/Equal Opportunity Institution
c:\circ\datedue.pm3-p.1

THE INTERNATIONAL LAW OF HUMAN RIGHTS IN AFRICA
Basic Documents and Annotated Bibliography

Preface

The Universal Declaration of Human Rights which was adopted by the General Assembly of the United Nations in 1948 set the standard for international and regional human rights instruments.* For instance, most of the provisions of both the International Covenant on Civil and Political Rights (1966) and the International Covenant on Economic, Social and Cultural Rights (1966) can be traced to provisions in the Universal Declaration of Human Rights. Equally, both the European Convention for the Protection of Human Rights and Fundamental Freedoms (1950) and the European Social Charter (1961) are similar in content to the International Covenant on Civil and Political Rights and the International Covenant on Economic, Social and Cultural Rights respectively. Also the American Convention on Human Rights (1969) is in important respects similar to the two International Covenants and European instruments mentioned above. Finally, on 27th June, 1981 at Nairobi, Kenya, the Assembly of Heads of State and Government of the Organisation of African Unity adopted the African Charter on Human and Peoples' Rights; and this instrument was also partly inspired by the Universal Declaration of Human Rights. It should however be noted, as is evidenced by some of the writing in the bibliography at the end of this book, that the idea that human beings should have certain rights had been accepted in Africa and elsewhere long before 1948. Nevertheless the scope and content of such rights varied over time and space.

With the coming into force of the African Charter of Human and Peoples' Rights** and with it a heightened interest in human rights in Africa, we considered it appropriate to bring together important human rights documents of African origin and concern. The term documents refers to Conventions, Resolutions, Declarations and Recommendations of both international (nota-

---

*The Charter of the United Nations particularly Articles 1, 13, 55, 56, 62, 68 and 76 provided a basis for the formulation of the Declaration.
**It came into force in October, 1986.

bly the U.N. and I.L.O.) and regional (O.A.U., Southern African States etc.) institutions and groupings. We also have included a few studies which we thought would aid and enlighten further work on human rights in Africa. For a similar reason, the International Court of Justice's Advisory Opinion on South African Presence in Namibia (1970) has been added to the collection. It is our hope that this compilation will stimulate greater discussion and analysis of human rights in Africa and that this will lead eventually to an effective respect, promotion and protection of human rights in Africa. More particularly, the work of the main implementing organ of the African Charter on Human and Peoples' Rights (the African Commission on Human and Peoples' Rights) can be facilitated by this compilation. Under Article 45 of the Charter the Commission is mandated, inter alia, 'to collect documents, undertake studies and researches on African problems in the field of human and peoples' rights . . .'. Equally, under Article 60 the Commission is expected to draw inspiration from international human and peoples' rights instruments, particularly those from Africa. Furthermore, the Commission is required, under Article 61, to consider 'other general or special international conventions, laying down rules expressly recognized by member states of the Organization of African Unity, [and] African practices consistent with international norms on human and peoples' rights . . .'. Many of the documents and instruments referred to in the above provisions are either reproduced or listed in this compilation. Also what has been or should be researched into can be determined, to a great extent, by the bibliography.

The book is divided into six parts. Part I contains African Instruments. Although only a few provisions of the Charter of the Organisation of African Unity have direct bearing on human rights, the whole Charter has been reproduced because we consider it so basic to Africa. Excerpts from the Third ACP-EEC Convention signed at Lomé on 8 December 1984 are included in this part because (1) it can be viewed rightly as aimed at the protection and promotion of human rights even though 'human rights' appear only in the preamble and (2) 44 African countries are parties to it.* The almost universal – and our particular – desire for an early end to Apartheid led us to devote part II to instruments on Southern Africa. In Part III the reader is presented with Global Instruments, some of which form a useful background to the whole collection. Part IV is devoted to Communications Concerning Human Rights. The United Nations deal with human rights complaints mainly through the Human Rights Commission of the Economic and Social Council. The Resolutions in this section of the book outline the procedure for dealing with Human Rights Communications by the Commission on Human Rights and its Sub-Commission on Prevention of Discrimination and Protection of Minorities. A

---

*The length of the Convention prevents its reproduction.

bibliography on Human Rights in English and French can be found in Part V. The first section of this part covers works of a general nature that can be said to be of universal concern whilst the second section concentrates on human rights in Africa. A similar distinction obtains in the section devoted to French materials. Part VI contains the Appendices, showing the status of ratification of Treaties by African countries and their reservations, declarations and objections.

This book has been made possible through the assistance, financial or otherwise of: The Stichting European Human Rights Foundation, London; York University, Toronto; International Institute of Human Rights, Strasbourg; International Labour Organisation, Geneva; The Hague Academy of International Law, The Hague; the Canadian Human Rights Foundation, Montreal; and The Netherlands Institute of Human Rights, Utrecht. We also are indebted to the University of Limburg through the Research and Study Group of its International Law Department for research, financial and secretarial assistance. We are grateful to all these institutions for their assistance. As regards individuals, we are grateful to Prof. Theo van Boven of the University of Limburg and former Director of the United Nations Division (now Centre) of Human Rights for his encouragement and in providing us with some of the documents. Fons Coomans of the same University kept drawing our attention to work on Human Rights in French. He also led us to the rich collection of work on human rights of the Netherlands Institute on Human Rights (SIM) from where most of the items under the bibliography in French were compiled, and we are extremely grateful to him. We also are thankful to Agnes Martijn for typing sections of the book.

Table of Contents

Preface V

PART I: AFRICAN INTERNATIONAL INSTRUMENTS 1

Treaties 3

1. African Charter on Human and Peoples' Rights (1981) 5
2. OAU Convention Governing the Specific Aspects of Refugee Problems in Africa (1969) 20
3. Charter of the OAU (1963) 28

Other Instruments 35

4. Law of Lagos (1961) 37
5. Declaration on the Problem of Subversion (1965) 47
6. Principles Concerning Treatment of Refugees (1966) 49
7. African Legal Process and the Individual (1971) 56
8. OAU Lagos Plan of Action for Food and Energy (1980) 60
9. Recommendations of the Gaborone Seminar on Human Rights and Development in Africa (1982) 70
10. ACP/EEC (Lomé III) Convention – Excerpts (1984) 73

PART II: INSTRUMENTS ON SOUTHERN AFRICA 79

Treaties 81

11. International Convention on the Suppression and Punishment of the Crime of *Apartheid* (1973) 83

12. International Convention against *Apartheid* in Sports (1986)	88

Other Instruments 97

13. The Freedom Charter (1955)	99
14. Lusaka Manifesto on Southern Africa (1969)	104
15. The International Court of Justice Advisory Opinion on South African Presence in Namibia (1970)	111
16. OAU Declaration of Dar es Salaam on Southern Africa (1975)	151

PART III: GLOBAL INSTRUMENTS 157

17. U.N. Charter Articles Pertaining to Human Rights	159

The International Bill of Human Rights 161

18. Universal Declaration of Human Rights (1948)	163
19. International Covenant on Economic, Social and Cultural Rights (1966)	168
20. International Covenant on Civil and Political Rights (1966)	175
21. Optional Protocol to the International Covenant on Civil and Political Rights (1966)	187

Treaties 191

22. Convention on the Prevention and Punishment of the Crime of Genocide (1966)	193
23. Convention concerning Freedom of Association and Protection of the Right to Organise (1948)	196
24. Convention concerning the Application of the Principles of the Right to Organise and to Bargain Collectively (1949)	203
25. Convention relating to the Status of Refugees (1951)	208
26. Convention on the Political Rights of Women (1952)	227
27. Convention on Consent to Marriage, Minimum Age for Marriage and Registration of Marriages (1962)	230
28. International Convention on the Elimination of All Forms of Racial Discrimination (1965)	234
29. Protocol relating to the Status of Refugees (1966)	243
30. Convention on the Elimination of All Forms of Discrimination against Women (1979)	248
31. Convention Against Torture and Other Cruel, Inhuman or Degrading Treatment or Punishment (1984)	258

Other Instruments 271

32. Statute of the Office of the U.N. High Commissioner for Refugees (1950) 273
33. Standard Minimum Rules for the Treatment of Prisoners (1955) 277
34. Declaration on the Granting of Independence to Colonial Countries and Peoples (1960) 296
35. General Assembly Resolution on 'Permanent Sovereignty Over Natural Resources' (1962) 298
36. Declaration on Territorial Asylum (1967) 301
37. Proclamation of Teheran (1968) 303
38. Declaration on Social Progress and Development (1969) 307
39. Declaration on Principles of International Law concerning Friendly Relations and Co-operation among States in accordance with the U.N. Charter (1970) 320
40. Universal Declaration on the Eradication of Hunger and Malnutrition (1974) 326
41. Declaration on the Establishment of a New International Economic Order (1974) 332
42. Programme of Action for the Establishment of a New International Economic Order (1974) 335
43. Charter of Economic Rights and Duties of States (1974) 347
44. Code of Conduct for Law Enforcement Officials (1979) 356
45. Declaration on the Elimination of All Forms of Intolerance and of Discrimination Based on Religion or Belief (1981) 362
46. Declaration on the Human Rights of Individuals who are not Nationals of the Country in which they live (1985) 365
47. List of other Global Instruments 370

PART IV: HUMAN RIGHTS COMMUNICATIONS 373

48. ECOSOC Resolution 728 F (xxviii) of 1959 375
49. ECOSOC Resolution 1235 (xlii) of 1967 377
50. ECOSOC Resolution 1503 (xlviii) of 1970 379
51. Resolution 1 (xxiv) of the Sub-Commission on Prevention of Discrimination and Protection of Minorities 382

PART V: BIBLIOGRAPHY 385

XII

PART VI: APPENDICES   405

I. Status of Ratification of Some of the Instruments as at 31 December
   1986   407

II. Declarations, Reservations and Objections   410

PART I

African International Instruments

Treaties

1.

African Charter on Human and Peoples' Rights

Adopted by the 18th Assembly of the Heads of State and Government of the Organization of African Unity (OAU) on 27 June 1981 at Nairobi, Kenya. Not yet entered into force.* As published in U.S. Congress, House of Representatives, Committee on Foreign Affairs, *Human Rights Docs.*, 1983, pp. 155 *et seq.*. See also 21 *I.L.M.*, 1982, pp. 59 *et seq.*. For the Charter of the OAU, see p. 1047, *I.O.I.*, II.H.1.a., and Louis B. Sohn, *Basic Documents of African Regional Organizations,* Oceana Publications, Inc., Dobbs Ferry, N.Y., 1981, Vol. I.

Preamble

The African States members of the Organization of African Unity, parties to the present convention entitled "African Charter on Human and Peoples' Rights",

Recalling Decision 115 (XVI) of the Assembly of Heads of State and Government at its Sixteenth Ordinary Session held in Monrovia, Liberia, from 17 to 20 July 1979 on the preparation of a "preliminary draft on an African Charter on Human and Peoples' Rights providing *inter alia* for the establishment of bodies to promote and protect human and peoples' rights";

Considering the Charter of the Organization of African Unity, which stipulates that "freedom, equality, justice and dignity are essential objectives for the achievement of the legitimate aspirations of the African peoples";

Reaffirming the pledge they solemnly made in Article 2 of the said Charter to eradicate all forms of colonialism from Africa, to coordinate and intensify their cooperation and efforts to achieve a better life for the peoples of Africa and to promote international cooperation having due regard to the Charter of the United Nations and the Universal Declaration of Human Rights;

Taking into consideration the virtues of their historical tradition and the values of African civilization which should inspire and characterize their reflection on the concept of human and peoples' rights;

Recognizing on the one hand, that fundamental human rights stem from the attributes of human beings, which justifies their national and international protection and on the other hand that the

---

*Entry into force requires ratification by a simple majority of OAU Member States.

reality and respect of peoples rights should necessarily guarantee human rights;

Considering that the enjoyment of rights and freedoms also implies the performance of duties on the part of everyone;

Convinced that it is henceforth essential to pay a particular attention to the right to development and that civil and political rights cannot be dissociated from economic, social and cultural rights in their conception as well as universality and that the satisfaction of economic, social and cultural rights is a guarantee for the enjoyment of civil and political rights;

Conscious of their duty to achieve the total liberation of Africa, the peoples of which are still struggling for their dignity and genuine independence, and undertaking to eliminate colonialism, neocolonialism, apartheid, zionism and to dismantle aggressive foreign military bases and all forms of discrimination, particularly those based on race, ethnic group, color, sex, language, religion or political opinions;

Reaffirming their adherence to the principles of human and peoples' rights and freedoms contained in the declarations, conventions and other instruments adopted by the Organization of African Unity, the Movement of Non-Aligned Countries and the United Nations;

Firmly convinced of their duty to promote and protect human and peoples' rights and freedoms taking into account the importance traditionally attached to these rights and freedoms in Africa;

Have agreed as follows:

Part I: Rights and Duties

Chapter I—Human and Peoples' Rights

Article 1

The Member States of the Organization of African Unity parties to the present Charter shall recognize the rights, duties and freedoms enshrined in this Charter and shall undertake to adopt legislative or other measures to give effect to them.

Article 2

Every individual shall be entitled to the enjoyment of the rights and freedoms recognized and guaranteed in the present Charter without distinction of any kind such as race, ethnic group, color, sex, language, religion, political or any other opinion, national and social origin, fortune, birth or other status.

Article 3

1. Every individual shall be equal before the law.
2. Every individual shall be entitled to equal protection of the law.

Article 4

Human beings are inviolable. Every human being shall be entitled to respect for his life and the integrity of his person. No one may be arbitrarily deprived of this right.

Article 5

Every individual shall have the right to the respect of the dignity inherent in a human being and to the recognition of his legal status. All forms of exploitation and degradation of man particularly slavery, slave trade, torture, cruel, inhuman or degrading punishment and treatment shall be prohibited.

Article 6

Every individual shall have the right to liberty and to the security of his person. No one may be deprived of his freedom except for reasons and conditions previously laid down by law. In particular, no one may be arbitrarily arrested or detained.

Article 7

1. Every individual shall have the right to have his cause heard. This comprises:
    (a) the right to an appeal to competent national organs against acts of violating his fundamental rights as recognized and guaranteed by conventions, laws, regulations and customs in force;
    (b) the right to be presumed innocent until proved guilty by a competent court or tribunal;
    (c) the right to defence, including the right to be defended by counsel of his choice;
    (d) the right to be tried within a reasonable time by an impartial court or tribunal.
2. No one may be condemned for an act or omission which did not constitute a legally punishable offence at the time it was committed. No penalty may be inflicted for an offence for which no provision was made at the time it was committed. Punishment is personal and can be imposed only on the offender.

Article 8

Freedom of conscience, the profession and free practice of religion shall be guaranteed. No one may, subject to law and order, be submitted to measures restricting the exercise of these freedoms.

Article 9

1. Every individual shall have the right to receive information.
2. Every individual shall have the right to express and disseminate his opinions within the law.

Article 10

1. Every individual shall have the right to free association provided the he abides by the law.
2. Subject to the obligation of solidarity provided for in Article 29 no one may be compelled to join an association.

Article 11

Every individual shall have the right to assemble freely with others. The exercise of this right shall be subject only to necessary restrictions provided for by law in particular those enacted in the interest of national security, the safety, health, ethics and rights and freedoms of others.

Article 12

1. Every individual shall have the right to freedom of movement and residence within the borders of a State provided he abides by the law.
2. Every individual shall have the right to leave any country including his own, and to return to his country. This right may only be subject to restrictions, provided for by law for the protection of national security, law and order, public health or morality.
3. Every individual shall have the right, when persecuted, to seek and obtain asylum in other countries in accordance with laws of those countries and international conventions.
4. A non-national legally admitted in a territory of a State Party to the present Charter, may only be expelled from it by virtue of a decision taken in accordance with the law.
5. The mass expulsion of non-nationals shall be prohibited. Mass explusion shall be that which is aimed at national, racial, ethnic or religious groups.

Article 13

1. Every citizen shall have the right to participate freely in the government of his country, either directly or through freely chosen representatives in accordance with the provisions of the law.
2. Every citizen shall have the right of equal access to the public service of his country.
3. Every individual shall have the right of access to public property and services in strict equality of all persons before the law.

Article 14

The right to property shall be guaranteed. It may only be encroached upon in the interest of public need or in the general interest of the community and in accordance with the provisions of appropriate laws.

Article 15

Every individual shall have the right to work under equitable and satisfactory conditions, and shall receive equal pay for equal work.

Article 16

1. Every individual shall have the right to enjoy the best attainable state of physical and mental health.
2. States parties to the present Charter shall take the necessary

measures to protect the health of their people and to ensure that they receive medical attention when they are sick.

Article 17

1. Every individual shall have the right to education.
2. Every individual may freely, take part in the cultural life of his community.
3. The promotion and protection of morals and traditional values recognized by the community shall be the duty of the State.

Article 18

1. The family shall be the natural unit and basis of society. It shall be protected by the State which shall take care of its physical health and moral.
2. The State shall have the duty to assist the family which is the custodian of morals and traditional values recognized by the community.
3. The State shall ensure the elimination of every discrimination against women and also censure the protection of the rights of the woman and the child as stipulated in international declarations and conventions.
4. The aged and the disabled shall also have the right to special measures of protection in keeping with their physical or moral needs.

Article 19

All peoples shall be equal; they shall enjoy the same respect and shall have the same rights. Nothing shall justify the domination of a people by another.

Article 20

1. All peoples shall have the right to existence. They shall have the unquestionable and inalienable right to self-determination. They shall freely determine their political status and shall pursue their economic and social development according to the policy they have freely chosen.
2. Colonized or oppressed peoples shall have the right to free themselves from the bonds of domination by resorting to any means recognized by the international community.
3. All peoples shall have the right to the assistance of the States parties to the present Charter in their liberation struggle against foreign domination, be it political, economic or cultural.

Article 21

1. All peoples shall freely dispose of their wealth and natural resources. This right shall be exercised in the exclusive interest of the people. In no case shall a people be deprived of it.
2. In case of spoliation the dispossessed people shall have the right to the lawful recovery of its property as well as to an adequate compensation.

3. The free disposal of wealth and natural resources shall be exercised without prejudice to the obligation of promoting international economic cooperation based on mutual respect, equitable exchange and the principles of international law.

4. States parties to the present Charter shall individually and collectively exercise the right to free disposal of their wealth and natural resources with a view to strengthening African unity and solidarity.

5. States parties to the present Charter shall undertake to eliminate all forms of foreign economic exploitation particularly that practiced by international monopolies so as to enable their peoples to fully benefit from the advantages derived from their national resources.

Article 22

1. All peoples shall have the right to their economic, social and cultural development with due regard to their freedom and identity and in the equal enjoyment of the common heritage of mankind.

2. States shall have the duty, individually or collectively, to ensure the exercise of the right to development.

Article 23

1. All peoples shall have the right to national and international peace and security. The principles of solidarity and friendly relations implicitly affirmed by the Charter of the United Nations and reaffirmed by that of the Organization of African Unity shall govern relations between States.

2. For the purpose of strengthening peace, solidarity and friendly relations, States parties to the present Charter shall ensure that:

(a) any individual enjoying the right of asylum under Article 12 of the present Charter shall not engage in subversive activities against his country of origin or any other State party to the present Charter;

(b) their territories shall not be used as bases for subversive or terrorist activities against the people of any other State party to the present Charter.

Article 24

All peoples shall have the right to a general satisfactory environment favorable to their development.

Article 25

States parties to the present Charter shall have the duty to promote and ensure through teaching, education and publication, the respect of the rights and freedoms contained in the present Charter and to see to it that these freedoms and rights as well as corresponding obligations and duties are understood.

Article 26

States parties to the present Charter shall have the duty to guarantee the independence of the Courts and shall allow the establishment and improvement of appropriate national institutions entrusted with the promotion and protection of the rights and freedoms guaranteed by the present Charter.

Chapter II—Duties

Article 27

1. Every individual shall have duties towards his family and society, the State and other legally recognized communities and the international community.
2. The rights and freedoms of each individual shall be exercised with due regard to the rights of others, collective security, morality and common interest.

Article 28

Every individual shall have the duty to respect and consider his fellow beings without discrimination, and to maintain relations aimed at promoting, safeguarding and reinforcing mutual respect and tolerance.

Article 29

The individual shall also have the duty:
1. To preserve the harmonious development of the family and to work for the cohesion and respect of the family; to respect his parents at all times, to maintain them in case of need;
2. To serve his national community by placing his physical and intellectual abilities at its service;
3. Not to compromise the security of the State whose national or resident he is;
4. To preserve and strengthen social and national solidarity, particularly when the latter is threatened;
5. To preserve and strengthen the national independence and the territorial integrity of his country and to contribute to its defence in accordance with the law;
6. To work to the best of his abilities and competence, and to pay taxes imposed by law in the interest of the society;
7. To preserve and strengthen positive African cultural values in his relations with other members of the society, in the spirit of tolerance, dialogue and consultation and, in general, to contribute to the promotion of the moral well being of society;
8. To contribute to the best of his abilities, at all times and at all levels, to the promotion and achievement of African unity.

Part II: Measures of Safeguard

Chapter I—Establishment and Organization of the African Commission on Human and Peoples' Rights

Article 30

An African Commission on Human and Peoples' Rights, hereinafter called "the Commission", shall be established within the Organization of African Unity to promote human and peoples' rights and ensure their protection in Africa.

Article 31

1. The Commission shall consist of eleven members chosen from amongst African personalities of the highest reputation, known for their high morality, integrity, impartiality and competence in matters of human and peoples' rights; particular consideration being given to persons having legal experience.
2. The members of the Commission shall serve in their personal capacity.

Article 32

The Commission shall not include more than one national of the same State.

Article 33

The members of the Commission shall be elected by secret ballot by the Assembly of Heads of State and Government, from a list of persons nominated by the States parties to the present Charter.

Article 34

Each State party to the present Charter may not nominate more than two candidates. The candidates must have the nationality of one of the States parties to the present Charter. When two candidates are nominated by a State, one of them may not be a national of that State.

Article 35

1. The Secretary General of the Organization of African Unity shall invite States parties to the present Charter at least four months before the elections to nominate candidates;
2. The Secretary General of the Organization of African Unity shall make an alphabetical list of the persons thus nominated and communicate it to the Heads of State and Government at least one month before the elections.

Article 36

The members of the Commission shall be elected for a six year period and shall be eligible for re-election. However, the term of office of four of the members elected at the first election shall terminate after two years and the term of office of the three others, at the end of four years.

Article 37

Immediately after the first election, the Chairman of the Assembly of Heads of State and Government of the Organization of African Unity shall draw lots to decide the names of those members referred to in Article 36.

Article 38

After their election, the members of the Commission shall make a solemn declaration to discharge their duties impartially and faithfully.

Article 39

1. In case of death or resignation of a member of the Commission, the Chairman of the Commission shall immediately inform the Secretary General of the Organization of African Unity, who shall declare the seat vacant from the date of death or from the date on which the resignation takes effect.
2. If, in the unanimous opinion of other members of the Commission, a member has stopped discharging his duties for any reason other than a temporary absence, the Chairman of the Commission shall inform the Secretary General of the Organization of African Unity, who shall then declare the seat vacant.
3. In each of the cases anticipated above, the Assembly of Heads of State and Government shall replace the member whose seat became vacant for the remaining period of his term unless the period is less than six months.

Article 40

Every member of the Commission shall be in office until the date his successor assumes office.

Article 41

The Secretary General of the Organization of African Unity shall appoint the Secretary of the Commission. He shall also provide the staff and services necessary for the effective discharge of the duties of the Commission. The Organization of African Unity shall bear the costs of the staff and services.

Article 42

1. The Commission shall elect its Chairman and Vice Chairman for a two year period. They shall be eligible for re-election.
2. The Commission shall lay down its rules of procedure.
3. Seven members shall form a quorum.
4. In case of an equality of votes, the Chairman shall have a casting vote.
5. The Secretary General may attend the meetings of the Com-

mission. He shall neither participate in deliberations nor shall he be entitled to vote. The Chairman of the Commission may, however, invite him to speak.

Article 43

In discharging their duties, members of the Commission shall enjoy diplomatic privileges and immunities provided for in the General Convention on the Privileges and Immunities of the Organization of African Unity.

Article 44

Provision shall be made for the emoluments and allowances of the members of the Commission in the Regular Budget of the Organization of African Unity.

Chapter II—Mandate of the Commission

Article 45

The functions of the Commission shall be:
1. To promote Human and Peoples' Rights and in particular:
   (a) to collect documents, undertake studies and researches on African problems in the field of human and peoples' rights, organize seminars, symposia and conferences, disseminate information, encourage national and local institutions concerned with human and peoples' rights, and should the case arise, give its views or make recommendations to Governments.
   (b) to formulate and lay down, principles and rules aimed at solving legal problems relating to human and peoples' rights and fundamental freedoms upon which African Governments may base their legislations.
   (c) co-operate with other African and international institutions concerned with the promotion and protection of human and peoples' rights.
2. Endure the protection of human and peoples' rights under conditions laid down by the present Charter.
3. Interpret all the provisions of the present Charter at the request of a State party, an institution of the OAU or an African Organization recognized by the OAU.
4. Perform any other tasks which may be entrusted to it by the Assembly of Heads of State and Government.

Chapter III—Procedure of the Commission

Article 46

The Commission may resort to any appropriate method of investigation; it may hear from the Secretary General of the Organization of African Unity or any other person capable of enlightening it.

Communication From States

Article 47

If a State party to the present Charter has good reasons to believe that another State party to this Charter has violated the provisions of the Charter, it may draw, by written communication, the attention of that State to the matter. This communication shall also be addressed to the Secretary General of the OAU and to the Chairman of the Commission. Within three months of the receipt of the communication, the State to which the communication is addressed shall give the enquiring State, written explanation or statement elucidating the matter. This should include as much as possible relevant information relating to the laws and rules of procedure applied and applicable, and the redress already given or course of action available.

Article 48

If within three months from the date on which the original communication is received by the State to which it is addressed, the issue is not settled to the satisfaction of the two States involved through bilateral negotiation or by any other peaceful procedure, either State shall have the right to submit the matter to the Commission through the Chairman and shall notify the other States involved.

Article 49

Notwithstanding the provisions of Article 47, if a State party to the present Charter considers that another State party has violated the provisions of the Charter, it may refer the matter directly to the Commission by addressing a communication to the Chairman, to the Secretary General of the Organization of African Unity and the State concerned.

Article 50

The Commission can only deal with a matter submitted to it after making sure that all local remedies, if they exist, have been exhausted, unless it is obvious to the Commission that the procedure of achieving these remedies would be unduly prolonged.

Article 51

1. The Commission may ask the States concerned to provide it with all relevant information.
2. When the Commission is considering the matter, States concerned may be represented before it and submit written or oral representation.

Article 52

After having obtained from the States concerned and from other sources all the information it deems necessary and after having tried all appropriate means to reach an amicable solution based on the respect of Human and Peoples' Rights, the Commission shall prepare, within a reasonable period of time from the notification referred to in Article 48, a report stating the facts and its findings. This report shall be sent to the States concerned and communicated to the Assembly of Heads of State and Government.

Article 53

While transmitting its report, the Commission may make to the Assembly of Heads of State and Government such recommendations as it deems useful.

Article 54

The Commission shall submit to each ordinary Session of the Assembly of Heads of State and Government a report on its activities.

Other Communications

Article 55

1. Before each Session, the Secretary of the Commission shall make a list of the communications other than those of States parties to the present Charter and transmit them to the members of the Commission, who shall indicate which communications should be considered by the Commission.

2. A communication shall be considered by the Commission if a simple majority of its members so decide.

Article 56

Communications relating to human and peoples' rights referred to in Article 55 received by the Commission, shall be considered if they:

1. Indicate their authors even if the latter request anonymity,
2. Are compatible with the Charter of the Organization of African Unity or with the present Charter,
3. Are not written in disparaging or insulting language directed against the State concerned and its institutions or to the Organization of African Unity,
4. Are not based exclusively on news discriminated through the mass media,
5. Are sent after exhausting local remedies, if any, unless it is obvious that this procedure is unduly prolonged,
6. Are submitted within a reasonable period from the time local remedies are exhausted or from the date the Commission is seized of the matter, and
7. Do not deal with cases which have been settled by these States involved in accordance with the principles of the Charter of the United Nations, or the Charter of the Organization of African Unity or the provisions of the present Charter.

Article 57

Prior to any substantive consideration, all communications shall be brought to the knowledge of the State concerned by the Chairman of the Commission.

Article 58

1. When it appears after deliberations of the Commission that one or more communications apparently relate to special cases which reveal the existence of a series of serious or massive violations of human and peoples' rights, the Commission shall draw the attention of the Assembly of Heads of State and Government to these special cases.
2. The Assembly of Heads of State and Government may then request the Commission to undertake an in-depth study of these cases and make a factual report, accompanied by its findings and recommendations.
3. A case of emergency duly noticed by the Commission shall be submitted by the latter to the Chairman of the Assembly of Heads of State and Government who may request an in-depth study.

Article 59

1. All measures taken within the provisions of the present Chapter shall remain confidential until such a time as the Assembly of Heads of State and Government shall otherwise decide.
2. However, the report shall be published by the Chairman of the Commission upon the decision of the Assembly of Heads of State and Government.
3. The report on the activities of the Commission shall be published by its Chairman after it has been considered by the Assembly of Heads of State and Government.

Chapter IV—Applicable Principles

Article 60

The Commission shall draw inspiration from international law on human and people's rights, particularly from the provisions of various African instruments on human and peoples' rights, the Charter of the United Nations, the Charter of the Organization of African Unity, the Universal Declaration of Human Rights, other instruments adopted by the United Nations and by African countries in the field of human and peoples' rights as well as from the provisions of various instruments adopted within the Specialized Agencies of the United Nations of which the parties to the present Charter are members.

Article 61

The Commission shall also take into consideration, as subsidiary measures to determine the principles of law, other general or special international conventions, laying down rules expressly recognized by member states of the Organization of African Unity, African practices consistent with international norms on human and people's rights, customs generally accepted as law, general principles of law recognized by African states as well as legal precedents and doctrine.

Article 62

Each state party shall undertake to submit every two years, from the date the present Charter comes into force, a report on the legislative or other measures taken with a view to giving effect to the rights and freedoms recognized and guaranteed by the present Charter.

Article 63

1. The present Charter shall be open to signature, ratification or adherence of the member states of the Organization of African Unity.
2. The instruments of ratification or adherence to the present Charter shall be deposited with the Secretary General of the Organization of African Unity.
3. The present Charter shall come into force three months after the reception by the Secretary General of the instruments of ratification or adherence of a simple majority of the member states of the Organization of African Unity.

Part III: General Provisions

Article 64

1. After the coming into force of the present Charter, members of the Commission shall be elected in accordance with the relevant Articles of the present Charter.
2. The Secretary General of the Organization of African Unity shall convene the first meeting of the Commission at the Headquarters of the Organization within three months of the constitution of the Commission. Thereafter, the Commission shall be convened by its Chairman whenever necessary but at least once a year.

Article 65

For each of the States that will ratify or adhere to the present Charter after its coming into force, the Charter shall take effect three months after the date of the deposit by that State of its instrument of ratification or adherence.

Article 66

Special protocols or agreements may, if necessary, supplement the provisions of the present Charter.

Article 67

The Secretary General of the Organization of African Unity shall inform member states of the Organization of the deposit of each instrument of ratification or adherence.

Article 68

The present Charter may be amended if a State party makes a written request to that effect to the Secretary General of the Organization of African Unity. The Assembly of Heads of State and Government may only consider the draft amendment after all the States parties have been duly informed of it and the Commission has given its opinion on it at the request of the sponsoring State. The amendment shall be approved by a simple majority of the States parties. It shall come into force for each State which has accepted it in accordance with its constitutional procedure three months after the Secretary General has received notice of the acceptance.

2.

OAU CONVENTION GOVERNING THE SPECIFIC ASPECTS OF REFUGEE PROBLEMS IN AFRICA

Adopted by the Assembly of Heads of State and Government at its Sixth Ordinary Session (Addis Ababa, 10 September 1969)

Entry into Force: 20 June 1974, in accordance with Article XI
Text: United Nations Treaty Series No. 14 691

PREAMBLE

We, the Heads of State and Government assembled in the city of Addis Ababa, from 6-10 September 1969,

1. *Noting with concern* the constantly increasing numbers of refugees in Africa and desirous of finding ways and means of alleviating their misery and suffering as well as providing them with a better life and future,

2. *Recognizing* the need for and essentially humanitarian approach towards solving the problems of refugees,

3. *Aware*, however, that refugee problems are a source of friction among many Member States, and desirous of eliminating the source of such discord,

4. *Anxious* to make a distinction between a refugee who seeks a peaceful and normal life and a person fleeing his country for the sole purpose of fomenting subversion from outside,

5. *Determined* that the activities of such subversive elements should be discouraged, in accordance with the Declaration on the Problem of Subversion and Resolution on the Problem of Refugees adopted at Accra in 1965,

6. *Bearing* in mind that the Charter of the United Nations and the Universal Declaration of Human Rights have affirmed the principle that human beings shall enjoy fundamental rights and freedoms without discrimination,

7. *Recalling* Resolution 2312 (XXII) of 14 December 1967 of the United

Nations General Assembly, relating to the Declaration on Territorial Asylum,

8. *Convinced* that all the problems of our continent must be solved in the spirit of the Charter of the Organization of African Unity and in the African context,

9. *Recognizing* that the United Nations Convention of 28 July 1951, as modified by the Protocol of 31 January 1967, constitutes the basic and universal instrument relating to the status of refugees and reflects the deep concern of States for refugees and their desire to establish common standards for their treatment,

10. *Recalling* Resolutions 26 and 104 of the OAU Assemblies of Heads of State and Government, calling upon Member States of the Organization who had not already done so to accede to the United Nations Convention of 1951 and to the Protocol of 1967 relating to the Status of Refugees, and meanwhile to apply their provisions to refugees in Africa,

11. *Convinced* that the efficiency of the measures recommended by the present Convention to solve the problem of refugees in Africa necessitates close and continuous collaboration between the Organization of African Unity and the Office of the United Nations High Commissioner for Refugees,

Have agreed as follows:

Article I

Definition of the term "Refugee"

1. For the purposes of this Convention, the term "refugee" shall mean every person who, owing to well-founded fear of being persecuted for reasons of race, religion, nationality, membership of a particular social group or political opinion, is outside the country of his nationality and is unable or, owing to such fear, is unwilling to avail himself of the protection of that country, or who, not having a nationality and being outside the country of his former habitual residence as a result of such events is unable or, owing to such fear, is unwilling to return to it.

2. The term "refugee" shall also apply to every person who, owing to external agression, occupation, foreign domination or events seriously disturbing public order in either part or the whole of his country of origin or nationality, is compelled to leave his place of habitual residence in order to seek refuge in another place outside his country of origin or nationality.

3. In the case of a person who has several nationalities, the term "a country of which he is a national" shall mean each of the countries of

which he is a national, and a person shall not be deemed to be lacking the protection of the country of which he is a national if, without any valid reason based on well-founded fear, he has not availed himself of the protection of one of the countries of which he is a national.

4. This Convention shall cease to apply to any refugee if:

(a) he has voluntarily re-availed himself of the protection of the country of his nationality, or,

(b) having lost his nationality, he has voluntarily reacquired it, or,

(c) he has acquired a new nationality, and enjoys the protection of the country of his new nationality, or,

(d) he has voluntarily re-established himself in the country which he left or outside which he remained owing to fear of persecution, or,

(e) he can no longer, because the circumstances in connection with which he was recognized as a refugee have ceased to exist, continue to refuse to avail himself of the protection of the country of his nationality, or,

(f) he has committed a serious non-political crime outside his country of refuge after his admission to that country as a refuge, or,

(g) he has seriously infringed the purposes and objectives of this Convention.

5. The provisions of this Convention shall not apply to any person with respect to whom the country of asylum has serious reasons for considering that:

(a) he has committed a crime against peace, a war crime, or a crime against humanity, as defined in the international instruments drawn up to make provision in respect of such crimes;

(b) he committed a serious non-political crime outside the country of refuge prior to his admission to that country as a refugee;

(c) he has been guilty of acts contrary to the purposes and principles of the Organization of African Unity;

(d) he has been guilty of acts contrary to the purposes and principles of the United Nations.

6. For the purposes of this Convention, the Contracting State of Asylum shall determine whether an applicant is a refugee.

Article II

Asylum

1. Member States of the OAU shall use their best endeavours consistent with their respective legislations to receive refugees and to secure the settle-

ment of those refugees who, for well-founded reasons, are unable or unwilling to return to their country of origin or nationality.

2. The grant of asylum to refugees is a peaceful and humanitarian act and shall not be regarded as an unfriendly act by any Member State.

3. No person shall be subjected by a Member State to measures such as rejection at the frontier, return or expulsion, which would compel him to return to or remain in a territory where his life, physical integrity or liberty would be threatened for the reasons set out in Article I, paragraphs 1 and 2.

4. Where a Member State finds difficulty in continuing to grant asylum to refugees, such Member State may appeal directly to other Member States and through the OAU, and such other Member States shall in the spirit of African solidarity and international co-operation take appropriate measures to lighten the burden of the Member State granting asylum.

5. Where a refugee has not received the right to reside in any country of asylum, he may be granted temporary residence in any country of asylum in which he first presented himself as a refugee pending arrangement for his resettlement in accordance with the preceding paragraph.

6. For reasons of security, countries of asylum shall, as far as possible, settle refugees at a reasonable distance from the frontier of their country of origin.

Article III

Prohibition of Subversive Activities

1. Every refugee has duties to the country in which he finds himself, which require in particular that he conforms with its laws and regulations as well as with measures taken for the maintenance of public order. He shall also abstain from any subversive activities against any Member State of the OAU.

2. Signatory States undertake to prohibit refugees residing in their respective territories from attacking any State Member of the OAU, by any activity likely to cause tension between Member States, and in particular by use of arms, through the press, or by radio.

Article IV

Non-Discrimination

Member States undertake to apply the provisions of this Convention to all refugees without discrimination as to race, religion, nationality, membership of a particular social group or political opinions.

Article V

Voluntary Repatriation

1. The essentially voluntary character of repatriation shall be respected in all cases and no refugee shall be repatriated against his will.

2. The country of asylum, in collaboration with the country of origin, shall make adequate arrangements for the safe return of refugees who request repatriation.

3. The country of origin, on receiving back refugees, shall facilitate their resettlement and grant them the full rights and privileges of nationals of the country, and subject them to the same obligations.

4. Refugees who voluntarily return to their country shall in no way be penalized for having left it for any of the reasons giving rise to refugee situations. Whenever necessary, an appeal shall be made through national information media and through the Administrative Secretary-General of the OAU, inviting refugees to return home and giving assurance that the new circumstances prevailing in their country of origin will enable them to return without risk and to take up a normal and peaceful life without fear of being disturbed or punished, and that the text of such appeal should be given to refugees and clearly explained to them by their country of asylum.

5. Refugees who freely decide to return to their homeland, as a result of such assurances or on their own initiative, shall be given every possible assistance by the country of asylum, the country of origin, voluntary agencies and international and intergovernmental organizations, to facilitate their return.

Article VI

Travel Documents

1. Subject to Article III, Member States shall issue to refugees lawfully staying in their territories travel documents in accordance with the United Nations Convention relating to the Status of Refugees and the Schedule and Annex thereto, for the purpose of travel outside their territory, unless compelling reasons of national security or public order otherwise require. Member States may issue such a travel document to any other refugee in their territory.

2. Where an African country of second asylum accepts a refugee from a country of first asylum, the country of first asylum may be dispensed from issuing a document with a return clause.

3. Travel documents issued to refugees under previous international agreements by States Parties thereto shall be recognized and treated by Member States in the same way as if they had been issued to refugees pursuant to this Article.

Article VII

Co-operation of the National Authorities with the Organization of African Unity

In order to enable the Administrative Secretary-General of the Organization of African Unity to make reports to the competent organs of the Organization of African Unity, Member States undertake to provide the Secretariat in the appropriate form with information and statistical data requested concerning:

(a) the condition of refugees;

(b) the implementation of this Convention, and

(c) laws, regulations and decrees which are, or may hereafter be, in force relating to refugees.

Article VIII

Co-operation with the Office of the United Nations High Commissioner for Refugees

1. Member States shall co-operate with the Office of the United Nations High Commissioner for Refugees.

2. The present Convention shall be the effective regional complement in Africa of the 1951 United Nations Convention on the Status of Refugees.

Article IX

Settlement of Disputes

Any dispute between States signatories to this Convention relating to its interpretation or application, which cannot be settled by other means, shall be referred to the Commission for Mediation, Conciliation and Arbitration of the Organization of African Unity, at the request of any one of the Parties to the dispute.

Article X

Signature and Ratification

1. This Convention is open for signature and accession by all Member States of the Organization of African Unity and shall be ratified by signatory States in accordance with their respective constitutional processes. The

instruments of ratification shall be deposited with the Administrative Secretary-General of the Organization of African Unity.

2. The original instrument, done if possible in African languages, and in English and French, all texts being equally authentic, shall be deposited with the Administrative Secretary-General of the Organization of African Unity.

3. Any independent African State, Member of the Organization of African Unity, may at any time notify the Administrative Secretary-General of the Organization of African Unity of its accession to this Convention.

Article XI

Entry into force

This Convention shall come into force upon deposit of instruments of ratification by one-third of the Member States of the Organization of African Unity.

Article XII

Amendment

This Convention may be amended or revised if any member State makes a written request to the Administrative Secretary-General to that effect, provided however that the proposed amendment shall not be submitted to the Assembly of Heads of State and Government for consideration until all Member States have been duly notified of it and a period of one year has elapsed. Such an amendment shall not be effective unless approved by at least two-thirds of the Member States Parties to the present Convention.

Article XIII

Denunciation

1. Any Member State Party to this Convention may denounce its provisions by a written notification to the Administrative Secretary-General.

2. At the end of one year from the date of such notification, if not withdrawn, the Convention shall cease to apply with respect to the denouncing State.

Article XIV

Upon entry into force of this Convention, the Administrative Secretary-General of the OAU shall register it with the Secretary-General of the United Nations, in accordance with Article 102 of the Charter of the United Nations.

Article XV

Notifications by the Administrative Secretary-General of the Organization of African Unity

The Administrative Secretary-General of the Organization of African Unity shall inform all Members of the Organization:

(a) of signatures, ratifications and accessions in accordance with Article X;

(b) of entry into force, in accordance with Article XI;

(c) of requests for amendments submitted under the terms of Article XII;

(d) of denunciations, in acccordance with Article XIII.

IN WITNESS WHEREOF we, the Heads of African State and Government, have signed this Convention.

1. Algeria
2. Botswana
3. Burundi
4. Cameroon
5. Central African Republic
6. Chad
7. Congo (Brazzaville)
8. Congo (Kinshasa)
9. Dahomey
10. Equatorial Guinea
11. Ethiopia
12. Gabon
13. Gambia
14. Ghana
15. Guinea
16. Ivory Coast
17. Kenya
18. Lesotho
19. Liberia
20. Libya
21. Madagascar
22. Malawi
23. Mali
24. Mauritania
25. Mauritius
26. Morocco
27. Niger
28. Nigeria
29. Rwanda
30. Senegal
31. Sierra Leone
32. Somalia
33. Sudan
34. Swaziland
35. Togo
36. Tunisia
37. Uganda
38. United Arab Republic
39. United Republic of Tanzania
40. Upper Volta
41. Zambia

DONE in the City of Addis Ababa this 10th day of September 1969.

3.

Charter of the Organization of African Unity

> Signed at Addis Ababa on 25 May 1963. Entered into force on 13 September 1963. See also 479 *U.N.T.S.*, pp. 39 *et seq.*. Headquarters of the Organization are at Addis Ababa.

We, the Heads of African States and Governments assembled in the City of Addis Ababa, Ethiopia;
Convinced that it is the inalienable right of all people to control their own destiny;
Conscious of the fact that freedom, equality, justice and dignity are essential objectives for the achievement of the legitimate aspirations of the African peoples;
Conscious of our responsibility to harness the natural and human resources of our continent for the total advancement of our peoples in spheres of human endeavour;
Inspired by a common determination to promote understanding among our peoples and co-operation among our states in response to the aspirations of our peoples for brotherhood and solidarity, in a larger unity transcending ethnic and national differences;
Convinced that, in order to translate this determination into a dynamic force in the cause of human progress, conditions for peace and security must be established and maintained;
Determined to safeguard and consolidate the hard-won independence as well as the sovereignty and territorial integrity of our states, and to fight against neo-colonialism in all its forms;
Dedicated to the general progress of Africa;
Persuaded that the Charter of the United Nations and the Universal Declaration of Human Rights, to the principles of which we reaffirm our adherence, provide a solid foundation for peaceful and positive co-operation among states;
Desirous that all African States should henceforth unite so that the welfare and well-being of their peoples can be assured;
Resolved to reinforce the links between our states by establishing and strengthening common institutions;
Have agreed to the present Charter.

ESTABLISHMENT

Art. I. 1. The High Contracting Parties do by the present Charter establish an Organization to be known as the *Organization of African Unity.*
2. The Organization shall include the Continental African States, Madagascar and other Islands surrounding Africa.

PURPOSES

Art. II. 1. The Organization shall have the following purposes:
    (*a*) to promote the unity and solidarity of the African States;
    (*b*) to co-ordinate and intensify their co-operation and efforts to achieve a better life for the peoples of Africa;
    (*c*) to defend their sovereignty, their territorial integrity and independence;
    (*d*) to eradicate all forms of colonialism from Africa; and
    (*e*) to promote international co-operation, having due regard to the Charter of the United Nations and the Universal Declaration of Human Rights.

2. To these ends, the Member States shall co-ordinate and harmonise their general policies especially in the following fields:
    (*a*) political and diplomatic co-operation;
    (*b*) economic co-operation, including transport and communications;
    (*c*) educational and cultural co-operation;
    (*d*) health, sanitation, and nutritional co-operation;
    (*e*) scientific and technical co-operation; and
    (*f*) co-operation for defense and security.

In July 1981, the Eighteenth Assembly of Heads of State and Government at its meeting in Nairobi approved unanimously a Charter on Human Rights and Peoples' Rights. Article 63(3) provides, that the Charter shall enter into force after ratification by a simple majority of OAU member states.

As of 1 March 1982, four out of fifty member states had deposited instruments of ratification. For the text see 21 *I.L.M.* 1982, pp. 59 *et seq.*.

PRINCIPLES

Art. III. The Member States, in pursuit of the purposes stated in Article II, solemnly affirm and declare their adherence to the following principles:
1. the sovereign equality of all Member States;
2. non-interference in the internal affairs of states;
3. respect for the sovereignty and territorial integrity of each state and for its inalienable right to independent existence;
4. peaceful settlement of disputes by negotiation, mediation, conciliation or arbitration;
5. unreserved condemnation, in all its forms, of political assassination as well as of subversive activities on the part of neighbouring states or any other state;
6. absolute dedication to the total emancipation of the African territories which are still dependent;
7. affirmation of a policy of non-alignment with regard to all blocs.

MEMBERSHIP

Art. IV. Each independent sovereign African State shall be entitled to become a Member of the Organization.

RIGHTS AND DUTIES OF MEMBER STATES

Art. V. All Member States shall enjoy equal rights and have equal duties.

Art. VI. The Member States pledge themselves to observe scrupulously the principles enumerated in Article III of the present Charter.

INSTITUTIONS

Art. VII. The Organization shall accomplish its purposes through the following principal institutions:
1. the Assembly of Heads of State and Government;
2. the Council of Ministers;
3. the General Secretariat;
4. the Commission of Mediation, Conciliation and Arbitration.

THE ASSEMBLY OF HEADS OF STATE AND GOVERNMENT

Art. VIII. The Assembly of Heads of State and Government shall be the supreme organ of the Organization. It shall, subject to the provisions of this Charter, discuss matters of common concern to Africa with a view to co-ordinating and harmonizing the general policy of the Organization. It may in addition review the structure, functions and acts of all the organs and any specialized agencies which may be created in accordance with the present Charter.

> See note at Article II, *supra*.

Art. IX. The Assembly shall be composed of the Heads of State and Government or their duly accredited representatives and it shall meet at least once a year. At the request of any Member State and approval by the majority of the Member States, the Assembly shall meet in extraordinary session.

Art. X. 1. Each Member State shall have one vote.
2. All resolutions shall be determined by a two-thirds majority of the Members of the Organization.
3. Questions of procedure shall require a simple majority. Whether or not a question is one of procedure shall be determined by a simple majority of all Member States of the Organization.
4. Two-thirds of the total membership of the Organization shall form a quorum at any meeting of the Assembly.

Art. XI. The Assembly shall have the power to determine its own rules of procedure.

> The rules of procedure referred to in this Article were approved by the Assembly of Heads of State and Government at Addis Ababa, Ethiopia, in July 1964. For the text see L.B. Sohn, *Basic Documents of African Regional Organizations*, Oceana Publications, Inc., Dobbs Ferry, N.Y. 1971, Vol. I, p. 77.

THE COUNCIL OF MINISTERS

Art. XII. 1. The Council of Ministers shall consist of Foreign Ministers or such other Ministers as are designated by the governments of Member States.
2. The Council of Ministers shall meet at least twice a year. When requested by any Member State and approved by two-thirds of all Member States, it shall meet in extraordinary session.

Art. XIII. 1. The Council of Ministers shall be responsible to the Assembly of Heads of State and Government. It shall be entrusted with the responsibility of preparing conferences of the Assembly.
2. It shall take cognisance of any matter referred to it by the Assembly. It shall be entrusted with the implementation of the decision of the Assembly of Heads of State and Government. It shall co-ordinate inter-African co-operation in accordance with the instructions of the Assembly and in conformity with Article II (2) of the present Charter.

Art. XIV. 1. Each Member State shall have one vote.
2. All resolutions shall be determined by a simple majority of the members of the Council of Ministers.
3. Two-thirds of the total membership of the Council of Ministers shall form a quorum for any meeting of the Council.

Art. XV. The Council shall have the power to determine its own rules of procedure.

> The rules of procedure referred to in this Article were adopted by the Council of Foreign Ministers at Dakar, Senegal, on 11 August 1963.

GENERAL SECRETARIAT

Art. XVI. There shall be an Administrative Secretary-General of the Organization, who shall be appointed by the Assembly of Heads of State and Government. The Administrative Secretary-General shall direct the affairs of the Secretariat.

Art. XVII. There shall be one or more Assistant Secretaries-General of the Organization, who shall be appointed by the Assembly of Heads of State and Government.

Art. XVIII. The functions and conditions of services of the Secretary-General, of the Assistant Secretaris-General and other employees of the Secretariat shall be governed by the provisions of this Charter and the regulations approved by the Assembly of Heads of State and Government.

1. In the performance of their duties the Administrative Secretary-General and the staff shall not seek or receive instructions from any government or from any other authority external to the Organization. They shall refrain from any action which might reflect on their position as international officials responsible only to the Organization.

2. Each member of the Organization undertakes to respect the exclusive character of the responsibilities of the Administrative Secretary-General and the Staff and not to seek to influence them in the discharge of their responsibilities.

> The regulations referred to in this Article were adopted by the Council of Foreign Ministers at Dakar on 11 August 1963.

COMMISSION OF MEDIATION, CONCILIATION AND ARBITRATION

Art. XIX. Member States pledge to settle all disputes among themselves by peaceful means and to this end decide to establish a Commission of Mediation, Conciliation and Arbitration, the composition of which and conditions of service shall be defined by a separate Protocol to be approved by the Assembly of Heads of State and Government. Said Protocol shall be regarded as forming an integral part of the present Charter.

SPECIALIZED COMMISIONS

Article XX. The Assembly shall establish such Specialized Commissions as it may deem necessary, including the following:
1. Economic and Social Commission;
2. Educational, Scientific, Cultural and Health Commission;
3. Defence Commission.

> The Charter originally provided for five Specialized Commissions. In 1967 it was agreed to reduce the number to three.

Art. XXI. Each Specialized Commission referred to in Article XX shall be composed of the Ministers concerned or other Ministers or Plenipotentiaries designated by the governments of the Member States.

Art. XXII. The functions of the Specialized Commissions shall be carried out in accordance with the provisions of the present Charter and of the regulations approved by the Council of Ministers.

THE BUDGET

Art. XXIII. The budget of the Organization prepared by the Administrative Secretary-General shall be approved by the Council of Ministers. The budget shall be provided by contributions from Member States in accordance with the scale of assessment of the United Nations; provided, however, that no Member State shall be assessed an amount exceeding twenty percent of the yearly regular budget of the Organization. The Member States agree to pay their respective contributions regularly.

SIGNATURE AND RATIFICATION OF CHARTER

Art. XXIV. 1. This Charter shall be open for signature to all independent sovereign African States and shall be ratified by the signatory states in accordance with their respective constitutional processes.

2. The original instrument, done, if possible in African languages, in English and French, all texts being equally authentic, shall be deposited with the Government of Ethiopia which shall transmit certified copies thereof to all independent sovereign African States.

3. Instruments of ratification shall be deposited with the Government of Ethiopia, which shall notify all signatories of each such deposit.

ENTRY INTO FORCE

Art. XXV. This Charter shall enter into force immediately upon receipt by the Government of Ethiopia of the instruments of ratification from two thirds of the signatory states.

REGISTRATION OF THE CHARTER

Art. XXVI. This Charter shall, after due ratification, be registered with the Secretariat of the United Nations through the Government of Ethiopia in conformity with Article 102 of the Charter of the United Nations.

INTERPRETATION OF THE CHARTER

Art. XXVII. Any question which may arise concerning the interpretation of this Charter shall be decided by a vote of two thirds of the Assembly of Heads of State and Government of the Organization.

ADHESION AND ACCESSION

Art. XXVIII. 1. Any independent sovereign African State may at time notify the Administrative Secretary-General of its intention to adhere or accede to this Charter.

2. The Administrative Secretary-General shall, on receipt of such notification, communicate a copy of it to all the Member States. Admission shall be decided by a simple majority of the Member States. The decision of each Member State shall be transmitted to the Administrative Secretary-General, who shall, upon receipt of the required number of votes, communicate the decision to the state concerned.

MISCELLANEOUS

Art. XXIX. The working languages of the Organization and all its institutions shall be, if possible African languages, English and French.

Art. XXX. The Administrative Secretary-General may accept on behalf of the Organization gifts, bequests and other donations made to the Organization, provided that this is approved by the Council of Ministers.

Art. XXXI. The Council of Ministers shall decide on the privileges and immunities to be accorded to the personnel of the Secretariat in the respective territories of the Member States.

CESSATION OF MEMBERSHIP

Art. XXXII. Any state which desires to renounce its membership shall forward a written notification to the Administrative Secretary-General. At the end of one year from the date of such notification, if not withdrawn, the Charter shall cease to apply with respect to the renouncing state, which shall thereby cease to belong to the Organization.

AMENDMENT OF THE CHARTER

Art. XXXIII. This Charter may be amended or revised if any Member State makes a written request to the Administrative Secretary-General to that effect; provided, however, that the proposed amendment is not submitted to the Assembly for consideration until all the Member States have been duly notified of it and a period of one year has elapsed. Such an amendment shall not be effective unless approved by at least two-thirds of all the Member States.

In faith whereof, We, the Heads of African State and Government, have signed this Charter.

Other Instruments

4.

LAW OF LAGOS

(The International Commission of Jurists is a non-governmental organisation which is concerned with the protection and promotion of human rights all over the world. In 1961 it sponsored a conference on the Rule of Law, which was held in Lagos, Nigeria. The Law of Lagos is the result of that conference).

The African Conference on the Rule of Law consisting of 194 judges, practising lawyers and teachers of law from 23 African nations as well as 9 countries of other continents,

Assembled in Lagos, Nigeria, in January 1961 under the aegis of the International Commission of Jurists,

Having discussed freely and frankly the Rule of Law with particular reference to Africa, and

Having reached conclusions regarding Human Rights in relation to Government security, Human Rights in relation to aspects of criminal and administrative law, and the responsibility of the Judiciary and of the Bar for the protection of the rights of the individual in society,

NOW SOLEMNLY

Recognizes that the Rule of Law is dynamic concept which should be employed to safeguard and advance the will of the people and the political rights of the individual and to establish social, economic, educational and cultural conditions under which the individual may achieve his dignity and realize his legitimate aspirations in all countries, whether dependent or independent,

Reaffirms the Act of Athens and the Declaration of Delhi with special reference to Africa and

Declares

1. That the principles embodied in the Conclusions of the Conference which

are annexed hereto should apply to any society, whether free or otherwise, but that the Rule of Law cannot be fully realized unless legislative bodies have been established in accordance with the will of the people who have adopted their Constitution freely;

2. That in order to maintain adequately the Rule of Law all Governments should adhere to the principle of democratic representation in their Legislatures;

3. That fundamental human rights, especially the right to personal liberty, should be written and entrenched in the Constitutions of all countries and that such personal liberty should not in peacetime be restricted without trial in a Court of Law;

4. That in order to give full effect to the Universal Declaration of Human Rights of 1948, this Conference invites the African Governments to study the possibility of adopting an African Convention of Human Rights in such a manner that the Conclusions of this Conference will be safeguarded by the creation of a court of appropriate jurisdiction and that resourse thereto be made available for all persons under the jurisdiction of the signatory States;

5. That in order to promote the principles and the practical application of the Rule of Law, the judges, practising lawyers and teachers of law in African countries should take steps to establish branches of the International Commission of Jurists.

This Resolution shall be known as the Law of Lagos.

Done at Lagos this 7th day of January 1961.

CONCLUSIONS

COMMITTEE I

Human Rights and Government Security – The Legislative, Executive and Judiciary

I

1. The exigencies of modern society necessitate the practice of the Legislature delegating to the Executive the power to make rules having the force of legislation.

2. The power of the Executive to make rules or regulations having legislative effect should derive from the express mandate of the Legislature; these rules and regulations should be subject to approval by that body. The object and scope of such executive power should be clearly defined.

3. The Judiciary should be given the jurisdiction to determine in every case

upon application whether the circumstances have arisen or the conditions have been fulfilled under which such power is to be or has been exercised.

4. Every constitution should provide that, except during a period of emergency, legislation should as far as possible be delegated only in respect of matters of economic and social character and that the exercise of such powers should not infringe upon fundamental human rights.

5. The proclamation of a state of emergency is a matter of most serious concern as it directly affects and may infringe upon human rights. It is the sense of the Conference that the dangers of survival of the nation such as arise from a sudden military challenge may call for urgent and drastic measures by the Executive which by the nature of things are susceptible only to *a posteriori* legislative ratification and judicial review. In any other case, however, it is the Parliament duly convened for the purpose that should declare whether or not the state of emergency exists. Wherever it is impossible or inexpedient to summon Parliament for this purpose, for example during Parliamentary recess, the Executive should be competent to declare a state of emergency, but in such a case Parliament should meet as soon as possible thereafter.

6. The Conference is of the opinion that real danger exists when, to quote the words of the General Rapporteur, 'The citizenry, whether by legislative or executive action, or abuse of the judicial process, are made to live as if in a perpetual state of emergency.'

7. The Conference feels that in all cases of the exercise of emergency powers any person who is aggrieved by the violation of his rights should have access to the courts for determination whether the power has been lawfully exercised.

II

The Conference, having considered the relative rights and obligations of legislative, executive and judicial institutions and their functions as affecting human rights and government security with particular reference to the observance of the Rule of Law in both independent and dependent countries in Africa and elsewhere; and having taken cognizance of allegations that discriminatory legislation based on race, colour or creed exists to the detriment of fundamental human rights of large sections of the population,

Requests the International Commission of Jurists to investigate, examine, consider and report on the legal conditions in Africa and elsewhere with particular regard to the existence of the Rule of Law and the observation of fundamental human rights.

COMMITTEE II

Human Rights and Aspects of Criminal and Administrative Law

The Rule of Law is of universal validity and application as it embraces those institutions and principles of justice which are considered minimal to the assurance of human rights and the dignity of man.

Further as a preamble to these *Conclusions* it is decided to adopt the following text from the *Conclusions* of the Second Committee of the International Congress of Jurists, New Delhi, India, 1959:

'The Rule of Law depends not only on the provision of adequate safeguards against abuse of power by the Executive, but also on the existence of effective government capable of maintaining law and order and of ensuring adequate social and economic conditions of life for the society.'

'The following propositions relating to the Executive and the Rule of Law are accordingly formulated on the basis of the certain conditions which are either satisfied, or in the case of newly independent countries still struggling with difficult economic and social problems are in process of being satisfied. These conditions require the existence of an Executive invested with sufficient power and resources to discharge its functions with efficiency and integrity. They require the existence of a Legislature elected by democratic process and not subject, either in the manner of its election or otherwise, to manipulation by the Executive. They require the existence of an independent Judiciary which will discharge its duties fearlessly. They finally call for the earnest endeavour of government to achieve such social and economic conditions within a society as will ensure a reasonable standard of economic security, social welfare and education for the mass of the people.'

1. Taking full cognizance of and incorporating herein by reference Clause III 3*(a)* of the *Conclusions* of the First Committee of the above-mentioned International Congress of Jurists in New Delhi* it is recognized and agreed that legislation authorizing administrative action by the Executive should not be discriminatory with respect to race, creed, sex or other such reasons and any such discriminatory provisions contained in legislation are considered contrary to the Rule of Law.

2. While recognizing that inquiry into the merits of the propriety of an individual administrative act by the Executive may in many cases not be

---

[1]"The Legislative must ... not discriminate in its laws in respect of individuals, classes of persons, or minority groups on the ground of race, religion, sex or other such reasons not affording a proper basis for making a distinction between human beings, classes, or minorities.'

appropriate for the ordinary courts, it is agreed that there should be available to the person aggrieved a right of access to:
(a) a hierarchy of administrative courts of independent jurisdiction; or
(b) where these do not exist, to an administrative tribunal subject to the overriding authority of the ordinary courts.

3. The minimum requirements for such administrative action and subsequent judicial review as recommended in paragraph 2 above are as follows:
(a) that the full reasons for the action of the Executive be made known to the person aggrieved; and
(b) that the aggrieved person shall be given a fair hearing; and
(c) that the grounds given by the Executive for its action shall not be regarded as conclusive but shall be objectively considered by the court.

4. It is desirable that, whenever reasonable in the prevailing circumstances, the action of the Executive shall be suspended while under review by the courts.

5. (i) No person of sound mind shall be deprived of his liberty except upon a charge of a specific criminal offence; further, except during a public emergency, preventive detention without trial is held to be contrary to the Rule of Law.

(ii) During a period of public emergency, legislation often authorizes preventive detention of an individual if the Executive finds that public security so requires. Such legislation should provide the individual with safeguards against continuing arbitrary confinement by requiring a prompt administrative hearing and decision upon the need and justification for detention with a right to judicial review. It should be required that any declaration of public emergency by the Executive be reported to and subject to ratification by the Legislature. Moreover, both the declaration of public emergency and any consequent detention of individuals should be effective only for a specified and limited period of time (not exceeding six months).

(iii) Extension of the period of public emergency should be effected by the Legislature only after careful and deliberate consideration of the necessity therefore. Finally, during any period of public emergency the Executive should only take such measures as are reasonably justifiable for the purpose of dealing with the situation which exists during that period.

6. The courts and magistrates shall permit an accused person to be or to remain free pending trial except in the following cases which are deemed proper grounds for refusing bail:
(a) in the case of a very grave offence;
(b) if the accused is likely to interfere with witnesses or impede the course of justice;
(c) if the accused is likely to commit the same or other offences;
(d) if the accused may fail to appear for trial.

7. The power to grant bail is a judicial function which shall not be subject to

control by the Executive. Although a court should hear and consider the views and representations of the Executive, the fact that investigation of the case is being continued is not a sufficient ground for refusing bail. Bail should be commensurate with the economic means of the accused, and, whether by appeal or independent application, a higher court should have the power to release provisionally an accused person who has been denied bail by the lower court.

8. After conviction and pending review, the trial or appellate court should have discretionary power to admit the convicted person to bail subject to the grounds set forth in paragraph 6 above.

9. It is recommended that greater use be made of the summons requiring appearance in court to answer a criminal charge in place of arrest and consequent necessity for bail and provisional release.

COMMITTEE III

The Responsibility of the Judiciary and of the Bar for the Protection of the Rights of the Individual in Society

The Conference reaffirms the *Conclusions* reached by the Fourth Committee of the International Congress of Jurists, New Delhi, India, 1959, which are appended hereto; and having regard to the particular problems of emerging States, wishes to emphasize certain points in particular, and to add others.

1. In a free society practising the Rule of Law, it is essential that the absolute independence of the Judiciary be guaranteed. Members of the legal profession in any country have, over and above their ordinary duties as citizens, a special duty to seek ways and means of securing in their own country the maximum degree of independence for the Judiciary.

2. It is recognized that in different countries there are different ways of appointing, promoting and removing judges by means of action taken by the Executive and Legislative powers. It is not recommended that these powers should be abrogated where they have been universally accepted over a long period as working well – provided that they conform to the principles expressed in Clauses II, III, IV and V of the Report of the Fourth Committee at New Delhi.

3. In respect of any country in which the methods of appointing, promoting and removing judges are not yet fully settled, or do not ensure the independence of the Judiciary, it is recommended:

(a) that these powers should not be put into the hands of the Executive or the Legislative, but should be entrusted exclusively to an independent organ

such as the Judicial Service Commission of Nigeria or the *Conseil supérieur de la magistrature* in the African French-speaking countries;

(b) that in any country in which the independency of the Judiciary is not already fully secured in accordance with these principles, they should be implemented immediately in respect of all judges, especially those having criminal jurisdiction.

4. It is recommended that all customary, traditional or local law should be administered by the ordinary courts of the land, and emphasized that for so long as that law is administered by special courts, all the principles enunciated here and at New Delhi, for safeguarding the Rule of Law, apply to those courts.

5. The practice, whereby in certain territories judicial powers, especially in criminal matters, are exercised by persons who have no adequate legal training or experience, or who as administrative officers are subject to the control of the Executive is one which falls short of the Rule of Law.

6. (a) To maintain the respect for the Rule of Law it is necessary that the legal profession should be free from any interference;

(b) In countries where an organized Bar exists, the lawyers themselves should have the right to control the admission to the profession and the discipline of the members according to rules established by law;

(c) In countries where an organized Bar does not exist, the power to discipline lawyers should be exercised by the Judiciary in consultation with senior practising lawyers and never by the Executive.

7. The Conference, reaffirms Clause X of the *Conclusions* of the Fourth Committee at New Delhi, and recommends that all steps should be taken to ensure equal access to law for both rich and poor, especially by a provision for and an organization of a system of Legal Aid in both criminal and civil matters.

8. The Conference expressly reaffirms the principle that retroactive legislation especially in criminal matters is inconsistent with the Rule of Law.

Appendix

REPORT OF COMMITTEE IV INTERNATIONAL CONGRESS OF JURISTS, NEW DELHI, 1959

The Judiciary and the Legal Profession under the Rule of Law

Clause I

An independent Judiciary is an indispensable requisite of a free society under the Rule of Law. Such independence implies freedom from interference by the

Executive or Legislative with the exercise of the judicial function, but does not mean that the judge is entitled to act in an arbitrary manner. His duty is to interpret the law and the fundamental principles and assumptions that underlie it. It is implicit in the concept of independence set out in the present paragraph that provision should be made for the adequate remuneration of the Judiciary and that a judge's right to the remuneration settled for his office should not during his term of office be altered to his disadvantage.

Clause II

There are in different countries varying ways in which the Judiciary are appointed, re-appointed (where re-appointment arises) and promoted, involving the Legislative, Executive, the Judiciary itself, in some countries the representatives of the practising legal profession, or a combination of two or more of these bodies. The selection of judges by election and particularly by re-election, as in some countries, presents special risks to the independence of the Judiciary which are more likely to be avoided only where tradition has circumscribed by prior agreement the list of candidates and has limited political controversy. There are also potential dangers in exclusive appointment by the Legislative, Executive, or Judiciary, and where there is on the whole general satisfaction with calibre and independence of judges it will be found that either in law or in practice there is some degree of co-operation (or at least consultation) between the Judiciary and the authority actually making the appointment.

Clause III

The principle of irremovability of the Judiciary, and their security of tenure until death or until a retiring age fixed by statute is reached, is an important safeguard of the Rule of Law. Although it is not impossible for a judge appointed for a fixed term to assert his independence, particularly if he is seeking re-appointment, he is subject to greater difficulties and pressure than a judge who enjoys security of tenure for his working life.

Clause IV

The reconciliation of the principle of irremovability of the Judiciary with the possibility of removal in exceptional circumstances necessitates that the ground for removal should be before a body of judicial character assuring at least the same safeguards to the judge as would be accorded to an accused person in a criminal trial.

Clause V

The considerations set out in the preceding paragraph should apply to: (1) the ordinary civil and criminal Courts; (2) administrative Courts or constitutional

Courts, not being subordinate to the ordinary Courts. The members of administrative tribunals, whether professional lawyers or laymen, as well as laymen exercising other judicial functions (juries, assessors, Justices of the Peace, etc.) should only be appointed and removable in accordance with the spirit of these considerations, in so far as they are applicable to their particular positions. All such persons have in any event the same duty of independence in the performance of their judicial function.

Clause VI

It must be recognized that the Legislative has responsibility for fixing the general framework and laying down the principles of organization of judicial business and that, subject to the limitations on delegations of legislative power which have been dealt with elsewhere, it may delegate part of this responsibility to the Executive. However, the exercise of such responsibility by the Legislative including any delegation to the Executive should not be employed as an indirect method of violating the independence of the Judiciary in the exercise of its judicial functions.

Clause VII

It is essential to the maintenance of the Rule of Law that there should be an organized legal profession free to manage its own affairs. But it is recognized that there may be general supervision by the Courts and that there may be regulations governing the admission to and pursuit of the legal profession.

Clauses VIII

Subject to his professional obligation to accept assignments in appropriate circumstances, the lawyer should be free to accept any case which is offered to him.

Clause IX

While there is some difference of emphasis between various countries as to the extent to which a lawyer may be under a duty to accept a case it is conceived that:

    1. Wherever a man's life, liberty, property or reputation are at stake he should be free to obtain legal advice and representation; if this principle is to become effective, it follows that lawyers must be prepared frequently to defend persons associated with unpopular causes and minority views with which they themselves may be entirely out of sympathy;

    2. Once a lawyer has accepted a brief he should not relinquish it to the detriment of his client without good and sufficient cause;

    3. It is the duty of a lawyer which he should be able to discharge without fear of consequences to press upon the Court any argument of law or of fact which he may think proper for the due presentation of the case by him.

Clause X

Equal access to law for the rich and poor alike is essential to the maintenance of the Rule of Law. It is, therefore, essential to provide adequate legal advice and representation to all those, threatened as to their life, liberty, property or reputation who are not able to pay for it. This may be carried out in different ways and is on the whole at present more comprehensively observed in regard to criminal as opposed to civil cases. It is necessary, however, to assert the full implications of the principle, in particular in so far as 'adequate' means legal advice or representation by lawyers of the requisite standing and experience. This is a question which cannot be altogether dissociated from the question of adequate remuneration for the services rendered. The primary obligation rests on the legal profession to sponsor and use its best effort to ensure that adequate legal advice and representation are provided. An obligation also rests upon the State and the community to assist the legal profession in carrying out this responsibility.

5.

DECLARATION ON THE PROBLEM OF SUBVERSION

The Assembly of Heads of State and Government meeting in its Second Ordinary Session in Accra, Ghana, from 21 to 25 October 1965,

Desirous of consolidating the fraternal links that unite us,

SOLEMNLY UNDERTAKE:

1. Not to tolerate in conformity with article 3, paragraph 5, of the Charter, any subversion originating in our countries against another Member State of the Organization of African Unity;

2. Not to tolerate the use of our territories for any subversive activity directed from outside Africa against any Member States of the Organization of African Unity;

3. To oppose collectively and firmly by every means at our disposal every form of subversion conceived, organized or financed by foreign powers against Africa, OAU or its Member States individually;

4. *(a)* To resort to *bilateral or multilateral consultation* to settle all differences between two or more Member States of the Organization of African Unity;

(b) To refrain from conducting any *press or radio campaigns* against any Member States of the Organization of African Unity; and to resort instead to the procedure laid down in the Charter and the Protocol of Mediation, Conciliation, and Arbitration of the Organization of African Unity;

5. *(a)* Not to create dissension within or among Member States by fomenting or aggravating racial, religious, linguistic, ethnic, or other differences;

(b) To combat all forms of activity of this kind;

6. To observe strictly the *principles of international law* with regard to all *political refugees* who are nationals of any Member States of the Organization of African Unity;

7. To endeavour to promote, through bilateral and multilateral consultation the return of refugees to their countries of origin with the consent of both the refugees concerned and their governments;

8. To continue to guarantee the safety of political refugees from non-independent African territories, and to support them in their struggle to liberate their countries.

6.

PRINCIPLES CONCERNING TREATMENT OF REFUGEES*

As adopted by the Asian-African Legal Consultative Committee at its Eighth Session, Bangkok 1966

ARTICLE I

Definition of the term 'Refugee'

A refugee is a person who, owing to persecution or well-founded fear of persecution for reasons of race, colour, religion, political belief or membership of a particular social group:

(a) leaves the State of which he is a national, or the Country of his nationality, or, if he has no nationality, the State or Country of which he is a habitual resident; or,

(b) being outside such State or Country, is unable or unwilling to return to it or to avail himself of its protection.

Exceptions

(1) A person having more than one nationality shall not be a refugee if he is in a position to avail himself of the protection of any State or Country of which he is a national.

(2) A person who prior to his admission into the Country of refuge, has committed a crime against peace, a war crime, or a crime against humanity or a serious non-political crime or has committed acts contrary to the purposes and principles of the United Nations shall not be a refugee.

---

*Text: Report of the Eighth Session of the Asian-African Legal Consultative Committee held in Bangkok from 8 to 17 August 1966, page 335.

Explanation

The dependants of a refugee shall be deemed to be refugees.

Explanation

The expression 'leaves' includes voluntary as well as involuntary leaving.

* Text: Report of the Eighth Session of the Asian-African Legal Consultative Committee held in Bangkok from 8 to 17 August 1966, page 335.

Notes

(i) The Delegation of Ghana reserved its position on this Article.

(ii) The Delegations of Iraq, Pakistan and the United Arab Republic expressed the view that, in their opinion, the definition of the term 'Refugee' includes a person who is obliged to leave the State of which he is a national under the pressure of an illegal act or as a result of invasion of such State, wholly or partially, by an alien with a view to occupying the State.

(iii) The Delegations of Ceylon and Japan expressed the view that in their opinion the expression 'persecution' means something more than discrimination or unfair treatment but includes such conduct as shocks the conscience of civilized nations.

(iv) The Delegations of Japan and Thailand expressed the view that the word 'and' should be substituted for the word 'or' in the last line of paragraph *(a)*.

(v) In Exception (2) the words 'prior to his admission into the Country of refuge' were inserted by way of amendment to the original text of the Draft Article on the proposal of the Delegation of Ceylon and accepted by the Delegations of India, Indonesia, Japan and Pakistan. The Delegations of Iraq and Thailand did not accept the amendment.

(vi) The Delegation of Japan proposed insertion of the following additional paragraph in the Article in relation to proposal under note (iv):
'A person who was outside of the State of which he is a national or the Country of his nationality, or if he has no nationality, the State or the Country of which he is a habitual resident, at the time of the events which caused him to have a well-founded fear of above-mentioned persecution and is unable or unwilling to return to it or to avail himself of its protection shall be considered a refugee.'

The Delegations of Ceylon, India, Indonesia, Iraq and Pakistan were of the view that this additional paragraph was unnecessary. The Delegation of Thailand reserved its position on this paragraph.

ARTICLE II

Loss of Status as Refugee

1. A refugee shall lose his status as refugee if:
   (i) he voluntarily returns permanently to the State of which he was a national or the Country of his nationality, to the State or the Country of which he was a habitual resident; or
   (ii) he has voluntarily re-availed himself of the protection of the State or Country of his nationality; or
   (iii) he voluntarily acquires the nationality of another State or Country and is entitled to the protection of that State or Country.

2. A refugee shall lose his status as a refugee if he does not return to the State of which he is a national, or to the Country of his nationality, or, if he has no nationality, to the State or Country of which he was a habitual resident, or if he fails to avail himself of the protection of such State or Country after the circumstances in which he became a refugee have ceased to exist.

Explanation

It would be for the State of asylum of the refugee to decide whether the circumstances in which he became a refugee have ceased to exist.

Notes

(i) The Delegations of Iraq and the United Arab Republic reserved their position on paragraph 1 (iii).

(ii) The Delegation of Thailand wished it to be recorded that the loss of status as a refugee under paragraph 1 (ii) will take place only when the refugee has successfully re-availed himself of the protection of the State of his nationality because the right of protection was that of his country and not that of the individual.

ARTICLE III

Asylum to a Refugee

1. A State has the sovereign right to grant or refuse asylum in its territory to a refugee.
2. The exercise of the right to grant such asylum to a refugee shall be

respected by all other States and shall not be regarded as an unfriendly act.

3. No one seeking asylum in accordance with these Principles should, except for overriding reasons of national security or safeguarding the populations, be subjected to measures such as rejection at the frontier, return or expulsion which would result in compelling him to return to or remain in a territory if there is a well-founded fear of persecution endangering his life, physical integrity or liberty in that territory.

4. In cases where a State decides to apply any of the above-mentioned measures to a person seeking asylum, it should grant provisional asylum under such conditions as it may deem appropriate, to enable the person thus endangered to seek asylum in another country.

ARTICLE IV

Right of Return

A refugee shall have the right to return if he so chooses to the State of which he is a national or to the country of his nationality and in this event it shall be the duty of such State or Country to receive him.

ARTICLE V

Right to compensation

1. A refugee shall have the right to receive compensation from the State or the Country which he left or to which he was unable to return.

2. The compensation referred to in paragraph 1 sall be for such loss as bodily injury, deprivation of personal liberty in denial of human rights, death of dependants of the refugee or of the person whose dependant the refugee was, and destruction of or damage to property and assets, caused by the authorities of the State or Country, public officials or mob violence.

Notes

(i) The Delegations of Pakistan and the United Arab Republic were of the view that the word 'also' should be inserted before the words 'such loss' in paragraph 2.

(ii) The Delegations of India and Japan expressed the view that the words 'deprivation of personal liberty in denial of human rights', should be omitted.

(iii) The Delegations of Ceylon, Japan and Thailand suggested that the words 'in the circumstances in which the State would incur state responsibility for such treatment to aliens under international law' should be added at the end of paragraph 2.

(iv) The Delegations of Ceylon, Japan, Pakistan and Thailand expressed the view that compensation should be payable also in respect of the denial of the refugee's right to return to the State of which he is a national.

(v) The Delegation of Ceylon was opposed to the inclusion of the words 'or country' in this Article.

(vi) The Delegations of Ceylon, Ghana, India and Indonesia were of the view that in order to clarify the position, the words 'arising out of events which gave rise to the refugee leaving such State or Country' should be added to paragraph 2 of this Article after the words 'mob violence'.

ARTICLE VI

Minimum Standard of Treatment

1. A State shall accord to refugees treatment in no way less favourable than that generally accorded to aliens in similar circumstances.

2. The standard of treatment referred to in the preceding clause shall include the rights relating to aliens contained in the Final Report of the Committee on the status of aliens, annexed to these principles, to the extent that they are applicable to refugees.

3. A refugee shall not be denied any rights on the ground that he does not fulfill requirements which by their nature a refugee is incapable of fulfilling.

4. A refugee shall not be denied any rights on the ground that there is no reciprocity in regard to the grant of such rights between the receiving State and the State or Country of nationality of the refugee or, if he is stateless, the State or Country of his former habitual residence.

Notes

(i) The Delegations of Iraq and Pakistan were of the view that a refugee should generally be granted the standard of treatment applicable to the nationals of the country of asylum.

(ii) The Delegation of Indonesia reserved its position on paragraph 3 of the Article.

(iii) The Delegations of Indonesia and Thailand reserved their position on paragraph 4 of the Article.

ARTICLE VII

Obligations

A refugee shall not engage in subversive activities endangering the national security of the country of refuge, or in activities inconsistent with or against the principles and purposes of the United Nations.

Notes

(i) The Delegations of India, Japan and Thailand were of the view that the words 'or any other country' should be added after the words 'the country of refuge' in this Article. The other Delegations were of the view that such addition was not necessary.

(ii) The Delegation of Iraq was of the view that the inclusion of the words 'or in activities inconsistent with or against the principles and purposes of the United Nations' was inappropriate as in this Article what was being dealt with was the right and obligation of the refugee and not that of the State.

ARTICLE VIII

Expulsion and Deportation

1. Save in the national or public interest or on the ground of violation of the conditions of asylum, the State shall not expel a refugee.
2. Before expelling a refugee, the State shall allow him a reasonable period within which to seek admission into another State. The State shall, however, have the right to apply during the period such internal measures as it may deem necessary.
3. A refugee shall not be deported or returned to a State or Country where his life or liberty would be threatened for reasons of race, colour, religion, political belief or membership of a particular social group.

Notes

(i) The Delegation of Ceylon, Ghana and Japan did not accept the text of paragraph 1. In the views of these Delegations the text of this paragraph should read as follows:

> 'A state shall not expel or deport a refugee save on ground of national security or public order, or a violation of any of the vital or fundamental conditions of asylum.'

(ii) The Delegations of Ceylon and Ghana were of the view that in paragraph 2 the words 'as generally applicable to aliens under such circumstances' should be added at the end of the paragraph after the word 'necessary'.

ARTICLE IX

Nothing in these Articles shall be deemed to impair any higher rights and benefits granted or which may hereafter be granted by a State to refugees.

7.

ECONOMIC COMMISSION FOR AFRICA CONFERENCE OF AFRICAN JURISTS ON AFRICAN LEGAL PROCESS AND THE INDIVIDUAL

Addis Ababa, 19–23 April 1971

Text of all substantive Resolutions adopted by the Conference

RESOLUTION 1

The process of arrest and detention

The Conference of African Jurists on African Legal Process and the Individual, concerning the process of arrest and detention, affirms the resolutions of the Lagos Conference in this regard, and deplores and condemns any legislation which permits detention without trial, emphasizes the importance of respecting the provisions regarding the conditions of arrest and detention contained in various criminal codes, and urges that respect for these provisions be extended as far as possible to all kinds of arrest and detention, and that all places of detention shall be subject to frequent and regular judicial inspection, and that in the recruitment and employment of law enforcement officers attention be paid to their suitability, qualifications, training and that their remuneration be improved, recommends to this end the establishment of an Institute of Comparative Law, under the auspices of the Organization of African Unity, with the co-operation of the United Nations and its competent specialized agencies and of all inter-governmental and non-governmental organizations concerned with the problem, charged with:
(1) the scientific study and development of law in Africa; and
(2) the holding at regular intervals (once or twice a year in various African countries in turn) of study and research sessions on African law lasting two or three weeks at a time; and
(3) the promotion of research into problems of African law and the publication of an African Journal of Comparative Law to be used for the

widespread dissemination of the results of research, and of information regarding legal developments.

RESOLUTION 2

The judicial process: Access to courts, trial, review, judicial remedies and the Ombudsman

The Conference of African Jurists on African Legal Process and the Individual, reaffirms the resolutions of the United Nations Seminar held at Mexico (1961) stressing that *ampare, habeas corpus, mandado de seguaraça* and other means of defending human rights are enduring and essential juridical institutions for the survival of any civilized community, recognizes and recommends that a many-sided approach must be undertaken to overcome the economic, social and human factors which create a gap between the principle that the courts should be readily accessible to all and the actualities of present-day judicial facilities in Africa, declares that among the measures that should be undertaken are:

(1) An extensive simplification of the rules of procedure especially in relation to the institution or commencement of legal proceedings by any person in particular, illiterate or needy persons;
(2) A sustained programme of civic education designed to communicate a better knowledge of legal rights and duties and thus promote the awareness of remedies which would enable the ordinary man to defend his rights and in which judges, magistrates, lawyers and law students have a leading role to play;
(3) A determined effort to minimize the cost of judicial proceedings and to bring justice and the individual closer together by increasing the number of courts and extending the use of circuit courts;
(4) A thoughtful Africanization of law and procedure so as to increase their understanding;
(5) The establishment of adequate machinery for the provision of legal aid to persons who otherwise could not afford to prosecute or defend their rights in court;
(6) A scrupulous respect for the basic elements of fair hearing including the enforcement of such safeguards as the protection of witnesses, litigants and counsel; the presumption of innocence; the protection afforded by the principle *ne bis in idem* and against self-incrimination; the holding of trials in public and the curtailment of delays in disposing of cases;
(7) (a) The settlement of all judicial business in the ordinary courts of the land and the abolition of all exceptional tribunals;

(b) The development of an adequate system for the settlement of administrative problems and of administrative courts with a channel of appeals to the highest courts in the land;

(c) Where appropriate the creation of the office of an Ombudsman; and

(d) The introduction of some code of non-contentious administrative procedure and appropriate machinery for its enforcement.

RESOLUTION 3

The judicial process: Independence of the judiciary, the executive and the judiciary and international judicial processes

The Conference of African Jurists on African Legal Process and the Individual, after considering the important questions regarding the independence of the judiciary, the relations between the judiciary and the executive, and possible international judicial processes, affirms the resolutions in this regard of the following Conferences: the Lagos Conference of January 1961, the Rio de Janeiro Conference of 1962, the Bangkok Conference of 1965, and the Dakar Conference of 1967, all held under the auspices of the International Commission of Jurists, endorses the recommendations of the United Nations Seminar on the establishment of regional commissions on human rights with special reference to Africa, held in Cairo 1969; and recommends as follows:

(1) That the independence of the judiciary be guaranteed in order to ensure the impartiality of justice;

(2) That attention be paid to the social and economic factors that promote stability and that jurists should acknowledge the fact that they have a vested interest and a professional or technical commitment to the task of nation-building and that problems of political morality and the prevalence of the spirit of justice within their State are the business of lawyers;

(3) That steps be taken to agree to an early date upon a comprehensive code of judicial ethics, which also takes account of relations between the judiciary and the police; and

(4) That in exercise of political power all authority be subordinated to law and that the protection of human rights should be the primary concern of all the principal organs of the State;

(5) with a view to promoting the better protection of human rights, the Conference recommend further:

(i) that an African Commission on Human Rights be established and charged with the responsibility of collecting and circulating information relating to legislation and decisions concerning human rights in annual reports devoted to the question of civil rights in Africa;

(ii) that an African Convention on Human Rights be concluded;

(iii) that every effort be made to harmonize legislation in the different African countries in this regard;

(iv) that an Advisory Body be established to which recourse may be had for the interpretation of the terms of the African Convention on Human Rights; and

(v) that the various African States be urged to take speedy measures to accede to or ratify the International Covenant on Civil and Political Rights, the International Covenant on Economic, Social and Cultural Rights, the International Convention on the Elimination of all forms of racial discrimination and the OAU Convention governing specific aspects of refugee problems in Africa;

(6) The Conference welcomes the recommendations of the aforesaid United Nations Seminar held in Cairo in 1969 entrusting the Organization of African Unity with the establishment of a Commission for Human Rights for Africa and invites the Organization of African Unity to hasten the implementation of the said recommendations taking account of existing international instruments that have been drafted by the United Nations in this connection.

RESOLUTION 4

Provision of legal services to individuals

The Conference of African Jurists on African Legal Process and the Individual, on the question of legal aid, the Conference emphasizes that it is essential to the fair and impartial administration of justice that rich and poor alike should have equal access to the courts and to the assistance of trained legal personnel and that this consideration imposes an obligation on governments and on the legal profession to devise adequate machinery for ensuring that the ideal of equal justice before the law becomes a living reality that supports the development of a spirit of justice in the society.

8.

EXTRACTS FROM THE PLANS OF ACTION ADOPTED BY THE OAU SPECIAL ECONOMIC SUMMIT HELD IN LAGOS, NIGERIA (APRIL 1980)

PLAN OF ACTION FOR FOOD

Over the last two decades, and at a time the African Continent is facing a rapid growth in population and urbanisation, the food and agriculture situation in Africa has undergone a drastic deterioration; the food production and consumption per person has fallen below nutritional requirements.

The shortfall in food production, coupled with high levels of post-harvest losses and periodic severe shortages, have led to rapidly increasing dependence on food imports, resulting in a drain on foreign exchange resources and creating serious major constraints in financing the development of African economies. At the root of the food problem in Africa is the fact that Governments have not usually accorded the necessary priority to agriculture both in the allocation of resources, and in giving sufficient attention to policies for the promotion of productivity and improvement of rural life.

For an improvement of the food situation in Africa, the fundamental requisite is a strong political will to channel a greatly increased volume of resources to agriculture, to carry through essential reorientations of social systems, to apply policies that will induce small farmers and members of agricultural cooperatives to achieve higher levels of productivity, and to set up effective machineries for the formation of relevant programmes and for their execution. The development of agriculture, however, should not be considered in isolation, but rather integrated within the economic and social development processes. Emphasis should also be put on the latter aspect, particularly the problem of improving the conditions of rural life.

For an effective agricultural revolution in Africa it is essential to involve the youth, and to arrest the rural to urban drift. Policies have to consistently emphasize the need not only to improve the living conditions on the farms but also to increase farm real incomes as a means of making agriculture more attractive and remunerative. New dimensions of inter-country cooperation are called for, but primary responsibility for a break-through in food and agriculture lies with individual Governments operating in their respective national contexts.

Over the years 1980–85, the objective should be to bring about immediate improvement in the food situation and to lay the foundations for the achievement of self-sufficiency in cereals and in livestock and fish products. Priority action should be directed at securing a substantial reduction in food wastage, attaining a markedly higher degree of food security, and bringing about a large and sustained increase in the production of food, especially of tropical cereals with due emphasis on the diversification of agricultural production. Urgent measures are recommended in each of these areas.

Losses

The objective should be to make significant progress towards the achievement of a 50% reduction in post-harvest losses.
Recommended action includes:
- careful assessment of the extent of food losses;
- formulation of national policies for food loss reduction;
- mass media campaigns to educate the public on methods of reducing food waste;
- construction of appropriate storage, processing and other facilities;
- establishment of central technical units;
- promotion (through research, infrastructural development, and incentives to farmers and fishermen) of improved methods of drying, preservation, storage, pest control, and processing;
- improvement of livestock routes and holding grounds;
- training of technical staff for food loss control work, preferably through subregional/regional institutions, seminars and workshops.

Security

Most African countries should aim, as a first step, at setting up national strategic food reserves of the order of 10% of total food production.

Urgent steps should be taken by every African country to adopt a coherent national food security policy. National policies must be translated into concrete actions, such as early construction of storage facilities, creation of grain reserves, improvement of grain stock management and better forecasting and early warning systems. The need for collective self-reliance will require subregional food security arrangements similar to the one initiated in the Sahelian zone. In addition, it is recommended that African countries should examine the feasibility of setting up an African Food Relief Support with a view to assist membercountries in times of food emergency.

Production

Food development must be promoted in an integrated manner, and should take into consideration the problem of transportation and distribution of farm products at the level of consumers. And food self-sufficiency should take into consideration the nutritional values of foodstuffs and solve simultaneously the problems of under- and malnutrition.

The set-up of agricultural production should be based on adequate and realistic agrarian reform programmes consistent with the political and social conditions prevailing in respective countries. Improved organization of agricultural production must be given a priority so as to increase agricultural production and productivity.

The OAU, in cooperation with the ECA, FAO, IFAD, WFP and other relevant international organizations, should carry out studies and make recommendations to the next economic summit on the establishment of regional food trade and distribution organizations.

Crops

All African countries should adopt necessary measures for the implementation of the regional food plan for Africa adopted by African Ministers of Agriculture. The main immediate objective should be to bring about quantitative and qualitative improvement in food crops production (cereals, fruits, tubers, oil seeds, vegetables etc.), with a view to replacing a sizeable proportion of the presently imported products. Besides, the production of these food products should be encouraged in countries which have the potential for these crops. More particularly so as to replace the increasing demand for wheat and barley, special attention should be given to the cultivation of cereals such as millet, maize and sorghum.

Areas in which urgent action is recommended include:
- promotion of better agricultural practices, particularly the intensive use of improved input packages and plant protection measures;
- modification of the techno-economic structures of production so as to provide the small farmers and members of agricultural cooperatives with the necessary incentives to increase production;
- better utilization of water for irrigated cereals on on-going irrigation schemes, and initiation of new schemes;
- soil and water conservation;
- flood control and drainage;
- intensification of the use of improved hand tools and drought animals, and promotion of mechanized farming where justified;
- physical infrastructural development, including the building of small

bridges, dams, access and feeder roads and the improvement of education, health and other social facilities, much of which at this stage should, as far as possible, be undertaken through voluntary self-help participation.

Livestock

The main areas in which increased support is recommended in the immediate future are:
- training: establishment of subregional training centres and workshops on livestock production, slaughterhouse practices, and poultry and small stock development;
- animal health: establishment of specialized trypanosomiasis control units, improving productivity of trypanotolerant breeds, and integrated development of areas freed from tsetse; establishment of vaccine production facilities and an effective regional quarantine system; establishment of subregional research centres in tick-borne disease; and improvement of laboratory services and disease surveillance systems;
- animal breeding;
- control and eradication of foot-and-mouth disease;
- controlled grazing and range management;
- development of animal feed; and,
- infrastructural development.

Fisheries

The target should be to increase annual fish production from African waters by one million tons by 1985, which should permit a rise of one kilogram in the level of average annual fish consumption per person between now and 1985.

Incomes/Prices

It is strongly recommended that governments undertake the formulation and application of effective and coherent policies to ensure that prices of farm inputs and farm produce provide an adequate incentive for increasing food production, particularly by small farmers, while safeguarding the interest of the poorer consumers at the same time. Similarly, the individual activities entailed in the recommended programme of action should be designed and implemented with a view to ensuring a beneficial income distribution impact on the rural poor. In particular, efforts should be made to reduce the widening gaps in income between the rich and the poor in the rural area.

Forestry

The objective should be to integrate forestry more closely with agriculture, to ensure adequate supplies of fuel wood and to increase the contribution of forest resources in industrialization.

Research

Science and technology has a pivotal role in the development of agriculture, especially in connection with agronomic research, training and extension. Within the context of agronomic research, special emphasis should be placed on the improvement of livestock, sheep and poultry breeds, as well as the improvement of selected seeds, fertilizers, pesticides and other chemicals suitable for African conditions.

Agricultural research is crucial to the transformation of agriculture in Africa. National research systems should be strengthened, as also inter-country cooperative research programmes.

Agricultural research is crucial to the transformation of agriculture in Africa. National research systems should be strengthened, as also inter-country cooperative research programmes. Agricultural research work should be geared so as to support the objective of food self-sufficiency, and liaison between research and extension should be made more effective. It was therefore recommended that:

- Agricultural research should put more emphasis on the development and spread of new technologies than has occurred in the past.
- Biological innovation such as plant and livestock breeding and control of agricultural pests could substantially increase agricultural production and output in Africa. They provide more productive plant and animal species and other husbandry techniques and should be emphasized in agricultural research programmes.
- Research has in the past addressed itself to a narrow spectrum of food crops and has neglected a number of food crops indigenous to Africa. Such crops are grown by a large number of the rural population and constitute a major proportion of their diet. This situation should be rectified.
- Research should also be intensified in the area of root crops, tubers and soya beans; and into the improvement of production and nutritional values of all food crops.
- Research should also continue for export crops which not only bring in foreign exchange necessary for development but also provide raw materials for our industries.
- Special attention should be given to problems affecting food production in the semi-arid areas in order to stabilize production in this fragile eco-

system. Research should develop adapted crop varieties and production systems that ensure optimal utilisation of the limited soil and water resources.

Services

Rational exploitation and development of natural resources, especially forestry and wildlife, should be promoted as a means of improving food supply in the regions within the context of integrated rural development programmes.

Strong institutions should be developed for rural development planning and monitoring, data collection, provision of agricultural credit and inputs, efficient transport, marketing, agro-industrial development, and storage and processing.

Agricultural mechanisation has a priority role in the increase of agricultural production and in the modernization of farms. However, this problem must be studied very carefully and should be related to industrial development so that it will not further increase the dependency of African countries on the developed world. In the process of agricultural mechanization, special emphasis should be put on animal traction in countries that have not yet reached the appropriate level of motorization.

Resources

Total investments required over the 1980–85 period for the implementation of the proposed programmes amount to about $21.400 m at 1979 prices. In addition, expenditures for inputs would rise by about $560 m over the same period. This level of expenditure will form only part of the total expenditure requirements of the agriculture sector for the 1980s as contained in the document, Regional Food Plan for Africa (AFPLAN), approved by the Ministers of Agriculture in Arusha, Tanzania, in 1978 and endorsed by Heads of State in the Monrovia Declaration in 1979. Additional resources will be necessary to cover the latter half of the decade which is not covered in this Plan of Action for only 1980–85.

All African countries reaffirm their support for IFAD and WFP. They appeal to the international community to place more resources at the disposal of these organizations which should accord top requests coming from African Countries.

It should be desirable to aim at financing at least 50% of the investment requirements with domestic resources. Governments should set up specific yearly goals for food and agriculture, and set up effective national and regional machineries to monitor progress towards them. At the regional level, monitoring should be an inter-agency exercise involving OAU, ECA, FAO, WFC and UNDP.

In the context of the new strategy and targets in food and agriculture, it will be necessary for a reappraisal to be made of the on-going projects that are financed from external sources with a view to ensuring that they too do contribute to the realization of these new objectives.

PLAN OF ACTION FOR ENERGY

(a) Short-term

Hydrocarbons supplies to African countries:
– Everything possible should be done to ensure stable and guaranteed supplies of oil to African countries.
– Arrangements must also be made for African oil-producing countries to increase their assistance to other African countries wherever possible in the training of cadres and technical staff and in prospecting for and exploiting of oil deposits.
– It is also recommended that African experts should be placed at the disposal of memberstates who so desire, in accordance with the 1974 OAU Declaration on Cooperation, Development and Economic Independence.
– With regard to oil prices, and to demonstrate African solidarity, various ways of integrating the impact of oil prices, particularly on the balance of payments, can be suggested, such as preferential tariffs, a compensation fund financed from African and possibly external contributions, including the planned OPEC Fund to offset partially balance-of-payments deficits and finance development projects.
– It should be noted the lack of storage and distribution infrastructure, the existence of middlemen and the shortage of senior technical staff. To reduce the risk of misdirection of supplies, there should be direct negotiations between producing and importing countries.
– To alleviate the difficulties caused by monetary transactions, it is suggested that the possibility of importing countries being allowed to pay in local currency or to use bartering be studied.

(b) Medium- and long-term

Fossil fuels:
– Intensification of geological and geophysical exploration in non-producing countries;
– Evaluation of known hydrocarbon resources and their potential;
– Offshore exploration for hydrocarbons;
– Development of known coal-bearing areas and exploration of new regions with similar geological conditions;

- Assessment of coal reserves and integration of coal utilization in national energy planning;
- Establishment of machinery to coordinate activities and formulate policies for national development and utilization of hydrocarbons;
- Establishment of training and research-institutions in the field of fossil fuels exploration, development and utilization.

Development of hydropower resources:
- Inventory of hydropower resources in all African countries, taking into account their integrated utilization such as electricity production, irrigation, fisheries, navigation, etc.:
- Surveys of hydroelectric power plants and master-plans at the scale of whole river basins for an optimum exploitation of the resources, which should include rural electrification;
- Development of economically attractive small-scale hydroelectric power schemes for rural areas;
- Need for neighbouring countries to exploit hydroelectric installations jointly; (In that connection, certain commonly neglected parameters should be taken into account, such as the need to protect the environment, health problems and the relocation of the people who have to be moved.)
- Evaluation of the needs to be satisfied since the investment required is large. As far as the conveyance of energy over long distances was concerned, the advantages of direct current should be considered in the future;
- Study on internationalizing the status of installations from the point of view of ensuring safe supplies of electrical energy;
- When finance is being sought, projects should be given a subregional and possibly regional character so as to make better use of the priority often given to undertakings of that type;
- In the search for solutions to the energy problem, priority should be given in sites with great hydro-potential, since their enormous potential would make it possible to consider interconnecting a large number of African countries;
- Establishment of national boards for rural electrification;
- Promotion of standardization in power supply equipment and expansion of interconnection of grids (including a decrease in number of existing voltage levels);
- Manufacture of electrical equipment suitable to the needs of African countries by utilizing local raw materials.

Development of new and renewable sources of energy:
- Intensification of geothermal exploration with the use of modern exploitation methods;
- Continuation of scientific and technological research for industrial applica-

tion of geothermal resources as a source of generating electricity, for heating, cooking processes, extraction of minerals and production of water and steam;
- Establishment of geothermal power-generating pilot plants;
- Surveys of the possibilities and feasibilities of harnessing tidal, wave and ocean thermal energy, including research into the techniques to be used for such forms of energy;
- Intensification of research on economic conversion of solar energy into mechanical or electrical energy; examination of potentialities of solar heating systems and solar distillation of saline water; development of instruments for measuring solar radiation and establishment of modern stations;
- Establishment of subregional and regional machinery for cooperation and coordination of solar energy activities in Africa.

Utilization of nuclear energy:
- Nuclear-fuel producing countries should think of conserving their resources for the future.
- The necessary technical cadres should be trained and research encouraged so as to follow technological development in the field and be able to make the right choice when the time comes.
- Future thought should be given to using the uranium produced in Africa as a source of energy by building nuclear power stations in the form of joint projects among neighbouring countries in view of the size of the plants which would probably be available.

Proposals

In order to implement the proposed plan of action rapidly and efficiently it is recommended:

1. Urgent establishment of an African Energy Commission responsible for:
   (a) Coordinating all activities being undertaken in the of the field of energy in Africa, assisting African States in the formulation and coordination of energy policies and programmes and in disseminating of data and information pertaining the energy on the continent;
   (b) Promoting the preparation as a matter of urgency of an exhaustive inventory of all energy resources on the continent;
   (c) Promote the establishment of an African Nuclear Energy Agency with a view to follow development in nuclear technology, formulate and harmonize nuclear energy development programmes in Africa and provide manpower training in the nuclear field.
   (d) promote the establishment of a Regional Geothermal Energy Centre, to assist African countries to explore and exploit their geothermal resources;

(e) To establish an appropriate framework for the implementation of recommendations made at earlier meetings in the field of energy.

2. Possible establishment of an African Energy Development Fund designed specifically to finance the implementation of energy projects in Africa.

3. Urgent establishment of a Regional Solar Energy Centre, the objectives of which are outlined in the constitution already approved by the ECA Fifth Conference of Ministers, held in Rabat in March 1979. In this connection, it is urgent to invite the member-states to accelerate the signature of the said constitution in order to make the Centre operational as soon as possible.

4. Particular attention should be paid to renewable energy resources, such as solar energy, wind energy, biogas and geothermal energy, and research and development in these fields should be intensified.

5. Special attention should be given to reafforestation following the intensive use of wood for heating and of charcoal as the main sources of energy.

6. The highest priority should be given to the use of hydroelectric resources, particularly by developing small hydroelectric power stations.

7. National arrangements for controlling and managing activities involving hydrocarbons should be strengthened.

8. The African countries should take joint action to develop and use the energy resources available in the continent, through cooperation and solidarity, with a view to safeguarding their economic development and survival.

9. Priority should be given to the rapid implementation of the recommendations and resolutions already adopted on energy problems.

9.

RECOMMENDATIONS OF THE GABORONE SEMINAR ON HUMAN RIGHTS AND DEVELOPMENT IN AFRICA

The 'African Seminar on Human Rights and Development' was organized at the University College of Botswana, Gaborone from May 24 to 29, 1982.

REPORTS OF WORKING GROUPS

Working Group on the African Charter

1) The conference welcomes the adoption of the Charter on Human and People's Rights and strongly urges its rapid ratification by African States;
2) All National and Pan-African organizations, groups and individuals who are concerned with the promotion and protection of human rights, particularly the Inter-African Union of Lawyers, should work for the ratification of the Charter;
3) They should also disseminate the contents of the Charter to all the people in their states;
4) Governmental and non-governmental national human rights commissions should be created in African States;
5) There is a need to devise methods for dealing with emergency cases of human rights violations in the operations of the African Human Rights Commission;
6) African Universities and research institutions should undertake research on the provisions of the Charter, particularly from the point of view of its implementation and its relationship to African Constitutions and other international human rights instruments;
7) All members of professions who are concerned with the preservation of human life and human rights, particularly members of the legal profession, should be familiarised with the African Charter;
8) The text of the Charter should be publicised in the mass media and disseminated in and through educational institutions.

Working Group on Women

We in this working group recommend drastic changes including the following: African governments should agree in writing to pursue all appropriate means and without delay a policy of eliminating discrimination against women and to this end undertake:
1) To embody the principle of equality of men and women in their national constitutions and other appropriate legislation if not yet incorporated therein, and to ensure, through law and other appropriate means, the practical realisation of the principle;
2) To adopt appropriate legislative and other measures including sanctions where appropriate prohibiting all forms of discrimination against women;
3) To establish legal protections of the rights of women on an equal basis with men to ensure through competent national tribunals and other public institutions the effective protection of women against any act of discrimination;
4) To take all appropriate measures, including legislation to modify or abolish existing regulations, customs and practices which constitute discrimination against women;
5) Government shall take all appropriate measures to modify the social and cultural pattern of conduct of men and women, with a view to achieving the elimination of prejudices and customary and all other practices which are based on the idea of inferiority or superiority of either sex or on stereotyped roles for men and women. E.g. this could include measures such as the research into the relationship of the dominant prevailing culture of male supremacy and creating an information network and data bank for these findings. Such information will be used for public education purposes.

Working Group on Education, Research and Information

The working group recommends that:
1) Human rights education be implemented in African countries through all education programmes (non-formal; formal; all levels of the school education system; pre-service and in-service vocational and professional education and training);
2) Existing institutions and structures be used to encourage/promote the teaching and education of human rights (these structures may include for example relevant social service organizations such as National Red Cross, Church organizations, rehabilitation divisions, public relations offices, etc.);
3) Simple, relevant teaching aids be developed locally. These should include audio-visual aids;

4) Human rights education take an integrated interdisciplinary approach mainly;
5) International organizations be requested to support meaningful human rights education programmes including the production of relevant teaching material;
6) Urgent re-examination of goals of current research vis-a-vis African problems;
7) Encouragement of research in the field of economic, social and cultural rights;
8) Encourage compilation of all human rights materials in our respective countries as a foundation towards organization of research and information;
9) The setting up of local documentation centres or to improve existing resources;
10) Cooperation with efforts at the international level such as Human Rights Information and Documentation Systems (HURIDOCS) to identify and document human rights material and co-ordinate these efforts with the regional system (the Pan-African Documentation and information System-PADIS, which is supported by UNECA).
11) To encourage support by international, regional and national organizations in support of seminars, workshops, conferences, meetings such as this one for several advantageous reasons relating to education research and information.

10.

A.C.P./E.E.C. (LOMÉ III) CONVENTION (EXCERPTS)

Contracting Parties to the Treaty establishing the European Coal and Steel Community and the Treaty establishing the European Economic Community, hereinafter referred to as 'the Community', the States of the Community being hereinafter referred to as 'Member States',

and the Council and Commission of the European Communities,

of the one part, and

Her Majesty the Queen of Antigua and Barbuda,
The Head of State of the Bahamas,
The Head of State of Barbados,
Her Majesty the Queen of Belize,
The President of the People's Republic of Benin,
The President of the Republic of Botswana,
and other states, hereinafter referred to as 'ACP States',

of the other part,

Having regard to the Treaty establishing the European Economic Community and the Treaty establishing the European Coal and Steel Community, on the one hand, and the Georgetown Agreement constituting the group of African, Caribbean and Pacific States, on the other;

Anxious to reinforce, on the basis of complete equality between partners and in their mutual interest, close and continuing co-operation in a spirit of international solidarity;

Wishing to demonstrate their common desire to maintain and develop the friendly relations existing between their countries, in accordance with the principles of the Charter of the United Nations;

Reaffirming their adherence to the principles of the said Charter and their faith in fundamental human rights, in the dignity and worth of the human person, in the equal rights of men and women and of nations large and small;

Resolved to step up their common efforts to contribute towards international co-operation and to the solution of international problems of economic, social, intellectual and humanitarian nature, in conformity with the aspirations of the international community towards the establishment of a new, more just and more balanced economic order;

Resolved to make, through their co-operation, a significant contribution to the economic development and social progess of the ACP States and to the greater well-being of their populations;

Have decided to conclude this Convention and to this end have designated as their Plenipotentiaries:

[...]

CHAPTER 1

Objectives and principles of co-operation

Article 1

The Community and its Member States, of the one part, and the ACP States, of the other part (hereinafter referred to as the Contracting Parties), hereby conclude this co-operation Convention in order to promote and expedite the economic, cultural and social development of the ACP States and to consolidate and diversify their relations in a spirit of solidarity and mutual interest.

The Contracting Parties thereby affirm their undertaking to continue, strengthen and render more effective the system of co-operation established under the first and second ACP-EEC Conventions and confirm the special character of their relations, based on their reciprocal interest, and the specific nature of their co-operation.

The Contracting Parties hereby express their resolve to intensify their effort to create, with a view to a more just and balanced international economic order, a model for relations between developed and developing states and to work together to affirm in the international context the principles underlying their co-operation.

[...]

Article 4

Support shall be provided in ACP-EEC co-operation for the ACP States' own efforts to achieve more self-reliant and self-sustained development based on their cultural and social values, their human capacities, their natural resources and their economic potential in order to promote the ACP States' social and economic progress and the well-being of their population through the satisfaction of their basic needs, the recognition of the role of women and the enhancement of people's capacities, with respect for their dignity.

[...]

CHAPTER 2

Objectives and guidelines of the Convention in the main areas of co-operation

Article 10

Co-operation shall be aimed at supporting development in the ACP States, a process centred on man himself and rooted in each people's culture. It shall back up the policies and measures adopted by those States to enhance their human resources, increase their own creative capacities and promote their cultural identities. Co-operation shall also encourage participation by the population in the design and execution of development operations.

Account shall be taken, in the various fields of co-operation, and at all the different stages of the operations executed, of the cultural dimension and social implications of such operations.

[...]

Article 12

Agricultural co-operation shall be aimed at the pursuit of food self-sufficiency and food security in the ACP States, developing and organizing their productive systems, improving the living standards and conditions and the life styles of the rural population and achieving the balanced development of rural areas.

Operations in this field shall be designed and executed to support the agricultural and food policies or strategies adopted by the ACP States.

[...]

Article 19

The Community shall contribute towards the ACP States' own development efforts by providing adequate financial resources and appropriate technical assistance aimed at stepping up those States' capacities for self-reliant and integrated economic, social and cultural development and also at helping to raise their population's standard of living and well-being.

Such contribution shall be made on predictable and regular bases. They shall be accorded on the most liberal terms possible for the Community. Particular account shall be taken of the situation of the least-developed ACP States.

[...]

(Agricultural co-operation and food security)

[...]

Article 26

Co-operation in the agricultural and rural sector, that is arable farming, livestock production, fisheries and forestry, shall be aimed, inter alia, at:
- supporting that ACP States' efforts to increase their degree of self-sufficiency in food, in particular by strengthening the capacity of the ACP States to provide their population with sufficient food and ensure a satisfactory level of nutrition;
- reinforcing food security at national, regional and inter-regional level;
- guaranteeing the rural population incomes that will significantly improve their standard of living;
- promoting the active participation of the rural population in their own development by organizing small farmers into associations and integrating them more effectively into national and international economic activity;
- creating satisfactory living conditions and a satisfactory life style in the rural environment, notably by developing social and cultural activities;
- improving rural productivity, notably by transfers of appropriate technology and the rational exploitation of plant and animal resources;
- reducing post-harvest losses;
- diversifying job-creating rural activities and expanding activities that back up production;
- improving production by on-the-spot processing of the products of agriculture, including livestock farming, and fisheries and forestry;
- ensuring a balance between food crops and export crops;

- developing agricultural research tailored to the natural and human environment of the country and the region and meeting extension service needs;
- in the context of the above objective, protecting the natural environment, particularly through specific operations to control drought and desertification.

[...]

Article 123

1. Co-operation shall support the ACP States' efforts aimed at enhancing the work of women, improving their living conditions, expanding their role and promoting their status in the production and development process.

2. Particular attention shall be given to access by women to all aspects of training, to more advanced technology, to credit and to co-operative organizations, and to appropriate technology aimed at alleviating the arduous nature of their tasks.

[...]

Article 214

Technical co-operation shall provide support for educational and training operations in accordance with Article 119.

PART II

Instruments on Southern Africa

Treaties

11.

INTERNATIONAL CONVENTION ON THE SUPPRESSION AND PUNISHMENT OF THE CRIME OF *APARTHEID*

Annex to GA Res. 3068 (XXVIII) of 30 November 1973. Opened for signature on the same day. Entered into force on 18 July 1976. For the Parties to the Convention see *I.O.I.*, I. App. *infra*. A World Conference for Action against *Apartheid* was held at Lagos, Nigeria, from 22 to 26 August 1977. See *U.N. Doc.* A/CONF. 91.

The States Parties to the present Convention,
Recalling the provisions of the Charter of the United Nations, in which all Members pledged themselves to take joint and separate action in co-operation with the Organization for the achievement of universal respect for, and observance of, human rights and fundamental freedoms for all without distinction as to race, sex, language or religion,
Considering the Universal Declaration of Human Rights, which states that all human beings are born free and equal in dignity and rights and that everyone is entitled to all the rights and freedoms set forth in the Declaration, without distinction of any kind, such as race, colour or national origin,
Considering the Declaration on the Granting of Independence to Colonial Countries and Peoples, in which the General Assembly stated that the process of liberation is irresistible and irreversible and that, in the interests of human dignity, progress and justice, an end must be put to colonialism and all practices of segregation and discrimination associated therewith,
Observing that, in accordance with the International Convention on the Elimination of All Forms of Racial Discrimination, States particularly condemn racial segregation and *apartheid* and undertake to prevent, prohibit and eradicate all practices of this nature in territories under their jurisdiction,
Observing that, in the Convention on the Prevention and Punishment of the Crime of Genocide, certain acts which may also be qualified as acts of *apartheid* constitute a crime under international law,
Observing that, in the Convention on the Non-Applicability of Statutory Limitations to War Crimes and Crimes Against Humanity, „inhuman acts resulting from the policy of *apartheid*" are qualified as crimes against humanity.
Observing that the General Assembly of the United Nations has adopted a number of resolutions in which the policies and practices of *apartheid* are condemned as a crime against humanity,
Observing that the Security Council has emphasized that *apartheid*, its continued intensification and expansion, seriously disturb and threaten international peace and security,
Convinced that an International Convention on the Suppression and Punishment of the Crime of *Apartheid* would make it possible to take more effective measures at the international and national levels with a view to the suppression and punishment of the crime of *apartheid*,
Have agreed as follows:

Article I

1. The States Parties to the present Convention declare that *apartheid* is a crime against humanity and that inhuman acts resulting from the policies and practices of *apartheid* and similar policies and practices of racial segregation and discrimination, as defined in article II of the Convention, are crimes violating the principles of international law, in particular the purposes and principles of the Charter of the United Nations, and constituting a serious threat to international peace and security.
2. The States Parties to the present Convention declare criminal those organizations, institutions and individuals committing the crime of *apartheid*.

Article II

For the purpose of the present Convention, the term „the crime of *apartheid*", which shall include similar policies and practices of racial segregation and discrimination as practised in southern Africa, shall apply to the following inhuman acts committed for the purpose of establishing and maintaining domination by one racial group of persons over any other racial group of persons and systematically oppressing them:
(*a*) Denial to a member or members of a racial group or groups of the right to life and liberty of person:
(i) By murder of members of a racial group or groups;
(ii) By the infliction upon the members of a racial group or groups of serious bodily or mental harm by the infringement of their freedom or dignity, or by subjecting them to torture or to cruel, inhuman or degrading treatment or punishment;
(iii) By arbitrary arrest and illegal imprisonment of the members of a racial group or groups;
(*b*) Deliberate imposition on a racial group or groups of living conditions calculated to cause its or their physical destruction in whole or in part;
(*c*) Any legislative measures and other measures calculated to prevent a racial group or groups from participation in the political, social, economic and cultural life of the country and the deliberate creation of conditions preventing the full development of such a group or groups, in particular by denying to members of a racial group or groups basic human rights and freedoms, including the right to work, the right to form recognized trade unions, the right to education, the right to leave and to return to their contry, the right to a nationality, the right to freedom of movement and residence, the right to freedom of opinion and expression, and the right to freedom of peaceful assembly and association;
(*d*) Any measures, including legislative measures, designed to divide the population along racial lines by the creation of separate reserves and ghettos for the members of a racial group or groups, the prohibition of mixed marriages among members of various racial groups, the expropriation of landed property belonging to a racial group or groups or to members thereof;
(*e*) Exploitation of the labour of the members of a racial group or groups, in particular by submitting them to forced labour;
(*f*) Persecution of organizations and persons, by depriving them of fundamental rights and freedoms, because they oppose *apartheid*.

Article III

International criminal responsibility shall apply, irrespective of the motive involved, to individuals, members of organizations and institutions and representatives of the State, whether residing in the territory of the State in which the acts are perpetrated or in some other State, whenever they:
(*a*) Commit, participate in, directly incite or conspire in the commission of the acts mentioned in article II of the present Convention;
(*b*) Directly abet, encourage or co-operate in the commission of the crime of *apartheid*.

Article IV

The States Parties to the present Convention undertake:
(*a*) To adopt any legislative or other measures necessary to suppress as well as to prevent any encouragement of the crime of *apartheid* and similar segregationist policies or their manifestations and to punish persons guilty of that crime;
(*b*) To adopt legislative, judicial and administrative measures to prosecute, bring to trial and punish in accordance with their jurisdiction persons responsible for, or accused of, the acts defined in article II of the present Convention, whether or not such persons reside in the territory of the State in which the acts are committed or are nationals of that State or of some other State or are stateless persons.

Article V

Persons charged with the acts enumerated in article II of the present Convention may be tried by a competent tribunal of any State Party to the Convention which may acquire jurisdiction over the person of the accused or by an international penal tribunal having jurisdiction with respect to those States Parties which shall have accepted its jurisdiction.

Article VI

The States Parties to the present Convention undertake to accept and carry out in accordance with the Charter of the United Nations the decisions taken by the Security Council aimed at the prevention, suppression and punishment of the crime of *apartheid*, and to cooperate in the implementation of decisions adopted by other competent organs of the United Nations with a view to achieving the purposes of the Convention.

Article VII

1. The States Parties to the present Convention undertake to submit periodic reports to the group established under article IX on the legislative, judicial, administrative or other measures that they have adopted and that give effect to the provisions of the Convention.
2. Copies of the reports shall be transmitted through the Secretary-General of the United Nations to the Special Committee on *Apartheid*.

Article VIII

Any State Party to the present Convention may call upon any competent organ of the United Nations to take such action under the Charter of the United Nations as it considers appropriate for the prevention and suppression of the crime of *apartheid*.

Article IX

1. The Chairman of the Commission on Human Rights shall appoint a group consisting of three members of the Commission on Human Rights, who are also representatives of States Parties to the present Convention, to consider reports submitted by States Parties in accordance with article VII.
2. If, among the members of the Commission on Human Rights, there are no representatives of States Parties to the present Convention or if there are fewer than three such representatives, the Secretary-General of the United Nations shall, after consulting all States Parties to the Convention, designate a representative of the State Party or representatives of the States Parties which are not members of the Commission on Human Rights to take part in the work of the group established in accordance with paragraph 1 of this article, until such time as representatives of the States Parties to the Convention are elected to the Commission on Human Rights.
3. The group may meet for a period of not more than five days, either before the opening or after the closing of the session of the Commission on Human Rights, to consider the reports submitted in accordance with article VII.

Article X

1. The States Parties to the present Convention empower the Commission on Human Rights:
(*a*) To request United Nations organs, when transmitting copies of petitions under article 15 of the International Convention on the Elimination of All Forms of Racial Discrimination, to draw its attention to complaints concerning acts which are enumerated in article II of the present Convention;
(*b*) To prepare, on the basis of reports from competent organs of the United Nations and periodic reports from States Parties to the present Convention, a list of individuals, organizations, institutions and representatives of States which are alleged to be responsible for the crimes enumerated in article II of the Convention, as well as those against whom legal proceedings have been undertaken by States Parties to the Convention;
(*c*) To request information from the competent United Nations organs concerning measures taken by the authorities responsible for the administration of Trust and Non-Self-Governing Territories, and all other Territories to which General Assembly resolution 1514 (XV) of 14 December 1960 applies, with regard to such individuals alleged to be responsible for crimes under article II of the Convention who are believed to be under their territorial and administrative jurisdiction.
2. Pending the achievement of the objectives of the Declaration on the Granting of Independence to Colonial Countries and Peoples, contained in General Assembly resolution 1514 (XV), the provisions of the present Convention shall in no way limit the right of petition granted to those peoples by other international instruments or by the United Nations and its specialized agencies.

Article XI

1. Acts enumerated in article II of the present Convention shall not be considered political crimes for the purpose of extradition.
2. The States Parties to the present Convention undertake in such cases to grant extradition in accordance with their legislation and with the treaties in force.

Article XII

Disputes between States Parties arising out of the interpretation, application or implementation of the present Convention which have not been settled by negotiation shall, at the request of the States Parties to the dispute, be brought before the International Court of Justice, save where the parties to the dispute have agreed on some other form of settlement.

Article XIII

The present Convention is open for signature by all States. Any State which does not sign the Convention before its entry into force may accede to it.

Article XIV

1. The present Convention is subject to ratification. Instruments of ratification shall be deposited with the Secretary-General of the United Nations.
2. Accession shall be effected by the deposit of an instrument of accession with the Secretary-General of the United Nations.

Article XV

1. The present Convention shall enter into force on the thirtieth day after the date of the deposit with the Secretary-General of the United Nations of the twentieth instrument of ratification or accession.
2. For each State ratifying the present Convention or acceding to it after the deposit of the twentieth instrument of ratification or instrument of accession, the Convention shall enter into force on the thirtieth day after the date of the deposit of its own instrument of ratification or instrument of accession.

Article XVI

A State Party may denounce the present Convention by written notification to the Secretary-General of the United Nations. Denunciation shall take effect one year after the date of receipt of the notification by the Secretary-General.

Article XVII

1. A request for the revision of this Convention may be made at any time by any State Party by means of a notification in writing addressed to the Secretary-General of the United Nations.
2. The General Assembly of the United Nations shall decide upon the steps, if any, to be taken in respect of such request.

Article XVIII

The Secretary-General of the United Nations shall inform all States of the following particulars:
(a) Signatures, ratifications and accessions under articles XIII and XIV;
(b) The date of entry into force of the present Convention under article XV;
(c) Denunciations under article XVI;
(d) Notifications under article XVII.

Article XIX

1. The present Convention, of which the Chinese, English, French, Russian and Spanish texts are equally authentic, shall be deposited in the archives of the United Nations.
2. The Secretary-General of the United Nations shall transmit certified copies of the present Convention to all States.

12.

INTERNATIONAL CONVENTION AGAINST *APARTHEID* IN SPORTS

(Adopted by (U.N.) General Assembly Resolution 40/64 G of 10 December 1985 and opened for signature and ratification on 16 May 1986. As at 21 August 1986, 64 States had signed the Convention.)

The States Parties to the present Convention,

Recalling the provisions of the Charter of the United Nations, in which all Members pledged themselves to take joint and separate action, in co-operation with the Organization, for the achievement of universal respect for, and observance of, human rights and fundamental freedoms for all without distinction as to race, sex, language or religion,

Considering that the Universal Declaration of Human Rights proclaims that all human beings are born free and equal in dignity and rights and that everyone is entitled to all the rights and freedoms set forth in the Declaration without distinction of any kind, particularly in regard to race, colour or national origin,

Observing that, in accordance with the International Convention on the Elimination of All Forms of Racial Discrimination, States Parties to that Convention particularly condemn racial segregation and *apartheid* and undertake to prevent, prohibit and eradicate all practices of this nature in all fields,

Observing that the General Assembly of the United Nations has adopted a number of resolutions condemning the practice of *apartheid* in sports and has affirmed its unqualified support for the Olympic principle that no discrimination be allowed on the grounds of race, religion or political affiliation and that merit should be the sole criterion for participation in sports activities,

Considering that the International Declaration against *Apartheid* in Sports, which was adopted by the General Assembly on 14 December 1977, solemnly affirms the necessity for the speedy elimination of *apartheid* in sports,

Recalling the provisions of the International Convention on the Suppression and Punishment of the Crime of *Apartheid* and recognizing, in particular, that participation in sports exchanges with teams selected on the basis of *apartheid*

directly abets and encourages the commission of the crime of *apartheid,* as defined in that Convention,

Resolved to adopt all necessary measures to eradicate the practice of *apartheid* in sports and to promote international sports contacts based on the Olympic principle,

Recognizing that sports contact with any country practising *apartheid* in sports condones and strengthens *apartheid* in violation of the Olympic principle and thereby becomes the legitimate concern of all Governments,

Desiring to implement the principles embodied in the International Declaration against *Apartheid* in Sports and to secure the earliest adoption of practical measures to that end,

Convinced that the adoption of an International Convention against *Apartheid* in Sports would result in more effective measures at the international and national levels, with a view to eliminating *apartheid* in sports,

Have agreed as follows:

Article 1

For the purposes of the present Convention:

(a) The expression *'apartheid'* shall mean a system of institutionalized racial segregation and discrimination for the purpose of establishing and maintaining domination by one racial group of persons over another racial group of persons and systematically oppressing them, such as that pursued by South Africa, and *'apartheid* in sports' shall mean the application of the policies and practices of such a system in sports activities, whether organized on a professional or an amateur basis;

(b) The expression 'national sports facilities' shall mean any sports facility operated within the framework of a sports programme conducted under the auspices of a national government;

(c) The expression 'Olympic principle' shall mean the principle that no discrimination be allowed on the grounds of race, religion or political affiliation;

(d) The expression 'sports contracts' shall mean any contract concluded for the organization, promotion, performance or derivative rights, including servicing, of any sports activity;

(e) The expression 'sports bodies' shall mean any organization constituted to organize sports activities at the national level, including national Olympic committees, national sports federations or national governing sports committees;

(f) The expression 'team' shall mean a group of sportsmen organized for the purpose of participating in sports activities in competition with other such organized groups;

(g) The expression 'sportsmen' shall mean men and women who participate in sports activities on an individual or team basis, as well as managers, coaches, trainers and other officials whose functions are essential for the operation of a team;

Article 2

States Parties strongly condemn *apartheid* and undertake to pursue immediately by all appropriate means the policy of eliminating the practice of *apartheid* in all its forms from sports.

Article 3

States Parties shall not permit sports contact with a country practising *apartheid* and shall take appropriate action to ensure that their sports bodies, teams, and individual sportsmen do not have such contact.

Article 4

States Parties shall take all possible measures to prevent sports contact with a country practising *apartheid* and shall ensure that effective means exist for bringing about compliance with such measures.

Article 5

States Parties shall refuse to provide financial or other assistance to enable their sports bodies, teams and individual sportsmen to participate in sports activities in a country practising *apartheid* or with teams or individual sportsmen selected on the basis of *apartheid*.

Article 6

Each State Party shall take appropriate action against its sports bodies, teams and individual sportsmen that participate in sports activities in a country practising *apartheid* or with teams representing a country practising *apartheid*, which in particular shall include:
 (a) Refusal to provide financial or other assistance for any purpose to such sports bodies, teams and individual sportsmen;
 (b) Restriction of access to national sports facilities by such sports bodies, teams and individual sportsmen;
 (c) Non-enforceability of all sports contracts which involve sports activities in a country practising *apartheid* or with teams or individual sportsmen selected on the basis of *apartheid;*

(d) Denial and withdrawal of national honours or awards in sports to such teams and individual sportsmen;
(e) Denial of official receptions in honour of such teams or sportsmen.

Article 7

States Parties shall deny visas and/or entry to representatives of sports bodies, teams and individual sportsmen representing a country practising *apartheid*.

Article 8

States Parties shall take all appropriate action to secure the expulsion of a country practising *apartheid* from international and regional sports bodies.

Article 9

States Parties shall take all appropriate measures to prevent international sports bodies from imposing financial or other penalties on affiliated bodies which, in accordance with United Nations resolutions, the provisions of the present Convention and the spirit of the Olympic principle, refuse to participate in sports with a country practising *apartheid*.

Article 10

1. States Parties shall use their best endeavours to ensure universal compliance with the Olympic principle of non-discrimination and the provisions of the present Convention.
2. Towards this end, States Parties shall prohibit entry into their countries of members of teams and individual sportsmen participating or who have participated in sports competitions in South Africa and shall prohibit entry into their countries of representatives of sports bodies, members of teams and individual sportsmen who invite on their own initiative sports bodies, teams and sportsmen officially representing a country practising *apartheid* and participating under its flag. States Parties may also prohibit entry of representatives of sports bodies, members of teams or individual sportsmen who maintain sports contacts with sports bodies, teams or sportsmen representing a country practising *apartheid* and participating under its flag. Prohibition of entry should not violate the regulations of the relevant sports federations which support the elimination of *apartheid* in sports and shall apply only to participation in sports activities.
3. States Parties shall advise their national representatives to international

sports federations to take all possible and practical steps to prevent the participation of the sports bodies, teams and sportsmen referred to in paragraph 2 above in international sports competitions and shall, through their representatives in international sports organizations, take every possible measure:

(a) To ensure the expulsion of South Africa from all federations in which it still holds membership as well as to deny South Africa reinstatement to membership in any federation from which it has been expelled;

(b) In case of national federations condoning sports exchanges with a country practising *apartheid,* to impose sanctions against such national federations including, if necessary, expulsion from the relevant international sports organization and exclusion of their representatives from participation in international sports competitions.

4. In cases of flagrant violations of the provisions of the present Convention, States Parties shall take appropriate action as they deem fit, including, where necessary, steps aimed at the exclusion of the responsible national sports governing bodies, national sports federations or sportsmen of the countries concerned from international sports competition.

5. The provisions of the present article relating specifically to South Africa shall cease to apply when the system of *apartheid* is abolished in that country.

Article 11

1. There shall be established a Commission against *Apartheid* in Sports (hereinafter referred to as 'the Commission') consisting of fifteen members of high moral character and committed to the struggle against *apartheid,* particular attention being paid to participation of persons having experience in sports administration, elected by the States Parties from among their nationals, having regard to the most equitable geographical distribution and the representation of the principal legal systems.

2. The members of the Commission shall be elected by secret ballot from a list of persons nominated by the States Parties. Each State Party may nominate one person from among its own nationals.

3. The initial election shall be held six months after the date of the entry into force of the present Convention. At least three months before the date of each election, the Secretary-General of the United Nations shall address a letter to the States Parties inviting them to submit their nominations within two months. The Secretary-General shall prepare a list in alphabetical order of all persons thus nominated, indicating the States Parties which have nominated them, and shall submit it to the States Parties.

4. Elections of the members of the Commission shall be held at a meeting of States Parties convened by the Secretary-General at United Nations Head-

quarters. At that meeting, for which two thirds of the States Parties shall constitute a quorum, the persons elected to the Commission shall be those nominees who obtain the largest number of votes and an absolute majority of the votes of the representatives of States Parties present and voting.

5. The members of the Commission shall be elected for a term of four years. However, the terms of nine of the members elected at the first election shall expire at the end of two years; immediately after the first election, the names of these nine members shall be chosen by lot by the Chairman of the Commission.

6. For the filling of casual vacancies, the State Party whose national has ceased to function as a member of the Commission shall appoint another person from among its nationals, subject to the approval of the Commission.

7. States Parties shall be responsible for the expenses of the members of the Commission while they are in performance of Commission duties.

Article 12

1. States Parties undertake to submit to the Secretary-General of the United Nations, for consideration by the Commission, a report on the legislative, judicial, administrative or other measures which they have adopted to give effect to the provisions of the present Convention within one year of its entry into force and thereafter every two years. The Commission may request further information from the States Parties.

2. The Commission shall report annually through the Secretary-General to the General Assembly of the United Nations on its activities and may make suggestions and general recommendations based on the examination of the reports and information received from the States Parties. Such suggestions and recommendations shall be reported to the General Assembly together with comments, if any, from States Parties concerned.

3. The Commission shall examine, in particular, the implementation of the provisions of article 10 of the present Convention and make recommendations on action to be undertaken.

4. A meeting of States Parties shall be convened by the Secretary-General at the request of a majority of the States Parties to consider further action with respect to the implementation of the provisions of article 10 of the present Convention. In cases of flagrant violation of the provisions of the present Convention, a meeting of States Parties shall be convened by the Secretary-General at the request of the Commission.

Article 13

1. Any State Party may at any time declare that it recognizes the competence

of the Commission to receive and examine complaints concerning breaches of the provisions of the present Convention submitted by States Parties which have also made such a declaration. The Commission may decide on the appropriate measures to be taken in respect of breaches.

2. States Parties against which a complaint has been made, in accordance with paragraph 1 of the present article, shall be entitled to be represented and take part in the proceedings of the Commission.

Article 14

1. The Commission shall meet at least once a year.
2. The Commission shall adopt its own rules of procedure.
3. The secretariat of the Commission shall be provided by the Secretary-General of the United Nations.
4. The meetings of the Commission shall normally be held at United Nations Headquarters.
5. The Secretary-General shall convene the initial meeting of the Commission.

Article 15

The Secretary-General of the United Nations shall be the depositary of the present Convention.

Article 16

1. The present Convention shall be open for signature at United Nations Headquarters by all States until its entry into force.
2. The present Convention shall be subject to ratification, acceptance or approval by the signatory States.

Article 17

The present Convention shall be open for accession by all States.

Article 18

1. The present Convention shall enter into force on the thirtieth day after the date of deposit with the Secretary-General of the United Nations of the twenty-seventh instrument of ratification, acceptance, approval or accession.
2. For each State ratifying, accepting, approving or acceding to the present Convention after its entry into force, the Convention shall enter into force on the thirtieth day after the date of deposit of the relevant instrument.

Article 19

Any dispute between States Parties arising out of the interpretation, application or implementation of the present Convention which is not settled by negotiation shall be brought before the International Court of Justice at the request and with the mutual consent of the States Parties to the dispute, save where the Parties to the dispute have agreed on some other form of settlement.

Article 20

1. Any State Party may propose an amendment or revision to the present Convention and file it with the depositary. The Secretary-General of the United Nations shall thereupon communicate the proposed amendment or revision to the States Parties with a request that they notify him whether they favour a conference of States Parties for the purpose of considering and voting upon the proposal. In the event that at least one third of the States Parties favour such a conference, the Secretary-General shall convene the conference under the auspices of the United Nations. Any amendment or revision adopted by the majority of the States Parties present and voting at the conference shall be submitted to the General Assembly of the United Nations for approval.

2. Amendments or revisions shall come into force when they have been approved by the General Assembly and accepted by a two-thirds majority of the States Parties, in accordance with their respective constitutional processes.

3. When amendments or revisions come into force, they shall be binding on those States Parties which have accepted them, other States Parties still being bound by the provisions of the present Convention and any earlier amendment or revision which they have accepted.

Article 21

A State Party may withdraw from the present Convention by written notification to the depositary. Such withdrawal shall take effect one year after the date of receipt of the notification by the depositary.

Article 22

The present Convention has been concluded in Arabic, Chinese, English, French, Russian and Spanish, all texts being equally authentic.

Other Instruments

13.

THE FREEDOM CHARTER

Adopted at Kliptown, Transvaal, 26 June 1955

The idea of a national convention where South Africans of all races and colour would be represented was first conceived in 1953. Various organisations and groups were asked to indicate how they would like the country to be governed. Finally on 25th and 26th June 1955 a 'Congress of the People' was held in Klipfontein (Kliptown) near Johannesburg and 'The Freedom Charter' was adopted on the latter date. It incorporated the responses of the organisations and groups and set out guidelines and principles as to how South Africa should be governed in the future.

The Congress was convened and attended by the African National Congress (ANC), South African Coloured People's Organisation (SACPO), the Congress of Democrats (COD: an organisation of whites), The Indian Congress and the newly formed South African Congress of Trade Unions (SACTU) (Kairos, p. 17). 2,888 delegates from throughout South Africa attended the Congress which was 'perhaps the most representative gathering ever held in the country'. (Mission To South Africa, The Commonwealth Report 1986, Annex 4. This Report does not mention SACTU as one of the Conveners of the Congress).

In 1956 Chief Albert Luthuli, Nelson Mandela, Ruth First and 153 other participants and leaders of the Congress were prosecuted in what was called the 'High Treason Case'. '105 of the accused were Africans, 23 whites, 21 Indians and 7 coloured people' (Kairos, p. 19). The case ended in an ignominious defeat for the apartheid regime for 'after a trial lasting more than four years all the accused persons were acquitted but the ANC and the Congress of Democrats were banned while the other two organisations were effectively prevented from legal operation by the banning of their leaders' (Mission To South Africa, The Commonwealth Report 1986, Annex 4).

Note. Rudi Oomen's translation from Dutch into English of 'Kairos' was taken into account in writing the introductory note; and we are grateful to him.

We, the People of South Africa, declare for all our country and the world to know:
that South Africa belongs to all who live in it, black and white, and that no government can justly claim authority unless it is based on the will of all the people;
that our people have been robbed of their birthright to land, liberty and peace by a form of government founded on injustice and inequality;
that our country will never be prosperous or free until all our people live in brotherhood, enjoying equal rights and opportunities;
that only a democratic state, based on the will of all the people, can secure to all their birthright without distinction of colour, race, sex or belief;
And therefore, we, the people of South Africa, black and white together – equals, countrymen and brothers – adopt this Freedom Charter. And we pledge ourselves to strive together, sparing neither strength nor courage, until the democratic changes here set out have been won.

THE PEOPLE SHALL GOVERN!

Every man and woman shall have the right to vote for and to stand as a candidate for all bodies which make laws;
All people shall be entitled to take part in the administration of the country;
The rights of the people shall be the same, regardless of race, colour or sex.
All bodies of minority rule, advisory boards, councils and authorities shall be replaced by democratic organs of selfgovernment.

ALL NATIONAL GROUPS SHALL HAVE EQUAL RIGHTS!

There shall be equal status in the bodies of state, in the courts and in the schools for all national groups and races;
All people shall have equal right to use their own languages, and to develop their own folk culture and customs;
All national groups shall be protected by law against insults to their race and national pride;
The preaching and practice of national, race or colour discrimination and contempt shall be a punishable crime;
All apartheid laws and practices shall be set aside.

THE PEOPLE SHALL SHARE IN THE COUNTRY'S WEALTH!

The national wealth of our country, the heritage of all South Africans, shall be restored to the people;
The mineral wealth beneath the soil, the banks and monopoly industry shall be transferred to the ownership of the people as a whole;
All other industry and trade shall be controlled to assist the well-being of the people;
All people shall have equal rights to trade where they choose, to manufacture and to enter all trades, crafts and professions.

THE LAND SHALL BE SHARED AMONG THOSE WHO WORK IT!

Restrictions of land ownership on a racial basis shall be ended, and all the land redivided amongst those who work it, to banish famine and land hunger;
The state shall help the peasants with implements, seed, tractors and dams to save the soil and assist the tillers;
Freedom of movement shall be guaranteed to all who work on the land;
All shall have the right to occupy land wherever they choose;
People shall not be robbed of their cattle, and forced labour and farm prisons shall be abolished.

ALL SHALL BE EQUAL BEFORE THE LAW!

No one shall be imprisoned, deported or restricted without a fair trial;
No one shall be condemned by the order of any Government official;
The courts shall be representative of all the people;
Imprisonment shall be only for serious crimes against the people, and shall aim at re-education, not vengeance;
The police force and army shall be open to all on an equal basis and shall be the helpers and protectors of the people;
All laws which discriminate on grounds of race, colour or belief shall be repealed.

ALL SHALL ENJOY EQUAL HUMAN RIGHTS!

The law shall guarantee to all their right to speak, to organise, to meet together, to publish, to preach, to worship and to educate their children;
The privacy of the house from police raids shall be protected by law;

All shall be free to travel without restriction from country-side to town, from province to province, and from South Africa abroad;

Pass Laws, permits and all other laws restricting these freedoms shall be abolished.

THERE SHALL BE WORK AND SECURITY!

All who work shall be free to form trade unions, to elect their officers and to make wage agreements with their employers;

The state shall recognise the right and duty of all to work, and to draw full unemployment benefits;

Men and women of all races shall receive equal pay for equal work;

There shall be a forty-hour working week, a national minimum wage, paid annual leave, and sick leave for all workers, and maternity leave on full pay for all working mothers;

Miners, domestic workers, farm workers and civil servants shall have the same rights as all other who work;

Child labour, compound labour, the tot system and contract labour shall be abolished.

THE DOORS OF LEARNING AND OF CULTURE SHALL BE OPENED!

The government shall discover, develop and encourage national talent for the enhancement of our cultural life;

All the cultural treasures of mankind shall be open to all, by free exchange of books, ideas and contact with other lands;

The aim of education shall be to teach the youth to love their people and their culture, to honour human brotherhood, liberty and peace;

Education shall be free, compulsory, universal and equal for all children;

Higher education and technical training shall be opened to all by means of state allowances and scholarships awarded on the basis of merit;

Adult illiteracy shall be ended by a mass state eduction plan;

Teachers shall have all the rights of other citizens;

The colour bar in cultural life, in sport and in education shall be abolished.

THERE SHALL BE HOUSES, SECURITY AND COMFORT!

All people shall have the right to live where they choose, to be decently housed, and to bring up their families in comfort and security;

Unused housing space to be made available to the people;

Rent and prices shall be lowered, food plentiful and no one shall go hungry;

A preventive health scheme shall be run by the state;

Free medical care and hospitalisation shall be provided for all, with special care for mothers and young children;

Slums shall be demolished, and new suburbs built where all have transport, roads, lighting, playing fields, creches and social centres;

The aged, the orphans, the disabled and the sick shall be cared for by the state;

Rest, leisure and recreation shall be the right of all;

Fenced locations and ghettoes shall be abolished, and laws which break up families shall be repealed.

THERE SHALL BE PEACE AND FRIENDSHIP!

South Africa shall be a fully independent state, which respects the rights and sovereignty of all nations;

South Africa shall strive to maintain world peace and the settlement of all international disputes by negotiation – not war;

Peace and friendship amongst all our people shall be secured by upholding the equal rights, opportunities and status of all;

The people of the protectorates – Basutoland, Bechuanaland and Swaziland shall be free to decide for themselves their own future;

The right of all the peoples of Africa to independence and self-government shall be recognised, and shall be the basis of close co-operation.

Let all who love their people and their country now say, as we say here: 'THESE FREEDOMS WE WILL FIGHT FOR, SIDE BY SIDE. THROUGHOUT OUR LIVES, UNTIL WE HAVE WON OUR LIBERTY.'

14.

LUSAKA MANIFESTO ON SOUTHERN AFRICA: JOINT STATEMENT BY THIRTEEN GOVERNMENTS, LUSAKA (APRIL 1969)

The Manifesto is a joint statement agreed by representatives of Burundi, Central African Republic, Chad, Congo Republic, Congo (Kinshasa), now Zaire, Ethiopia, Kenya, Rwanda, Somalia, Sudan, Tanzania, Uganda, and Zambia, at the Conference of East and Central African States in April, 1969.

1. When the purpose and the basis of States' International policies are misunderstood, there is introduced into the world a new and unnecessary disharmony. Disagreements, conflicts of interest, or different assessments of human priorities, already provoke an excess of tension in the world, and disastrously divide mankind at a time when united action is necessary to control modern technology and put it to the service of man. It is for this reason that, discovering widespread misapprehension of our attitudes and purposes in relation to Southern Africa, we, the leaders of East and Central African States meeting at Lusaka, April 16, 1969, have agreed to issue this Manifesto.

2. By this Manifesto we wish to make clear, beyond all shadow of doubt, our acceptance of the belief that all men are equal, and have equal rights to human dignity and respect, regardless of colour, race, religion, or sex. We believe that all men have the right and the duty to participate, as equal members of the society, in their own government. We do not accept that any individual or group has any right to govern any other group of sane adults, without their consent, and we affirm that only the people of a society, acting together as equals, can determine what is, for them, a good society and a good social, economic, or political organization.

3. On the basis of these beliefs we do not accept that any one group within a society has the right to rule any society without the continuing consent of all the citizens. We recognize that at any one time there will be, within every society, failures in the implementation of these ideals. We recognize that for the sake of order in human affairs, there may be transitional arrangements while a transformation from group inequalities to individual equality is being effected. But we affirm that without an acceptance of these ideals – without a

commitment to these principles of human equality and self-determination – there can be no basis for peace and justice in the world.

4. None of us would claim that within our own States we have achieved that perfect social, economic and political organization which would ensure a reasonable standard of living for all our people and establish individual security against avoidable hardship or miscarriage of justice. On the contrary, we acknowledge that within our own States the struggle towards human brotherhood and unchallenged human dignity is only beginning. It is on the basis of our commitments to human equality and human dignity, not on the basis of achieved perfection, that we take our stand of hostility towards the colonialism and racial discrimination which is being practised in Southern Africa. It is on the basis of their commitment to these universal principles that we appeal to other members of the human race for support.

5. If the commitment to these principles existed among the States holding power in Southern Africa, any disagreement we might have about the rate of implementation, or about isolated acts of policy, would be matters affecting only our individual relationships with the States concerned. If these commitments existed, our States would not be justified in the expressed and active hostility towards the regimes of Southern Africa such as we have proclaimed and continue to propagate.

6. The truth is, however, that in Mozambique, Angola, Rhodesia, South-West Africa, and the Republic of South Africa, there is an open and continued denial of the principles of human equality and national self-determination. This is not a matter of failure in the implementation of accepted human principles. The effective administrations in all these territories are not struggling towards these difficult goals. They are fighting the principles; they are deliberately organizing their societies so as to try to destroy the hold of these principles in the minds of men. It is for this reason that we believe the rest of the world must be interested. For the principle of human equality, and all that flows from it, is either universal or it does not exist. The dignity of all men is destroyed when the manhood of any human being is denied.

7. Our objectives in Southern Africa stem from our commitment to this principle of human equality. We are not hostile to the Administrations of these States because they are manned and controlled by white people. We are hostile to them because they are systems of minority control which exist as a result of, and in the pursuance of, doctrines of human inequality. What we are working for is the right of self-determination for the people of those territories. We are working for a rule in those countries which is based on the will of all the people, and an acceptance of the equality of every citizen.

8. Our stand towards Southern Africa thus involves a rejection of racialism, not a reversal of the existing racial domination. We believe that all the peoples who have made their homes in the countries of Southern Africa are Africans,

regardless of the colour of their skins; and we would oppose a racialist majority government which adopted a philosophy of deliberate and permanent discrimination between its citizens on grounds of racial origin. We are not talking racialism when we reject the colonialism and apartheid policies now operating in those areas; we are demanding an opportunity for all the people of these States, working together as equal individual citizens, to work out for themselves the institutions and the system of government under which they will, by general consent, live together and work together to build a harmonius society.

9. As an aftermath of the present policies it is likely that different groups within these societies will be self-conscious and fearful. The initial political and economic organizations may well take account of these fears, and this group self-consciousness. But how this is to be done must be a matter exclusively for the peoples of the country concerned, working together. No other nation will have a right to interfere in such affairs. All that the rest of the world has a right to demand is just what we are now asserting – that the arrangements within any State which wishes to be accepted into the community of nations must be based on an acceptance of the principles of human dignity and equality.

10. To talk of the liberation of Africa is thus to say two things. First, that the peoples in the territories still under colonial rule shall be free to determine for themselves their own institutions of self-government. Secondly, that the individuals in Southern Africa shall be freed from an environment poisoned by the propaganda of racialism, and given an opportunity to be men – not white men, brown men, yellow man, or black men.

11. Thus the liberation of Africa for which we are struggling does not mean a reverse racialism. Nor is it an aspect of African Imperialism. As far as we are concerned the present boundaries of the States of Southern Africa are the boundaries of what will be free and independent African States. There is no question of our seeking or accepting any alterations to our own boundaries at the expense of these future free African nations.

12. On the objective of liberation as thus defined, we can neither surrender nor compromise. We have always referred and we still prefer, to achieve it without physical violence. We would prefer to negotiate rather than destroy, to talk rather than kill. We do not advocate violence, we advocate an end to the violence against human dignity which is now being perpetrated by the oppressors of Africa. If peaceful progress to emancipation were possible, or if changed circumstances were to make it possible in the future, we would urge our brothers in the resistance movements to use peaceful methods of struggle even at the cost of some compromise on the timing of change. But while peaceful progress is blocked by actions of those at present in power in the States of Southern Africa, we have no choice but to give to the peoples of those territories all the support of which we are capable in their struggle against their oppressors. This is why the signatory states participate in the movement for the

liberation of Africa under the aegis of the Organization of African Unity. However, the obstacle to change is not the same in all the countries of Southern Africa, and it follows therefore, that the possibility of continuing the struggle through peaceful means varies from one country to another.

13. In *Mozambique* and *Angola,* and in so-called *Portuguese Guinea,* the basic problem is not racialism but a pretence that Portugal exists in Africa. Portugal is situated in Europa; the fact that it is a dictatorship is a matter for the Portuguese to settle. But no decree of the Portuguese dictator, nor legislation passed by any Parliament in Portugal, can make Africa part of Europe. The only thing which could convert a part of Africa into a constituent unit in a union which also includes a European State would be the freely expressed will of the people of that part of Africa. There is no such popular will in the Portuguese colonies. On the contrary, in the absence of any opportunity to negotiate a road to freedom, the peoples of all three territories have taken up arms against the colonial power. They have done this despite the heavy odds against them, and despite the great suffering they know to be involved.

14. Portugal, as a European State, has naturally its own allies in the context of the ideological conflict between West and East. However, in our context, the effect of this is that Portugal is enabled to use her resources to pursue the most heinous war and degration of man in Africa. The present Manifesto must, therefore, lay bare the fact that the inhuman commitment of Portugal in Africa and her ruthless subjugation of the people of Mozambique, Angola and so-called Portuguese Guinea, is not only irrelevant to the ideological conflict of power-politics, but is also diametrically opposed to the politics, the philosophies and the doctrines practised by her Allies in the conduct of their own affairs at home. The peoples of Mozambique, Angola and, Portuguese Guinea are not interested in Communism or Capitalism; they are interested in their freedom. They are demanding an acceptance of the principles of independence on the basis of majority rule, and for many years they called for discussions on this issue. Only when their demand for talks was continually ignored did they begin to fight. Even now, if Portugal should change her policy and accept the principle of self-determination, we would urge the Liberation Movements to desist from their armed struggle and co-operate in the mechanics of a peaceful transfer of power from Portugal to the peoples of the African territories.

15. The fact that many Portuguese citizens have immigrated to these African countries does not affect this issue. Future immigration policy will be a matter for the independent Governments when these are established. In the meantime we would urge the Liberation Movements to reiterate their statements that all those Portuguese people who have made their homes in Mozambique, Angola or Portuguese Guinea, and who are willing to give their future loyalty to those states, will be accepted as citizens. And an independent Mozambique,

Angola, or Portuguese Guinea may choose to be as friendly with Portugal as Brazil is. That would be the free choice of a free people.

16. In Rhodesia the situation is different insofar as the metropolitan power has acknowledged the colonial status of the territory. Unfortunately, however, it has failed to take adequate measures to re-assert its authority against the minority which has seized power with the declared intention of maintaining white domination. The matter cannot rest there. Rhodesia, like the rest of Africa, must be free, and its independence must be on the basis of majority rule. If the colonial power is unwilling or unable to effect such a transfer of power to the people, then the people themselves will have no alternative but to capture it as and when they can. And Africa has no alternative but to support them. The question which remains in Rhodesia is therefore whether Britain will re-assert her authority in Rhodesia and then negotiate the peaceful progress to majority rule before independence. In so far as Britain is willing to make this second commitment, Africa will co-operate in her attempts to re-assert her authority. This is the method of progress which we would prefer; it could involve less suffering for all the people of Rhodesia, both black and white. But until there is some firm evidence that Britain accepts the principle of independence on the basis of majority rule and is prepared to take whatever steps are necessary to make it a reality, then Africa has no choice but to support the struggle for the people's freedom by whatever means are open.

17. Just as a settlement of the Rhodesian problem with a minimum of violence is a British responsibility, so a settlement in South West Africa with a minimum of violence is a United Nations responsibility. By every canon of international law, and by every precedent, South West Africa should by now have been a sovereign, independent State with a Government based on majority rule. South West Africa was a German colony until 1919, just as Tanganyika, Rwanda and Burundi, Togoland and Cameroon were German colonies. It was a matter of European politics that when the Mandatory System was established after Germany had been defeated, the administration of South West Africa was given to the white minority Government of South Africa, while the other ex-German colonies in Africa were put into the hands of the British, Belgian, or French Governments. After the Second World War every mandated territory except South West Africa was converted into a Trusteeship Territory and has subsequently gained independence. South Africa, on the other hand, has persistently refused to honour even the international obligation it accepted in 1919, and has increasingly applied to South West Africa the inhuman doctrines and organization of apartheid.

18. The United Nations General Assembly has ruled against this action and in 1966 terminated the Mandate under which South Africa had a legal basis for its occupation and domination of South West Africa. The General Assembly declared that the territory is now the direct responsibility of the United

Nations and set up an *ad hoc* Committee to recommend practical means by which South West Africa would be administered, and the people enabled to exercise self-determination and to achieve independence.

19. Nothing could be clearer than this decision – which no permanent member of the Security Council voted against. Yet, since that time no effective measures have been taken to enforce it. South West Africa remains in the clutches of the most ruthless minority government in Africa. Its people continue to be oppressed and those who advocate even peaceful progress to independence continue to be persecuted. The world has an obligation to use its strength to enforce the decision which all the countries co-operated in making. If they do this there is hope that the change can be effected without great violence. If they fail, then sooner or later the people of South West Africa will take the law into their own hands. The people have been patient beyond belief, but one day their patience will be exhausted. Africa, at least, will then be unable to deny their call for help.

20. The Republic of South Africa is itself an independent sovereign State and a Member of the United Nations. It is more highly developed and richer than any other nation in Africa. On every legal basis its internal affairs are a matter exclusively for the people of South Africa. Yet the purpose of law is people and we assert that the actions of the South African Government are such that the rest of the world has a responsibility to take some action in defence of humanity.

21. There is one thing about South African oppression which distinguishes it from other oppressive régimes. The apartheid policy adopted by its government, and supported to a greater or lesser extent by almost all its white citizens, is based on a rejection of man's humanity. A position of privileges or the experience of oppression in the South African society depends on the one thing which it is beyond the power of any man to change. It depends upon a man's colour, his parentage, and his ancestors. If you are black you cannot escape this categorisation; nor can you escape it if you are white. If your are a black milionaire and a brilliant political scientist, you are still subject to the pass laws, and still excluded from political activity. If you are white, even protests against the system and an attempt to reject segregation, will lead you only to the segregation and the comparative comfort of a white jail. Beliefs, abilities, and behaviour are all irrelevant to a man's status; everything depends upon race. Manhood is irrelevant. The whole system of government and society in South Africa is based on the denial of human equality. And the system is maintained by a ruthless denial of the human rights of the majority of the population and thus, inevitably of all.

22. These things are known and are regularly condemned in the Councils of the United Nations and elsewhere. But it appears that to many countries international law takes precedence over humanity; therefore no action follows

the words. Yet even if international law is held to exclude active assistance to the South African opponents of apartheid, it does not demand that the comfort and support of human and commercial intercourse should be given to a government which rejects the manhood of most of humanity. South Africa should be excluded from the United Nations Agencies, and even from the United Nations itself. It should be ostracized by the world community. It should be isolated from world trade patterns and left to be self-sufficient if it can. The South African Government cannot be allowed both to reject the very concept of mankind's unity, and to benefit by the strength given through friendly international relations. And certainly Africa cannot acquiesce in the maintenance of the present policies against people of African descent.

23. The signatories of this Manifesto assert that the validity of the principles of human equality and dignity extend to the Republic of South Africa just as they extend to the colonial territories of Southern Africa. Before a basis for peaceful development can be established in this continent, these principles must be acknowledged by every nation, and in every State there must be a deliberate attempt to implement them.

15.

THE INTERNATIONAL COURT OF JUSTICE DELIVERS ITS ADVISORY OPINION ON THE LEGAL CONSEQUENCES FOR STATES OF THE CONTINUED PRESENCE OF SOUTH AFRICA IN NAMIBIA (SOUTH WEST AFRICA) NOTWITHSTANDING SECURITY COUNCIL RESOLUTION 276 (1970)[1]

A summary of the Opinion is provided in the form of a communique from the I.C.J. The Separate Opinion of Vice-President Ammoun[2] (of Lebanon) is reproduced here for the depth of its analysis of and its instruction on the human rights issues raised by the case. 'These are', in Judge Ammoun's words, 'the sovereignty of dependent peoples, ... the right of peoples to self-determination and decolonization, equality between nations and between individuals, racial discrimination as expressed in the doctrine of apartheid in South Africa and in Namibia, in sum, the whole body of human rights and their imperative universal character'.[3]

Text of I.C.J. communique, 21 June 1971

Today, 21 June 1971, the International Court of Justice delivered its Advisory Opinion on the above question.

In answer to the question put by the Security Council of the United Nations, 'What are the legal consequences for States of the continued presence of South Africa in Namibia notwithstanding Security Council resolution 276 (1970)?', the Court is of opinion,

by 13 votes to 2,

(1) that, the continued presence of South Africa in Namibia being illegal, South Africa is under obligation to withdraw its administration from Namibia immediately and thus put an end to its occupation of the Territory; by 11 votes to 4,

---

1. Reports of Judgments, Advisory Opinions and Orders of the International Court of Justice, 1971.
2. Ibid., pp. 55–88.
3. Ibid., p. 55.

(2) that States Members of the United Nations are under obligation to recognize the illegality of South Africa's presence in Namibia and the invalidity of its acts on behalf of or concerning Namibia, and to refrain from any acts and in particular any dealings with the Government of South Africa implying recognition of the legality of, or lending support or assistance to, such presence and administration;

(3) that it is incumbent upon States which are not Members of the United Nations to give assistance, within the scope of subparagraph (2) above, in the action which has been taken by the United Nations with regard to Namibia.

Analysis of the advisory opinion

COURSE OF THE PROCEEDINGS

paragraphs 1–18 of the Advisory Opinion

The Court first recalls that the request for the advisory opinion emanated from the United Nations Security Council, which decided to submit it by resolution 284 (1970) adopted on 29 July 1970. The Court goes on to recapitulate the different steps in the subsequent proceedings.

It refers in particular to the three Orders of 26 January 1971 whereby the Court decided not to accede to the objections raised by the Government of South Africa against the participation in the proceedings of three Members of the Court. These objections were based on statements which the Judges in question had made in a former capacity as representatives of their Governments in United Nations organs dealing with matters concerning Namibia, or on their participation in the same capacity in the work of those organs. The Court came to the conclusion that none of the three cases called for the application of Article 17, paragraph 2, of its Statute.

OBJECTIONS AGAINST THE COURT'S DEALING WITH THE QUESTION

paras. 19–41 of the Advisory Opinion

The Government of South Africa contended that the Court was not competent to deliver the opinion, because Security Council resolution 284 (1970) was invalid for the following reasons: (a) two permanent members of the Council abstained during the voting (Charter of the United Nations, Art. 27. para. 3); (b) as the question related to a dispute between South Africa and other Members of the United Nations, South Africa should have been invited to participate in the discussion (Charter, Art. 32) and the proviso requiring members of the Security Council which are parties to a dispute to abstain from voting should have been observed (Charter, Art. 27, para. 3). The Court points out that (a) for a long period the voluntary abstention of a permanent member has consistently been interpreted as not constituting a bar to the adoption of resolutions by the Security Council, (b) the question of Namibia was placed on the agenda of the Council as a situation and the South African Government failed to draw the Council's attention to the necessity in its eyes of treating it as a dispute.

In the alternative the Government of South Africa maintained that even if the Court had competence it should nevertheless, as a matter of judicial propriety, refuse to give the opinion requested, on account of political pressure to which, it was contended, the Court had been or might be subjected. On 8 February 1971, at the opening of the public sittings, the President of the Court declared that it would not be proper for the Court to entertain those observations, bearing as they did on the very nature of the Court as the principal judicial organ of the United Nations, an organ which, in that capacity, acts only on the basis of law, independently of all outside influences or interventions whatsoever.

The Government of South Africa also advanced another reason for not giving the advisory opinion requested: that the question was in reality contentious, because it related to an existing dispute between South Africa and other States. The Court considers that it was asked to deal with a request put forward by a United Nations organ with a view to seeking legal advice on the consequences of its own decisions. The fact that, in order to give its answer, the Court might have to pronounce on legal questions upon which divergent views exist between South Africa and the United Nations does not convert the cease into a dispute between States. (There was therefore no necessity to apply Article 83 of the Rules of Court, according to which, if an advisory opinion is requested upon a legal question 'actually pending between two or more States', Article 31 of the Statute, dealing with judges ad hoc, is applicable; the Government of South Africa having requested leave to choose a judge ad hoc, the Court heard its observations on that point on 27 January 1971 but, in the light of the above considerations, decided by the Order of 29 January 1971 not to accede to that request.)

In sum, the Court saw no reason to decline to answer the request for an advisory opinion.

HISTORY OF THE MANDATE

paras. 42–86 of the Advisory Opinion

Refuting the contentions of the South African Government and citing its own pronouncements in previous proceedings concerning South West Africa (Advisory Opinions of 1950, 1955 and 1956; Judgment of 1962), the Court recapitulates the history of the Mandate.

The mandates system established by Article 22 of the Covenant of the League of Nations was based upon two principles of paramount importance: the principle of non-annexation and the principle that the well-being and development of the peoples concerned formed a sacred trust of civilization. Taking the developments of the past half-century into account, there can be little doubt that the ultimate objective of the sacred trust was self-determination and independence. The mandatory was to observe a number of obligations and the Council of the League was to see that they were fulfilled. The rights of the mandatory as such had their foundation in those obligations.

When the League of Nations was dissolved, the raison d'être and original object of these obligations remained. Since their fulfilment did not depend on the existence of the League, they could not be brought to an end merely because the supervisory organ had ceased to exist. The Members of the League had not declared, or accepted even by implication, that the mandates would be cancelled or lapse with the dissolution of the League.

The last resolution of the League Assembly and Article 80, paragraph 1, of the United Nations Charter maintained the obligations of mandatories. The International Court of Justice has consistently recognized that the Mandate survived the demise of the League, and South Africa also admitted as much for a number of years. Thus the supervisory element, which is an essential part of the Mandate, was bound to survive. The United Nations suggested a system of supervision which would not exceed that which applied under the mandates system, but this proposal was rejected by South Africa.

RESOLUTIONS BY THE GENERAL ASSEMBLY AND THE SECURITY COUNCIL

paras. 87–116 of the Advisory Opinion

Eventually, in 1966, the General Assembly of the United Nations adopted resolution 2145 (XXI), whereby it decided that the Mandate was terminated and that South Africa had no other right to administer the Territory. Subsequently the Security Council adopted various resolutions including resolution 276 (1970) declaring the continued presence of South Africa in Namibia illegal. Objections challenging the validity of these resolutions having been raised, the Court points out that it does not possess powers of judicial review or appeal in relation to the United Nations organs in question. Nor does the validity of their resolutions form the subject of the request for advisory opinion. The Court nevertheless, in the exercise of its judicial function, and since these objections have been advanced, considers them in the course of its reasoning before determining the legal consequences arising from those resolutions.

It first recalls that the entry into force of the United Nations Charter established a relationship between all Members of the United Nations on the one side, and each mandatory Power on the other, and that one of the fundamental principles governing that relationship is that the party which disowns or does not fulfil its obligations cannot be recognized as retaining the rights which it claims to derive from the relationship. Resolution 2145 (XXI) determined that there had been a material breach of the Mandate, which South Africa had in fact disavowed.

It has been contended (a) that the Covenant of the League of Nations did not confer on the Council of the League power to terminate a mandate for misconduct of the mandatory and that United Nations could not derive from the League greater powers than the latter itself had: (b) that, even if the Council of the League had possessed the power of revocation of the Mandate, it could not have been exercised unilaterally but only in co-operation with the Mandatory; (c) that resolution 2145 (XXI) made pronouncements which the General Assembly, not being a judicial organ, was not competent to make; (d) that a detailed factual investigation was called for; (e) that one part of resolution 2145 (XXI) decided in effect a transfer of territory.

The Court observes (a) that, according to a general principle of international law (incorporated in the Vienna Convention on the Law of Treaties), the right to terminate a treaty on account of breach must be presumed to exist in respect of all treaties, even if unexpressed; (b) that the consent of the wrongdoer to such a form of termination cannot be required; (c) that the United Nations, as a successor to the League, acting through its competent organ, must be seen above all as the supervisory institution competent to pronounce on the conduct of the Mandatory; (d) that the failure of South Africa to comply with the obligation to submit to supervision cannot be disputed; (e) that the General Assembly was not making a finding on facts, but formulating a legal situation; it would not be correct to assume that, because it is in principle vested with recommendatory powers, it is debarred from adopting, in special cases within the framework of its competence, resolutions which make determinations or have operative design.

The General Assembly, however, lacked the necessary powers to ensure the withdrawal of South Africa from the Territory and therefore, acting in accordance with Article 11, paragraph 2, of the Charter, enlisted the co-operation of the Security Council. The Council for its part, when it adopted the resolutions concerned, was acting in the exercise of what it deemed to be its primary responsibility for the maintenance of peace and security. Article 24 of the Charter vests in the Security Council the necessary authority. Its decisions were taken in conformity with the purposes and principles of the Charter, under Article 25 of which it is for member States to comply with those decisions, even those members of the Security Council which voted against them and those Members of the United Nations who are not members of the Council.

LEGAL CONSEQUENCES FOR STATES OF THE CONTINUED PRESENCE OF SOUTH AFRICA IN NAMIBIA

paras. 117–127 and 133 of the Advisory Opinion

The Court stresses that a binding determination made by a competent organ of the United Nations to the effect that a situation is illegal cannot remain without consequence.

South Africa, being responsible for having created and maintained that situation, has the obligation to put an end to it and withdraw its administration from the Territory. By occupying the Territory without title, South Africa incurs international responsibilities arising from a continuing violation of an international obligation. It also remains accountable for any violations of the rights of the people of Namibia, or of its obligations under international law towards other States in respect of the exercise of its powers in relation to the Territory.

The member States of the United Nations are under obligation to recognize the illegality and invalidity of South Africa's continued presence in Namibia and to refrain from lending any support or any form of assistance to South Africa with reference to its occupation of Namibia. The precise determination of the acts permitted – what measures should be selected, what scope they should be given and by whom they should be applied – is a matter which lies within the competence of the appropriate political organs of the United Nations acting within their authority under the Charter. Thus it is for the Security Council to determine any further measures consequent upon the decisions already taken by it. The Court in consequence confines itself to giving advice on those dealings with the Government of South Africa which, under the Charter of the United Nations and general international law, should be considered as inconsistent with resolution 276 (1970) because they might imply recognizing South Africa's presence in Namibia as legal:

(a) Member States are under obligation (subject to (d)) below to abstain from entering into treaty relations with South Africa in all cases in which the Government of South Africa purports to act on behalf of or concerning Namibia. With respect to existing bilateral treaties, member States must abstain from invoking or applying these treaties or provisions of treaties concluded by South Africa on behalf of or concerning Namibia which involve active inter-governmental co-operation. With respect to multilateral treaties, the same rule cannot be applied to certain general conventions such as those with humanitarian character, the non-performance of which may adversely affect the people of Namibia: it will be for the competent international organs to take specific measures in this respect.

(b) Member States are under obligation to abstain from sending diplomatic or special missions to South Africa including in their jurisdiction the territory of Namibia, to abstain from sending consular agents to Namibia, and to withdraw any such agents already there; and to make it clear to South Africa that the maintenance of diplomatic or consular relations does not imply any recognition of its authority with regard to Namibia.

(c) Member States are under obligation to abstain from entering into economic and other forms of relations with South Africa on behalf of or concerning Namibia which may entrench its authority over the territory.

(d) However, non-recognition should not result in depriving the people of Namibia of any advantages derived from international co-operation. In particular, the illegality or invalidity of acts performed by the Government of South Africa on behalf of or concerning Namibia after the termination of the Mandate cannot be extended to such acts as the registration of births, deaths and marriages.

As to States not members of the United Nations, although they are not bound by Articles 24 and 25 of the Charter, they have been called upon by resolution 276 (1970) to give assistance in the action which has been taken by the United Nations with regard to Namibia. In the view of the Court, the termination of the Mandate and the declaration of the illegality of South Africa's presence in Namibia are opposable to all States in the sense of barring erga omnes the legality of the situation which is maintained in violation of international law. In particular, no State which enters into relations with South Africa concerning Namibia may expect the United Nations or its Members to recognize the validity or effects of any such relationship. The Mandate having been terminated by a decision of the international organization in which the supervisory authority was vested, it is for non-member States to act accordingly. All States should bear in mind that the entity injured by the illegal presence of South Africa in Namibia is a people which must look to the international community for assistance in its progress, towards the goals for which the sacred trust was instituted.

Accordingly, the Court has given the replies reproduced above.

PROPOSITIONS BY SOUT AFRICA CONCERNING THE SUPPLY OF FURTHER FACTUAL INFORMATION AND THE POSSIBLE HOLDING OF A PLEBISCITE

paras. 128–132 of the Advisory Opinion

The Government of South Africa had expressed the desire to supply the Court with further factual information concerning the purposes and objectives of its policy of separate development, contending that to establish a breach of its substantive international obligations under the Mandate it would be necessary to prove that South Africa had failed to exercise its powers with a view to promoting the well-being and progress of the inhabitants. The Court found that no factual evidence was needed for the purpose of determining whether the policy of apartheid in Namibia was in conformity with the international obligations assumed by South Africa. It is undisputed that the official governmental policy pursued by South Africa in Namibia is to achieve a complete physical separation of races and ethnic groups. This means the enforcement of distinctions, exclusions, restrictions and limitations exclusively based on grounds of race, colour, descent or national or ethnic origin which constitute a denial of fundamental human rights. This the Court views as a flagrant violation of the purposes and principles of the Charter of the United Nations.

The Government of South Africa had also submitted a request that a plebiscite should be held in the Territory of Namibia under the joint supervision of the Court and the Government of South Africa. The Court having concluded that no further evidence was required, that the Mandate had been validly terminated and that in consequence South Africa's presence in Namibia was illegal and its acts on behalf of or concerning Namibia illegal and invalid, it was not able to entertain this proposal.

By a letter of 14 May 1971 the President informed the representatives of the States and organizations which had participated in the oral proceedings that the Court had decided not to accede to the two above-mentioned requests.

DECLARATION AND SEPARATE OR DISSENTING OPINIONS

Sub-paragraph 1 of the operative clause of the Advisory Opinion (illegality of the presence of South Africa in Namibia; see pages C99 and C100) was adopted by 13 votes to 2. Sub-paragraphs 2 and 3 were adopted by 11 votes to 4.

Judge Sir Gerald Fitzmaurice (dissenting opinion) considers that the Mandate was not validly revoked, that the Mandatory is still subject to the obligations of the Mandate whatever these may be, and that States Members of the United Nations are bound to respect the position unless and until it is changed by lawful means.

Judge Gros (dissenting opinion) disagrees with the Court's conclusions as to the legal validity and effects of General Assembly resolution 2145 (XXI), but considers that South Africa ought to agree to negotiate on the conversion of the Mandate into a United Nations trusteeship.

Judges Petren and Onyeama (separate opinions) voted for sub-paragraph 1 of the operative clause but against sub-paragraphs 2 and 3, which in their view ascribe too broad a scope to the effects of non-recognition.

SEPARATE OPINION OF VICE-PRESIDENT AMMOUN

[Translation]

1. The Security Council having requested from the International Court of Justice, within the framework of the latter's advisory jurisdiction, an authoritative opinion concerning the legal consequences of the continued presence of South Africa in Namibia (formerly South West Africa) notwithstanding the termination in 1966 of the tutelary Mandate which the League of Nations had conferred upon that Power in 1920, the Court has been called upon to pronounce, for the first time in regard to certain fundamental principles of international law, on a number of problems raised by the request for an opinion. These are, in particular, the sovereignty of dependent peoples, the mandate institution, its nature and its objects, the right of peoples to self-determination and decolonization, equality between nations and between individuals, racial discrimination as expressed in the doctrine of *apartheid* in South Africa and in Namibia and, in sum, the whole body of human rights and their imperative universal character.

All these notions are the outward expression of a new body of international law, the consequence of an irreversible social and political evolution of the modern world. The Court, in its Advisory Opinion, has not overlooked them. In my view, however, it has not always gone far enough in spelling out the legal conclusions to which they point.

Furthermore, I find that neither the reasons given for the operative part nor the wording of those paragraphs are sufficiently explicit and decisive in regard to the legal qualification of the presence of South Africa in Namibia and the obligations for States that flow therefrom.

I have therefore felt it my duty to compose this separate opinion with a view to contributing to the Advisory Opinion of the Court, whose views I share, some further support, however modest it may be.

2. The Republic of South Africa, having, like certain other States, availed itself of Article 66 of the Statute of the Court in order to furnish information in connection with the request for an advisory opinion, presented itself as a party to a dispute between it and the majority of States which had taken part in voting the United Nations General Assembly and Security Council resolutions relating to Namibia. On that ground, it requested permission to choose a judge *ad hoc* to participate, with the Members of the Court, in the giving of the opinion.

Having rejected South Africa's application by a majority decision in an Order made on 29 January 1971, the Court has explained that one of its reasons lay in the absence of a dispute between parties. To justify the appointment of a judge *ad hoc*, not only would a dispute have had to be present but there would have had to be on the Bench no judge of the nationality of one of the parties while the Bench did include a judge of the nationality of the opposing party. But what, in the present proceedings, would have been the identity of that opposing party? The States which voted against South Africa? But in that case those which voted for South Africa are *in the same interest* as it, within the meaning of Article 31 of the Statute, and as such are already represented. To have ignored this and allowed South Africa a judge *ad hoc* would in such circumstances have contravened the rule of that very equality which the Statute seeks to safeguard through the institution of judges *ad hoc*. *A fortiori* this rules out any discretionary power that some might wish to deduce from Article 68 of the Statute, for the Court may not, on the pretext of interpretation, contravene the fundamental rule and *raison d'être* of that institution. In any case, if the opinion of the minority had been accepted, the Court ought, in my view, to have permitted the choice of a judge *ad hoc* both for South Africa and for Namibia. The legal personality of Namibia would thus have been judicially recognized and Namibia would have appeared for the first time in international proceedings [1].

Namibia, even at the periods when it had been reduced to the status of a German colony or was subject to the South African Mandate, possessed a legal personality which was denied to it only by the law now obsolete. It was considered by the Powers of the day as a merely geographical concept taking its name from its location in the South-West of the African Continent. It nevertheless constituted a subject of law that was distinct from the German State, possessing national sovereignty but lacking the exercise thereof. The institution of the Mandate, *a fortiori*, did not connote the annexation of the country which was subject to it, as the Court has made clear by its reference to its earlier Advisory Opinion of 18 July 1950. Sovereignty, which is inherent in every people, just as liberty is inherent in every human being, therefore did not cease to belong to the people subject to mandate. It had simply, for a time, been rendered inarticulate and deprived of freedom of expression. General Smuts, the Prime Minister of the Union of South Africa, already recognized this in his study on what was to be the mandate institution [2]. As the beneficiaries on whose behalf the mandate agreements were to be concluded, it was right that some of the peoples who were to be subjected to them should be consulted on the selection of the mandatory. That is what was stipulated in paragraph 4 of Article 22 of the Covenant, for the peoples severed from the Ottoman Empire. In fact the commission of inquiry, reduced to its American members, King and Crane, conducted such consultations in Lebanon, Syria, Palestine and Iraq; the United Kingdom and France having declined the American President Woodrow Wilson's invitation to take part because they had come to an agreement as to the allocation of the mandates and were already in position on the spot. The majority of the populations consulted demanded immediate independence, but the right of peoples to self-determination had not yet come to maturity and it was only in the wake of the Second World War that the four countries mentioned were to obtain their independence.

The opinion expressed by Paul Fauchille, writing in 1922, deserves

---

[1] It was only as an observer that Namibia was admitted to the United Nations Economic Commission for Africa.
[2] *The League of Nations: A Practical Suggestion.*

attention solely as a historical illustration, since today it has lost all relevance. "It seems clear," he averred, "that, whereas in the case of mandates of the second and third categories full sovereignty is attributed to the Mandatory, there is in the case of mandates of the first category, as in a protectorate properly so called, a sharing of sovereignty between the independent communities or nations and the Mandatory [1]." Fauchille thus assimilated "B" and "C" Mandates to the colonies of his period. He conceived of a sharing of sovereignty in the case of "A" Mandates, whereas it must surely be agreed that sovereignty is indivisible, as is liberty, and that all that is conceivable is a distinction between the possession of sovereignty and its exercise. Stoyanovsky, writing three years later, took a more accurate view when he upheld the notion of virtual sovereignty residing in a people deprived of its exercise by domination or tutelage [2]. Those were also the views of Paul Pic [3].

It is true that the Namibians' status of a people, which was recognized by the General Assembly of the United Nations in its resolution 2372 (XXII) of 12 June 1968, has been disputed by the South African Government so as to justify dividing—and ruling—the country under the euphemism of separate development, known in Afrikaans as *apartheid*. But the Namibian people, whose existence and unity the Court has, in its turn, recognized in the present Advisory Opinion, has itself asserted its international personality by taking up the struggle for freedom. Since South Africa has opposed the achievement of the objects of the Mandate and blocked Namibia's path to independence and the enjoyment of its full sovereignty, Namibia has decided to fight. The legitimacy of the Namibian national struggle has been recognized in four resolutions of the General Assembly [4] and in Security Council resolution 269 (1969). This struggle, by analogy, continues the line of those waged by other members of the international community, during the First World War, before they were recognized as States, such as the Polish, Czech and Slovak peoples; or of the French national movement [1] at the time when France was under the domination of Nazi Germany.

In law, the legitimacy of the peoples' struggle cannot be in any doubt, for it follows from the right of self-defence, inherent in human nature, which is confirmed by Article 51 of the United Nations Charter. It is also an accepted principle that self-defence may be collective; thus we see the other peoples of Africa, members of the Organization of African Unity, associated with the Namibians in their fight for freedom. The rightness of this is also confirmed by the Universal Declaration of Human Rights, which stresses in its preamble that "it is essential, if man is not to be compelled to have recourse, as a last resort, to rebellion against

---

[1] *Traité de droit international public*, 1922, Vol. I, p. 298.
[2] *La théorie générale des mandats internationaux*, 1925, pp. 83 ff.
[3] "Le régime des mandats d'après le traité de Versailles", *Revue générale de droit international public*, 1923, 2nd Series, IV, No. 5, p. 334.
[4] Resolutions 2372 (XXII), 2403 (XXIII), 2498 (XXIV) and 2517 (XXIV).
[1] These are the terms used by L. Cavaré, *Droit international public positif*, Vol. II, 2nd ed., pp. 334 f.

tyranny and oppression, that human rights should be protected by the rule of law".

The struggle of the Namibian people thus takes its place within the framework of international law, not least because the struggle of peoples in general has been one, if not indeed the primary factor in the formation of the customary rule whereby the right of peoples to self-determination is recognized. I could therefore have wished that the Court, like the General Assembly and the Security Council, had mentioned in its Opinion the legitimate struggle of the Namibian people. But its silence on this subject does not exclude its agreement, since it has referred to the relevant resolutions of the other two organs of the United Nations.

The Court has not mentioned the General Assembly's decision to the effect that "henceforth South West Africa comes under the direct responsibility of the United Nations" (para. 4 of General Assembly resolution 2145 (XXI)). That should have been said in order to make clear the nature of the relationships between the Organization, on the one hand, and Namibia and the Republic of South Africa on the other. Nor has the Court referred to the setting-up of a United Nations Council for South West Africa (para. 6 of the same resolution), the name of which was changed by resolution 2372 (XXII) to United Nations Council for Namibia and which resolution 2248 (S-V) had vested with powers of statehood. These are the powers which it was for the Mandatory to exercise until the expiry of the Mandate, and they entitle the Council, acting on behalf of the United Nations, to exercise legislative competence and administrative authority in Namibia as well as to represent it diplomatically and exercise diplomatic protection of its nationals. It is to this body that it would in other circumstances have fallen to choose a judge *ad hoc* for Namibia, and it might also have presented the Court with a written statement and an oral statement as did the Government of South Africa. However it did not receive the communication referred to in Article 66 which would have authorized it to do so.

3. The revocation of South Africa's Mandate for Namibia which was decided upon by the General Assembly of the United Nations is based on three grounds which are mentioned in the fifth paragraph of the preamble to resolution 2145 (XXI) of 27 October 1966, reading as follows:

> "*Convinced* that the administration of the mandated Territory by South Africa has been conducted in a manner contrary to the Mandate, the Charter of the United Nations and the Universal Declaration of Human Rights."

The General Assembly had reached this decision after finding, in the eighth paragraph of the preamble to the same resolution,

> "... that all the efforts of the United Nations to induce the Government of South Africa to fulfil its obligations in respect of the administration of the Mandated Territory and to ensure the well-being and security of the indigenous inhabitants have been of no avail".

The revocation of the Mandate was thus explicitly based on three grounds relating to international instruments of the first importance. In refusing, quite rightly, to question the formal or intrinsic validity of the resolutions concerned, the Court nevertheless felt it necessary to refute the arguments advanced in this connection by certain States. In doing this it had in addition to direct its consideration to each of the three grounds stated in resolution 2145 (XXI) as justifying the termination of the Mandate and entailing the illegality of the presence in Namibia of the South African authorities thus bereft of title.

The Court considered the first ground, namely that of the violation of Article 22 of the Covenant of the League of Nations and of Article 2 of the mandate agreement, according to which:

> "The Mandatory shall promote to the utmost the material and moral well-being and the social progress of the inhabitants of the territory subject to the present Mandate."

The Court could not content itself with finding that the Mandatory had violated this obligation, for it was called upon to deduce the legal consequences of the illegal presence of South Africa in Namibia, and these consequences differ in nature and in number according to whether there was a violation of the relatively limited texts constituting the mandate instruments, or a violation of the obligations flowing from the constitutional Charter of the United Nations and the Universal Declaration of Human Rights.

Furthermore, the principles and purposes of the United Nations must be observed by all its organs: by the General Assembly and the Security Council and, no less, by the International Court of Justice, as also by each of the member States.

Now, we are told that these principles have been violated, these purposes gravely neglected. And when the political organs have fulfilled their obligations, by denouncing and condemning these violations and this grave neglect, the International Court of Justice owed it to itself to discharge its own obligations by not closing its eyes to conduct infringing the principles and rights which it is its duty to defend.

Again, the Court could not remain an unmoved witness in face of the evolution of modern international law which is taking place in the United Nations through the implementation and the extension to the whole world of the principles of equality, liberty and peace in justice which are embodied in the Charter and in the Universal Declaration of Human Rights.

The Court is not a law-making body. It declares the law. But it is a law discernible from the progress of humanity, not an obsolete law, a vestige of the inequalities between men, the domination and colonialism which were rife in international relationships up to the beginning of this century but are now disappearing, thanks to the struggle being waged by the peoples and to the extension to the ends of the world of the universal community of mankind.

Thus, in addition to the violation of the stipulations of the Mandate, the Court did not omit consideration of the other two grounds for its termination. By referring, like resolution 2145 (XXI), to the Charter of the United Nations and the Universal Declaration of Human Rights, the Court has asserted the imperative character of the right of peoples to self-determination and also of the human rights whose violation by the South African authorities it has denounced. It appears to me, however, that its reasoning and conclusions, to which, as I have said, I subscribe, leave room for explanations which, expressed in the separate opinions, may serve to strengthen those conclusions.

4. With regard to the survival of the Mandate after the dissolution of the League and the taking-over by the United Nations of supervision of the Mandatory's administration, which the Court has justified by legal arguments drawn from consideration of the purposes and objects of the Mandate in the light of the texts and *travaux préparatoires* and from an analysis of the pertinent Charter articles, referring also herein to certain of its earlier decisions (the Advisory Opinions of 1950, 1955 and 1956, and the Judgment of 1962), I would like to add one general observation which seems to me to be essential; it relates to the very nature of the tutelary-mandate institution and its place in the evolution of humanity.

Historians [1] have outlined the upward march of mankind from the time when *homo sapiens* appeared on the face of the globe, first of all in the Near East in what was the land of Canaan, up to the age of the greatest thinkers and, more particularly, throughout the whole history of social progress, from the slavery of Antiquity to man's inevitable, irreversible drive towards equality and freedom. This march is like time itself. It never stops. Nothing can stand in its way for long. The texts, whether they be laws, constitutions, declarations, covenants or charters, do but define it and mark its successive phases. They are a mere record of it. In other words, the progressive rights which men and peoples enjoy are the result much less of those texts than of the human progress to which they bear witness.

The institution of tutelage, succeeding colonialization and preceding and preparing the way for sovereign independence, has its place in this upward march, at one stage of which this concept of guardianship was born, in 1920; at the following stage, it was due to end. The provisions of Article 22 of the Covenant and the terms of the mandate agreements, whether they define the purposes of tutelage or specify the assistance to be given to backward peoples to enable them to catch up the vanguard of more developed peoples, give expression to this kinetic reality. Woodrow Wilson, and even the South African General Smuts, and the French Minister Simon, were imbued with this truth when they admitted that mandates must have an end, or are revocable. And so, to revert to the arguments set forth in the Advisory Opinion, I could have wished that the revocability of the Mandate, which has been so strongly contested, had been more fully justified by reference to the nature of tutelage and in consideration of the universal context in which it finds its place. Considering its nature and purposes, the duration of the tutelary Mandate

---

[1] See in particular H. G. Wells. *Outline of History*.

could not be determined at will by the party charged or entrusted with it. When the General Assembly, representing the international community once the League had ceased to do so, decided the revocation of that Mandate, with effect *erga omnes* in view of the Mandate's objective institutional character, that revocation was also binding on the extremely small number of States which had opposed it or, by expressing doubts and reservations, withheld their approval. For how could South Africa's Mandate, with its organs and structures, having lapsed for the quasi-unanimity of States, survive in the eyes of some others? An institution is a creature of reason which either exists or does not: it cannot at one and the same time be and not be. That would be no less curious than if a State admitted by majority vote to the United Nations should be a Member for some but not for others.

5. Recognition of the right of peoples to self-determination is expressed by the Court in paragraph 52 of the Advisory Opinion. It is there stated, *inter alia*, that:

> "Furthermore, the subsequent development of international law, in regard to non-self-governing territories, as enshrined in the Charter of the United Nations, made the principle of self-determination applicable to all of them. ... A further important stage in this development was the Declaration on the Granting of Independence to Colonial Countries and Peoples (General Assembly resolution 1514 (XV) of 14 December 1960), which embraces all peoples and territories which 'have not yet attained independence'."

The Opinion is not lacking in persuasive force; it would have possessed still more if it had retraced the path whereby this right of peoples has made its entry into positive international law and had determined exactly what were the factors which have gone into its making. I refer in particular to the fight of the peoples for freedom and independence, which has been going on ever since there have been conquering and dominating peoples and subject but unsubjugated peoples. To confine ourselves to modern times, we may mention the historic declarations proclaimed at the end of the eighteenth century, the provisions of present-day charters and covenants from the Atlantic Charter and the United Nations Charter to the Pact of Bogotá and the Charter of the Organization of African Unity, the repeated declarations of Bandung and of the non-aligned countries meeting in Belgrade and Cairo, the declaration contained in resolution 1514 (XV) of the General Assembly of the United Nations and, finally the two solemn Declarations which marked the close of the work of the United Nations during the first 25 years of its existence: resolution 2625 (XXV), adopted unanimously on 24 October 1970, on the principles of international law concerning friendly relations and co-operation between States in accordance with the Charter of the United Nations, and resolution 2627 (XXV), adopted on the same day on the occasion of the 25th anniversary of the United Nations. Would these international or universal instruments have seen the light of day if it had not been for the heroic fight of peoples aspiring with all their hearts after freedom and independence? If there is any "general practice" which might be held, beyond dispute, to constitute law within the meaning of Article 38, paragraph 1 *(b)*, of the Statute of the Court, it must surely be that which is made up of the conscious action of the peoples themselves, engaged in a determined struggle. This struggle continues for the purpose of asserting, yet once more, the right of self-determination, more particularly in southern Africa and, specifically, Namibia. Indeed one is bound to recognize that the right of peoples to self-determination, before being written into charters that were not granted but won in bitter struggle, had first been written painfully, with the blood of the peoples, in the finally awakened conscience of humanity. And without those same peoples, mainly of Asia and Africa, who since the Second World War have streamed into the new international Organization, the first of a universalist character, would it have been possible to achieve that impressive number of declarations and resolutions whereby the great principles they had helped consecrate have been translated into law and applied to the reshaping of international relations?

As for the "general practice" of States to which one traditionally refers when seeking to ascertain the emergency of customary law, it has, in the case of the right of peoples to self-determination, become so widespread as to be not merely "general" but universal, since it has been enshrined in the Charter of the United Nations (Art. 1, para. 2, and Art. 55) and confirmed by the texts that have just been mentioned: pacts, declarations and resolutions, which, taken as a whole, epitomize the unanimity of States in favour of the imperative right of peoples to self-determination. There is not one State, it should be emphasized, which has not, at least once, appended its signature to one or other of these texts, or which has not supported it by its vote. The confirmed rightness of this practice is moreover evinced by the great number of States— no less than 55—which, since the consecration by the Charter of the right of self-determination, have benefited from it, after having ensured, by the struggles and the strivings of their peoples, its definitive embodiment in both the theory and the practice of the new law. If any doubts had remained on this matter in the mind of the States Members of the United Nations, they would not have resolved to proclaim the legitimacy of the struggle of peoples—and more specifically the Namibian people—to make good their right of self-determination. If this right is still not recognized as a juridical norm in the practice of a few rare States or the writings of certain even rarer theoreticians, the attitude of the former is explained by their concern for their traditional interests, and that of the latter by a kind of extreme respect for certain long-entrenched postulates of classic international law. Law is a living deed, not a brilliant honours-list of past writers whose work of course compels respect but who cannot, except for a few great minds, be thought to have had such a vision of the future that they could always see beyond their own times. Everything goes to show how difficult it is to free ourselves from the servitudes of a past through which we have ourselves lived and from traditions we have always respected. It is, then, a page of history which needs turning that must be seen in attachment to an outdated law which denies the resolutions of the United Nations the authority with which the Charter has invested them, which authority has been reinforced by the almost unanimous will of the peoples of the world. That will is incomparably more decisive than that of the five or six Powers which have asserted opposite conceptions while relying on a claim to representativity whose lack of legal basis they must confess. Facts, therefore, have got the better of their last-ditch resistance, and in the last two sentences of paragraph 52 of the Advisory Opinion one may see an allusion to this struggle: one perhaps over-discreet, but at all events the Opinion has written *finis* to the matter.

6. The violation of human rights has not come to an end in any part of the world; to realize that fact one need only consult the archives of the European Court of Human Rights, the Human Rights Commission of the United Nations or the International Commission of Jurists, or simply read the world press. Violations of personal freedom and human dignity, the racial, social or religious discrimination which constitutes the most serious of violations of human rights since it annihilates the two-fold basis provided by equality and liberty, all still resist the currents of liberation in each of the five continents. That is certainly no reason why we should close our eyes to the conduct of the South African authorities. The facts mentioned before the Court in relation to the request for an advisory opinion cannot be ignored, seeing that consideration of them is important for the determination of the legal consequences of the illegal presence of South Africa in Namibia.

The Advisory Opinion takes judicial notice of the Universal Declaration of Human Rights. In the case of certain of the Declaration's provisions, attracted by the conduct of South Africa, it would have been an improvement to have dealt in terms with their comminatory nature, which is implied in paragraphs 130 and 131 of the Opinion by the references to their violation.

In its written statement the French Government, alluding to the obligations which South Africa accepted under the Mandate and assumed on becoming a Member of the United Nations, and to the norms laid down in the Universal Declaration of Human Rights, stated that there was no doubt that the Government of South Africa had, in a very real sense, systematically infringed those rules and those obligations. Nevertheless, referring to the mention by resolution 2145 (XXI) of the Universal Declaration of Human Rights, it objected that it was plainly impossible for non-compliance with the norms it enshrined to be sanctioned with the revocation of the Mandate, inasmuch as that Declaration was not in the nature of a treaty binding upon States.

Although the affirmations of the Declaration are not binding *qua* international convention within the meaning of Article 38, paragraph 1 *(a)*, of the Statute of the Court, they can bind States on the basis of custom within the meaning of paragraph 1 *(b)* of the same Article, whether because they constituted a codification of customary law as was said in respect of Article 6 of the Vienna Convention on the Law of Treaties, or because they have acquired the force of custom through a general practice accepted as law, in the words of Article 38, paragraph 1 *(b)*, of the Statute. One right which must certainly be considered a pre-existing binding customary norm which the Universal Declaration of Human Rights codified is the right to equality, which by common consent has ever since the remotest times been deemed inherent in human nature.

The equality demanded by the Namibians and by other peoples of every colour, the right to which is the outcome of prolonged struggles to make it a reality, is something of vital interest to us here, on the one hand because it is the foundation of other human rights which are no more than its corollaries and, on the other, because it naturally rules out racial discrimination and *apartheid*, which are the gravest of the facts with which South Africa, as also other States, stands charged. The attention I am devoting to it in these observations can therefore by no means be regarded as exaggerated or out of proportion.

It is not by mere chance that in Article 1 of the Universal Declaration of the Rights of Man there stands, so worded, this primordial principle or axiom: "All human beings are born free and equal in dignity and rights."

From this first principle flow most rights and freedoms.

Of all human rights, the right to equality is far and away the most important. It is also the one which has been longest recognized as a natural right; it may even be said that the doctrine of natural law was born in ancient times with the concept of human equality as its first element. It has been part of natural law ever since Zeno of Sidon [1] and his earliest disciples. It is in countries outside Europe that the provenance of the concept itself, as also of its most ardent present-day defenders, must be sought. Like the Christianity which later espoused the same premises, the philosophy of Zeno reflected the revolt of the humble and the oppressed. "Stoic liberty," Hegel teaches us in his *Phenomenology of the Mind*, "arose in a time of fear and slavery." Equality was not to the liking of the Greeks up to and including the time of Plato and Aristotle, who both found words to justify inequality and slavery [2], whereas for the Stoics: "man is a slave neither by nature nor by conquest." When Zeno died, his work was completed, and the notion of equality definitively received and propagated throughout the world of that era by his disciples [3], the distant forerunners of the eighteenth-century philosophers. Two streams

---

[1] According to Diogenes Laertes, a statue was erected to him in that city, as also in Athens, where he had gone to teach and where he founded the school which first bore his name but was later called the Stoic school.

[2] For Aristotle, reason was a privilege of which certain people, for instance slaves, are deprived. His advice to his pupil Alexander, who was not yet called the Great, was "to treat Greeks as members of the family, the *Barbarians* as animals . . .".

Yet had not the *Barbarians* already probed space, predicted eclipses and given names to the signs of the Zodiac; divided time into months, into weeks; invented the alphabet; and were they not soon to give the world the first really humane philosophy: namely, that founded upon equality?

[3] G. Rodier, *Etudes de philosophie grecque*, 1969, p. 231.

The disciples of Zeno were, many of them, his fellow countrymen: Zeno, the second of that name, and Boëthus, both also of Sidon; Antipater, of Tyre; Apollonios, also of Tyre; Chrysippos, of Phoenician Cyprus; Herillos, of Carthage; Cato, of Utica; Perseus, friend of Zeno; Posidonios, of Hama in Syria, a Phoenician halting-place on the road to Babylon; Diogenes, of Babylon; Panetios, a pupil of Antipater of Tyre, who was born in Rhodes, a Phoenicio-Greek meeting-place as also was Cyprus, where Cicero and Pompey came to follow his teaching.

of thought had become established on the two opposite shores of the Mediterranean, a Graeco-Roman stream represented by Epictetus, Lucan, Cicero and Marcus Aurelius; and an Asian and African stream, comprising the monks of Sinai and Saint John Climac, Alexandria with Plotinus and Philo the Jew, Carthage to which Saint Augustine gave new lustre; the two streams flowed together in Spain with Seneca. The stoic philosophy, sowing for the first time in mankind's history the seeds of equality between men and between nations, influenced the greatest of the Roman jurisconsults who were of Phoenician origin, Papinius and Ulpian, and then the doctors of Christianity [1] through whom it was eventually transmitted to the Age of Reason [2]. The ground was thus prepared for the legislative and constitutional process which began with the first declarations or bills of rights in America and Europe, continued with the constitutions of the nineteenth century, and culminated in positive international law in the San Francisco, Bogotá and Addis Ababa charters, and in the Universal Declaration of Human Rights which has been confirmed by numerous resolutions of the United Nations, in particular the abovementioned declarations adopted by the General Assembly in resolutions 1514 (XV), 2625 (XXV) and 2627 (XXV). The Court in its turn has now confirmed it.

7. The Charter has consecrated the principle of equality in even more categorical terms than it uses for the right of peoples to self-determination by reaffirming in its preamble the faith of the United Nations in the equal rights of nations large and small, and by declaring in Article 2, paragraph 1, that "The Organization is based on the principle of the sovereign equality of all its Members". The General Assembly has many times had occasion to affirm the right to equality and the fundamental rights which derive therefrom. This has been the case every time that the General Assembly has decided that it had competence notwithstanding the claim by States that such rights did not enjoy the protection of international law and therefore fell within their own national jurisdiction. Thus South Africa has regularly sought to rely on its domestic jurisdiction, denying the competence of the United Nations whenever since 1946, at session after session, it has been accused of practising *apartheid* in violation of the right to equality. The successive resolutions of the General Assembly rejecting this contention by South Africa have given it to be understood that the equality and fundamental rights violated by *apartheid* constitute obligations which are in fact placed under the protection of international law and as such fall within the competence of the United Nations.

---

[1] Bertrand Russell, in his *History of Western Philosophy*, pp. 275 f., writes: "By nature, the stoics held, all human beings are equal ... Christianity took this part of the stoic teachings."

[2] For this flowering of the concept of equality in the ancient land of Phoenicia, its adoption by the Graeco-Roman world and Christianity, and its development through the vicissitudes of time, the following works may be consulted: Bertrand Russell, *op. cit.*; Emile Bréhier, *Histoire de la philosophie*, Vol. 2, pp. 228 and 234; Rodis-Lewis, *La morale stoïcienne*, pp. 11 and 74; G. Rodier, *Etudes de philosophie grecque*, pp. 219, 220 and 231; Fritz Schulz, *History of Roman Legal Science*, p. 67; Ernest Renan, *Histoire des origines du christianisme*.

Only recently, on 26 May 1971, the Special Committee on Apartheid decided to oppose any dialogue with South Africa unless based on prior recognition of the equality of the Black population.

For the rest, how is it possible not to recognize the binding force of principles and rights which the international community has agreed that it is legitimate to defend by force of arms? That is what the General Assembly and the Security Council have been affirming ever since 1966 in proclaiming the legitimacy of the Namibian people's struggle, and that of all other dependent peoples, to defend their rights. What is more, in its resolution 2396 (XXIII) of 2 December 1968, the General Assembly, making specific reference to human rights and the struggle for their implementation, reaffirmed—

". . . its recognition of the legitimacy of the struggle of the peoples of South Africa for all human rights."

This resolution, adopted unanimously but for the two votes of South Africa and Portugal, demonstrates that the international community as a whole deems it legitimate to defend human rights by force of arms; it thus considers them to be peremptory rights endowed with effective sanction, or in other words that they are part and parcel of positive international law. The opposition of two States, Portugal and South Africa, does not diminish the legal authority of that resolution, because they could not be expected to go to the heroic length of condemning themselves. The Security Council in its turn, in resolution 282 (1970) ordering an embargo on the shipment of arms to South Africa, recognized—

". . . the legitimacy of the struggle of the oppressed people of South Africa in pursuance of their human and political rights as set forth in the Charter of the United Nations and [in] the Universal Declaration of Human Rights".

This concordance of view between the General Assembly and the Security Council offers final confirmation of the binding nature of human rights.

It will also be noted that the General Assembly equated acts which result from the policy of *apartheid* and thus violate the fundamental laws of equality and liberty, and nearly all other human rights, to war crimes and crimes against humanity when, in the International Convention of 26 November 1968, it declared them liable to prosecution without statutory limitation. Thus, in the eyes of the international community, violations of human rights by the practice of *apartheid*, itself a violation of equality and of the rights which are its corollaries, are no less punishable than the crimes against humanity and war crimes upon which the Charter of the Nuremberg Tribunal visited sanctions. General Assembly resolution 2074 (XX) even condemned *apartheid* as constituting "a crime against humanity". For how can States—other than Portugal and South Africa, so often denounced by the United Nations—cast doubt on a tenet to which they have all subscribed, namely that human rights are binding in character? How true is what the Catholic philosopher Jacques Maritain once wrote:

> "... underlying the stealthy, perpetual urge to transform societies is the fact that man possesses inalienable rights while the possibility of claiming actually to exercise now this one, now that, is yet denied him by those vestiges of inhumanity which remain embedded in the social structures of every era [1]".

The particular human rights whose violation by the practice of *apartheid* is punishable for the same reason and on the same terms as war crimes, and such crimes against humanity as genocide, will be indentified when, at the end of section 8, I come in the course of the argument to deal with the various acts which go to make up *apartheid*.

8. The Court could not refrain from ascertaining the real nature of the practice of *apartheid*, which is not merely contrary to the Mandatory's obligation to ensure the moral and material well-being and social progress of the population under Mandate, but also contravenes the principles of equality and liberty, and the other rights deriving therefrom for individuals and peoples alike. The condemnation of *apartheid*, if it were only taken into account as a violation of the Mandate, would not be radical, as it should be. For it is not only practised by the former mandatory State of South Africa, nor only in the former mandated territory of Namibia. It is more widespread. It is applied in countries which are not under tutelage. It should be delineated and punished as any other attempt upon human equality and individual or national liberty would be. It should be apprehended, in the General Assembly's words, as a crime against humanity, committed in this case against the Namibian people. The breach of the obligation to submit a report to the satisfaction of the Council of the League, or to transmit the petitions of the inhabitants, both of which are obligations bound up with the safeguards for the due performance of the principal obligations assumed by the trustee-Mandatory as such, is not laden with the same degree of gravity as the violation of the latter themselves. It is therefore inadmissible to choose the easy way out and justify the revocation of the Mandate by reference to the refusal to report to the General Assembly or transmit petitions, or even the refusal to collaborate with the committees set up by the United Nations, while at the same time overlooking the gravest violations by failing to make the effort to adduce the proofs thereof, on the hollow pretext that a State has not been given an opportunity of producing factual evidence, when both the written and the oral proceedings contain superabundant proof. This point was grasped by the General Assembly when, with the exception of South Africa and Portugal, it unanimously took account of the breach not only of the Mandate, but also of the Charter and the Universal Declaration of Human Rights. As is plain from the texts of its many

---

[1] *Autour de la Déclaration universelle des droits de l'homme*, Unesco, 1948, p. 16.

resolutions, what decided the United Nations to penalize South Africa's conduct was much less the non-compliance over reports and petitions than the flagrant violation of the most essential principles of humanity, principles protected by the sanction of international law: equality, of which *apartheid* is the negation; freedom, which finds expression in the right of peoples to self-determination; and the dignity of the human person, which has been profoundly injured by the measures applied to non-White human beings.

That point having been made clear, a reply must nevertheless be given to two objections raised in connection with the practice of *apartheid* and the necessity of denouncing it with a view to determining the legal consequences.

When, in the first place, it is maintained that the request for advisory opinion formulated by the Security Council is not concerned with *apartheid*, it is surely forgotten that the application of that doctrine has been the underlying cause of the United Nations' action ever since the earliest days, from the raising of the question by India in 1946 to resolution 2145 (XXI) of 1966, which revoked the Mandate, and those adopted since. Resolution 2145 (XXI), which was reaffirmed by the Security Council resolution, 276 (1970), to which resolution 284 (1970) requesting the opinion of the Court refers, contains the following paragraph:

> "*Reaffirming* its resolution 2074 (XX) of 17 December 1965, in particular paragraph 4 thereof which condemned the policies of *apartheid* and racial discrimination practised by the Government of South Africa in South West Africa as constituting a crime against humanity."

In view of this, can it still be said that the request for the Court's opinion does not entitle it to deal with the subject of *apartheid*?

Nor is it any excuse for evading examination of the practice of *apartheid* in Namibia to plead the absence of material proof of the application of that policy to the detriment of the Namibian people; for such proof, quite apart from ministerial admissions on the part of South Africa, is to be found in abundance in the documentation of the proceedings. After reproducing some of these admissions, I will cite the official texts of the South African Government which demonstrate the facts of the matter and reveal the explanation, which is that the policy of *apartheid* has been applied not, as South Africa claims, in the interest of the population formerly under Mandate, but to the prejudice of that population and in the interest of the mandatory State and its own nationals.

In the matter of admissions, four successive Prime Ministers from 1948 to the present day, Dr. Malan, Mr. Strijdom, Dr. Verwoerd and Mr. Vorster, have defined their concept of the *apartheid* policy, as applicable in both South Africa and Namibia, in declarations which offer proof conclusive. In a speech made in April 1948, Dr. Malan asked:

> "Will the European race in the future be able to maintain its rule, its purity and its civilization, or will it float along until it vanishes

for ever, without honour, in the Black sea of South Africa's Non-European population?... As a result of foreign influences the demand for the removal of all colour bar and segregation measures is being pressed more and more continuously and vehemently; and all this means nothing less that that the White race will lose its ruling position..."

In April 1955 Mr. Strijdom, describing his policy in Parliament, stated:

"I am being as blunt as I can. I am making no excuses. Either the White man dominates or the Black man takes over... The only way the Europeans can maintain supremacy is by domination..."

Dr. Verwoerd likewise stated to Parliament in 1958:

"Dr. Malan said it, and Mr. Strijdom said it, and I have said it repeatedly and I want to say it again: The policy of *apartheid* moves consistently in the direction of more and more separate development with the ideal of total separation in all spheres."

Later Dr. Verwoerd went into greater detail in a speech on 25 January 1963:

"Reduced to its simplest form the problem is nothing else than this: We want to keep South Africa White... Keeping it White can only mean one thing, namely White domination, not leadership, not guidance, but control, supremacy. If we are agreed that it is the desire of the people that the White man should be able to continue to protect himself by White domination... we say that it can be achieved by separate development."

Finally, in May 1965, the present Prime Minister, Mr. Vorster, then Minister of Justice, declared:

"In this Parliament, whose business it is to decide the destiny of the Republic of South Africa, Whites, and Whites only, will have the right to sit."

Such declarations would afford ample proof of what the practice of *apartheid* means and what the motives of those who devised it were. But the Ministers whose declarations are here reproduced have not appeared before the Court to certify their full authenticity or to explain and comment upon them. I therefore turn to the official texts which have been promulgated and published, and which constitute at one and the same time material proof and an admission; their mere enumeration, even though not exhaustive, demonstrates the various forms in which the unlawfulness of *apartheid* is manifested and the corresponding human rights which have been violated.

The chief texts possessing this probative effect are the following:

1. The Bantu Trust and Land Act of 1936, concerning reserves for

Africans which constitute permanent territorial segregation; it thus encroached upon personal liberty, freedom of movement, freedom of residence and the right to own property (Universal Declaration of Human Rights, Arts. 1, 13 and 17).

2. The Natives (Urban Areas) Proclamation of 1951, amended in 1954, under which Black persons may not, with a few exceptions, reside in urban areas; this Proclamation infringes the same rights as the Bantu Trust and Land Act.

3. The Native Reserve Regulations of 1924 and 1938, which forbade Africans in the reserves to leave them or return to them without special authorization; this also violates the human rights mentioned above.

4. The Native Administration Proclamation of 1922, which forbids Africans to circulate without a pass; this violates the right to freedom of movement (Art. 13).

5. The Native Building Workers Act of 1951, which encroaches upon the principles of equality and liberty (Art. 1).

6. The Prohibition of Political Interference Act of 1968, which, in violation of democratic freedoms, prohibits parties of racially mixed membership (Art. 21).

7. The South West Africa Affairs Amendment Act of 1949, which flouted the political rights of the Africans (Art. 21).

8. The Master and Servants Proclamation of 1920, which makes the breach of a contract of employment a punishable offence; this constitutes an infringement of the right to work and an affront to human dignity, and virtually reintroduces forced labour (Arts. 1 and 23).

9. The Prohibition of Mixed Marriages Ordinance of 1953, which regards marriages between Blacks and Whites as void; this is another affront to human dignity and violates the principles of equality as well as the rights of the family (Arts. 1 and 16).

10. The Terrorism Act of 1967, intended to enforce *apartheid* through severe repression, which violates the most sacred principles of criminal law, namely the rule *nullum crimen sine lege*, the rules relating to the definition of principal and accessory, the non-retroactivity of penal laws and of penalties, the presumption of innocence, and the rule of *res judicata*.

11. The Suppression of Communism Act of 1950, extended to Namibia, which has the same unlawful characteristics as the Terrorism Act.

It is, in sum, not without interest to recall that the Commission on Human Rights, in its resolution 3 (XXIV) of 1968, denounced the laws and practices of *apartheid* and *condemned*—

> "...the Government of South Africa for its perpetuation and intensification of the inhuman policy of *apartheid*, in complete and flagrant violation of the Charter of the United Nations and the Universal Declaration of Human Rights".

In the light of the foregoing it is justifiable to consider that the General Assembly was not mistaken when, in resolution 395 (V) of 2 December 1950, it emphasized that any system of racial segregation, such as *apart-*

heid, is necessarily based on doctrines of racial discrimination. The Assembly was no less categorical in its Declaration on the Elimination of All Forms of Racial Discrimination, adopted by resolution 1904 (XVIII). This Declaration condemns racial discrimination and *apartheid* as violating human rights. It was adopted unanimously. Given this general agreement of States, some of which have the fullest possible means of investigation at their disposal, it is difficult to understand how the material existence of the illegalities they denounce can be doubted.

Furthermore, the condemnation of *apartheid* has passed the stage of declarations and entered the phase of binding conventions. The International Convention on the Elimination of All Forms of Racial Discrimination—naturally including *apartheid*—adopted by the General Assembly on 21 December 1965, came into force on 4 January 1969.

9. South Africa has not only contested the material existence of the facts but also the interpretation placed upon them by the General Assembly and the Security Council. Its point of view—rejected by all States, even those which question the validity of the measures taken against South Africa—is that its administration has been designed with the precise aim of realising the objectives of the Mandate, these being to promote the well-being and social progress of the inhabitants; that accordingly *apartheid*, or the separate development of these populations was, given their stage of social evolution, instituted in their own interest: that the measures which have been deemed contrary to the provisions of the Charter and to the Universal Declaration of Human Rights, in particular by resolution 2145 (XXI) revoking the Mandate, were justified by the socio-anthropological circumstances and are directed solely to the accomplishment of the mission entrusted to South Africa.

The Court, in paragraph 131 of the Advisory Opinion, has very justly adduced the textual proof which exists of the unlawfulness of the practice of *apartheid*. Concrete proof could likewise be drawn from the facts already in the Court's possession. When it is possible to refer to such proofs, it is even better to present them in order to reinforce, if need be, the decisiveness of the Court's findings. In this connection I propose to deal with two questions which the Court has not touched upon but which afford opportunities for further clarification: in order, first, to meet the assertion that the Namibian people is not a people and, secondly, to refute the claim that *apartheid* corresponds to the Mandatory's obligation of promoting the well-being and social progress of the people under Mandate.

10. The argument to which South Africa clings most tenaciously is that of the disparity of the various ethnic groups in Namibia. In order to justify the policy of *apartheid* applied not only in the Republic of South Africa but also in Namibia, successive Pretoria governments have put forward the argument that the natives in the south-west of Africa have never formed a people, and that, because of the ethnic and sociological differences which divide them and set them against each other, only the policy of separate development based upon their tribal institutions could ensure their social well-being and progress. This assertion has been used to

buttress denials by the South African Government that it pursued a policy of racial discrimination and has also permitted it to reject any accusation that it violated the provisions of the Mandate and the Charter or contravened the Universal Declaration of Human Rights. I therefore propose to show that the premise upon which South Africa bases this justification of its methods of administration in Namibia is a false one; that the Namibian people, ultimate heir of an ancient civilization which in its heyday rivalled anything in Europe, had, before the days of the colonial régime, taken part in the making of great empires, notwithstanding the multiplicity of the elements of which it, like so many other peoples, is composed.

How many of the peoples that have come into being, throughout history and in our times, have not in fact been made up of a variety of human elements? Multiplicity of ethnic entities has been no obstacle to the formation of peoples and States in Africa. Not to mention the ancient States of Ghana, Mali, Bornu, Axum, Kivu, Benin and that of the Bantus, or the Congo State of the Berlin Conference, it cannot be denied that a large number of the 30 or so States liberated since 1960 are multiracial. India, China and Pakistan offer similar examples in Asia. Many States of Europe also preserve what is sometimes no faded memory of a now complete process of union: for example, Switzerland, Czechoslovakia, Yugoslavia, or the United Kingdom from the Norse invasions down to the reigns of Henry VIII (incorporation of Wales in England) and Queen Anne (union with Scotland). Moreover, is not even the South Africa of today governed by a White minority formed by the union of immigrants of different national origins—Germans, English, Dutch and several others? Whereas the people of Namibia, which always used to be the master of the country, is nowadays united by common aspirations, the legal foundation of nationhood, towards a life of independence and freedom, whatever may be the political régime which it will select after obtaining independence.

If we take a look at the historical facts, we shall see, in the first place, what legality used to be taken to mean in Africa and what it was which used to be called "African law" as opposed to "the public law of Europe"; an African law illustrated—if one can apply the term—in the monstrous blunder committed by the authors of the Act of Berlin, the results of which have not yet disappeared from the African political scene. It was a monstrous blunder and a flagrant injustice to consider Africa south of the Sahara as *terrae nullius*, to be shared out among the Powers for occupation and colonization, when even in the sixteenth century Vitoria had written that Europeans could not obtain sovereignty over the Indies by occupation, for they were not *terra nullius*.

By one of fate's ironies, the declaration of the 1885 Berlin Congress which held the dark continent to be *terrae nullius* related to regions which had seen the rise and development of flourishing States and empires. One should be mindful of what Africa was before there fell upon it the two greatest plagues in the recorded history of mankind: the slave-trade, which ravaged Africa for centuries on an unprecedented scale; and colonialism, which exploited humanity and natural wealth to a relentless extreme. Before these terrible plagues overran their continent, the African peoples had founded States and even empires of a high level of civilization. Only Abyssinia, by its savage resistance, escaped the slave-trade and repelled colonialism, preserving its venerable institutions of State. States less ancient but structurally no less developed than the country of the Negus have nothing to show today but ruins enshrining faint impressions of the past. It is just and pertinent that they be recalled here one by one, beginning, in the first centuries of the Christian era, with the empire of Ghana, the power and wealth of which was unequalled in Western Europe after the fall of the Roman Empire. The empire of Mali, which covered territories more vast than Europe at a time when a considerable part of the latter was a feudal and often feuding patchwork; at the centre of this empire shone a university more ancient than any of Europe, the University of Timbuktu, of which it was said, in illustration of its splendour, that the profit there obtained from the sale of manuscripts exceeded that derived from any economic activity. The State of Bornu, the prosperity of which was still such in the nineteenth century, when visited by an English traveller shortly before its conquest, that the situation of the most humble citizen appeared to him happy and comfortable. The Great Lake civilizations, where traces can be found of roads, irrigation canals, dykes and aqueducts, of a remarkable level of technical skill. Passing on, without pausing to consider the civilizations of Axum, Kivu and Benin, we come to that of Southern Africa. On the banks of the Zambezi, in the same areas as are now dominated by the Republic of South Africa, the Portuguese found, to quote Barboza, "richer trade than in any other part of the world". This is a flattering comparison, for it was made when the Italian republics were at their splendid apogee. In Zimbabwe, the present Rhodesia, gigantic ruins, which call to mind the bastions at Nuragus or Mycenae, bear witness to its ancient grandeur. Its empire extended, into what is now the Republic of South Africa, on both banks of the Limpopo, including the present Transvaal and the sites of Pretoria and Johannesburg. To sum up, let us recall what Raimondo Luraghi has written:

> "Thus, at the time of the arrival of the Portuguese, a chequered history had unrolled for centuries and millennia between the Sahara desert and South Africa—a history of civilized peoples, comparable to that of the great empires of Latin America or of Europe in the most brilliant days of Antiquity and the Middle Ages."

Furthermore, African civilization was not merely material. To give some idea of the high intellectual level of these discredited, unknown or ignored peoples I would quote the work written by Father Placide Tempels, a Belgian Franciscan, on the Bantu people, who still live in Namibia in large numbers. Father Tempels called his book *Philisophie bantoue*, because he had observed the ontological nature of their thinking, based upon awareness of self— on the "know thyself", may I add, of Thales, the Phoenician philosopher who was adopted by the Greeks and ranked among the Seven Sages of their land. "To that intense spiritual doctrine which quickens and nourishes souls within the Catholic church," writes Placide Tempels, "a striking analogy may be found in the ontological thinking of the Bantus." The latter are in fact one of those same great ethnic groups which inhabit the immense territories to which colonialism still desperately clings, that is to say from Mozambique and Angola to Zimbabwe, South Africa and Namibia. And it is these very populations which the South African Government claims are made up of tribes of diverse origins which are incapable of uniting, and which do not deserve the title of a people which the United Nations has attributed to them.

11. Having done justice to the contention that separate development or *apartheid* is a necessity on account of the diversity of ethnic composition precluding on the part of the inhabitants a potentiality for nationhood, I shall now turn to the argument that the measures of discrimination adopted by the South African authorities can be justified in terms of the stage of social evolution reached by the Namibians.

The second paragraph of Article 2 of the mandate agreement provides that:

> "The Mandatory shall promote to the utmost the material and moral well-being and the social progress of inhabitants of the territory subject to the present Mandate."

Here then is an obligation which the Mandatory has to carry out "to the utmost" *[par tous les moyens en son pouvoir]*. To that end the first paragraph of the same Article confers upon him "full power of administration and legislation over the territory subject to the present Mandate".

This means that, rightly or wrongly, the Council of the League of Nations deliberately conferred a power of discretion on the Mandatory. It was however a power of discretion in the legal sense of the term, thus evidently not an arbitrary power but one necessarily subordinate to certain limitations which flow from the overriding principles and rules of law, more particularly the rights of peoples and individuals.

South Africa contends that bad faith would be the only ground upon which criticism could be levelled against its use of that power. This implies that South Africa could be pardoned for irresponsible inaction or neglect, whether serious or slight; for the misuse of law; or for a wilful misinterpretation of the provisions of Article 22 of the Covenant, the Mandate and the United Nations Charter which is alleged to justify racial discrimination and *apartheid*, *de facto* annexation of the Territory of Namibia, and legislative, administrative or judicial measures contrary to the tenets of both national and international law, the principles of the Charter and the Universal Declaration of Human Rights.

But in fact there is no escaping the dialectical necessity of comparing the responsibility of an authority administering a country placed under its guardianship with that of other authorities entrusted with the administration of their own countries or the interests of their nationals. The latter are expected in public law to provide good government and, in the area of personal rights, to model their conduct on that of the *bonus paterfamilias*; they are for that reason the more to be blamed for any abuse of law or misuse of power. In short, the international judge cannot be denied the right of determining in all circumstances whether proper use has been made of the discretionary power; whether, in the opinion of the international tribunal, it has been exercised with a view to the promotion of the well-being and social progress of the population, or whether the mandatory State has done its utmost to fulfil its obligations. This implies ascertaining whether racial discrimination, *apartheid* and related measures, blameworthy in themselves, can be justified on account of local or temporary circumstances, usually of a social nature, and the interests of the population in question. To pass an opinion in these various situations, a judge cannot rely on his personal judgment, which is bound to be subjective and vary according to the mentality of each judge, his legal, philosophical and ethical outlook, his views on natural law and his cultural and social background. An objective criterion or standard is clearly necessary. Such a criterion is afforded by the general conduct of States and international organizations as a whole. Should the judge further decide to derive criteria from municipal precedents, which abound in such examples as the notion of the *bonus paterfamilias* already mentioned, or from powerful moral trends in a given country, they must still be acceptable to other countries in general or be already enshrined in the universal conscience of mankind. And in fact it can be said that the many resolutions, adopted over nearly a quarter of a century, which condemn racial discrimination and *apartheid* in South Africa and, as later extended, in Namibia, disclose an objective standard which the South African Government is required to apply. The same can be said with reference to the other human rights. To this the firm attitude of the international community has borne witness whenever it has taken a stand against their infringement. Indeed, the mere perusal of the texts I have mentioned is edifying in this regard.

12. I now come to the legal consequences of the presence of South Africa in Namibia. In order to determine what these are, that presence must first of all be legally classified. Is it a matter of mere peaceful intervention? Or of a military occupation degenerating into aggression? Or a colonial war? For the legal consequences differ in international law according to whether it falls within one or another of these classifications.

The representatives of a certain number of States who have had occasion to speak in the Security Council have stated that the occupation of Namibia by the Republic of South Africa is an aggression. The representatives who so argued were those of Algeria, Colombia, Hungary, Nepal, Nigeria, the Soviet Union, the United Arab Republic, and Zambia [1]. Similarly the other African States stated at Addis Ababa in 1966 that it was a military occupation, which is the mark of aggression according to all the definitions which have been given of that term. And the representative of the United States of America, in the written statement submitted to the Court, expressed the following view:

"The territory is occupied by force against the will of the international authority entitled to administer it. Such occupation is as much belligerent occupation as the hostile occupation of the territory of another State."

---

[1] See S/PV. 1387-1395.

An armed force which violates the frontiers of a country indisputably commits an aggression. What then is the position as to belligerent occupation of a whole territory, to which the representative of the United States refers?

The General Assembly has made matters clear: in resolution 2131 (XX) it said that "armed intervention is synonymous with aggression".

The representative of Pakistan was more emphatic in his oral statement of 15 February last. He rightly viewed the act of using force with the object of frustrating the right of self-determination as an act of aggression, which is all the more grave in that the right of self-determination is a norm of the nature of *jus cogens*, derogation from which is not permissible under any circumstances.

I hasten to recall that the Security Council has used terms no less forceful. It described the occupation of Namibia as illegal. In its resolution 269 (1969), following the General Assembly, it recognized "the legitimacy of the struggle of the people of Namibia against the illegal presence of the South African authorities in the territory"; a legitimate struggle against what, if not against an aggression? This is a logical interpretation, no refutation of which is possible. It follows not only from the logic of things but also from the actual text of the Charter. For Article 51 only authorizes self-defence *[légitime défense]* or legitimate struggle in cases of response to armed attack *[agression armée]*. Thus once the Security Council proclaims the legitimacy of a defence or of a struggle against a foreign occupier, it is an armed attack *[agression armée]* which is in question, and the occupier's act cannot consequently be anything other than an aggression *[agression]*. It is in this context that one must understand the Council's expression, mentioned by the Court in paragraph 109 of the Opinion, "that the continued occupation of the territory of Namibia by the South African authorities constitutes an aggressive encroachment on the authority of the United Nations".

The aggression committed by South Africa with regard to Namibia is the more serious in that, *de facto* and notwithstanding the South African Government's denials, it has turned into a veritable annexation. This can be indisputably proved by facts which cannot be denied. I will quote the more important of these, the meaning and significance of which it is easy to discern:

(1) The South West Africa Affairs Amendment Act of 1949 deleted all references to the Mandate from the Constitution of the Territory.

(2) The South African Government contends that it occupies the Territory of South West Africa by conquest or by acquisitive prescription.

(3) In the 16 following pieces of legislation, the "Union", or the "State", or the "Republic" of South Africa is defined as including South West Africa:

(a) the Terrorism Act of 1967;
(b) the Border Control Act of 1967;
(c) the War Pensions Act of 1967;
(d) the Wool Act of 1967;
(e) the Armaments Development and Production Act of 1968;
(f) the Human Sciences Research Act of 1968;

(g) the Professional Engineers' Act of 1968;
(h) the Companies Amendment Act of 1969;
(i) the Land Bank Amendment Act of 1969;
(j) the National Monuments Act of 1969;
(k) the Births, Marriages and Deaths Registration Act of 1970;
(l) the Land Survey Act of 1970;
(m) the Land Surveyors' Registration Act of 1970;
(n) the Maintenance Act of 1970;
(o) the National Supplies Procurement Act of 1970;
(p) the Reciprocal Enforcement of Maintenance Orders Act of 1970.

(4) The South West Africa Affairs Amendment Act of 1949 effects annexation at constitutional level, by providing for representation of the Namibians in the Pretoria Parliament.

The annexation of Namibia by South Africa is definitely an act of aggression. A memorable example of that kind of aggression is recorded in the historic Moscow Declaration of 30 October 1943 in which the Soviet Union, the United States, the United Kingdom and China qualified the occupation and annexation of Austria by Hitlerite Germany as aggression and solemnly declared their refusal to recognize it. The fact that the annexation of a territory by the mere movement of troops or by the presence of foreign troops is ranked as an act of aggression by that Declaration means that the word aggression covers a wider range than the notion of armed attack *stricto sensu*. This is easily understandable, inasmuch as occupation and annexation achieve the ultimate aims of aggression, bringing about the destruction of the entity which was the latter's target. As a matter of definition, can the occupation of Austria with a view to its annexation be classified as aggression, and the occupation and subsequent annexation of Namibia not be so regarded? This was what the Court has sought to exclude, when in paragraph 109 of the Opinion it recalled that in operative paragraph 3 of resolution 269 (1969) the Security Council decided "that the continued occupation of the territory of Namibia by the South African authorities constitutes an aggressive encroachment on the authority of the United Nations". The General Assembly had stated earlier in resolution 2074 (XX) that "any attempt to annex a part or the whole of the Territory of South West Africa constitutes an act of aggression". For while the law of former times, as in the 1885 Act of Berlin and the Treaties of Bardo and Algéciras and numerous other treaties, tolerated conquest and annexation, of which South Africa's conduct appears to be one of the last examples, modern law, that of the United Nations Charter, the Pact of Bogotá and the Charter of Addis Ababa, condemns them beyond reprieve. Annexation is nothing less than the negation of the new law of self-determination. Thus the United Nations has reiterated that acquisition of a territory may not be effected by the use or the threat of force. In its recent resolution 2628 (XXV), of 4 November 1970, the General Assembly "reaffirms that the acquisition of territories by force is inadmissible", and that consequently the occupied territories must be restored. None the less, South Africa has throughout, and even before the Court, sought to justify its continued occupation of Namibia by claiming to be there by right of conquest or by the effect of acquisitive prescription. The Court has dismissed this claim in paragraphs 85 and 86 of the Opinion. The most categorical argument on the point would have been that conquest and acquisitive prescription have totally disappeared from the new law which has condemned war and proclaimed the inalienability of sovereignty.

13. The presence of South Africa in Namibia having thus been defined as illegal and warlike, and, in short, regarded as aggression, what are the legal consequences of this?

The recognition by the United Nations of the legitimacy of the Namibian people's struggle against the South African aggression is nothing less than a recognition of belligerency. For the recognizing States, namely the States Members of the United Nations, it transforms the hostilities between a State and another subject of law, which the Namibian people is, into an international war. Consequently, when there is aggression by a State against a people for the purpose of subjugating it by force, then whatever its manifestations, it cannot be denied that it has the character of a war, or at least of a state of belligerency[1], with all the legal effects attaching thereto, including in particular the status of neutrality imposed on third-party States.

If the provisions of the Charter concerning collective security could have been implemented according to the letter and in the spirit of the San Francisco Conference, there would have been no place for neutrality, at least among States Members of the United Nations. The Charter provided on the one hand for an international army (Arts. 43 to 47) and disarmament (Art. 11, para. 1; Art. 26, and Art. 47, para. 1). But military preparations have been neglected since 1948, and in place of disarmament, which is in the doldrums, there has from the beginning been an intensive process of nuclear and conventional armament spreading into the wars being carried on more or less all over the world. On the other hand, there were the provisions concerning collective security (Arts. 39 et seq.), the executive counterpart of which was to be the international army. The fate of the new institution intended to put an end to wars was no better than that described above. The Security Council's action has been paralysed by the veto, or by the fear of a veto as in the Namibia question. Consequently, neutrality persists so long as wars are tolerated, whether deliberately or through weakness. This applies particularly in the case of the States Members which, evading the obligations deriving from the United Nations resolutions, for some reason or another, are at least under an obligation not to hinder the activities of or the measures adopted by the Organization of which they are Members.

The obligations of States not participating in hostilities, which constitute the status of neutrality, are applicable in the case of mere belli-

---

[1] L. Cavaré wrote as follows concerning colonial protectorates: "If the protected country retains its personality, then there is a war in the international meaning of the term and the laws of war must be applied" (*Droit international public positif*, Vol. I, 3rd ed., p. 551). *A fortiori*, this is the case for Namibia even before it was recognized by the United Nations by resolution 2372 (XXII). See also above section 2.

gerency just as in the case of war. This would be relevant if it were considered that the relations between South Africa and Namibia are only a state of belligerency between communities, one of which is not yet a State. The classic example of this is the War of Secession in the United States. Therefore, whether the Namibians are regarded as being in a state of war or in a state of insurrection against South Africa, recognized by the international community, the obligations of third States are clear: those States are bound by the status of neutrality as it derives from the 1871 Washington Rules, and Conventions V and XIII adopted by the 1907 Hague Peace Conference—which have become binding rules of customary law—and from the relevant provisons of the laws and customs of war. This means: abstention and impartiality.

In order to define the concept of impartiality, a distinction must be made between the aggressor and the victim of aggression[1]. A noteworthy example is that of the policy adopted by the United States of America, which led to the promulgation of the Cash and Carry and Lend-Lease Acts. These Acts were exceptions to the general rules of neutrality, founded on a desire to assist the victims of aggression[2]. With regard to certain Western States which continue to supply South Africa with arms, ammunition and war material, their attitude contravenes the status of neutrality, from which they have previously benefited[3], for instead of the obligation of impartiality being interpreted by them in favour of the victim, it is violated for the benefit of the aggressor. They should abstain from such deliveries. Security Council resolution 282 (1970), pronouncing the arms embargo against South Africa alone, is in line with international practice.

14. The obligation of abstention entailed by the status of neutrality must be defined having regard to the development of modern armaments and the variety of means of assistance which may be supplied to the belligerents. The different prohibitions imposed by international law

---

[1] G. Schwarzenberger explains the distinction in these words in connection with the implementation of the Briand-Kellogg Pact:

> "Parties to the Kellogg Pact which remain at peace with the aggressor are entitled, by way of reprisal, to depart from the observance of strict neutrality between the Pact-breaker and his victim and to discriminate against the aggressor."

As examples in support of this rule he cites the Destroyer Deal between the United States and Great Britain, and the "Aid Britain" Act of 1941. He adds in a relevant comparison:

> "As with Members of the United Nations (Art. 2 (5) of the Charter), parties to treaties may even be under a legal duty to discriminate against an aggressor State." (*A Manual of International Law*, Vol. I, 4th ed., p. 185.)

[2] See E. Castrén, *The Present Law of War and Neutrality*, 1954, pp. 451 and 477, who mentions that:

> "The purpose may be to assist the victim of aggression ... in which case American writers have used the expression 'supporting State' " (p. 451).

[3] R. Sherwood, in his book of memoirs entitled *Roosevelt and Hopkins*, writes on p. 221, of Churchill's overjoyed gratitude: "... and from this came the vast concept which Churchill later described as 'a new Magna Charta ... the most unselfish and unsordid financial act of any country in all history'."

may moreover duplicate and reinforce or may supplement those laid down in the relevant Security Council resolutions, on account of violation of the Charter and of international law. States may thus be under various obligations by virtue of more than one source of obligation. Examples of such prohibitions are:

(1) The prohibition of all military assistance, not only *de facto*, but also in implementation of a treaty of alliance or of bilateral or multilateral defence. The obligations contained in those treaties cannot prevail over the obligation not to assist an aggressor State. A treaty which enabled assistance to be given to an aggressor would be immoral and contrary to international order, and could not therefore be tolerated by the international community. Further, treaties of alliance generally provide that they do not operate unless it is the other signatory which was attacked.

(2) The prohibition of the supply of nuclear or conventional arms and of all ammunition; of the supply of ships, aircraft or other military machines, and of armed or transport helicopters; of rockets, missiles and electronic equipment which can be put to military uses; of all arms capable of being used against guerillas, including napalm, chemical and bacteriological weapons, and gases of all sorts. As in the case of treaties of alliance or defence, agreements for the supply of any of the foregoing may not be implemented in favour of the aggressor, for any reason whatsoever, whether of joint defence or of economic necessity.

(3) The prohibition of the supply of spare parts and any equipment capable of being used for the production or maintenance of arms or ammunition or nuclear devices, and patents or licences relating thereto.

(4) The prohibition of the emigration or despatch of technicians for work in the armaments industry, or for the training of military personnel; on the transmission of military or technical information, including information relating to the peaceful uses of nuclear energy, on account of the possibility of its being adapted to military purposes.

(5) The prohibition of the supply of oil and petroleum products and of natural gas on account of their vital importance for war. If this prohibition is such as to harm South African industry, that can only be a more effective way of bringing South Africa to put an end to its aggression [1].

(6) The prohibition of the supply of all facilities for the transport of the above-mentioned arms; machinery, munitions and other products.

(7) The prohibition of all economic, industrial or financial assistance, in the form of gifts, loans, credit, advances or guarantees, or in any other form [1]. This prohibition is not confined to States. It naturally extends to institutions in which States have voting rights, such as the International Bank for Reconstruction and Development, the International Develop-

---

[1] On the subject of oil supplies see Professor Erik Castrén, *The Present Law of War and Neutrality*, 1954, p. 474.

[1] See in connection with prohibitions of a financial nature, Professor Paul Reuter, *op. cit.*, p. 321.

ment Association and the International Finance Corporation; as is well known, the International Bank for Reconstruction and Development has deliberately disregarded the resolutions of the General Assembly and the Security Council, by continuing to grant South Africa aid amounting to hundreds of millions of dollars, which is in fact aid to the illegal activity of the South African authorities in Namibia, contrary to the objects and purposes of the United Nations [2].

All the above prohibitions apply to States and to associations of States and to public and private international organizations.

Furthermore, governments must show due diligence in preventing any individual or collective act contrary to neutrality. This obligation relates to nationals and subjects, and to foreign residents. Showing due diligence means that adequate measures must be taken, including legislative measures providing for penalties. For a State which undertakes an obligation commits its own subjects and those who live under its law and must employ every kind of means, legislative, administrative and judicial, by which it governs. It is not therefore sufficient to refuse diplomatic protection to those who transgress, as has been suggested by the Government of the United States.

It is by taking these measures, which are dictated by the status of neutrality, that States, and in particular those which are, politically and financially speaking, the Great Powers, will bring South Africa to abandon its present policy, in the interests of justice, peace and international co-operation.

15. It was to be desired that the Court should deduce all the legal consequences from the aggression observed by the Security Council. The request made of it was not confined to the effect of resolution 276 (1970), referred to in resolution 284 (1970) requesting the opinion. The legal consequences upon which it had to pronounce are all those resulting from the very presence of South Africa in Namibia, which is the first point mentioned in resolution 284 (1970), and which is conditioned by resolution 276 (1970). That presence was the justification for resolutions 282 (1970) and 283 (1970), which the Court could not leave out of account as not falling within the request for advisory opinion. For resolution 283 (1970) re-affirms, first resolution 276 (1970) and secondly resolution 282 (1970), in the following terms:

> "*Re-affirming* its resolution 282 (1970) on the arms embargo against the Government of South Africa and the significance of that resolution with regard to the territory and people of Namibia, . . ."

---

[2] The specialized agencies in which the voting is based on the democratic rule of one State, one vote, have all decided to refrain from any support to South Africa: for example, Unesco, ILO, FAO and WHO. The recalcitrant attitude of the IBRD and the IMF is to be explained by the multiple voting system on a capitalist basis which operates therein, by which the financial Great Powers have a number of votes calculated according to the size of their share in the capital of these two institutions. These Powers are primarily the States which the General Assembly has described as commercial partners of South Africa. In future, States ought to take it as a matter of course that they should bring their attitude in these institutions into line with decisions of the United Nations.

These two resolutions, 282 (1970) and 283 (1970), concerning the illegal presence of South Africa in Namibia were, what is more, adopted before the request for opinion; resolution 283 (1970) was adopted solely because of that illegal presence, which is the principal subject-matter of the request for opinion, and resolution 282 (1970) had in view *apartheid* beyond the frontiers of South Africa, as well as the policies of that Government in southern Africa, including Namibia. Resolution 282 (1970) reads as follows:

> "*Reiterating* its condemnation of the evil and abhorrent policies of *apartheid* and the measures being taken by the Government of South Africa to enforce and extend those policies beyond its borders,
>
> . . . .
>
> "*Gravely concerned* by the persistent refusal of the Government of South Africa to abandon its racist policies and to abide by the resolutions of the Security Council and of the General Assembly on this question and others relating to southern Africa . . ."

This latter paragraph of resolution 282 (1970), by making reference to "the resolutions of the Security Council", contemplated resolution 276 (1970) in particular.

16. Although the Court has made no mention of resolutions 282 (1970) and 283 (1970), it has nonetheless reached conclusions which do not differ in substance from those which follow from those two resolutions and from the status of neutrality.

I will begin with economic consequences, namely those enumerated in resolution 283 (1970) and the more complete set, resulting from the status of neutrality, which are mentioned in section 14, paragraph 7, of the present separate opinion. The Advisory Opinion has not failed to express the view, in the operative clause, that member States of the United Nations are under obligation "to refrain from any acts and in particular any dealings with the Government of South Africa . . . lending support or assistance to" South Africa. The prohibition of economic assistance provided for in resolution 283 (1970) and by the status of neutrality has thus been substantially adopted by the Opinion of the Court.

It is clear from a reading of the whole of the Opinion that the operative clause is integrally connected with the reasoning, and is explained by the reasoning. But even in the light of the reasoning, there are missing details which it might have been useful to clear up. The question arose whether the legal consequences which the Court was called upon to deduce should be summed up in a few major rules, or whether they should be laid down in terms as detailed as possible. The Court has chosen the first solution, leaving it to the political organs to effect the application thereof. This does not seem to me to be quite what the Security Council wanted. Of course any analytical formulation carried to extremes would have failed to be exhaustive, and might sometimes have overlooked circumstances which were necessarily unforeseeable. Nonetheless, a more complete enumeration, but one which did not lose itself in detail, might have been more satisfying, and would have been more surely effective in stopping at the source those interpretations which are sometimes made to suit national tendencies or interests.

The possible clarifications to supplement the Opinion may, in consequence of what has been said above, be deduced from what is laid down by the status of neutrality, and by resolution 283 (1970). Although not mentioned in the Advisory Opinion, this resolution is covered by the rule which has there been laid down *erga omnes*, namely that the decisions of the Security Council are imperatively binding by virtue of Article 25 of the Charter. The following is a not exhaustive list of the prohibitions of an economic kind which result therefrom:

(1) States should debar themselves and should forbid their nationals, subjects and foreign residents, under penalties, from having any part in South African companies or undertakings registered or established in Namibian territory, or having in that territory branches, representatives or agencies, either by way of technical participation or on the financial level by the acquisition of stocks, shares or bonds.

(2) States should not authorize the shares and bonds of such companies to be quoted on the Stock Exchange, or any dealings therein to be effected. Otherwise, they would be facilitating the disposal of assets acquired by misappropriation or spoliation, taking into account the civil or commercial responsibilities attaching thereto.

(3) The exploitation of the petroleum, diamond, gold and other resources of the soil and sub-soil of Namibia, its territorial waters or its continental shelf, carried out by South Africa or its nationals, or with its authorization, is equivalent to the seizure of Namibian assets by, or with the co-operation of, the occupying authority, and the Republic of South Africa must therefore render an account to the future State of Namibia of the income and taxes which it has derived or collected from such sources. Any States which have obtained profit from these exploitations, either in the form of concessions or in the form of participation in the invested capital, may be held jointly responsible with South Africa towards Namibia. These States and their subjects must refrain from acquiring any of the production of these exploitations, in order not to incur civil responsibility by being involved either as receivers or as purchasers, with notice, of assets not belonging to the vendor.

17. Turning to military matters, it should be observed that the passage in the operative clause of the Opinion forbidding any support or assistance to South Africa is drawn in very general terms. By mentioning "any acts" and "any dealings with the Government of South Africa", it clearly includes military support, and such support, being indisputably the most serious and the most heavy with consequences, must therefore be forbidden before any other form of support. Any supply of arms, munitions or war material, and any technical or scientific military assistance, are hereafter prohibited. This rule applies to all States, and none of them can evade it on any ground whatsoever, e.g., economic or strategic interests.

As in the case of economic consequences, the details of the military support which is prohibited remain to be determined. Like resolution 283 (1970), resolution 282 (1970) is a binding decision by virtue of Article 25, already referred to; the more so in that resolution 282 (1970) is related, as has been stated, to resolution 276 (1970) through resolution 283 (1970).

In any event, the acts of military support or assistance from which States must refrain are those the prohibition of which is dictated by resolution 282 (1970) and by the status of neutrality mentioned in Section 14, paragraphs 1 to 6, of this separate opinion. Under each of the three documents in question—the Court's Opinion, resolution 282 (1970) and the status of neutrality—what matters is that no assistance shall be given to an aggressor: consequently, the measures to be applied must be the same, in order to meet the same need.

Certain governments, in order to some extent to evade the embargo on arms and material for land, sea and aerial warfare, have drawn a distinction between arms and war material destined for internal use, in other words for repression—to which they admit the prohibition would apply—and arms and material allocated to external defence, which they contend would be excluded from the embargo.

This distinction is condemned by the facts of the case. In the various wars waged by the colonial Powers and mandatory States, heavy armaments and military aircraft were widely used. According to Mr. McBride, the Secretary General of the International Commission of Jurists, "heavy weapons were often employed to maintain a colonial régime, and they could be very useful to a régime like that in South Africa [1]". And armoured cars were in fact deployed at Sharpeville on 21 March 1960, when the South African police opened fire and according to the United Nations report, killed a large number of peaceful and unarmed Black demonstrators while fighter aircraft flew overhead. The anniversary of that day was proclaimed by the General Assembly as the *International Day for the Elimination of Racial Discrimination*. Of course, as a diplomat observed, "it is not possible to transform submarines into amphibious vehicles in order to use them for land operations". However, no one can be unaware that in the course of colonial wars there have been bombardments by naval units or aircraft of ports, towns, villages or concentrations of people. That is why the supply of any arms capable of reinforcing South Africa's military potential must be forbidden, particularly since it is this material strength which enables it to maintain its presence in Namibia notwithstanding resolution 276 (1970).

18. Furthermore, the illegal presence of South Africa in Namibia opens up possibilities of wide application of Article 103 of the Charter. The obligations of Members of the United Nations under the Charter, contemplated by that Article, clearly include obligations resulting from the provisions of the Charter and from its purposes, and also those laid down by the binding decisions of the organs of the United Nations. Among such decisions are those of the Security Council, namely resolutions 282 (1970) and 283 (1970). Since Article 103 applies both to past and future commitments, the following, whatever their date [1], can no longer be relied on

---

[1] *Ad Hoc* Sub-Committee of the Security Council, S/AC. 17/SR. 14, meeting of 24 June 1970.

[1] See hereon L. Cavaré, *op. cit.*, pp. 653 f.

against member States in their relationship with South Africa: military alliances, naval agreements or agreements relating to joint naval manœuvres, agreements to supply arms, war material and munitions, agreements for co-operation in the nuclear field for whatever purpose, as well as all treaties involving any assistance whatsoever calculated to facilitate the maintenance of South Africa's presence in Namibia, as is stated in paragraphs 119 et seq. of the Court's Opinion.

19. In conclusion, it should be emphasized that since 1967 the United Nations has been convinced that any assistance given to South Africa, even without being earmarked for any particular application, would nevertheless further the designs of South Africa both in South African territory and in Namibia. For the South African Government has been administering Namibia as an integral part of its territory since even before it was annexed thereto, applying to it its racial policy and its policy of colonial exploitation. Any financial, economic or military assistance is likely to promote the general development of that policy and consequently to tighten South Africa's hold over the Territory of Namibia. Thus it is that the General Assembly has adopted resolution upon resolution in order to dissuade member States of the United Nations from giving any assistance whatsoever to South Africa, even such as is not expressly intended to consolidate its presence in Namibia, for so long as it continues its policy of racial discrimination and *apartheid* in the geographical, political, economic and military ensemble of South and South West Africa. This was the purpose of resolutions 2307 (XXII), 2396 (XXIII), 2426 (XXIII) and 2506 (XXIV). In the same way, the two resolutions 282 (1970) and 283 (1970) of the Security Council concern South Africa no less than Namibia. It is in this sense that the Court's Opinion is to be understood; to do otherwise would be to run counter to reality.

(Signed) Fouad AMMOUN.

16.

O.A.U. DECLARATION OF DAR ES SALAAM ON SOUTHERN AFRICA

. The Council of Ministers of the OAU meetings in its 9th Extraordinary Session in Dar es Salaam from 7–10 April 1975 has made an in-depth study of the development in southern Africa in general and the situation in SA in particular. This evaluation was made with the specific objective in the region, namely, the total liquidation of the twin evils of colonialism and racism.

2. Though the OAU's position on these problems has repeatedly been made clear, the fast changing events in southern Africa make it imperative for the OAU to re-examine its strategy. Such reassessment is particularly crucial in the light of deliberate and calculated attempts by Africa's enemies to sow seeds of confusion among our ranks, and employing diversionary tactics with the view to undermining OAU's stand. It is therefore to the re-examination of the OAU's strategy for the liberation of Zimbabwe and Namibia as well as the abolition of the inhuman system of apartheid in SA that the Ministers have devoted their extraordinary session in Dar es Salaam. And they accordingly declare as follows:

3. The decisive defeat of Portuguese colonialism by the African liberation movements and the imminent independence of Mozambique and Angola has radically altered the balance of forces in southern Africa. The resultant fatal blow inflicted in the 'Unholy Alliance' of the Government in Pretoria with the Smith regime and the Portuguese colonialists has seriously undermined the geopolitical position of the SA regime. Freedom has come to the borders of SA and Namibia with the independence of Mozambique and Angola respectively. The buffer zones for the consolidation of colonialism and racism have ultimately crumbled.

4. Vorster's Government is faced with intensified international isolation as demonstrated by the decision of the UN General Assembly to bar the SA delegation from taking part in the proceedings of the 29th Session.

5. Recognizing that the liberation of Angola and Mozambique brings with it a radical change in the geography of the African freedom struggle, resulting in the intensification of the struggle against colonialism in Rhodesia and Nami-

bia, SA has been forced to review its policies towards its client States of Zimbabwe and Namibia. The apartheid regime of Vorster is therefore now engaged in new manoeuvres in an attempt to reduce, if not neutralize, the impact of the revolutionary changes that have taken place in the region. It is desperately attempting to break its isolation and to undermine international opposition to its illegal occupation of Namibia. SA is trying to camouflage the reality of the obnoxious system of racial oppression in SA by resorting to such highly orchestrated propaganda on the removal of 'petty-apartheid'. The aim of Vorster's Government in this exercise of whitewashing apartheid is clear: to deceive world public opinion into believing that some radical changes are taking place in his Republic of South Africa and thus reduce the regime's international isolation.

6. The OAU's full commitment to the objective of total liberation of the continent is unequivocal and unquestionable. There can never be any surrender or compromise on this goal. But the development in southern Africa necessitates that the OAU re-evaluate its approach for the purpose of achieving the desired goal. Such a re-examination becomes all the more urgent by the evidence of new tactics on the part of Vorster's regime in SA.

7. Above all, it is of the utmost importance that such a reassessment should have as its important prerequisite the maintenance and strengthening of unity and solidarity of Africa in confronting the new situation in southern Africa. The enemies of independent Africa realize that this unity is the most powerful weapon in the continent's arsenal. It is that unity and solidarity which Vorster, with his collaborators and supporters, are attempting to undermine. There Africa's urgent need to close its ranks in facing SA's new tactics becomes self-evident.

8. There are two main areas of conflict in southern Africa. The first is the confrontation with colonialism.

The second is the conflict with the system of apartheid which has rightly been declared by the UN as a crime against humanity. But whether we are dealing with the struggle against colonialism in Rhodesia or illegal occupation of Namibia or racist domination in SA, the main opponent of Africa is the same, the SA regime and the power it wields in the three areas. Thus the southern African problem is firstly SA as a colonialist power, and secondly SA as a racist society.

9. The OAU's objectives in Rhodesia, Namibia and SA have never changed. These objectives flow from the OAU's commitment to achieve the total independence on the basis of majority rule with respect to the two colonial territories. Concerning SA, the objective has been, and still is, the end of apartheid and the total elimination of racial discrimination. While the strategies and tactics in the attainment of this objective may change from one situation to another, and from time to time, the objective itself is constant and non-negotiable.

10. Africans cannot, and will never, acquiesce in the perpetuations of colonial and/or racist oppression in their continent. That is why any talk of detente with the apartheid regime is such nonsense that it should be treated with the contempt it deserves. What the OAU demands is the dismantling of the institutions of oppression and repression against the non-white people by the racist minority. Otherwise, Vorster's outcries about detente can only have one meaning in so far as the situation within SA is concerned. And this is that free and independent Africa should co-exist with apartheid and thus acquiesce in the daily humiliation, degradation, oppression, and repression of the African people in SA.

11. Africa has on many occasions decided as desire willingness to promote peaceful settlement to the problems of southern Africa, including that of SA. The liberation movements themselves have a long history of non-violent struggle. It is only the obduracy, intransigence and recalcitrance of the colonialist and racist regimes that forced them to resort to the armed struggle. Yet even at the eleventh hour, Africa proclaimed the Lusaka Manifesto was unambiguous in asserting the OAU's preference to achieve freedom and human dignity for our continent by peaceful means. But the OAU has also made it clear if peaceful progress towards its objective is blocked the OAU will support the armed struggle carried out by the peoples of the oppressed areas. This remains the unshakeable position of the OAU States as clearly defined by the Mogadishu Declaration.

OAU'S STRATEGY AGAINST COLONIALISM

12. In recent years the OAU has adopted and carried out several strategies against colonialism. When in 1969 the racist and colonial regimes ignored the Lusaka Manifesto, the OAU States adopted the Mogadishu Declaration in 1971 calling for the intensification of the armed struggle. This was followed by the Accra strategy of 1973 concentrating on the liberation of the Portuguese colonies. The victory over Portuguese colonialism which vindicated the Accra Strategy led Africa, in 1975, to adopt the Dar es Salaam Declaration by which the OAU has resolved to take advantage of the victories achieved by the freedom fighters of Mozambique, Angola, Guinea-Bissau and Cape Verde, Sao Tome and Principe for the advance of the freedom march further south, with particular emphasis on the liberation of Zimbabwe and Namibia. The Extraordinary Session of the Council of Ministers while unequivocally reaffirming this Declaration wishes to highlight the following:

13. The process of decolonization has gained such momentum as to make it irreversible. The new situation now requires the OAU to retain the initiative in its own hands and intensify, not relax, the pressures on SA's apartheid regime

which is now operating from a position of declining strength.

14. In SA lies the key to the complete decolonization of southern Africa. Therefore, the problem of the liberation of southern Africa must be examined within the context of a comprehensive strategy for the total liberation of the area, while recognizing that the specific factors in the three territories concerned – Zimbabwe, Namibia and SA – makes the liberation movements adopt different tactics.

(A) Zimbabwe

15. The OAU's objective in Zimbabwe is independence on the basis of majority rule. This can be achieved either peacefully or by violent means. Either way, Africa will lend its total support to the freedom fighters led by their nationalist movement – the African National Council. As long as the objectives of majority rule before independence is not compromised, the OAU would support all efforts made by the Zimbabwe nationalists to win independence by peaceful means. This may mean a holding of a constitutional conference where the nationalist forces will negotiate with the Smith regime. If that takes place, the OAU has the duty to do everything possible to assist the success of such negotiations, in constant consultation with the nationalists until and unless the Zimbabwean nationalists themselves are convinced that talks with Smith have failed. In this event, the freedom fighters will have to intensify the armed struggle with the material, financial and diplomatic assistance of independent Africa.

16. In considering the objectives of the OAU in Zimbabwe, it is important to properly evaluate the role of SA in that territory. SA has troops in Zimbabwe which help to maintain white minority rule. SA has frustrated the efforts of the international community by being the major sanctions buster. Both in its military and economic support of the Smith regime, SA continues to defy opposition from independent Africa and the UN. The apartheid regime must forthwith withdraw its military, political and economic support to the minority regime.

17. While the OAU accepts the task of helping in genuine negotiations in order to facilitate the transfer of power to the African majority, it must remain absolutely vigilant and undertake the necessary preparations for the intensification of the armed struggle should peaceful solution to the Zimbabwe conflict be blocked.

18. The Council of Ministers expressed its appreciation of the declaration by the ANC on the need for strengthening unity amongst the people of Zimbabwe as the most powerful weapon in their armoury in the struggle for immediate majority rule, and urges them to continue with vigilance, employing the double-strategy of full preparedness for intensifying the armed struggle while at the same time exploring the possibilities for peaceful change.

(B) Namibia

19. Africa's and the UN's position on the question of Namibia is unequivocal. SA's continued occupation of that land is illegal and all member-States of the UN are under obligation to refrain from doing anything which implies the legality of its administration. Africa must fulfil strictly this obligation to abstain from any action which may be construed as recognition or acceptance of SA's right to be in Namibia.

20. The OAU and the UN hold the unity and territorial integrity of Namibia sacrosant. Both organizations are working for the independence of the territory as a whole and are totally opposed to its fragmentation. Both organizations recognize SWAPO as the legitimate and authentic representative of the Namibian people. Despite the specific and unanimous demand of the Security Council, SA has not yet accepted withdrawing from Namibia. In fact the apartheid regime has consolidated its repressive rule in the territory and proceed with its bantustanization.

21. The 9th Extraordinary Session of the Council of Ministers reiterate their conviction that the only possible solution to the problem of Namibia lies in the implementation by SA of Security Council Resolution No. 366 (1974) of 17 December 1974. The African States, considering that the Security Council by its own decision is scheduled to convene on or about the 30 May 1975 to consider the question of Namibia, call upon the Council to take the necessary measures, including those envisaged under Chapter VII of the UN Charter with a view to effectively overcome SA's defiance and contempt of the UN's decisions. In the absence of SA's willingness to terminate its illegal occupation of Namibia, the OAU must assit the national liberation movement of Namibia, SWAPO, to intensify the armed struggle in Namibia. SWAPO should also be supported in every way possible.

The OAU strategy on apartheid

22. As regards SA, both the OAU and the UN are dedicated to the principle of full equality for all the people of the country, irrespective of race or colour. It is impossible for free Africa to acquiesce in the denial of human equality and human dignity which is represented by the philosophy and system of apartheid. Thus the OAU, like the UN, opposes the regime in SA, not because it is white, but because it rejects and fights against the principles of human equality and national self-determination.

23. The OAU has repeatedly warned that the apartheid regime constitutes a serious threat to international peace and security. This threat assumes graver proportions as the apartheid regime feels insecure. Despite Vorster's claims at the end of 1974 that given six months or so the world would be surprised by the

changes that would be initiated from within the apartheid republic, the situation has taken a turn for the worse as evidenced by the mass trial of students, the consolidation and strengthening of the 'Bantustans' and the vast increase of SA's military budget. Clearly, Vorster's regime is not about to depart from the doctrine of apartheid. Indeed, if anything, Vorster's measures have been designed to strengthen the security of the system of apartheid within SA.

24. Confronted with this unabashed determination of the apartheid regime to maintain its white supremacist system, the OAU's responsibility is clear. We must ostracize, and urge the rest of the world to ostracize, the SA regime as at present organized. Free Africa must maintain the economic, political and cultural boycott of SA. The OAU and the UN must work in concert for the extension of the boycott. We must, in brief, work for the total isolation, of the SA regime. There is no justification at all for changing this policy, as long as the apartheid policy continues. Nor is there anything for free Africa to talk to the leaders of the apartheid regime in connection with their policies in SA.

25. If and when the leaders of the apartheid regime of SA decide to abandon their racist policy they should initiate discussions with the liberation movements of SA. The regime should immediately and unconditionally release the nationalist leader, Nelson Mandela, and lift the restriction order on Robert Sobukwe as well as hundreds of other nationalist leaders who are now in SA jails or under restriction orders.

26. The 9th Extraordinary Session of the Council of Ministers of the OAU resolutely reaffirms free Africa's total rejection of apartheid and all its manifestations, including any so-called 'independent homelands' within SA. The puppet leaders of these so-called homelands should be denied invitations by independent African States. The Council underscores the importance of all independent African States to remain firmly united in the policy of isolating SA and ostracizing its apartheid regime. The Council reiterates its support to the national liberation movements of SA in their struggle in all its forms. It also calls for the intensification of international efforts with the co-operation of Governments, Inter-Governmental and Non-Governmental organizations for the eradication of apartheid.

27. Unprecedented opportunities and challenges prevail in SA following the collapse of the 500 year Portuguese colonialism. The OAU is determined to capitalize on the opportunities in order to bring closer the day when every inch of African soil will be free from colonial and racist domination. While being cognizant of the fact that SA stands as the final major obstacle, to Africa's march to liberation, the Council of Ministers reaffirms its unflinching determination to realize the freedom and independence of Zimbabwe and Namibia and the total destruction of apartheid and racial discrimination in SA.

PART III

Global Instruments

17.

U.N. CHARTER ARTICLES PERTAINING TO HUMAN RIGHTS

We the peoples of the United Nations, determined ... to reaffirm faith in fundamental human rights, in the dignity and worth of the human person, in the equal rights of men and women ... have resolved to combine our efforts to accomplish these aims ...

CHAPTER I. PURPOSES AND PRINCIPLES

Article 1

The Purposes of the United Nations are: ...
   3. To achieve international cooperation in solving international problems of an economic, social, cultural, or humanitarian character, and in promoting and encouraging respect for human rights and for fundamental freedoms for all without distinction as to race, sex, language, or religion ...

[...]

CHAPTER IV. THE GENERAL ASSEMBLY

Article 13

The General Assembly shall initiate studies and make recommendations for the purpose of: ...
   b. promoting international cooperation in the economic, social, cultural, educational, and health fields, and assisting in the realization of human rights and fundamental freedoms for all without distinction as to race, sex, language, or religion.

[...]

CHAPTER IX. INTERNATIONAL ECONOMIC AND SOCIAL COOPERATION

Article 55

With a view to the creation of conditions of stability and well-being which are necessary for peaceful and friendly relations among nations based on respect for the principle of equal rights and self-determination of peoples, the United Nations shall promote: ...

    c. universal respect for, and observance of, human rights and fundamental freedoms for all without distinction as to race, sex, language, or religion.

Article 56

All Members pledge themselves to take joint and separate action in cooperation with the Organization for the achievement of the purposes set forth in Article 55.

[...]

CHAPTER X. THE ECONOMIC AND SOCIAL COUNCIL

Article 62

The Economic and Social Council ... may make recommendations for the purpose of promoting respect for, and observance of, human rights and fundamental freedoms for all ...

[...]

Article 68

The Economic and Social Council shall set up commissions in economic and social fields and for the promotion of human rights ...

[...]

CHAPTER XII. INTERNATIONAL TRUSTEESHIP SYSTEM

Article 76

The basic objectives of the trusteeship system ... shall be ...

    c. to encourage respect for human rights and for fundamental freedoms for all without distinction as to race, sex, language, or religion ...

The international bill of human rights

18.

Universal Declaration of Human Rights

GA Res. 217 (III) of 10 December 1948.

Preamble

Whereas recognition of the inherent dignity and of the equal and inalienable rights of all members of the human family is the foundation of freedom, justice and peace in the world,

Whereas disregard and contempt for human rights have resulted in barbarous acts which have outraged the conscience of mankind, and the advent of a world in which human beings shall enjoy freedom of speech and belief and freedom from fear and want has been proclaimed as the highest aspiration of the common people,

Whereas it is essential, if man is not to be compelled to have recourse, as a last resort, to rebellion against tyranny and oppression, that human rights should be protected by the rule of law,

Whereas it is essential to promote the development of friendly relations between nations,

Whereas the peoples of the United Nations have in the Charter reaffirmed their faith in fundamental human rights, in the dignity and worth of the human person and in the equal rights of men and women and have determined to promote social progress and better standards of life in larger freedom,

Whereas Member States have pledged themselves to achieve, in co-operation with the United Nations, the promotion of universal respect for and observance of human rights and fundamental freedoms,

Whereas a common understanding of these rights and freedoms is of the greatest importance for the full realization of this pledge,

Now, therefore,

The General Assembly,

Proclaims this Universal Declaration of Human Rights as a common standard of achievement for all peoples and all nations, to the end that every individual and every organ of society, keeping this Declaration constantly in mind, shall strive by teaching and education to promote respect for these rights and freedoms and by progressive measures, national and international, to secure their universal and effective recognition and observance, both among the peoples of Member States themselves and among the peoples of territories under their jurisdiction.

Art. 1. All human beings are born free and equal in dignity and rights. They are endowed with reason and conscience and should act towards one another in a spirit of brotherhood.

Art. 2. Everyone is entitled to all the rights and freedoms set forth in this Declaration, without distinction of any kind, such as race, colour, sex, language, religion, political or other opinion, national or social origin, property, birth or other status.

Furthermore, no distinction shall be made on the basis of the political, jurisdictional or international status of the country or territory to which a person belongs, whether it be independent, trust, non-self-governing or under any other limitation of sovereignty.

Art. 3. Everyone has the right to life, liberty and the security of person.

Art. 4. No one shall be held in slavery or servitude; slavery and the slave trade shall be prohibited in all their forms.

Art. 5. No one shall be subjected to torture or to cruel, inhuman or degrading treatment or punishment.

Art. 6. Everyone has the right to recognition everywhere as a person before the law.

Art. 7. All are equal before the law and are entitled without any discrimination to equal protection of the law. All are entitled to equal protection against any discrimination in violation of this Declaration and against any incitement to such discrimination.

Art. 8. Everyone has the right to an effective remedy by the competent national tribunals for acts violating the fundamental rights granted him by the constitution or by law.

Art. 9. No one shall be subjected to arbitrary arrest, detention or exile.

Art. 10. Everyone is entitled in full equality to a fair and public hearing by an independent and impartial tribunal, in the determination of his rights and obligations and of any criminal charge against him.

Art. 11. 1. Everyone charged with a penal offence has the right to be presumed innocent until proved guilty according to law in a public trial at which he has had all the guarantees necessary for his defence.

2. No one shall be held guilty of any penal offence on account of any act or omission which did not constitute a penal offence, under national or international law, at the time when it was committed. Nor shall a heavier penalty be imposed than the one that was applicable at the time the penal offence was committed.

Art. 12. No one shall be subjected to arbitrary interference with his privacy, family, home or correspondence, nor to attacks upon his honour and reputation. Everyone has the right to the protection of the law against such interference or attacks.

Art. 13. 1. Everyone has the right to freedom of movement and residence within the borders of each State.

2. Everyone has the right to leave any country, including his own, and to return to his country.

Art. 14. 1. Everyone has the right to seek and to enjoy in other countries asylum from persecution.

2. This right may not be invoked in the case of prosecutions genuinely arising from non-political crimes or from acts contrary to the purposes and principles of the United Nations.

Art. 15. 1. Everyone has the right to a nationality.

2. No one shall be arbitrarily deprived of his nationality nor denied the right to change his nationality.

Art. 16. 1. Men and women of full age, without any limitation due to race, nationality or religion, have the right to marry and to found a family. They are entitled to equal rights as to marriage, during marriage and at its dissolution.

2. Marriage shall be entered into only with the free and full consent of the intending spouses.

3. The family is the natural and fundamental group unit of society and is entitled to protection by society and the State.

Art. 17. 1. Everyone has the right to own property alone as well as in association with others.

2. No one shall be arbitrarily deprived of his property.

Art. 18. Everyone has the right to freedom of thought, conscience and religion; this right includes freedom to change his religion or belief, and freedom either alone or in community with others and in public or private, to manifest his religion or belief in teaching, practice, worship and observance.

Art. 19. Everyone has the right to freedom of opinion and expression; this right includes freedom to hold opinions without interference and to seek, receive and impart information and ideas through any media and regardless of frontiers.

Art. 20. 1. Everyone has the right to freedom of peaceful assembly and association.

2. No one may be compelled to belong to an association.

Art. 21. 1. Everyone has the right to take part in the government of his country, directly or through freely chosen representatives.

2. Everyone has the right of equal access to public service in his country.

3. The will of the people shall be the basis of the authority of government; this will shall be expressed in periodic and genuine elections which shall be by universal and equal suffrage and shall be held by secret vote or by equivalent free voting procedures.

Art. 22. Everyone as a member of society, has the right to social security and is entitled to realization, through national effort and international co-operation and in accordance with the organization and resources of each State, of the economic, social and cultural rights indispensable for his dignity, and the free development of his personality.

Art. 23. 1. Everyone has the right to work, to free choice of employment, to just and favourable conditions of work and to protection against unemployment.

2. Everyone, without any discrimination, has the right to equal pay for equal work.

3. Everyone who works has the right to just and favourable remuneration ensuring for himself and his family an existence worthy of human dignity and supplemented, if necessary, by other means of social protection.

4. Everyone has the right to form and to join trade unions for the protection of his interests.

Art. 24. Everyone has the right to rest and leisure, including reasonable limitation of working hours and periodic holidays with pay.

Art. 25. 1. Everyone has the right to a standard of living adequate for the health and well-being of himself and of his family, including food, clothing, housing and medical care and necessary social services and the right to security in the event of unemployment, sickness, disability, widowhood, old age or other lack of livelihood in circumstances beyond his control.

2. Motherhood and childhood are entitled to special care and assistance. All children, whether born in or out of wedlock, shall enjoy the same social protection.

Art. 26. 1. Everyone has the right to education. Education shall be free, at least in the elementary and fundamental stages. Elementary education shall be compulsory. Technical and professional education shall be made generally available and higher education shall be equally accessible to all on the basis of merit.

2. Education shall be directed to the full development of the human personality and to the strengthening of respect for human rights and fundamental freedoms. It shall promote understanding, tolerance and friendship among all nations, racial or religious groups, and shall further the activities of the United Nations for the maintenance of peace.

3. Parents have a prior right to choose the kind of education that shall be given to their children.

Art. 27. 1. Everyone has the right freely to participate in the cultural life of the community, to enjoy the arts and to share in scientific advancement and its benefits.

2. Everyone has the right to the protection of the moral and material interests resulting from any scientific, literary, or artistic production of which he is the author.

Art. 28. Everyone is entitled to a social and international order in which the rights and freedoms set forth in this Declaration can be fully realized.

Art. 29. 1. Everyone has duties to the community in which alone the free and full development of his personality is possible.

2. In the exercise of his rights and freedoms, everyone shall be subject only to such limitations as are determined by law solely for the purpose of securing due recognition and respect for the rights and freedoms of others and of meeting the just requirements of morality, public order and the general welfare in a democratic society.

3. These rights and freedoms may in no case be exercised contrary to the purposes and principles of the United Nations.

Art. 30. Nothing in this Declaration may be interpreted as implying for any State, group or person any right to engage in any activity or to perform any act aimed at the destruction of any of the rights and freedoms set forth herein.

The International Covenants on Economic and Social Rights and on Civil and Political Rights were adopted by the General Assembly on 16 December 1966 and came into force on 3 January and 23 March 1976, respectively. As at 31 December 1985, 85 States had become States parties to the International Covenant on Economic, Social and Cultural Rights and 82 to the International Covenant on Civil and Political Rights.

The Covenants put into binding legal form the rights set forth in the Universal Declaration of Human Rights. States parties undertake to guarantee that the rights enumerated in the Covenants will be exercised without discrimination of any kind as to race, colour, sex, language, religion, political or other opinion, national or social origin, property, birth or other status.

Fourteen States parties have made the declaration provided for in article 41 of the Covenant on Civil and Political Rights recognizing the competence of the Human Rights Committee established under that Covenant to receive and consider complaints from a State party that another State party is not fulfilling the obligations it has undertaken under the Covenant. Both the State submitting the complaint and the State referred to in it must have made the declaration provided for in this article.

The Optional Protocol to the International Covenant on Civil and Political Rights, with 36 States parties as at 31 December 1985, entitles the Human Rights Committee, the organ established under the Covenant to supervise its implementation, to receive communications from individuals within the jurisdiction of States which have ratified the Covenant with regard to matters which concern States that are parties to the Optional Protocol.

19.

International Covenant on Economic, Social and Cultural Rights

Annex to GA Res. 2200 (XXI) of 16 December 1966. Opened for signature on 19 December 1966. Entered into force on 3 January 1976.

Preamble

The States Parties to the present Covenant,
Considering that, in accordance with the principles proclaimed in the Charter of the United Nations, recognition of the inherent dignity and of the equal and inalienable rights of all members of the human family is the foundation of freedom, justice and peace in the world,
Recognizing that these rights derive from the inherent dignity of the human person,
Recognizing that, in accordance with the Universal Declaration of Human Rights, the ideal of free human beings enjoying freedom from fear and want can only be achieved if conditions are created whereby everyone may enjoy his economic, social and cultural rights, as well as his civil and political rights,
Considering the obligation of States under the Charter of the United Nations to promote universal respect for, and observance of, human rights and freedoms,
Realizing that the individual, having duties to other individuals and to the community to which he belongs, is under a responsibility to strive for the promotion and observance of the rights recognized in the present Covenant,
Agree upon the following articles:

Part I

Art. 1. 1. All peoples have the right of self-determination. By virtue of that right they freely determine their political status and freely pursue their economic, social and cultural development.

2. All peoples may, for their own ends, freely dispose of their natural wealth and resources without prejudice to any obligations arising out of international economic co-operation, based upon the principle of mutual benefit, and international law. In no case may a people be deprived of its own means of subsistence.

3. The States Parties to the present Covenant, including those having responsibility for the administration of Non-Self-Governing and Trust Territories, shall promote the realization of the right of self-determination, and shall respect that right, in conformity with the provisions of the Charter of the United Nations.

Part II

Art. 2. 1. Each State Party to the present Covenant undertakes to take steps, individually and through international assistance and co-operation, especially economic and technical, to the maximum of its available resources, with a view to achieving progressively the full realization of the rights recognized in the present Covenant by all appropriate means, including particularly the adoption of legislative measures.

2. The States Parties to the present Covenant undertake to guarantee that the rights enunciated in the present Covenant will be exercised without discrimination of any kind as to race, colour, sex, language, religion, political or other opinion, national or social origin, property, birth or other status.

3. Developing countries, with due regard to human rights and their national economy, may determine to what extent they would guarantee the economic rights recognized in the present Covenant to non-nationals.

Art. 3. The States Parties to the present Covenant undertake to ensure the equal right of men and women to the enjoyment of all economic, social and cultural rights set forth in the present Covenant.

Art. 4. The States Parties to the present Covenant recognize that, in the enjoyment of those rights provided by the State in conformity with the present Covenant, the State may subject such rights only to such limitations as are determined by law only in so far as this may be compatible with the nature of these rights and solely for the purpose of promoting the general welfare in a democratic society.

Art. 5. 1. Nothing in the present Covenant may be interpreted as implying for any State, group or person any right to engage in any activity or to perform any act aimed at the destruction of any of the rights or freedoms recognized herein, or at their limitation to a greater extent than is provided for in the present Covenant.

2. No restriction upon or derogation from any of the fundamental human rights recognized or existing in any country in virtue of law, conventions, regulations or custom shall be admitted on the pretext that the present Covenant does not recognize such rights or that it recognizes them to a lesser extent.

Part III

Art. 6. 1. The States Parties to the present Covenant recognize the right to work, which includes the right of everyone to the opportunity to gain his living by work which he freely chooses or accepts, and will take appropriate steps to safeguard this right.

2. The steps to be taken by a State Party to the present Covenant to achieve the full realization of this right shall include technical and vocational guidance and training programmes, policies and techniques to achieve steady economic, social and cultural development and full and productive employment under conditions safeguarding fundamental political and economic freedoms to the individual.

Art. 7. The States Parties to the present Covenant recognize the right of everyone to the enjoyment of just and favourable conditions of work which ensure, in particular:

(*a*) Remuneration which provides all workers, as a minimum, with:
(i) Fair wages and equal remuneration for work of equal value without distinction of any kind, in particular women being guaranteed conditions of work not inferior to those enjoyed by men, with equal pay for equal work;
(ii) A decent living for themselves and their families in accordance with the provisions of the present Covenant;
(*b*) Safe and healthy working conditions;
(*c*) Equal opportunity for everyone to be promoted in his employment to an appropriate higher level, subject to no considerations other than those of seniority and competence;
(*d*) Rest, leisure and reasonable limitation of working hours and periodic holidays with pay, as well as remuneration for public holidays.

Art. 8. 1. The States Parties to the present Covenant undertake to ensure:
(*a*) The right of everyone to form trade unions and join the trade union of his choice, subject only to the rules of the organization concerned, for the promotion and protection of his economic and social interests. No restrictions may be placed on the exercise of this right other than those prescribed by law and which are

necessary in a democratic society in the interests of national security or public order or for the protection of the rights and freedoms of others;

(b) The right of trade unions to establish national federations or confederations and the right of the latter to form or join international trade-union organizations;

(c) The right of trade unions to function freely subject to no limitations other than those prescribed by law and which are necessary in a democratic society in the interests of national security or public order or for the protection of the rights and freedoms of others;

(d) The right to strike, provided that it is exercised in conformity with the laws of the particular country.

2. This article shall not prevent the imposition of lawful restrictions on the exercise of these rights by members of the armed forces or of the police or of the administration of the State.

3. Nothing in this article shall authorize States Parties to the International Labour Organisation Convention of 1948 concerning Freedom of Association and Protection of the Right to Organize to take legislative measures which would prejudice, or apply the law in such a manner as would prejudice, the guarantees provided for in that Convention.

Art. 9. The States Parties to the present Covenant recognize the right of everyone to social security, including social insurance.

Art. 10. The States Parties to the present Covenant recognize that:

1. The widest possible protection and assistance should be accorded to the family, which is the natural and fundamental group unit of society, particularly for its establishment and while it is responsible for the care and education of dependent children. Marriage must be entered into with the free consent of the intending spouses.

2. Special protection should be accorded to mothers during a reasonable period before and after childbirth. During such period working mothers should be accorded paid leave or leave with adequate social security benefits.

3. Special measures of protection and assistance should be taken on behalf of all children and young persons without any discrimination for reasons of parentage or other conditions. Children and young persons should be protected from economic and social exploitation. Their employment in work harmful to their morals or health or dangerous to life or likely to hamper their normal development should be punishable by law. States should also set age limits below which the paid employment of child labour should be prohibited and punishable by law.

Art. 11. 1. The States Parties to the present Covenant recognize the right of everyone to an adequate standard of living for himself and his family, including adequate food, clothing and housing, and to the continuous improvement of living conditions. The States Parties will take appropriate steps to ensure the realization of this right, recognizing to this effect the essential importance of international co-operation based on free consent.

2. The States Parties to the present Covenant, recognizing the fundamental right of everyone to be free from hunger, shall take, individually and through international co-operation, the measures, including specific programmes, which are needed:

(a) To improve methods of production, conservation and distribution of food by making full use of technical and scientific knowledge, by disseminating knowledge of the principles of nutrition and by developing or reforming agrarian systems in such a way as to achieve the most efficient development and utilization of natural resources;

(b) Taking into account the problems of both food-importing and food-exporting countries, to ensure an equitable distribution of world food supplies in relation to need.

Art. 12. 1. The States Parties to the present Covenant recognize the right of everyone to the enjoyment of the highest attainable standard of physical and mental health.

2. The steps to be taken by the States Parties to the present Covenant to achieve

the full realization of this right shall include those necessary for:

(*a*) The provision for the reduction of the stillbirth-rate and of infant mortality and for the healthy development of the child;

(*b*) The improvement of all aspects of environmental and industrial hygiene;

(*c*) The prevention, treatment and control of epidemic, endemic, occupational and other diseases;

(*d*) The creation of conditions which would assure to all medical service and medical attention in the event of sickness.

Art. 13. 1. The States Parties to the present Covenant recognize the right of everyone to education. They agree that education shall be directed to the full development of the human personality and the sense of its dignity, and shall strengthen the respect for human rights and fundamental freedoms. They further agree that education shall enable all persons to participate effectively in a free society, promote understanding, tolerance and friendship among all nations and all racial, ethnic or religious groups, and further the activities of the United Nations for the maintenance of peace.

2. The States Parties to the present Covenant recognize that, with a view to achieving the full realization of this right:

(*a*) Primary education shall be compulsory and available free to all;

(*b*) Secondary education in its different forms, including technical and vocational secondary education, shall be made generally available and accessible to all by every appropriate means, and in particular by the progressive introduction of free education;

(*c*) Higher education shall be made equally accessible to all, on the basis of capacity, by every appropriate means, and in particular by the progressive introduction of free education;

(*d*) Fundamental education shall be encouraged or intensified as far as possible for those persons who have not received or completed the whole period of their primary education;

(*e*) The development of a system of schools at all levels shall be actively pursued, an adequate fellowship system shall be established, and the material conditions of teaching staff shall be continuously improved.

3. The States Parties to the present Covenant undertake to have respect for the liberty of parents and, when applicable, legal guardians to choose for their children schools, other than those established by the public authorities, which conform to such minimum educational standards as may be laid down or approved by the State and to ensure the religious and moral education of their children in conformity with their own convictions.

4. No part of this article shall be construed so as to interfere with the liberty of individuals and bodies to establish and direct educational institutions, subject always to the observance of the principles set forth in paragraph 1 of this article and to the requirement that the education given in such institutions shall conform to such minimum standards as may be laid down by the State.

Art. 14. Each State Party to the present Covenant which, at the time of becoming a Party, has not been able to secure in its metropolitan territory or other territories under its jurisdiction compulsory primary education, free of charge, undertakes, within two years, to work out and adopt a detailed plan of action for the progressive implementation, within a reasonable number of years, to be fixed in the plan, of the principle of compulsory education free of charge for all.

Art. 15. 1. The States Parties to the present Covenant recognize the right of everyone:

(*a*) To take part in cultural life;

(*b*) To enjoy the benefits of scientific progress and its applications;

(*c*) To benefit from the protection of the moral and material interests resulting from any scientific, literary or artistic production of which he is the author.

2. The steps to be taken by the States Parties to the present Covenant to achieve the full realization of this right shall include those necessary for the conservation, the development and the diffusion of science and culture.

3. The States Parties to the present Covenant undertake to respect the freedom indispensable for scientific research and creative activity.

4. The States Parties to the present Covenant recognize the benefits to be derived from the encouragement and development of international contacts and cooperation in the scientific and cultural fields.

Part IV

Art. 16. 1. The States Parties to the present Covenant undertake to submit in conformity with this part of the Covenant reports on the measures which they have adopted and the progress made in achieving the observance of the rights recognized herein.

2. (*a*) All reports shall be submitted to the Secretary-General of the United Nations, who shall transmit copies to the Economic and Social Council for consideration in accordance with the provisions of the present Covenant;

(*b*) The Secretary-General of the United Nations shall also transmit to the specialized agencies copies of the reports, or any relevant parts therefrom, from States Parties to the present Covenant which are also members of these specialized agencies in so far as these reports, or parts therefrom, relate to any matters which fall within the responsibilities of the said agencies in accordance with their constitutional instruments.

Art. 17. 1. The States Parties to the present Covenant shall furnish their reports in stages, in accordance with a programme to be established by the Economic and Social Council within one year of the entry into force of the present Covenant after consultation with the States Parties and the specialized agencies concerned.

2. Reports may indicate factors and difficulties affecting the degree of fulfilment of obligations under the present Covenant.

3. Where relevant information has previously been furnished to the United Nations or to any specialized agency by any State Party to the present Covenant, it will not be necessary to reproduce that information, but a precise reference to the information so furnished will suffice.

Art. 18. Pursuant to its responsibilities under the Charter of the United Nations in the field of human rights and fundamental freedoms, the Economic and Social Council may make arrangements with the specialized agencies in respect of their reporting to it on the progress made in achieving the observance of the provisions of the present Covenant falling within the scope of their activities. These reports may include particulars of decisions and recommendations on such implementation adopted by their competent organs.

Art. 19. The Economic and Social Council may transmit to the Commission on Human Rights for study and general recommendation or, as appropriate, for information the reports concerning human rights submitted by States in accordance with articles 16 and 17, and those concerning human rights submitted by the specialized agencies in accordance with article 18.

Art. 20. The States Parties to the present Covenant and the specialized agencies concerned may submit comments to the Economic and Social Council on any general recommendation under article 19 or reference to such general recommendation in any report of the Commission on Human Rights or any documentation referred to therein.

Art. 21. The Economic and Social Council may submit from time to time to the General Assembly reports with recommendations of a general nature and a summary of the information received from the States Parties to the present Covenant and the specialized agencies on the measures taken and the progress made in achieving general observance of the rights recognized in the present Covenant.

Art. 22. The Economic and Social Council may bring to the attention of other organs of the United Nations, their subsidiary organs and specialized agencies concerned with furnishing technical assistance any matters arising out of the reports referred to in this part of the present Covenant which may assist such bodies in deciding, each within its field of competence, on the advisability of international measures likely to contribute to the effective progressive implementation of the present Covenant.

Art. 23. The States Parties to the present Covenant agree that international action for the achievement of the rights recognized in the present Covenant includes such methods as the conclusion of conventions, the adoption of recommendations, the furnishing of technical assistance and the holding of regional meetings and technical meetings for the purpose of consultation and study organized in conjunction with the Governments concerned.

Art. 24. Nothing in the present Covenant shall be interpreted as impairing the provisions of the Charter of the United Nations and of the constitutions of the specialized agencies which define the respective responsibilities of the various organs of the United Nations and of the specialized agencies in regard to the matters dealt with in the present Covenant.

Art. 25. Nothing in the present Covenant shall be interpreted as impairing the inherent of all peoples to enjoy and utilize fully and freely their natural wealth and resources.

Part V

Art. 26. 1. The present Covenant is open for signature by any State Member of the United Nations or member of any of its specialized agencies, by any State Party to the Statute of the International Court of Justice, and by any other State which has been invited by the General Assembly of the United Nations to become a party to the present Covenant.

2. The present Covenant is subject to ratification. Instruments of ratification shall be deposited with the Secretary-General of the United Nations.

3. The present Covenant shall be open to accession by any State referred to in paragraph 1 of this article.

4. Accession shall be effected by the deposit of an instrument of accession with the Secretary-General of the United Nations.

5. The Secretary-General of the United Nations shall inform all States which have signed the present Covenant or acceded to it of the deposit of each instrument of ratification or accession.

Art. 27. 1. The present Covenant shall enter into force three months after the date of the deposit with the Secretary-General of the United Nations of the thirty-fifth instrument of ratification or instrument of accession.

2. For each State ratifying the present Covenant or acceding to it after the deposit of the thirty-fifth instrument of ratification or instrument of accession, the present Covenant shall enter into force three months after the date of the deposit of its own instrument of ratification or instrument of accession.

Art. 28. The provisions of the present Covenant shall extend to all parts of federal States without any limitations or exceptions.

Art. 29. 1. Any State Party to the present Covenant may propose an amendment and file it with the Secretary-General of the United Nations. The Secretary-General shall thereupon communicate any proposed amendments to the States Parties to the present Covenant with a request that they notify him whether they favour a conference of States Parties for the purpose of considering and voting upon the proposals. In the event that at least one third of the States Parties favours such a conference, the Secretary-General shall convene the conference under the auspices of the United Nations. Any amendment adopted by a majority of the States Parties present and voting at the conference shall be submitted to the General Assembly of the United Nations for approval.

2. Amendments shall come into force when they have been approved by the General Assembly of the United Nations and accepted by a two-thirds majority of the States Parties to the present Covenant in accordance with their respective constitutional processes.

3. When amendments come into force they shall be binding on those States Parties which have accepted them, other States Parties still being bound by the provisions of the present Covenant and any earlier amendment which they have accepted.

Art. 30. Irrespective of the notifications made under article 26, paragraph 5, the

Secretary-General of the United Nations shall inform all States referred to in paragraph 1 of the same article of the following particulars:

(*a*) Signatures, ratifications and accessions under article 26;

(*b*) The date of the entry into force of the present Covenant under article 27 and the date of the entry into force of any amendments under article 29.

Art. 31. 1. The present Covenant, of which the Chinese, English, French, Russian and Spanish texts are equally authentic, shall be deposited in the archives of the United Nations.

2. The Secretary-General of the United Nations shall transmit certified copies of the present Covenant to all States referred to in article 26.

20.

International Covenant on Civil and Political Rights

Annex to GA Res. 2200 (XXI) of 16 December 1966. Opened for signature on 19 December 1966. Entered into force 23 March 1976.

Preamble

The States Parties to the present Covenant,
Considering that, in accordance with the principles proclaimed in the Charter of the United Nations, recognition of the inherent dignity and of the equal and inalienable rights of all members of the human family is the foundation of freedom, justice and peace in the world,
Recognizing that these rights derive from the inherent dignity of the human person,
Recognizing that, in accordance with the Universal Declaration of Human Rights, the ideal of free human beings enjoying civil and political freedom and freedom from fear and want can only be achieved if conditions are created whereby everyone may enjoy his civil and political rights, as well as his economic, social and cultural rights,
Considering the obligation of States under the Charter of the United Nations to promote universal respect for, and observance of, human rights and freedoms,
Realizing that the individual, having duties to other individuals and to the community to which he belongs, is under a responsibility to strive for the promotion and observance of the rights recognized in the present Covenant,
Agree upon the following articles:

Part I

Art. 1. 1. All peoples have the right of self-determination. By virtue of that right they freely determine their political status and freely pursue their economic, social and cultural development.

2. All peoples may, for their own ends, freely dispose of their natural wealth and resources without prejudice to any obligations arising out of international economic co-operation based upon the principle of mutual benefit, and international law. In no case may a people be deprived of its own means of subsistence.

3. The States Parties to the present Covenant, including those having responsibility for the administration of Non-Self-Governing and Trust Territories, shall promote the realization of the right of self-determination, and shall respect that right, in conformity with the provisions of the Charter of the United Nations.

Part II

Art. 2. 1. Each State Party to the present Covenant undertakes to respect and to to ensure to all individuals within its territory and subject to its jurisdiction the rights recognized in the present Covenant, without distinction of any kind, such as race, colour, sex, language, religion, political or other opinion, national or social origin, property, birth or other status.

2. Where not already provided for by existing legislative or other measures, each State Party to the present Covenant undertakes to take the necessary steps, in accordance with its constitutional processes and with the provisions of the present Covenant, to adopt such legislative or other measures as may be necessary to give effect to the rights recognized in the present Covenant.

3. Each State Party to the present Covenant undertakes:

(*a*) To ensure that any person whose rights or freedoms as herein recognized are violated shall have an effective remedy, notwithstanding that the violation has been committed by persons acting in an official capacity;

(*b*) To ensure that any person claiming such a remedy shall have his right thereto determined by competent judicial, administrative or legislative authorities, or by any other competent authority provided for by the legal system of the State, and to develop the possibilities of judicial remedy;

(*c*) To ensure that the competent authorities shall enforce such remedies when granted.

Art. 3. The States Parties to the present Covenant undertake to ensure the equal right of men and women to the enjoyment of all civil and political rights set forth in the present Covenant.

Art. 4. 1. In time of public emergency which threatens the life of the nation and the existence of which is officially proclaimed, the States Parties to the present Covenant may take measures derogating from their obligations under the present Covenant to the extent strictly required by the exigencies of the situation, provided that such measures are not inconsistent with their other obligations under international law and do not involve discrimination solely on the ground of race, colour, sex, language, religion or social origin.

2. No derogation from articles 6, 7, 8 (paragraphs 1 and 2), 11, 15, 16 and 18 may be made under this provision.

3. Any State Party to the present Covenant availing itself of the right of derogation shall immediately inform the other States Parties to the present Covenant, through the intermediary of the Secretary-General of the United Nations, of the provisions from which it has derogated and of the reasons by which it was actuated. A further communication shall be made, through the same intermediary, on the date on which it terminated such derogation.

Art. 5. 1. Nothing in the present Covenant may be interpreted as implying for any State, group or person any right to engage in any activity or perform any act aimed at the destruction of any of the rights and freedoms recognized herein or at their limitation to a greater extent than is provided for in the present Covenant.

2. There shall be no restriction upon or derogation from any of the fundamental human rights recognized or existing in any State Party to the present Covenant pursuant to law, conventions, regulations or custom on the pretext that the present Covenant does not recognize such rights or that it recognizes them to a lesser extent.

Part III

Art. 6. 1. Every human being has the inherent right to life. This right shall be protected by law. No one shall be arbitrarily deprived of his life.

2. In countries which have not abolished the death penalty, sentence of death may be imposed only for the most serious crimes in accordance with the law in force at the time of the commission of the crime and not contrary to the provisions of the present Covenant and to the Convention on the Prevention and Punishment of the Crime of Genocide. This penalty can only be carried out pursuant to a final judgement rendered by a competent court.

3. When deprivation of life constitutes the crime of genocide, it is understood that nothing in this article shall authorize any State Party to the present Covenant to derogate in any way from any obligation assumed under the provisions of the Convention on the Prevention and Punishment of the Crime of Genocide.

4. Anyone sentenced to death shall have the right to seek pardon or commutation of the sentence. Amnesty, pardon or commutation of the sentence of death may be granted in all cases.

5. Sentence of death shall not be imposed for crimes committed by persons below eighteen years of age and shall not be carried out on pregnant women.

6. Nothing in this article shall be invoked to delay or to prevent the abolition of capital punishment by any State Party to the present Covenant.

Art. 7. No one shall be subjected to torture or to cruel, inhuman or degrading treatment or punishment. In particular, no one shall be subjected without his free consent to medical or scientific experimentation.

Art. 8. 1. No one shall be held in slavery; slavery and the slave-trade in all their forms shall be prohibited.

2. No one shall be held in servitude.

3. (a) No one shall be required to perform forced or compulsory labour;

(b) Paragraph 3 (a) shall not be held to preclude, in countries where imprisonment with hard labour may be imposed as a punishment for a crime, by the performance of hard labour in pursuance of a sentence to such punishment by a competent court;

(c) For the purpose of this paragraph the term "forced or compulsory labour" shall not include:

(i) Any work or service, not referred to in sub-paragraph (b), normally required of a person who is under detention in consequence of a lawful order of a court, or of a person during conditional release from such detention;

(ii) Any service of a military character and, in countries where conscientious objection is recognized, any national service required by law of conscientious objectors;

(iii) Any service exacted in cases of emergency or calamity threatening the life or well-being of the community;

(iv) Any work or service which forms part of normal civil obligations.

Art. 9. 1. Everyone has the right to liberty and security of person. No one shall be subjected to arbitrary arrest or detention. No one shall be deprived of his liberty except on such grounds and in accordance with such procedure as are established by law.

2. Anyone who is arrested shall be informed, at the time of arrest, of the reasons for his arrest and shall be promptly informed of any charges against him.

3. Anyone arrested or detained on a criminal charge shall be brought promptly before a judge or other officer authorized by law to exercise judicial power and shall be entitled to trial within a reasonable time or to release. It shall not be the general rule that persons awaiting trail shall be detained in custody, but release may be subject to guarantees to appear for trial, at any other stage of the judicial proceedings, and, should occasion arise, for execution of the judgement.

4. Anyone who is deprived of his liberty by arrest or detention shall be entitled to take proceedings before a court, in order that that court may decide without delay on the lawfulness of his detention and order his release if the detention is not lawful.

5. Anyone who has been the victim of unlawful arrest or detention shall have an enforceable right to compensation.

Art. 10. 1. All persons deprived of their liberty shall be treated with humanity and with respect for the inherent dignity of the human person.

2. (a) Accused persons shall, save in exceptional circumstances, be segregated from convicted persons and shall be subject to separate treatment appropriate to their status as unconvicted persons;

(b) Accused juvenile persons shall be separated from adults and brought as speedily as possible for adjudication.

3. The penitentiary system shall comprise treatment of prisoners the essential aim of which shall be their reformation and social rehabilitation. Juvenile offenders shall be segregated from adults and be accorded treatment appropriate to their age and legal status.

Art. 11. No one shall be imprisoned merely on the ground of inability to fulfil a contractual obligation.

Art. 12. 1. Everyone lawfully within the territory of a State shall, within that territory, have the right to liberty of movement and freedom to choose his residence.

2. Everyone shall be free to leave any country, including his own.

3. The above-mentioned rights shall not be subject to any restrictions except those which are provided by law, are necessary to protect national security, public order *(ordre public)*, public health or morals or the rights and freedoms of others, and are consistent with the other rights recognized in the present Covenant.

4. No one shall be arbitrarily deprived of the right to enter his own country.

Art. 13. An alien lawfully in the territory of a State Party to the present Covenant may be expelled therefrom only in pursuance of a decision reached in accordance with law and shall, except where compelling reasons of national security otherwise require, be allowed to submit the reasons against his expulsion and to have his case reviewed by, and be represented for the purpose before, the competent authority or a person or persons especially designated by the competent authority.

Art. 14. 1. All persons shall be equal before the courts and tribunals. In the determination of any criminal charge against him, or of his rights and obligations in a suit at law, everyone shall be entitled to a fair and public hearing by a competent, independent and impartial tribunal established by law. The Press and the public may be excluded from all or part of a trial for reasons of morals, public order *(ordre public)* or national security in a democratic society, or when the interest of the private lives of the parties so requires, or to the extent strictly necessary in the opinion of the court in special circumstances where publicity would prejudice the interests of justice; but any judgement rendered in a criminal case or in a suit at law shall be made public except where the interest of juvenile persons otherwise requires or the proceedings concern matrimonial disputes or the guardianship of children.

2. Everyone charged with a criminal offence shall have the right to be presumed innocent until proved guilty according to law.

3. In the determination of any criminal charge against him, everyone shall be entitled to the following minimum guarantees, in full equality:

(*a*) To be informed promptly and in detail in a language which he understands of the nature and cause of the charge against him;

(*b*) To have adequate time and facilities for the preparation of his defence and to communicate with counsel of his own choosing;

(*c*) To be tried without undue delay;

(*d*) To be tried in his presence, and to defend himself in person or through legal assistance of his own choosing; to be informed, if he does not have legal assistance, of this right; and to have legal assistance assigned to him, in any case where the interests of justice so require, and without payment by him in any such case if he does not have sufficient means to pay for it;

(*e*) To examine, or have examined, the witnesses against him and to obtain the attendance and examination of witnesses on his behalf under the same conditions as witnesses against him;

(*f*) To have the free assistance of an interpreter if he cannot understand or speak the language used in court;

(*g*) Not to be compelled to testify against himself or to confess guilt.

4. In the case of juvenile persons, the procedure shall be such as will take account of their age and the desirability of promoting their rehabilitation.

5. Everyone convicted of a crime shall have the right to his conviction and sentence being reviewed by a higher tribunal according to law.

6. When a person has by a final decision been convicted of a criminal offence and when subsequently his conviction has been reversed or he has been pardoned on the ground that a new or newly discovered fact shows conclusively that there has been a miscarriage of justice, the person who has suffered punishment as a result of such conviction shall be compensated according to

law, unless it is proved that the non-disclosure of the unknown fact in time is wholly or partly attributable to him.

7. No one shall be liable to be tried or punished again for an offence for which he has already been finally convicted or acquitted in accordance with the law and penal procedure of each country.

Art. 15. 1. No one shall be held guilty of any criminal offence on account of any act or omission which did not constitute a criminal offence, under national or international law, at the time when it was committed. Nor shall a heavier penalty be imposed than the one that was applicable at the time when the criminial offence was committed. If, subsequent to the commission of the offence, provision is made by law for the imposition of a lighter penalty, the offender shall benefit thereby.

2. Nothing in this article shall prejudice the trial and punishment of any person for any act or omission which, at the time when it was committed, was criminal according to the general principles of law recognized by the community of nations.

Art. 16. Everyone shall have the right to recognition everywhere as a person before the law.

Art. 17. 1. No one shall be subjected to arbitrary or unlawful interference with his privacy, family, home or correspondence, nor to unlawful attacks on his honour and reputation.

2. Everyone has the right to the protection of the law against such interference or attacks.

Art. 18. 1. Everyone shall have the right to freedom of thought, conscience and religion. This right shall include freedom to have or to adopt a religion or belief of his choice, and freedom, either individually or in community with others and in public or private, to manifest his religion or belief in worship, observance, practice and teaching.

2. No one shall be subject to coercion which would impair his freedom to have or to adopt a religion or belief of his choice.

3. Freedom to manifest one's religion or beliefs may be subject only to such limitations as are prescribed by law and are necessary to protect public safety, order, health, or morals or the fundamental rights and freedoms of others.

4. The States Parties to the present Covenant undertake to have respect for the liberty of parents and, when applicable, legal guardians to ensure the religious and moral education of their children in conformity with their own convictions.

Art. 19. 1. Everyone shall have the right to hold opinions without interference.

2. Everyone shall have the right to freedom of expression; this right shall include freedom to seek, receive and impart information and ideas of all kinds, regardless of frontiers, either orally, in writing or in print, in the form of art, or through any other media of his choice.

3. The exercise of the rights provided for in paragraph 2 of this article carries with it special duties and responsibilities. It may therefore be subject to certain restrictions, but these shall only be such as are provided by law and are necessary:

(*a*) For respect of the rights or reputations of others;

(*b*) For the protection of national security or of public order (*ordre public*), or of public health or morals.

Art. 20. 1. Any propaganda for war shall be prohibited by law.

2. Any advocacy of national, racial or religious hatred that constitutes incitement to discrimination, hostility or violence shall be prohibited by law.

Art. 21. The right of peaceful assembly shall be recognized. No restrictions may may be placed on the exercise of this right other than those imposed in conformity with the law and which are necessary in a democratic society in the interests of national security or public safety, public order (*ordre public*), the protection of public health or morals or the protection of the rights and freedoms of others.

Art. 22. 1. Everyone shall have the right to freedom of association with others, including the right to form and join trade unions for the protection of his interests.

2. No restrictions may be placed on the exercise of this right other than those which are prescribed by law and which are necessary in a democratic society in the interests of national security or public safety, public order *(ordre public)*, the protection of public health or morals or the protection of the rights and freedoms of others. This article shall not prevent the imposition of lawful restrictions on members of the armed forces and of the police in their exercise of this right.

3. Nothing in this article shall authorize States Parties to the International Labour Organisation Convention of 1948 concerning Freedom of Association and Protection of the Right to Organize to take legislative measures which would prejudice, or to apply the law in such a manner as to prejudice, the guarantees provided for in that Convention.

Art. 23. 1. The family is the natural and fundamental group unit of society and is entitled to protection by society and the State.

2. The right of men and women of marriageable age to marry and to found a family shall be recognized.

3. No marriage shall be entered into without the free and full consent of the intending spouses.

4. States Parties to the present Covenant shall take appropriate steps to ensure equality of rights and responsibilities of spouses as to marriage, during marriage and at its dissolution. In the case of dissolution, provision shall be made for the necessary protection of any children.

Art. 24. 1. Every child shall have, without any discrimination as to race, colour, sex, language, religion, national or social origin, property or birth, the right to such measures of protection as are required by his status as a minor, on the part of his family, society and the State.

2. Every child shall be registered immediately after birth and shall have a name.

3. Every child has the right to acquire a nationality.

Art. 25. Every citizen shall have the right and the opportunity, without any of the distinctions mentioned in article 2 and without unreasonable restrictions:

(*a*) To take part in the conduct of public affairs, directly or through freely chosen representatives;

(*b*) To vote and to be elected at genuine periodic elections which shall be by universal and equal suffrage and shall be held by secret ballot, guaranteeing the free expression of the will of the electors;

(*c*) To have access, on general terms of equality, to public service in his country.

Art. 26. All persons are equal before the law and are entitled without any discrimination to the equal protection of the law. In this respect, the law shall prohibit any discrimination and guarantee to all persons equal and effective protection against discrimination on any ground such as race, colour, sex, language, religion, political or other opinion, national or social origin, property, birth or other status.

Art. 27. In those States in which ethnic, religious or linguistic minorities exist, persons belonging to such minorities shall not be denied the right, in community with the other members of their group, to enjoy their own culture, to profess and practice their own religion, or to use their own language.

Part IV

Art. 28. 1. There shall be established a Human Rights Committee (hereafter referred to in the present Covenant as the Committee). It shall consist of eighteen members and shall carry out the functions hereinafter provided.

2. The Committee shall be composed of nationals of the States Parties to the present Covenant who shall be persons of high moral character and recognized competence in the field of human rights, consideration being given to the usefulness of the participation of some persons having legal experience.

3. The members of the Committee shall be elected and shall serve in their personal capacity.

Art. 29. The members of the Committee shall be elected by secret ballot from a list of persons possessing the qualifications prescribed in article 28 and nominated for the purpose by the States Parties to the present Covenant.

2. Each State Party to the present Covenant may nominate not more than two persons. These persons shall be nationals of the nominating State.

3. A person shall be eligible for renomination.

Art. 30. 1. The initial election shall be held no later than six months after the date of the entry into force of the present Covenant.

2. At least four months before the date of each election to the Committee, other than an election to fill a vacancy declared in accordance with article 34, the Secretary-General of the United Nations shall address a written invitation to the States Parties to the present Covenant to submit their nominations for membership of the Committee within three months.

3. The Secretary-General of the United Nations shall prepare a list in alphabetical order of all the persons thus nominated, with an indication of the States Parties which have nominated them, and shall submit it to the States Parties to the present Covenant no later than one month before the date of each election.

4. Elections of the members of the Committee shall be held at a meeting of the States Parties to the present Covenant convened by the Secretary-General of the United Nations at the Headquarters of the United Nations. At that meeting, for which two thirds of the States Parties to the present Covenant shall constitute a quorum, the persons elected to the Committee shall be those nominees who obtain the largest number of votes and an absolute majority of the votes of the representatives of States Parties present and voting.

Art. 31. 1. The Committee may not include more than one national of the same State.

2. In the election of the Committee, consideration shall be given to equitable geographical distribution of membership and to the representation of the different forms of civilization and of the principal legal systems.

Art. 32. 1. The members of the Committee shall be elected for a term of four years. They shall be eligible for re-election if renominated. However, the terms of nine of the members elected at the first election shall expire at the end of two years; immediately after the first election, the names of these nine members shall be chosen by lot by the Chairman of the meeting referred to in article 30, paragraph 4.

2. Elections at the expiry of office shall be held in accordance with the preceding articles of this part of the present Covenant.

Art. 33. 1. If, in the unanimous opinion of the other members, a member of the Committee has ceased to carry out his functions for any cause other than absence of a temporary character, the Chairman of the Committee shall notify the Secretary-General of the United Nations, who shall then declare the seat of that member to be vacant.

2. In the event of the death or the resignation of a member of the Committee, the Chairman shall immediately notify the Secretary-General of the United Nations, who shall declare the seat vacant from the date of death or the date on which the resignation takes effect.

Art. 34. 1. When a vacancy is declared in accordance with article 33 and if the term of office of the member to be replaced does not expire within six months of the declaration of the vacancy, the Secretary-General of the United Nations shall notify each of the States Parties to the present Covenant, which may within two months submit nominations in accordance with article 29 for the purpose of filling the vacancy.

2. The Secretary-General of the United Nations shall prepare a list in alphabetical order of the persons thus nominated and shall submit it to the States Parties to the present Covenant. The election to fill the vacancy shall then take place in accordance with the relevant provisions of this part of the present Covenant.

3. A member of the Committee elected to fill a vacancy declared in accor-

dance with article 33 shall hold office for the remainder of the term of the member who vacated the seat on the Committee under the provisions of that article.

Art. 35. The members of the Committee shall, with the approval of the General Assembly of the United Nations, receive emoluments from United Nations resources on such terms and conditions as the General Assembly may decide, having regard to the importance of the Committee's responsibilities.

Art. 36. The Secretary-General of the United Nations shall provide the necessary staff and facilities for the effective performance of the functions of the Committee under the present Covenant.

Art. 37. 1. The Secretary-General of the United Nations shall convene the initial meeting of the Committee at the Headquarters of the United Nations.

2. After its initial meeting, the Committee shall meet at such times as shall be provided in its rules of procedure.

3. The Committee shall normally meet at the Headquarters of the United Nations or at the United Nations Office at Geneva.

Art. 38. Every member of the Committee shall, before taking up his duties, make a solemn declaration in open committee that he will perform his functions impartially and conscientiously.

Art. 39. 1. The Committee shall elect its officers for a term of two years. They may be re-elected.

2. The Committee shall establish its own rules of procedure, but these rules shall provide, *inter alia,* that:

(*a*) **Twelve members shall constitute a quorum;**

(*b*) Decisions of the Committee shall be made by a majority vote of the members present.

> Para. 2. The Committee held its first session in March 1977, at which it began, but did not complete, the drafting of its Rules of Procedure.

Art. 40. 1. The States Parties to the present Covenant undertake to submit reports on the measures they have adopted which give effect to the rights recognized herein and on the progress made in the enjoyment of those rights:

(*a*) Within one year of the entry into force of the present Covenant for the States Parties concerned;

(*b*) Thereafter whenever the Committee so requests.

2. All reports shall be submitted to the Secretary-General of the United Nations, who shall transmit them to the Committee for consideration. Reports shall indicate the factors and difficulties, if any, affecting the implementation of the present Covenant.

3. The Secretary-General of the United Nations may, after consultation with the Committee, transmit to the specialized agencies concerned copies of such parts of the reports as may fall within their field of competence.

4. The Committee shall study the reports submitted by the States Parties to the present Covenant. It shall transmit its reports, and such general comments as it may consider appropriate, to the States Parties. The Committee may also transmit to the Economic and Social Council these comments along with the copies of the reports it has received from States Parties to the present Covenant.

5. The States Parties to the present Covenant may submit to the Committee observations on any comments that may be made in accordance with paragraph 4 of this article.

Art. 41. 1. A State Party to the present Covenant may at any time declare under this article that it recognizes the competence of the Committee to receive and consider communications to the effect that a State Party claims that another State Party is not fulfilling its obligations under the present Covenant. Communications under this article may be received and considered only if submitted by a State Party which has made a declaration recognizing in regard to itself the competence of the Committee. No communication shall be received by the Committee if it concerns a State Party which has not made such a declaration. Communications received under this article shall be dealt with in accordance with the following procedure:

(*a*) If a State Party to the present Covenant considers that another State Party is not giving effect to the provisions of the present Covenant, it may, by written communication, bring the matter to the attention of that State Party. Within three months after the receipt of the communication, the receiving State shall afford the State which sent the communication an explanation or any other statement in writing clarifying the matter, which should include, to the extent possible and pertinent, reference to domestic procedures and remedies taken, pending, or available in the matter.
(*b*) If the matter is not adjusted to the satisfaction of both States Parties concerned within six months after the receipt by the receiving State of the initial communication, either State shall have the right to refer the matter to the Committee, by notice given to the Committee and to the other State.
(*c*) The Committee shall deal with a matter referred to it only after it has ascertained that all available domestic remedies have been invoked and exhausted in the matter, in conformity with the generally recognized principles of international law. This shall not be the rule where the application of the remedies is unreasonably prolonged.
(*d*) The Committee shall hold closed meetings when examining communications under this article.
(*e*) Subject to the provisions of sub-paragraph (*c*), the Committee shall make available its good offices to the States Parties concerned with a view to a friendly solution of the matter on the basis of respect for human rights and fundamental freedoms as recognized in the present Covenant.
(*f*) In any matter refferred to it, the Committee may call upon the States Parties concerned, referred to in sub-paragraph (*b*), to supply any relevant information.
(*g*) The States Parties concerned, referred to in sub-paragraph (*b*), shall have the right to be represented when the matter is being considered in the Committee and to make submissions orally and/or in writing.
(*h*) The Committee shall, within twelve months after the date of receipt of notice under sub-paragraph (*b*), submit a report:
(i) If a solution within the terms of sub-paragraph (*e*) is reached, the Committee shall confine its report to a brief statement of the facts and of the solution reached;
(ii) If a solution within the terms of sub-paragraph (*e*) is not reached, the Committee shall confine its report to a brief statement of the facts; the written submissions and record of the oral submissions made by the States Parties concerned shall be attached to the report.
In every matter, the report shall be communicated to the States Parties concerned.
2. The provisions of this article shall come into force when ten States Parties to the present Covenant have made declarations under paragraph 1 of this article. Such declarations shall be deposited by the States Parties with the Secretary-General of the United Nations, who shall transmit copies thereof to the other States Parties. A declaration may be withdrawn at any time by notification to the Secretary-General. Such a withdrawal shall not prejudice the consideration of any matter which is the subject of a communication already transmitted under this article; no further communication by any State Party shall be received after the notification of withdrawal of the declaration has been received by the Secretary-General, unless the State Party concerned has made a new declaration.

> Para. 2. Article 41 entered into force on 28 March 1979 for Austria, Canada, Denmark, the Federal Republic of Germany, Finland, Iceland, Italy, the Netherlands, New Zealand, Norway, Sweden and the United Kingdom of Great Britain and Northern Ireland.

Art. 42. 1. (*a*) If a matter referred to the Committee in accordance with article 41 is not resolved to the satisfaction of the States Parties concerned, the Committee may, with the prior consent of the States Parties concerned, appoint an *ad hoc* Conciliation Commission (hereinafter referred to as the Commission). The good offices of the Commission shall be made available to the States Parties concerned with a view to an amicable solution of the matter on the basis of respect for the present Covenant;

(b) The Commission shall consist of five persons acceptable to the States Parties concerned. If the States Parties concerned fail to reach agreement within three months on all or part of the composition of the Commission, the members of the Commission concerning whom no agreement has been reached shall be elected by secret ballot by a two-thirds majority vote of the Committee from among its members.

2. The members of the Commission shall serve in their personal capacity. They shall not be nationals of the States Parties concerned, or of a State not party to the present Covenant, or of a State Party which has not made a declaration under article 41.

3. The Commission shall elect its own Chairman and adopt its own rules of procedure.

4. The meetings of the Commission shall normally be held at the Headquarters of the United Nations or at the United Nations Office at Geneva. However, they may be held at such other convenient places as the Commission may determine in consultation with the Secretary-General of the United Nations and the States Parties concerned.

5. The secretariat provided in accordance with article 36 shall also service the commissions appointed under this article.

6. The information received and collated by the Committee shall be made available to the Commission and the Commission may call upon the States Parties concerned to supply any other relevant information.

7. When the Commission has fully considered the matter, but in any event not later than twelve months after having been seized of the matter, it shall submit to the Chairman of the Committee a report for communication to the States Parties concerned:

(a) If the Commission is unable to complete its consideration of the matter within twelve months, it shall confine its report to a brief statement of the status of its consideration of the matter;

(b) If an amicable solution to the matter on the basis of respect for human rights as recognized in the present Covenant is reached, the Commission shall confine its report to a brief statement of the facts and of the solution reached;

(c) If a solution within the terms of sub-paragraph (b) is not reached, the Commission's report shall embody its findings on all questions of fact relevant to the issues between the States Parties concerned, and its views on the possibilities of an amicable solution of the matter. This report shall also contain the written submissions and a record of the oral submissions made by the States Parties concerned;

(d) If the Commission's report is submitted under sub-paragraph (c), the States Parties concerned shall, within three months of the receipt of the report, notify the Chairman of the Committee whether or not they accept the contents of the report of the Commission.

8. The provisions of this article are without prejudice to the responsibilities of the Committee under article 41.

9. The States Parties concerned shall share equally all the expenses of the members of the Commission in accordance with estimates to be provided by the Secretary-General of the United Nations.

10. The Secretary-General of the United Nations shall be empowered to pay the expenses of the members of the Commission, if necessary, before reimbursement by the States Parties concerned, in accordance with paragraph 9 of this article.

Art. 43. The members of the Committee, and of the *ad hoc* conciliation commissions which may be appointed under article 42, shall be entitled to the facilities, privileges and immunities of experts on mission for the United Nations as laid down in the relevant sections of the Convention on the Privileges and Immunities of the United Nations.

Art. 44. The provisions for the implementation of the present Covenant shall apply without prejudice to the procedures prescribed in the field of human rights by or under the constituent instruments and the conventions of the United

Nations and of the specialized agencies and shall not prevent the States Parties to the present Covenant from having recourse to other procedures for settling a dispute in accordance with general or special international agreements in force between them.

Art. 45. The Committee shall submit to the General Assembly of the United Nations, through the Economic and Social Council, an annual report on its activities.

Part V

Art. 46. Nothing in the present Covenant shall be interpreted as impairing the provisions of the Charter of the United Nations and of the constitutions of the specialized agencies which define the respective responsibilities of the various organs of the United Nations and of the specialized agencies in regard to the matters dealt within the present Covenant.

Art. 47. Nothing in the present Covenant shall be interpreted as impairing the inherent right of all peoples to enjoy and utilize fully and freely their natural wealth and resources.

Part VI

Art. 48. 1. The present Covenant is open for signature by any State Member of the United Nations or member of any of its specialized agencies, by any State Party to the Statute of the International Court of Justice, and by any other State which has been invited by the General Assembly of the United Nations to become a party to the present Covenant.

2. The present Covenant is subject to ratification. Instruments of ratification shall be deposited with the Secretary-General of the United Nations.

3. The present Covenant shall be open to accession by any State referred to in paragraph 1 of this article.

4. Accession shall be effected by the deposit of an instrument of accession with the Secretary-General of the United Nations.

5. The Secretary-General of the United Nations shall inform all States which have signed this Covenant or acceded to it of the deposit of each instrument of ratification or accession.

Art. 49. 1. The present Covenant shall enter into force three months after the date of the deposit with the Secretary-General of the United Nations of the thirty-fifth instrument of ratification or instrument of accession.

2. For each State ratifying the present Covenant or acceding to it after the deposit of the thirty-fifth instrument of ratification or instrument of accession, the present Covenant shall enter into force three months after the date of the deposit of its own instrument of ratification or instrument of accession.

Art. 50. The provisions of the present Covenant shall extend to all parts of federal States without any limitations or exceptions.

Art. 51. 1. Any State Party to the present Covenant may propose an amendment and file it with the Secretary-General of the United Nations. The Secretary-General of the United Nations shall thereupon communicate any proposed amendments to the States Parties to the present Covenant with a request that they notify him whether they favour a conference of States Parties for the purpose of considering and voting upon the proposals. In the event that at least one third of the States Parties favours such a conference, the Secretary-General shall convene the conference under the auspices of the United Nations. Any amendment adopted by a majority of the States Parties present and voting at the conference shall be submitted to the General Assembly of the United Nations for approval.

2. Amendments shall come into force when they have been approved by the General Assembly of the United Nations and accepted by a two-thirds majority of the States Parties to the present Covenant in accordance with their respective constitutional processes.

3. When amendments come into force, they shall be binding on those States Parties which have accepted them, other States Parties still being bound by the provisions of the present Covenant and any earlier amendment which they have accepted.

Art. 52. Irrespective of the notifications made under article 48, paragraph 5, the Secretary-General of the United Nations shall inform all States referred to in paragraph 1 of the same article of the following particulars:

(*a*) Signatures, ratifications and accessions under article 48;

(*b*) The date of the entry into force of the present Covenant under article 49 and the date of the entry into force of any amendments under article 51.

Art. 53. 1. The present Covenant, of which the Chinese, English, French, Russian and Spanish texts are equally authentic, shall be deposited in the archives of the United Nations.

2. The Secretary-General of the United Nations shall transmit certified copies of the present Covenant to all States referred to in article 48.

21.

Optional Protocol to the International Covenant on Civil and Political Rights

Annex to GA Res. 2200 (XXI) of 16 December 1966. Opened for signature on 19 December 1966. Entered into force on 23 March 1976.

The States Parties to the present Protocol,
Considering that in order further to achieve the purposes of the Covenant on Civil and Political Rights (hereinafter referred to as the Covenant) and the implementation of its provisions it would be appropriate to enable the Human Rights Committee set up in part IV of the Covenant (hereinafter referred to as the Committee) to receive and consider, as provided in the present Protocol, communications from individuals claiming to be victims of violations of any of the rights set forth in the Covenant,
Have agreed as follows:

Art. 1. A State Party to the Covenant that becomes a party to the present Protocol recognizes the competence of the Committee to receive and consider communications from individuals subject to its jurisdiction who claim to be victims of a violation by that State Party of any of the rights set forth in the Covenant. No communication shall be received by the Committee if it concerns a State Party to the Covenant which is not a party to the present Protocol.

Art. 2. Subject to the provisions of article 1, individuals who claim that any of their rights enumerated in the Covenant have been violated and who have exhausted all available domestic remedies may submit a written communication to the Committee for consideration.

Art. 3. The Committee shall consider inadmissible any communication under the present Protocol which is anonymous, or which it considers to be an abuse of the right of submission of such communications or to be incompatible with the provisions of the Covenant.

Art. 4. 1. Subject to the provisions of article 3, the Committee shall bring any communications submitted to it under the present Protocol to the attention of the State Party to the present Protocol alleged to be violating any provision of the Covenant.
2. Within six months, the receiving State shall submit to the Committee written explanations or statements clarifying the matter and the remedy, if any, that may have been taken by that State.

Art. 5. 1. The Committee shall consider communications received under the present Protocol in the light of all written information made available to it by the individual and by the State Party concerned.
2. The Committee shall not consider any communication from an individual unless it has ascertained that:
(*a*) The same matter is not being examined under another procedure of international investigation or settlement;
(*b*) The individual has exhausted all available domestic remedies.

This shall not be the rule where the application of the remedies is unreasonably prolonged.

3. The Committee shall hold closed meetings when examining communications under the present Protocol.

4. The Committee shall forward its views to the State Party concerned and to the individual.

Art. 6. The Committee shall include in its annual report under article 45 of the Covenant a summary of its activities under the present Protocol.

Art. 7. Pending the achievement of the objectives of resolution 1514 (XV) adopted by the General Assembly of the United Nations on 14 December 1960 concerning the Declaration on the Granting of Independence to Colonial Countries and Peoples, the provisions of the present Protocol shall in no way limit the right of petition granted to these peoples by the Charter of the United Nations and other international conventions and instruments under the United Nations and its specialized agencies.

Art. 8. 1. The present Protocol is open for signature by any State which has signed the Covenant.

2. The present Protocol is subject to ratification by any State which has ratified or acceded to the Covenant. Instruments of ratification shall be deposited with the Secretary-General of the United Nations.

3. The present Protocol shall be open to accession by any State which has ratified or acceded to the Covenant.

4. Accession shall be effected by the deposit of an instrument of accession with the Secretary-General of the United Nations.

5. The Secretary-General of the United Nations shall inform all States which have signed the present Protocol or acceded to it of the deposit of each instrument of ratification or accession.

Art. 9. 1. Subject to the entry into force of the Covenant, the present Protocol shall enter into force three months after the date of the deposit with the Secretary-General of the United Nations of the tenth instrument of ratification or instrument of accession.

2. For each State ratifying the present Protocol or acceding to it after the deposit of the tenth instrument of ratification or instrument of accession, the present Protocol shall enter into force three months after the date of the deposit of its own instrument of ratification or instrument of accession.

Art. 10. The provisions of the present Protocol shall extend to all parts of federal States without any limitations or exceptions.

Art. 11. 1. Any State Party to the present Protocol may propose an amendment and file it with the Secretary-General of the United Nations. The Secretary-General shall thereupon communicate any proposed amendments to the States Parties to the present Protocol with a request that they notify him whether they favour a conference of States Parties for the purpose of considering and voting upon the proposal. In the event that at least one third of the States Parties favours such a conference, the Secretary-General shall convene the conference under the auspices of the United Nations. Any amendment adopted by a majority of the States Parties present and voting at the conference shall be submitted to the General Assembly of the United Nations for approval.

2. Amendments shall come into force when they have been approved by the General Assembly of the United Nations and accepted by a two-thirds majority of the States Parties to the present Protocol in accordance with their respective constitutional processes.

3. When amendments come into force, they shall be binding on those States Parties which have accepted them, other States Parties still being bound by the provisions of the present Protocol and any earlier amendment which they have accepted.

Art. 12. 1. Any State Party may denounce the present Protocol at any time by written notification addressed to the Secretary-General of the United Nations. Denunciation shall take effect three months after the date of receipt of the notification by the Secretary-General.

2. Denunciation shall be without prejudice to the continued application of the provisions of the present Protocol to any communication submitted under article 2 before the effective date of denunciation.

Art. 13. Irrespective of the notifications made under article 8, paragraph 5, of the present Protocol, the Secretary-General of the United Nations shall inform all States referred to in article 48, paragraph 1, of the Covenant of the following particulars:

(*a*) Signatures, ratifications and accessions under article 8;

(*b*) The date of the entry into force of the present Protocol under article 9 and the date of the entry into force of any amendments under article 11;

(*c*) Denunciations under article 12.

Art. 14. 1. The present Protocol, of which the Chinese, English, French, Russian and Spanish texts are equally authentic, shall be deposited in the archives of the United Nations.

2. The Secretary-General of the United Nations shall transmit certified copies of the present Protocol to all States referred to in article 48 of the Covenant.

Treaties

22.

Convention on the Prevention and Punishment of the Crime of Genocide

Annex to GA Res. 260-A (III) of 9 December 1948. Entered into force on 12 January 1951. See also Reservations to the Convention on the Prevention and Punishment of the Crime of Genocide, Advisory Opinion, *I.C.J. Reports* 1951, pp. 15 *et seq.*

The Contracting Parties,
  Having considered the declaration made by the General Assembly of the United Nations in its resolution 96 (I) dated 11 December 1946 that genocide is a crime under international law, contrary to the spirit and aims of the United Nations and condemned by the civilized world;
  Recognizing that at all periods of history genocide has inflicted great losses on humanity; and
  Being convinced that, in order to liberate mankind from such an odious scourge, international co-operation is required;
  Hereby agree as hereinafter provided.

Art. I. The Contracting Parties confirm that genocide, whether committed in time of peace or in time of war, is a crime under international law which they undertake to prevent and to punish.

Art. II. In the present Convention, genocide means any of the following acts committed with intent to destroy, in whole or in part, a national, ethnical, racial or religious group, as such:
  (*a*) Killing members of the group;
  (*b*) Causing serious bodily or mental harm to members of the group;
  (*c*) Deliberately inflicting on the group conditions of life calculated to bring about its physical destruction in whole or in part;
  (*d*) Imposing measures intended to prevent births within the group;
  (*e*) Forcibly transferring children of the group to another group.

Art. III. The following acts shall be punishable:
  (*a*) Genocide;
  (*b*) Conspiracy to commit genocide;
  (*c*) Direct and public incitement to commit genocide;
  (*d*) Attempt to commit genocide;
  (*e*) Complicity in genocide.

Art. IV. Persons committing genocide or any of the other acts enumerated in article III shall be punished, whether they are constitutionally responsible rulers, public officials or private individuals.

Art. V. The Contracting Parties undertake to enact, in accordance with their respective Constitutions, the necessary legislation to give effect to the provisions of the present Convention and, in particular, to provide effective penalties for persons guilty of genocide or any of the other acts enumerated in article III.

Art. VI. Persons charged with genocide or any of the other acts enumerated in article III shall be tried by a competent tribunal of the State in the territory of which the act was committed, or by such international penal tribunal as may have jurisdiction with respect to those Contracting Parties which shall have accepted its jurisdiction.

Art. VII. Genocide and the other acts enumerated in article III shall not be considered as political crimes for the purpose of extradition.

The Contracting Parties pledge themselves in such cases to grant extradition in accordance with their laws and treaties in force.

Art. VIII. Any Contracting Party may call upon the competent organs of the United Nations to take such action under the Charter of the United Nations as they consider appropriate for the prevention and suppression of acts of genocide or any of the other acts enumerated in article III.

Art. IX. Disputes between the Contracting Parties relating to the interpretation, application or fulfilment of the present Convention, including those relating to the responsibility of a State for genocide or any of the other acts enumerated in article III, shall be submitted to the International Court of Justice at the request of any of the parties to the dispute.

Art. X. The present Convention, of which the Chinese, English, French, Russian and Spanish texts are equally authentic, shall bear the date of 9 December 1948.

Art. XI. The present Convention shall be open until 31 December 1949 for signature on behalf of any Member of the United Nations and of any non-member State to which an invitation to sign has been addressed by the General Assembly.

The present Convention shall be ratified, and the instruments of ratification shall be deposited with the Secretary-General of the United Nations.

After 1 January 1950, the present Convention may be acceded to on behalf of any Member of the United Nations and of any non-member State which has received an invitation as aforesaid.

Instruments of accession shall be deposited with the Secretary-General of the United Nations.

Art. XII. Any Contracting Party may at any time, by notification addressed to the Secretary-General of the United Nations, extend the application of the present Convention to all or any of the territories for the conduct of whose foreign relations that Contracting Party is responsible.

Art. XIII. On the day when the first twenty instruments of ratification or accession have been deposited, the Secretary-General shall draw up a *procès-verbal* and transmit a copy of it to each Member of the United Nations and to each of the non-member States contemplated in article XI.

The present Convention shall come into force on the ninetieth day following the date of deposit of the twentieth instrument of ratification or accession.

Any ratification or accession effected subsequent to the latter date shall become effective on the ninetieth day following the deposit of the instrument of ratification or accession.

Art. XIV. The present Convention shall remain in effect for a period of ten years as from the date of its coming into force.

It shall thereafter remain in force for successive periods of five years for such Contracting Parties as have not denounced it at least six months before the expiration of the current period.

Denunciation shall be effected by a written notification addressed to the Secretary-General of the United Nations.

Art. XV. If, as a result of denunciations, the number of Parties to the present Convention should become less than sixteen, the Convention shall cease to be in force as from the date on which the last of these denunciations shall become effective.

Art. XVI. A request for the revision of the present Convention may be made at any time by any Contracting Party by means of a notification in writing addressed to the Secretary-General.

The General Assembly shall decide upon the steps, if any, to be taken in respect of such request.

Art. XVII. The Secretary-General of the United Nations shall notify all Members of the United Nations and the non-member States contemplated in article XI of the following:
    (*a*) Signatures, ratifications and accessions received in accordance with article XI;
    (*b*) Notifications received in accordance with article XII;
    (*c*) The date upon which the present Convention comes into force in accordance with article XIII;
    (*d*) Denunciations received in accordance with article XIV;
    (*e*) The abrogation of the Convention in accordance with article XV;
    (*f*) Notifications received in accordance with article XVI.

Art. XVIII. The original of the present Convention shall be deposited in the archives of the United Nations.
    A certified copy of the Convention shall be transmitted to all Members of the United Nations and to the non-member States contemplated in article XI.

Art. XIX. The present Convention shall be registered by the Secretary-General of the United Nations on the date of its coming into force.

23.

CONVENTION CONCERNING FREEDOM OF ASSOCIATION AND PROTECTION OF THE RIGHT TO ORGANISE*

The General Conference of the International Labour Organisation,

Having been convened at San Francisco by the Governing Body of the International Labour Office, and having met in its Thirty-first Session on 17 June 1948;

Having decided to adopt, in the form of a Convention, certain proposalsconcerning freedom of association and protection of the right to organise, which is the seventh item on the agenda of the session;

Considering that the Preamble to the Constitution of the International Labour Organisation declares 'recognition of the principle of freedom of association' to be a means of improving conditions of labour and of establishing peace;

Considering that the Declaration of Philadelphia reaffirms that 'freedom of expression and of association are essential to sustained progress';

Considering that the International Labour Conference, at its Thirtieth Session, unanimously adopted the principles which should form the basis for international regulation;

Considering that the General Assembly of the United Nations, at its Second Session, endorsed these principles and requested the International Labour Organisation to continue every effort in order that it may be possible to adopt one or several international Conventions;

adopts this ninth day of July of the year one thousand nine hundred and forty-eight the following Convention, which may be cited as the Freedom of Association and Protection of the Right to Organise Convention, 1948:

---

* ILO Convention n° 87, 9 July 1948. Entry into force, 4 July 1950.

PART I. FREEDOM OF ASSOCIATION

Article 1

Each Member of the International Labour Organisation for which this Convention is in force undertakes to give effect to the following provisions.

Article 2

Workers and employers, without distinction whatsoever, shall have the right to establish and, subject only to the rules of the organisation concerned, to join organisations of their own choosing without previous authorisation.

Article 3

1. Workers' and employers' organisations shall have the right to draw up their constitutions and rules, to elect their representatives in full freedom, to organise their administration and activities and to formulate their programmes.
2. The public authorities shall refrain from any interference which would restrict this right or impede the lawful exercise thereof.

Article 4

Workers' and employers' organisations shall not be liable to be dissolved or suspended by administrative authority.

Article 5

Workers' and employers' organisations shall have the right to establish and join federations and confederations and any such organisation, federation or confederation shall have the right to affiliate with international organisations of workers and employers.

Article 6

The provisions of Articles 2, 3 and 4 hereof apply to federations and confederations of workers' and employers' organisations.

Article 7

The acquisition of legal personality by workers' and employers' organisations, federations and confederations shall not be made subject to conditions of such a character as to restrict the application of the provisions of Articles 2, 3 and 4 hereof.

Article 8

1. In exercising the rights provided for in this Convention workers and employers and their respective organisations, like other persons or organised collectivities, shall respect the law of the land.
2. The law of the land shall not be such as to impair, nor shall it be so applied as to impair, the guarantees provided for in this Convention.

Article 9

1. The extent to which the guarantees provided for in this Convention shall apply to the armed forces and the police shall be determined by national laws or regulations.
2. In accordance with the principle set forth in paragraph 8 of article 19 of the Constitution of the International Labour Organisation the ratification of this Convention by any Member shall not be deemed to affect any existing law, award, custom or agreement in virtue of which members of the armed forces or the police enjoy any right guaranteed by this Convention.

Article 10

In this Convention the term 'organisation' means any organisation of workers or of employers for furthering and defending the interests of workers or of employers.

PART II. PROTECTION OF THE RIGHT TO ORGANISE

Each Member of the International Labour Organisation for which this Convention is in force undertakes to take all necessary and appropriate measures to ensure that workers and employers may exercise freely the right to organise.

PART III. MISCELLANEOUS PROVISIONS

Article 12

1. In respect of the territories referred to in Article 35 of the Constitution of the International Labour Organisation as amended by the Constitution of the International Labour Organisation Instrument of Amendment, 1946, other than the territories referred to in paragraphs 4 and 5 of the said article as so amended, each Member of the Organization which ratifies this Convention shall communicate to the Director-General of the International Labour Office with or as soon as possible after its ratification a declaration stating:
(a) The territories in respect of which it undertakes that the provisions of the Convention shall be applied without modification;
(b) The territories in respect of which it undertakes that the provisions of the Convention shall be applied subject to modifications, together with details of the said modifications;
(c) The territories in respect of which the Convention is inapplicable and in such cases the grounds on which it is inapplicable;
(d) The territories in respect of which it reserves its decision.

2. The undertakings referred to in sub-paragraphs *(a)* and *(b)* of paragraph 1 of this article shall be deemed to be an integral part of the ratification and shall have the force of ratification.

3. Any Member may at any time by a subsequent declaration cancel in whole or in part any reservations made in its original declaration in virtue of sub-paragraph *(b)*, *(c)* or *(d)* of paragraph 1 of this article.

4. Any Member may, at any time at which this Convention is subject to denunciation in accordance with the provisions of Article 16, communicate to the Director-General a declaration modifying in any other respect the terms of any former declaration and stating the present position in respect of such territories as it may specify.

Article 13

1. Where the subject matter of this Convention is within the self-governing powers of any non-metropolitan territory, the Member responsible for the international relations of that territory may, in agreement with the Government of the territory, communicate to the Director-General of the International Labour Office a declaration accepting on behalf of the territory the obligations of this Convention.

2. A declaration accepting the obligations of this Convention may be communicated to the Director-General of the International Labour Office:
(a) By two or more Members of the Organization in respect of any territory which is under their joint authority; or

(b) By any international authority responsible for the administration of any territory, in virtue of the Charter of the United Nations or otherwise, in respect of any such territory.

3. Declarations communicated to the Director-General of the International Labour Office in accordance with the preceding paragraphs of this article shall indicate whether the provisions of the Convention will be applied in the territory concerned without modification or subject to modifications; when the declaration indicates that the provisions of the Convention will be applied subject to modifications it shall give details of the said modifications.

4. The Member, Members or international authority concerned may at any time by a subsequent declaration renounce in whole or in part the right to have recourse to any modification indicated in any former declaration.

5. The Member, Members or international authority concerned may, at any time at which this Convention is subject to denunciation in accordance with the provisions of Article 16, communicate to the Director-General of the International Labour Office a declaration modifying in any other respect the terms of any former declaration and stating the present position in respect of the application of the Convention.

PART IV. FINAL PROVISIONS

Article 14

The formal ratifications of this Convention shall be communicated to the Director-General of the International Labour Office for registration.

Article 15

1. This Convention shall be binding only upon those Members of the International Labour Organization whose ratifications have been registered with the Director-General.

2. It shall come into force twelve months after the date on which the ratifications of two Members have been registered with the Director-General.

3. Thereafter, this Convention shall come into force for any Member twelve months after the date on which its ratification has been registered.

Article 16

1. A Member which has ratified this Convention may denounce it after the expiration of ten years from the date on which the Convention first comes into force, by an act communicated to the Director-General of the International

Labour Office for registration. Such denunciation shall not take effect until one year after the date on which it is registered.

2. Each Member which has ratified this Convention and which does not, within the year following the expiration of the period of ten years mentioned in the preceding paragraph, exercise the right of denunciation provided for in this article, will be found for another period of ten years and, thereafter, may denounce this Convention at the expiration of each period of ten years under the terms provided for in this article.

Article 17

1. The Director-General of the International Labour Office shall notify all Members of the International Labour Organization of the registration of all ratifications, declarations and denunciations communicated to him by the Members of the Organization.

2. When notifying the Members of the Organization of the registration of the second ratification communicated to him, the Director-General shall draw the attention of the Members of the Organization to the date upon which the Convention will come into force.

Article 18

The Director-General of the International Labour Office shall communicate to the Secretary-General of the United Nations for registration in accordance with Article 102 of the Charter of the United Nations full particulars of all ratifications, declarations and acts of denunciation registered by him in accordance with the provisions of the preceding articles.

Article 19

At the expiration of each period of ten years after the coming into force of this Convention, the Governing Body of the International Labour Office shall present to the General Conference a report on the working of this Convention and shall consider the desirability of placing on the agenda of the Conference the question of its revision in whole or in part.

Article 20

1. Should the Conference adopt a new Convention revising this Convention in whole or in part, then, unless the new Convention otherwise provides,
   (a) The ratification by a Member of the new revising Convention shall *ipso jure* involve the immediate denunciation of this Convention, notwith-

standing the provisions of Article 16 above, if and when the new revising Convention shall have come into force;

(b) As from the date when the new revising Convention comes into force this Convention shall cease to be open to ratification by the Members.

2. This Convention shall in any case remain in force in its actual form and content for those Members which have ratified it but have not ratified the revising Convention.

Article 21

The English and French versions of the text of this Convention are equally authoritative.

24.

CONVENTION CONCERNING THE APPLICATION OF THE PRINCIPLES OF THE RIGHT TO ORGANISE AND TO BARGAIN COLLECTIVELY

This Convention entered into force on 18 July 1951. For a fuller list of ILO Conventions and Recommendations see: International Labour Conventions and Recommendations 1919–1981. *Geneva; International Labour Office, 1982*

The General Conference of the International Labour Organisation,

Having been convened at Geneva by the Governing Body of the International Labour Office, and having met in its Thirty-second Session on 8 June 1949, and
Having decided upon the adoption of certain proposals concerning the application of the principles of the right to organise and to bargain collectively, which is the fourth item on the agenda of the session, and
Having determined that these proposals shall take the form of an international Convention,

adopts this first day of July of the year one thousand nine hundred and forty-nine the following Convention, which may be cited as the Right to Organise and Collective Bargaining Convention, 1949:

Article 1

1. Workers shall enjoy adequate protection against acts of anti-union discrimination in respect of their employment.
2. Such protection shall apply more particularly in respect of acts calculated to –
(a) make the employment of a worker subject to the condition, that he shall not join a union or shall relinquish trade union membership;
(b) cause the dismissal of or otherwise prejudice a worker by reason of union membership or because of participation in union activities outside working hours or, with the consent of the employer, within working hours.

Article 2

1. Workers' and employers' organisations shall enjoy adequate protection against any acts of interference by each other or each other's agents or members in their establishment, functioning or administration.
2. In particular, acts which are designed to promote the establishment of workers' organisations under the domination of employers or employers' organisations, or to support workers' organisations by financial or other means, with the object of placing such organisations under the control of employers or employers' organisations, shall be deemed to constitute acts of interference within the meaning of this Article.

Article 3

Machinery appropriate to national conditions shall be established, where necessary, for the purpose of ensuring respect for the right to organise as defined in the preceding Articles.

Article 4

Measures appropriate to national conditions shall be taken, where necessary, to encourage and promote the full development and utilisation of machinery for voluntary negotiation between employers or employers' organisations and workers' organisations, with a view to the regulation of terms and conditions of employment by means of collective agreements.

Article 5

1. The extent to which the guarantees provided for in this Convention shall apply to the armed forces and the police shall be determined by national laws or regulations.
2. In accordance with the principle set forth in paragraph 8 of article 19 of the Constitution of the International Labour Organisation the ratification of this Convention by any Member shall not be deemed to affect any existing law, award, custom or agreement in virtue of which members of the armed forces or the police enjoy any right guaranteed by this Convention.

Article 6

This Convention does not deal with the position of public servants engaged in the administration of the State, nor shall it be construed as prejudicing their rights or status in any way.

Article 7

The formal ratifications of this Convention shall be communicated to the Director-General of the International Labour Office for registration.

Article 8

1. This Convention shall be binding only upon those Members of the International Labour Organization whose ratifications have been registered with the Director-General.
2. It shall come into force twelve months after the date on which the ratifications of two Members have been registered with the Director-General.
3. Thereafter, this Convention shall come into force for any Member twelve months after the date on which its ratification has been registered.

Article 9

1. Declarations communicated to the Director-General of the International Labour Office in accordance with paragraph 2 of Article 35 of the Constitution of the International Labour Organization shall indicate:
 (a) The territories in respect of which the Member concerned undertakes that the provisions of the Convention shall be applied without modification;
 (b) The territories in respect of which it undertakes that the provisions of the Convention shall be applied subject to modifications, together with details of the said modifications;
 (c) The territories in respect of which the Convention is inapplicable and in such cases the grounds on which it is inapplicable;
 (d) The territories in respect of which it reserves its decision pending further consideration of the position.
2. The undertakings referred to in sub-paragraphs *(a)* and *(b)* of paragraph 1 of this article shall be deemed to be an integral part of the ratification and shall have the force of ratification.
3. Any Member may at any time by a subsequent declaration cancel in whole or in part any reservation made in its original declaration in virtue of sub-paragraph *(b), (c)* or *(d)* of paragraph 1 of this article.
4. Any Member may, at any time at which the Convention is subject to denunciation in accordance with the provisions of Article 11, communicate to the Director-General a declaration modifying in any other respect the terms of any former declaration and stating the present position in respect of such territories as it may specify.

Article 10

1. Declarations communicated to the Director-General of the International Labour Office in accordance with paragraphs 4 or 5 of Article 35 of the Constitution of the International Labour Organization shall indicate whether the provisions of the Convention will be applied in the territory concerned without modification or subject to modifications; when the declaration indicates that the provisions of the Convention will be applied subject to modifications, it shall give details of the said modifications.
2. The Member, Members or international authority concerned may at any time by a subsequent declaration renounce in whole or in part the right to have recourse to any modification indicated in any former declaration.
3. The Member, Members or international authority concerned may, at any time at which this Convention is subject to denunciation in accordance with the provisions of Article 11, communicate to the Director-General a declaration modifying in any other respect the terms of any former declaration and stating the present position in respect of the application of the Convention.

Article 11

1. A Member which has ratified this Convention may denounce it after the expiration of ten years from the date on which the Convention first comes into force, by an act communicated to the Director-General of the International Labour Office for registration. Such denunciation shall not take effect until one year after the date on which it is registered.
2. Each Member which has ratified this Convention and which does not, within the year following the expiration of the period of ten years mentioned in the preceding paragraph, exercise the right of denunciation provided for in this article, will be bound for another period of ten years and, thereafter, may denounce this Convention at the expiration of each period of ten years under the terms provided for in this article.

Article 12

1. The Director-General of the International Labour Office shall notify all Members of the International Labour Organisation of the registration of all ratifications, declarations and denunciations communicated to him by the Members of the Organization.
2. When notifying the Members of the Organization of the registration of the second ratification communicated to him, the Director-General shall draw the attention of the Members of the Organization to the date upon which the Convention will come into force.

Article 13

The Director-General of the International Labour Office shall communicate to the Secretary-General of the United Nations for registration in accordance with Article 102 of the Charter of the United Nations full particulars of all ratifications, declarations and acts of denunciations registered by him in accordance with the provisions of the preceding articles.

Article 14

At the expiration of each period of ten years after the coming into force of this Convention, the Governing Body of the International Labour Office shall present to the General Conference a report on the working of this Convention and shall consider the desirability of placing on the agenda of the Conference the question of its revision in whole or in part.

Article 15

1. Should the Conference adopt a new Convention revising this Convention in whole or in part, then, unless the new Convention otherwise provides,
(a) The ratification by a Member of the new revising Convention shall *ipso jure* involve the immediate denunciation of this Convention, notwithstanding the provisions of Article 11 above, if and when the new revising Convention shall have come into force;
(b) As from the date when the new revising Convention comes into force this Convention shall cease to be open to ratification by the Members.
2. This Convention shall in any case remain in force in its actual form and content for those Members which have ratified it but have not ratified the revising Convention.

Article 16

The English and French versions of the text of this Convention are equally authoritative.

25.

Convention relating to the Status of Refugees

> The Convention was adopted by the UN Conference on the Status of Refugees and Stateless Persons, held at Geneva from 2 to 25 July 1951. The Conference was convened pursuant to GA Res. 429 (V) of 14 December 1950.
> The Convention was signed on 28 July 1951. It entered into force on 22 April 1954. U.N. Doc. A/CONF.2/108. As published in *Collection of International Instruments concerning Refugees*, 2nd ed., published by the Office of the UNHCR — Geneva 1979, pp. 10 *et seq.*. With Annex.

PREAMBLE

The High Contracting Parties

Considering that the Charter of the United Nations and the Universal Declaration of Human Rights approved on 10 December 1948 by the General Assembly have affirmed the principle that human beings shall enjoy fundamental rights and freedoms without discrimination,

Considering that the United Nations has, on various occasions, manifested its profound concern for refugees and endeavoured to assure refugees the widest possible exercise of these fundamental rights and freedoms,

Considering that it is desirable to revise and consolidate previous international agreements relating to the status of refugees and to extend the scope of and the protection accorded by such instruments by means of a new agreement,

Considering that the grant of asylum may place unduly heavy burdens on certain countries, and that a satisfactory solution of a problem of which the United Nations has recognized the international scope and nature cannot therefore be achieved without international co-operation,

Expressing the wish that all States, recognizing the social and humanitarian nature of the problem of refugees, will do everything within their power to prevent this problem from becoming a cause of tension between States,

Noting that the United Nations High Commissioner for Refugees is charged with the task of supervising international conventions providing for the protection of refugees, and recognizing that the effective co-ordination of measures taken to deal with this problem will depend upon the cooperation of States with the High Commissioner,

Have agreed as follows:

CHAPTER I

GENERAL PROVISIONS

Article 1

Definition of the term "Refugee"

A. For the purposes of the present Convention, the term "refugee" shall apply to any person who:

(1) Has been considered a refugee under the Arrangements of 12 May 1926 and 30 June 1928 or under the Conventions of 28 October 1933 and 10 February 1938, the Protocol of 14 September 1939 or the Constitution of the International Refugee Organization;

Decisions of non-eligibility taken by the International Refugee Organization during the period of its activities shall not prevent the status of refugee being accorded to persons who fulfil the conditions of paragraph 2 of this section;

(2) As a result of events occuring before 1 January 1951 and owing to well-founded fear of being persecuted for reasons of race, religion, nationality, membership of a particular social group or political opinion, is outside the country of his nationality and is unable or, owing to such fear, is unwilling to avail himself of the protection of that country; or who, not having a nationality and being outside the country of his former habitual residence as a result of such events, is unable or, owing to such fear, is unwilling to return to it.

In the case of a person who has more than one nationality, the term "the country of his nationality" shall mean each of the countries of which he is a national, and a person shall not be deemed to be lacking the protection of the country of his nationality if, without any valid reason based on well-founded fear, he has not availed himself of the protection of one of the countries of which he is a national.

B. (1) For the purposes of this Convention, the words "events occurring before 1 January 1951" in Article 1, Section A, shall be understood to mean either

(a) "events occurring in Europe before 1 January 1951"; or

(b) "events occurring in Europe or elsewhere before 1 January 1951", and each Contracting State shall make a declaration at the time of signature, ratification or accession, specifying which of these meanings it applies for the purpose of its obligations under this Convention.

(2) Any Contracting State which has adopted alternative (*a*) may at any time extend its obligations by adopting alternative (*b*) by means of a notification addressed to the Secretary-General of the United Nations.

C. This Convention shall cease to apply to any person falling under the terms of section A if:

(1) He has voluntarily re-availed himself of the protection of the country of his nationality; or

(2) Having lost his nationality, he has voluntarily re-acquired it, or

(3) He has acquired a new nationality, and enjoys the protection of the country of his new nationality; or

(4) He has voluntarily re-established himself in the country which he left or outside which he remained owing to fear of persecution; or

(5) He can no longer, because the circumstances in connexion with which he has been recognized as a refugee have ceased to exist, continue to refuse to avail himself of the protection of the country of his nationality;

Provided that this paragraph shall not apply to a refugee falling under section A(1) of this Article who is able to invoke compelling reasons arising out of previous persecution for refusing to avail himself of the protection of the country of nationality;

(6) Being a person who has no nationality he is, because the circumstances in connexion with which he has been recognized as a refugee have ceased to exist, able to return to the country of his former habitual residence;

Provided that this paragraph shall not apply to a refugee falling under section A(1) of this Article who is able to invoke compelling reasons arising out of previous persecution for refusing to return to the country of his former habitual residence.

D. This Convention shall not apply to persons who are at present receiving from organs or agencies of the United Nations other than the United Nations High Commissioner for Refugees protection or assistance.

When such protection or assistance has ceased for any reason, without the position of such persons being definitively settled in accordance with the relevant resolutions adopted by the General Assembly of the United Nations, these persons shall *ipso facto* be entitled to the benefits of this Convention.

E. This Convention shall not apply to a person who is recognized by the competent authorities of the country in which he has taken residence as having the rights and obligations which are attached to the possession of the nationality of that country.

F. The provisions of this Convention shall not apply to any person with respect to whom there are serious reasons for considering that:

(a) he has committed a crime against peace, a war crime, or a crime against humanity, as defined in the international instruments drawn up to make provision in respect of such crimes;

(b) he has committed a serious non-political crime outside the country of refuge prior to his admission to that country as a refugee;

(c) he has been guilty of acts contrary to the purposes and principles of the United Nations.

Article 2

General obligations

Every refugee has duties to the country in which he finds himself, which require in particular that he conform to its laws and regulations as well as to measures taken for the maintenance of public order.

Article 3

Non-discrimination

The Contracting States shall apply the provisions of this Convention to refugees without discrimination as to race, religion or country of origin.

Article 4

Religion

The Contracting States shall accord to refugees within their territories treatment at least as favourable as that accorded to their nationals with respect to freedom to practise their religion and freedom as regards the religious education of their children.

Article 5

Rights granted apart from this Convention

Nothing in this Convention shall be deemed to impair any rights and benefits granted by a Contracting State to refugees apart from this Convention.

Article 6

The term "in the same circumstances"

For the purpose of this Convention, the term "in the same circumstances" implies that any requirements (including requirements as to length and conditions of sojourn or residence) which the particular individual would have to fulfil for the enjoyment of the right in question, if he were not a refugee, must be fulfilled by him, with the exception of requirements which by their nature a refugee is incapable of fulfilling.

Article 7

Exemption from reciprocity

1. Except where this Convention contains more favourable provisions, a Contracting State shall accord to refugees the same treatment as is accorded to aliens generally.

2. After a period of three years' residence, all refugees shall enjoy exemption from legislative reciprocity in the territory of the Contracting States.

3. Each Contracting State shall continue to accord to refugees the rights and benefits to which they were already entitled, in the absence of reciprocity, at the date of entry into force of this Convention for that State.

4. The Contracting States shall consider favourably the possibility of according to refugees, in the absence of reciprocity, rights and benefits beyond those to which they are entitled according to paragraphs 2 and 3, and to extending exemption from reciprocity to refugees who do not fulfil the conditions provided for in paragraphs 2 and 3.

5. The provisions of paragraphs 2 and 3 apply both to the rights and benefits referred to in Articles 13, 18, 19, 21 and 22 of this Convention and to rights and benefits for which this Convention does not provide.

Article 8

Exemption from exceptional measures

With regard to exceptional measures which may be taken against the person, property or interests of nationals of a foreign State, the Contracting States shall not apply such measures to a refugee who is formally a national of the said State solely on account of such nationality. Contracting States which, under their legislation, are prevented from applying the general principle expressed in this Article, shall, in appropriate cases, grant exemptions in favour of such refugees.

Article 9

Provisional measures

Nothing in this Convention shall prevent a Contracting State, in time of war or other grave and exceptional circumstances, from taking provisionally measures which it considers to be essential to the national security in the case of a particular person, pending a determination by the Contracting State that that person is in fact a refugee and that the continuance of such measures is necessary in his case in the interests of national security.

Article 10

Continuity of residence

1. Where a refugee has been forcibly displaced during the Second World War and removed to the territory of a Contracting State, and is resident there, the period of such enforced sojourn shall be considered to have been lawful residence within that territory.

2. Where a refugee has been forcibly displaced during the Second World War from the territory of a Contracting State and has, prior to the date of entry into force of this Convention, returned there for the purpose of taking up residence, the period of residence before and after such enforced displacement shall be regarded as one uninterrupted period for any purposes for which uninterrupted residence is required.

Article 11

Refugee seamen

In the case of refugees regularly serving as crew members on board a ship flying the flag of a Contracting State, that State shall give sympathetic consideration to their establishment on its territory and the issue of travel documents to them or their temporary admission to its territory particularly with a view to facilitating their establishment in another country.

CHAPTER II - JURIDICAL STATUS

Article 12

Personal status

1. The personal status of a refugee shall be governed by the law of the country of his domicile or, if he has no domicile, by the law of the country of his residence.

2. Rights previously acquired by a refugee and dependent on personal status, more particularly rights attaching to marriage, shall be respected by a Contracting State, subject to compliance, if this be necessary, with the formalities required by the law of that State, provided that the right in question is one which would have been recognized by the law of that State had he not become a refugee.

Article 13

Movable and immovable property

The Contracting States shall accord to a refugee treatment as favourable as possible and, in any event, not less favourable than that accorded to aliens generally in the same circumstances, as regards the acquisition of movable and immovable property and other rights pertaining thereto, and to leases and other contracts relating to movable and immovable property.

Article 14

Artistic rights and industrial property

In respect of the protection of industrial property, such as inventions, designs or models, trade marks, trade names, and of rights in literary, artistic and scientific works, a refugee shall be accorded in the country in which he has his habitual residence the same protection as is accorded to nationals of that country. In the territory of any other Contracting State, he shall be accorded the same protection as is accorded in that territory to nationals of the country in which he has his habitual residence.

Article 15

Right of association

As regards non-political and non-profit-making associations and trade unions the Contracting States shall accord to refugees lawfully staying in their territory the most favourable treatment accorded to nationals of a foreign country, in the same circumstances.

Article 16

Access to courts

1. A refugee shall have free access to the courts of law on the territory of all Contracting States.

2. A refugee shall enjoy in the Contracting State in which he has his habitual residence the same treatment as a national in matters pertaining to access to the Courts, including legal assistance and exemption from *cautio judicatum solvi.*

3. A refugee shall be accorded in the matters referred to in paragraph 2 in countries other than that in which he has his habitual residence the treatment granted to a national of the country of his habitual residence.

CHAPTER III

GAINFUL EMPLOYMENT

Article 17

Wage-earning employment

1. The Contracting State shall accord to refugees lawfully staying in their territory the most favourable treatment accorded to nationals of a foreign country in the same circumstances, as regards the right to engage in wage-earning employment.

2. In any case, restrictive measures imposed on aliens or the employment of aliens for the protection of the national labour market shall not be applied to a refugee who was already exempt from them at the date of entry into force of this Convention for the Contracting State concerned, or who fulfils one of the following conditions:

(a) He has completed three years' residence in the country,

(b) He has a spouse possessing the nationality of the country of residence. A refugee may not invoke the benefits of this provision if he has abandoned his spouse,

(c) He has one or more children possessing the nationality of the country of residence.

3. The Contracting States shall give sympathetic consideration to assim-

ilating the rights of all refugees with regard to wage-earning employment to those of nationals, and in particular of those refugees who have entered their territory pursuant to programmes of labour recruitment or under immigration schemes.

Article 18

Self-employment

The Contracting States shall accord to a refugee lawfully in their territory treatment as favourable as possible and, in any event, not less favourable than that accorded to aliens generally in the same circumstances, as regards the right to engage on his own account in agriculture, industry, handicrafts and commerce and to establish commercial and industrial companies.

Article 19

Liberal professions

1. Each Contracting State shall accord to refugees lawfully staying in their territory who hold diplomas recognized by the competent authorities of that State, and who are desirous of practising a liberal profession, treatment as favourable as possible and, in any event, not less favourable than that accorded to aliens generally in the same circumstances.

2. The Contracting States shall use their best endeavours consistently with their laws and constitutions to secure the settlement of such refugees in the territories, other than the metropolitan territory, for whose international relations they are responsible.

CHAPTER IV

WELFARE

Article 20

Rationing

Where a rationing system exists, which applies to the population at large and regulates the general distribution of products in short supply, refugees shall be accorded the same treatment as nationals.

Article 21

Housing

As regards housing, the Contracting States, in so far as the matter is regulated by laws or regulations or is subject to the control of public authorities, shall accord to refugees lawfully staying in their territory treatment as favourable as possible and, in any event, not less favourable than that accorded to aliens generally in the same circumstances.

Article 22

Public education

1. The Contracting States shall accord to refugees the same treatment as is accorded to nationals with respect to elementary education.

2. The Contracting States shall accord to refugees treatment as favourable as possible, and, in any event, not less favourable than that accorded to aliens generally in the same circumstances, with respect to education other than elementary education and, in particular, as regards access to studies, the recognition of foreign school certificates, diplomas and degrees, the remission of fees and charges and the award of scholarships.

Article 23

Public relief

The Contracting States shall accord to refugees lawfully staying in their territory the same treatment with respect to public relief and assistance as is accorded to their nationals.

Article 24

Labour legislation and social security

1. The Contracting States shall accord to refugees lawfully staying in their territory the same treatment as is accorded to nationals in respect of the following matters:

(a) In so far as such matters are governed by laws or regulations or are subject to the control of administrative authorities: remuneration, including family allowances where these form part of remuneration, hours of work, overtime arrangements, holidays with pay, restrictions on

home work, minimum age of employment, apprenticeship and training, women's work and the work of young persons, and the enjoyment of the benefits of collective bargaining;

(b) Social security (legal provisions in respect of employment injury, occupational diseases, maternity, sickness, disability, old age, death, unemployment, family responsibilities and any other contingency which, according to national laws or regulations, is covered by a social security scheme), subject to the following limitations:

  (i) There may be appropriate arrangements for the maintenance of acquired rights and rights in course of acquisition;

  (ii) National laws or regulations of the country of residence may prescribe special arrangements concerning benefits or portions of benefits which are payable wholly out of public funds, and concerning allowances paid to persons who do not fulfil the contribution conditions prescribed for the award of a normal pension.

2. The right to compensation for the death of a refugee resulting from employment injury or from occupational disease shall not be affected by the fact that the residence of the beneficiary is outside the territory of the Contracting State.

3. The Contracting States shall extend to refugees the benefits of agreements concluded between them, or which may be concluded between them in the future, concerning the maintenance of acquired rights and rights in the process of acquisition in regard to social security, subject only to the conditions which apply to nationals of the States signatory to the agreements in question.

4. The Contracting States will give sympathetic consideration to extending to refugees so far as possible the benefits of similar agreements which may at any time be in force between such Contracting States and non-contracting States.

CHAPTER V

ADMINISTRATIVE MEASURES

Article 25

Administrative assistance

1. When the exercise of a right by a refugee would normally require the assistance of authorities of a foreign country to whom he cannot have

recourse, the Contracting States in whose territory he is residing shall arrange that such assistance be afforded to him by their own authorities or by an international authority.

2. The authority or authorities mentioned in paragraph 1 shall deliver or cause to be delivered under their supervision to refugees such documents or certifications as would normally be delivered to aliens by or through their national authorities.

3. Documents or certifications so delivered shall stand in the stead of the official instruments delivered to aliens by or through their national authorities, and shall be given credence in the absence of proof to the contrary.

4. Subject to such exceptional treatment as may be granted to indigent persons, fees may be charged for the services mentioned herein, but such fees shall be moderate and commensurate with those charged to nationals for similar services.

5. The provisions of this Article shall be without prejudice to Articles 27 and 28.

Article 26

Freedom of movement

Each Contracting State shall accord to refugees lawfully in its territory the right to choose their place of residence and to move freely within its territory, subject to any regulations applicable to aliens generally in the same circumstances.

Article 27

Identity papers

The Contracting States shall issue identity papers to any refugee in their territory who does not possess a valid travel document.

Article 28

Travel documents

1. The Contracting States shall issue to refugees lawfully staying in their territory travel documents for the purpose of travel outside their territory

unless compelling reasons of national security or public order otherwise require, and the provisions of the Schedule to this Convention shall apply with respect to such documents. The Contracting States may issue such a travel document to any other refugee in their territory, they shall in particular give sympathetic consideration to the issue of such a travel document to refugees in their territory who are unable to obtain a travel document from the country of their lawful residence.

2. Travel documents issued to refugees under previous international agreements by parties thereto shall be recognized and treated by the Contracting States in the same way as if they had been issued pursuant to this article.

Article 29

Fiscal charges

1. The Contracting States shall not impose upon refugees duties, charges or taxes, of any description whatsoever, other or higher than those which are or may be levied on their nationals in similar situations.

2. Nothing in the above paragraph shall prevent the application to refugees of the laws and regulations concerning charges in respect of the issue to aliens of administrative documents including identity papers.

Article 30

Transfer of assets

1. A Contracting State shall, in conformity with its laws and regulations, permit refugees to transfer assets which they have brought into its territory, to another country where they have been admitted for the purposes of resettlement.

2. A Contracting State shall give sympathetic consideration to the application of refugees for permission to transfer assets wherever they may be and which are necessary for their resettlement in another country to which they have been admitted.

Article 31

Refugees unlawfully in the country of refuge

1. The Contracting States shall not impose penalties, on account of their illegal entry or presence, on refugees who, coming directly from a territory

where their life or freedom was threatened in the sense of Article 1, enter or are present in their territory without authorization, provided they present themselves without delay to the authorities and show good cause for their illegal entry or presence.

2. The Contracting States shall not apply to the movements of such refugees restrictions other than those which are necessary and such restrictions shall only be applied until their status in the country is regularized or they obtain admission into another country. The Contracting States shall allow such refugees a reasonable period and all the necessary facilities to obtain admission into another country.

Article 32

Expulsion

1. The Contracting States shall not expel a refugee lawfully in their territory save on grounds of national security or public order.

2. The expulsion of such a refugee shall be only in pursuance of a decision reached in accordance with due process of law. Except where compelling reasons of national security otherwise require, the refugee shall be allowed to submit evidence to clear himself, and to appeal to and be represented for the purpose before competent authority or a person or persons specially designated by the competent authority.

3. The Contracting States shall allow such a refugee a reasonable period within which to seek legal admission into another country. The Contracting States reserve the right to apply during that period such internal measures as they may deem necessary.

Article 33

Prohibition of expulsion or return ("refoulement")

1. No Contracting State shall expel or return ("refouler") a refugee in any manner whatsoever to the frontiers of territories where his life or freedom would be threatened on account of his race, religion, nationality, membership of a particular social group or political opinion.

2. The benefit of the present provision may not, however, be claimed by a refugee whom there are reasonable grounds for regarding as a danger to the security of the country in which he is, or who, having been convicted by a final judgment of a particularly serious crime, constitutes a danger to the community of that country.

Article 34

Naturalization

The Contracting States shall as far as possible facilitate the assimilation and naturalization of refugees. They shall in particular make every effort to expedite naturalization proceedings and to reduce as far as possible the charges and costs of such proceedings.

CHAPTER VI

EXECUTORY AND TRANSITORY PROVISIONS

Article 35

Co-operation of the national authorities with the United Nations

1. The Contracting States undertake to co-operate with the Office of the United Nations High Commissioner for Refugees, or any other agency of the United Nations which may succeed it, in the exercise of its functions, and shall in particular facilitate its duty of supervising the application of the provisions of this Convention.

2. In order to enable the Office of the High Commissioner or any other agency of the United Nations which may succeed it, to make reports to the competent organs of the United Nations, the Contracting States undertake to provide them in the appropriate form with information and statistical data requested concerning:

(a) the condition of refugees,

(b) the implementation of this Convention, and

(c) laws, regulations and decrees which are, or may hereafter be, in force relating to refugees.

Article 36

Information on national legislation

The Contracting States shall communicate to the Secretary-General of the United Nations the laws and regulations which they may adopt to ensure the application of this Convention.

Article 37

Relation to previous Conventions

Without prejudice to Article 28, paragraph 2, of this Convention, this Convention replaces, as between parties to it, the Arrangements of 5 July 1922, 31 May 1924, 12 May 1926, 30 June 1928 and 30 July 1935, the Conventions of 28 October 1933 and 10 February 1938, the Protocol of 14 September 1939 and the Agreement of 15 October 1946.

CHAPTER VII

FINAL CLAUSES

Article 38

Settlement of disputes

Any dispute between parties to this Convention relating to its interpretation or application, which cannot be settled by other means, shall be referred to the International Court of Justice at the request of any one of the parties to the dispute.

Article 39

Signature, ratification and accession

1. This Convention shall be opened for signature at Geneva on 28 July 1951 and shall thereafter be deposited with the Secretary-General of the United Nations. It shall be open for signature at the European Office of the United Nations from 28 July to 31 August 1951 and shall be re-opened for signature at the Headquarters of the United Nations from 17 September 1951 to 31 December 1952.

2. This Convention shall be open for signature on behalf of all States Members of the United Nations, and also on behalf of any other State invited to attend the Conference of Plenipotentiaries on the Status of Refugees and Stateless Persons or to which an invitation to sign will have been addressed by the General Assembly. It shall be ratified and the instruments of ratification shall be deposited with the Secretary-General of the United Nations.

3. This Convention shall be open from 28 July 1951 for accession by the States referred to in paragraph 2 of this Article. Accession shall be effected by the deposit of an instrument of accession with the Secretary-General of the United Nations.

Article 40

Territorial application clause

1. Any State may, at the time of signature, ratification or accession, declare that this Convention shall extend to all or any of the territories for the international relations of which it is responsible. Such a declaration shall take effect when the Convention enters into force for the State concerned.

2. At any time thereafter any such extension shall be made by notification addressed to the Secretary-General of the United Nations and shall take effect as from the ninetieth day after the day of receipt by the Secretary-General of the United Nations of this notification, or as from the date of entry into force of the Convention for the State concerned, whichever is the later.

3. With respect to those territories to which this Convention is not extended at the time of signature, ratification or accession, each State concerned shall consider the possibility of taking the necessary steps in order to extend the application of this Convention to such territories, subject, where necessary for constitutional reasons, to the consent of the governments of such territories.

Article 41

Federal clause

In the case of a Federal or non-unitary State, the following provisions shall apply:

(a) With respect to those Articles of this Convention that come within the legislative jurisdiction of the federal legislative authority, the obligations of the Federal Government shall to this extent be the same as those of Parties which are not Federal States,

(b) With respect to those Articles of this Convention that come within the legislative jurisdiction of constituent States, provinces or cantons which are not, under the constitutional system of the federation, bound to take legislative action, the Federal Government shall bring such Articles with a favourable recommendation to the notice of the appropriate authorities of States, provinces or cantons at the earliest possible moment.

(c) A Federal State Party to this Convention shall, at the request of any other Contracting State transmitted through the Secretary-General of the United Nations, supply a statement of the law and practice of the Federation and its constituent units in regard to any particular provision of the Convention showing the extent to which effect has been given to that provision by legislative or other action.

Article 42

Reservations

1. At the time of signature, ratification or accession, any State may make reservations to articles of the Convention other than to Articles 1, 3, 4, 16 (1), 33, 36-46 inclusive.

2. Any State making a reservation in accordance with paragraph 1 of this article may at any time withdraw the reservation by a communication to that effect addressed to the Secretary-General of the United Nations.

Article 43

Entry into force

1. This Convention shall come into force on the ninetieth day following the day of deposit of the sixth instrument of ratification or accession.

2. For each State ratifying or acceding to the Convention after the deposit of the sixth instrument of ratification or accession, the Convention shall enter into force on the ninetieth day following the date of deposit by such State of its instrument of ratification or accession.

Article 44

Denunciation

1. Any Contracting State may denounce this Convention at any time by a notification addressed to the Secretary-General of the United Nations.

2. Such denunciation shall take effect for the Contracting State concerned one year from the date upon which it is received by the Secretary-General of the United Nations.

3. Any State which has made a declaration or notification under Article 40 may, at any time thereafter, by a notification to the Secretary-General of the United Nations, declare that the Convention shall cease to extend to such territory one year after the date of receipt of the notification by the Secretary-General.

Article 45

Revision

1. Any Contracting State may request revision of this Convention at any time by a notification addressed to the Secretary-General of the United Nations.

2. The General Assembly of the United Nations shall recommend the steps, if any, to be taken in respect of such request.

Article 46

Notifications by the Secretary-General of the United Nations

The Secretary-General of the United Nations shall inform all Members of the United Nations and non-member States referred to in Article 39:

(a) of declarations and notifications in accordance with Section B of Article 1;

(b) of signatures, ratifications and accessions in accordance with Article 39;

(c) of declarations and notifications in accordance with Article 40;

(d) of reservations and withdrawals in accordance with Article 42;

(e) of the date on which this Convention will come into force in accordance with Article 43;

(f) of denunciations and notifications in accordance with Article 44;

(g) of requests for revision in accordance with Article 45.

IN FAITH WHEREOF the undersigned, duly authorized, have signed this Convention on behalf of their respective Governments,

DONE at Geneva, this twenty-eighth day of July, one thousand nine hundred and fifty-one, in a single copy, of which the English and French texts are equally authentic and which shall remain deposited in the archives of the United Nations, and certified true copies of which shall be delivered to all Members of the United Nations and to the non-member States referred to in Article 39.

26.

Convention on the Political Rights of Women

Annex to GA Res. 640 (VII) of 20 December 1952. The Convention was opened for signature in New York on 31 March 1953 and entered into force on 7 July 1954. 193 *U.N.T.S.*, pp. 135 *et seq.*, *G.A.O.R.*, 7th Session, Suppl. No. 20, (A/2361), p. 27.

The General Assembly,

Considering that the peoples of the United Nations are determined to promote equality of rights of men and women, in conformity with the principles embodied in the Charter;

Believing that an international convention on the political rights of women will constitute an important step towards the universal attainment of equal rights of men and women;

Reaffirming its resolution 56 (I) of 11 December 1946;

Decides to open the attached Convention for signature and ratification at the end of the present session.

ANNEX

CONVENTION ON THE POLITICAL RIGHTS OF WOMEN

The Contracting Parties,

Desiring to implement the principle of equality of rights for men and women contained in the Charter of the United Nations,

Recognizing that everyone has the right to take part in the government of his country directly or through freely chosen representatives, and has the right to equal access to public service in his country, and desiring to equalize the status of men and women in the enjoyment and exercise of political rights, in accordance with the provisions of the Charter of the United Nations and of the Universal Declaration of Human Rights,

Having resolved to conclude a Convention for this purpose,

Hereby agree as hereinafter provided:

Article I

Women shall be entitled to vote in all elections on equal terms with men, without any discrimination.

Article 2

Women shall be eligible for election to all publicly elected bodies, established by national law, on equal terms with men, without any discrimination.

Article 3

Women shall be entitled to hold public office and to exercise all public functions, established by national law, on equal terms with men, without any discrimination.

Article 4

1. This Convention shall be open for signature on behalf of any Member of the United Nations and also on behalf of any other State to which an invitation has been addressed by the General Assembly.

2. This Convention shall be ratified and the instruments of ratification shall be deposited with the Secretary-General of the United Nations.

Article 5

1. This Convention shall be open for accession to all States referred to in paragraph 1 of article 4.

2. Accession shall be effected by the deposit of an instrument of accession with the Secretary-General of the United Nations.

Article 6

1. This Convention shall come into force on the ninetieth day following the date of deposit of the sixth instrument of ratification or accession.

2. For each State ratifying or acceding to the Convention after the deposit of the sixth instrument of ratification or accession the Convention shall enter into force on the ninetieth day after deposit by such State of its instrument of ratification or accession.

Article 7

In the event that any State submits a reservation to any of the articles of this Convention at the time of signature, ratification or accession, the Secretary-General shall communicate the text of the reservation to all States which are or may become parties to this Convention. Any State which objects to the reservation may, within a period of ninety days from the date of the said communication (or upon the date of its becoming a party to the Convention), notify the Secretary-General that it does not accept it. In such case, the Convention shall not enter into force as between such State and the State making the reservation.

Article 8

1. Any State may denounce this Convention by written notification to the Secretary-General of the United Nations. Denunciation shall take effect one year after the date of receipt of the notification by the Secretary-General.

2. This Convention shall cease to be in force as from the date when the denunciation which reduces the number of parties to less than six becomes effective.

Article 9

Any dispute which may arise between any two or more Contracting States concerning the interpretation or application of this Convention, which is not settled by negotiation, shall at the request of any one of the parties to the dispute be referred to the International Court of Justice for decision, unless they agree to another mode of settlement.

Article 10

The Secretary-General of the United Nations shall notify all Members of the United Nations and the non-member States contemplated in paragraph 1 of article 4 of this Convention of the following:
- *a.* Signatures and instruments of ratifications received in accordance with article 4;
- *b.* Instruments of accession received in accordance with article 5;
- *c.* The date upon which this Convention enters into force in accordance with article 6;
- *d.* Communications and notifications received in accordance with article 7;
- *e.* Notifications of denunciation received in accordance with paragraph 1 of article 8;
- *f.* Abrogation in accordance with paragraph 2 of article 8.

Article 11

1. This Convention, of which the Chinese, English, French, Russian and Spanish texts shall be equally authentic, shall be deposited in the archives of the United Nations.

2. The Secretary-General of the United Nations shall transmit a certified copy to all Members of the United Nations and to the non-member States contemplated in paragraph 1 of article 4.

27.

CONVENTION ON CONSENT TO MARRIAGE, MINIMUM AGE FOR MARRIAGE AND REGISTRATION OF MARRIAGES

Opened for signature and ratification by General Assembly resolution 1763 A (XVII) of 7 November 1962; Entry into force: 9 December 1964, in accordance with article 6.

The Contracting States,

Desiring, in conformity with the Charter of the United Nations, to promote universal respect for, and observance of, human rights and fundamental freedoms for all, without distinction as to race, sex, language or religion,

Recalling that article 16 of the Universal Declaration of Human Rights states that:

'(1) Men and women of full age, without any limitation due to race, nationality or religion, have the right to marry and to found a family. They are entitled to equal rights as to marriage, during marriage and at its dissolution.'

'(2) Marriage shall be entered into only with the free and full consent of the intending spouses.',

Recalling further that the General Assembly of the United Nations declared, by resolution 843 (IX) of 17 December 1954, that certain customs, ancient laws and practices relating to marriage and the family were inconsistent with the principles set forth in the Charter of the United Nations and in the Universal Declaration of Human Rights,

Reaffirming that all States, including those which have or assume responsibility for the administration of Non-Self-Governing and Trust Territories until their achievement of independence, should take all appropriate measures with a view to abolishing such customs, ancient laws and practices by ensuring, *inter alia,* complete freedom in the choice of a spouse, eliminating completely child marriages and the betrothal of young girls before the age of puberty, establishing appropriate penalties where necessary and establishing a civil or other register in which all marriages will be recorded,

Hereby agree as hereinafter provided:

Article 1

1. No marriage shall be legally entered into without the full and free consent of both parties, such consent to be expressed by them in person after due publicity and in the presence of the authority competent to solemnize the marriage and of witnesses, as prescribed by law.

2. Notwithstanding anything in paragraph 1 above, it shall not be necessary for one of the parties to be present when the competent authority is satisfied that the circumstances are exceptional and that the party has, before a competent authority and in such manner as may be prescribed by law, expressed and not withdrawn consent.

Article 2

States parties to the present Convention shall take legislative action to specify a minimum age for marriage. No marriage shall be legally entered into by any person under this age, except where a competent authority has granted a dispensation as to age, for serious reasons, in the interest of the intending spouses.

Article 3

All marriages shall be registered in an appropriate official register by the competent authority.

Article 4

1. The present Convention shall, until 31 December 1963, be open for signature on behalf of all States Members of the United Nations or members of any of the specialized agencies, and of any other State invited by the General Assembly of the United Nations to become a party to the Convention.

2. The present Convention is subject to ratification. The instruments of ratification shall be deposited with the Secretary-General of the United Nations.

Article 5

1. The present Convention shall be open for accession to all States referred to in article 4, paragraph 1.

2. Accession shall be effected by the deposit of an instrument of accession with the Secretary-General of the United Nations.

Article 6

1. The present Convention shall come into force on the ninetieth day following the date of deposit of the eighth instrument of ratification or accession.
2. For each State ratifying or acceding to the Convention after the deposit of the eighth instrument of ratification or accession, the Convention shall enter into force on the ninetieth day after deposit by such State of its instrument of ratification or accession.

Article 7

1. Any Contracting State may denounce the present Convention by written notification to the Secretary-General of the United Nations. Denunciation shall take effect one year after the date of receipt of the notification by the Secretary-General.
2. The present Convention shall cease to be in force as from the date when the denunciation which reduces the number of parties to less than eight becomes effective.

Article 8

Any dispute which may arise between any two or more Contracting States concerning the interpretation or application of the present Convention which is not settled by negotiation shall, at the request of all the parties to the dispute, be referred to the International Court of Justice for decision, unless the parties agree to another mode of settlement.

Article 9

The Secretary-General of the United Nations shall notify all States Members of the United Nations and the non-member States contemplated in article 4, paragraph 1, of the present Convention of the following:
(a) Signatures and instruments of ratification received in accordance with article 4;
(b) Instruments of accession received in accordance with article 5;
(c) The date upon which the Convention enters into force in accordance with article 6;
(d) Notifications of denunciation received in accordance with article 7, paragraph 1;
(e) Abrogation in accordance with article 7, paragraph 2.

Article 10

1. The present Convention, of which the Chinese, English French, Russian and Spanish texts shall be equally authentic, shall be deposited in the archives of the United Nations.

2. The Secretary-General of the United Nations shall transmit a certified copy of the Convention to all States Members of the United Nations and to the non-member States contemplated in article 4, paragraph 1.

28.

International Convention on the Elimination of all Forms of Racial Discrimination

The International Convention on the Elimination of All Forms of Racial Discrimination was adopted by the General Assembly on 21 December 1965 and came into force on 4 January 1969. As at 31 December 1985, 131 States and Namibia (the United Nations Council for Namibia) had ratified or acceded to it.

The Convention set up the Committee on the Elimination of Racial Discrimination, composed of 18 experts, to review reports submitted by States parties to the Convention on measures they have taken to implement it, and to make general recommendations.

Article 14, paragraph 1, of the Convention provides that a State party may at any time declare that it recognizes the competence of the Committee on the Elimination of Racial Discrimination to receive and consider communications from individuals or groups of individuals within its jurisdiction claiming to be victims of a violation by the State party of any of the rights set forth in the Convention.

The coming into force of Article 14 on 3 December 1982 – when the tenth of the required 10 States parties to the Convention had made the declaration – enables individuals or groups of individuals to petition and state their grievances before an international organ, with the approval of the concerned State party to the Convention.

The States Parties to this Convention,

Considering that the Charter of the United Nations is based on the principles of the dignity and equality inherent in all human beings, and that all Member States have pledged themselves to take joint and separate action, in co-operation with the Organization, for the achievement of one of the purposes of the United Nations which is to promote and encourage universal respect for and observance of human rights and fundamental freedoms for all, without distinction as to race, sex, language or religion,

Considering that the Universal Declaration of Human Rights proclaims that all human beings are born free and equal in dignity and rights and that everyone is entitled to all the rights and freedoms set out therein, without distinction of any kind, in particular as to race, colour or national origin,

Considering that all human beings are equal before the law and are entitled to equal protection of the law against any discrimination and against any incitement to discrimination,

Considering that the United Nations has condemned colonialism and all practices of segregation and discrimination associated therewith, in whatever form and wherever they exist, and that the Declaration on the Granting of Independence to Colonial Countries and Peoples of 14 December 1960 (General Assembly resolution 1514 (XV)) has affirmed and solemnly proclaimed the necessity of bringing them to a speedy and unconditional end,

Considering that the United Nations Declaration on the Elimination of All Forms of Racial Discrimination of 20 November 1963 (General Assembly resolution 1904 (XVIII)) solemnly affirms the necessity of speedily eliminating racial discrimination throughout the world in all its forms and manifestations and of securing understanding of and respect for the dignity of the human person,

Convinced that any doctrine of superiority based on racial differentiation is scientifically false, morally condemnable, socially unjust and dangerous, and that there is no justification for racial discrimination, in theory or in practice, anywhere,

Reaffirming that discrimination between human beings on the grounds of race, colour or ethnic origin is an obstacle to friendly and peaceful relations among nations and is capable of disturbing peace and security among peoples and the harmony of persons living side by side even within one and the same State,

Convinced that the existence of racial barriers is repugnant to the ideals of any human society,

Alarmed by manifestations of racial discrimination still in evidence in some areas of the world and by governmental policies based on racial superiority or hatred, such as policies of *apartheid*, segregation or separation,

Resolved to adopt all necessary measures for speedily eliminating racial discrimination in all its forms and manifestations, and to prevent and combat racist doctrines and practices in order to promote understanding between races and to build an international community free from all forms of racial segregation and racial discrimination,

Bearing in mind the Convention concerning Discrimination in respect of Employment and Occupation adopted by the International Labour Organisation in 1958, and the Convention against Discrimination in Education adopted by the United Nations Educational, Scientific and Cultural Organization in 1960,

Desiring to implement the principles embodied in the United Nations Declaration on the Elimination of All Forms of Racial Discrimination and to secure the earliest adoption of practical measures to that end,

Have agreed as follows:

Part I

Art. 1. 1. In this Convention, the term "racial discrimination" shall mean any distinction, exclusion, restriction or preference based on race, colour, descent, or national or ethnic origin which has the purpose or effect of nullifying or impairing the recognition, enjoyment or exercise, on an equal footing, of human rights and fundamental freedoms in the political, economic, social, cultural or any other field of public life.

2. This Convention shall not apply to distinctions, exclusions, restrictions or preferences made by a State Party to this Convention between citizens and non-citizens.

3. Nothing in this Convention may be interpreted as affecting in any way the legal provisions of States Parties concerning nationality, citizenship or naturalization, provided that such provisions do not discriminate against any particular nationality.

4. Special measures taken for the sole purpose of securing adequate advancement of certain racial or ethnic groups or individuals requiring such protection as may be necessary in order to ensure such groups or individuals equal enjoyment or exercise of human rights and fundamental freedoms shall not be deemed racial discrimination, provided, however, that such measures do not, as a consequence, lead to the maintenance of separate rights for different racial groups and that they shall not be continued after the objectives for which they were taken have been achieved.

Art. 2. 1. States Parties condemn racial discrimination and undertake to pursue by all appropriate means and without delay a policy of eliminating racial discrimination in all its forms and promoting understanding among all races, and, to this end:

(*a*) Each State Party undertakes to engage in no act or practice of racial discrimination against persons, groups of persons or institutions and to ensure that all public authorities and public institutions, national and local, shall act in conformity with this obligation;

(*b*) Each State Party undertakes not to sponsor, defend or support racial discrimination by any persons or organizations;

(*c*) Each State Party shall take effective measures to review governmental, national and local policies, and to amend, rescind or nullify any laws and regulations which have the effect of creating or perpetuating racial discrimination wherever it exists;

(*d*) Each State Party shall prohibit and bring to an end, by all appropriate means, including legislation as required by circumstances, racial discrimination by any persons, group or organization;

(*e*) Each State Party undertakes to encourage, where appropriate, integrationist multi-racial organizations and movements and other means of eliminating barriers between races, and to discourage anything which tends to strengthen racial division.

2. States Parties shall, when the circumstances so warrant, take, in the social, economic, cultural and other fields, special and concrete measures to ensure the adequate development and protection of certain racial groups or individuals belonging to them, for the purpose of guaranteeing them the full and equal enjoyment of human rights and fundamental freedoms. These measures shall in no case entail as a consequence the maintenance of unequal or separate rights for different racial groups after the objectives for which they were taken have been achieved.

Art. 3. States Parties particularly condemn racial segregation and *apartheid* and undertake to prevent, prohibit and eradicate all practices of this nature in territories under their jurisdiction.

Art. 4. States Parties condemn all propaganda and all organizations which are based on ideas or theories of superiority of one race or group of persons of one colour or ethnic origin, or which attempt to justify or promote racial hatred and discrimination in any form, and undertake to adopt immediate and positive measures designed to eradicate all incitement to, or acts of, such discrimination and, to this end, with due regard to the principles embodied in the Universal Declaration of Human Rights and the rights expressly set forth in article 5 of this Convention, *inter alia:*

(*a*) Shall declare an offence punishable by law all dissemination of ideas based on racial superiority or hatred, incitement to racial discrimination, as well as all acts of violence or incitement to such acts against any race or group of persons of another colour or ethnic origin, and also the provision of any assistance to racist activities, including the financing thereof;

(*b*) Shall declare illegal and prohibit organizations, and also organized and all other propaganda activities, which promote and incite racial discrimination, and shall recognize participation in such organizations or activities as an offence punishable by law;

(*c*) Shall not permit public authorities or public institutions, national or local, to promote or incite racial discrimination.

Art. 5. In compliance with the fundamental obligations laid down in article 2 of this Convention, States Parties undertake to prohibit and to eliminate racial discrimination in all its forms and to guarantee the right of everyone, without distinction as to race, colour, or national or ethnic origin, to equality before the law, notably in the enjoyment of the following rights:

(*a*) The right to equal treatment before the tribunals and all other organs administering justice;

(*b*) The right to security of person and protection by the State against violence or bodily harm, whether inflicted by government officials or by any individual, group or institution;

(c) Political rights, in particular the rights to participate in elections—to vote and to stand for election—on the basis of universal and equal suffrage, to take part in the Government as well as in the conduct of public affairs at any level and to have equal access to public service;
(d) Other civil rights, in particular:
(i) The right to freedom of movement and residence within the border of the State;
(ii) The right to leave any country, including one's own, and to return to one's country;
(iii) The right to nationality;
(iv) The right to marriage and choice of spouse;
(v) The right to own property alone as well as in association with others;
(vi) The right to inherit;
(vii) The right to freedom of thought, conscience and religion;
(viii) The right to freedom of opinion and expression;
(ix) The right to freedom of peaceful assembly and association;
(e) Economic, social and cultural rights, in particular:
(i) The rights to work, to free choice of employment, to just and favourable conditions of work, to protection against unemployment, to equal pay for equal work, to just and favourable remuneration;
(ii) The right to form and join trade unions;
(iii) The right to housing;
(iv) The right to public health, medical care, social security and social services;
(v) The right to education and training;
(vi) The right to equal participation in cultural activities;
(f) The right of access to any place or service intended for use by the general public, such as transport, hotels, restaurants, cafés, theatres and parks.

Art. 6. States Parties shall assure to everyone within their jurisdiction effective protection and remedies, through the competent national tribunals and other State institutions, against any acts of racial discrimination which violate his human rights and fundamental freedoms contrary to this Convention, as well as the right to seek from such tribunals just and adequate reparation or satisfaction for any damage suffered as a result of such discrimination.

Art. 7. States Parties undertake to adopt immediate and effective measures, particularly in the fields of teaching, education, culture and information, with a view to combating prejudices which lead to racial discrimination and to promoting understanding, tolerance and friendship among nations and racial or ethnical groups, as well as to propagating the purposes and principles of the Charter of the United Nations, the Universal Declaration of Human Rights, the United Nations Declaration on the Elimination of All Forms of Racial Discrimination, and this Convention.

Part II

Art. 8. 1. There shall be established a Committee on the Elimination of Racial Discrimination (hereinafter referred to as the Committee) consisting of eighteen experts of high moral standing and acknowledged impartiality elected by States Parties from among their nationals, who shall serve in their personal capacity, consideration being given to equitable geographical distribution and to the representation of the different forms of civilization as well as of the principal legal systems.
2. The members of the Committee shall be elected by secret ballot from a list of persons nominated by the States Parties. Each State Party may nominate one person from among its own nationals.
3. The initial election shall be held six months after the date of the entry into force of this Convention. At least three months before the date of each election the Secretary-General of the United Nations shall address a letter to the States Parties inviting them to submit their nominations within two months. The Secretary-General shall prepare a list in alphabetical order of all persons thus nominated, indicating the States Parties which have nominated them, and shall submit it to the States Parties.

4. Elections of the members of the Committee shall be held at a meeting of States Parties convened by the Secretary-General at United Nations Headquarters. At that meeting, for which two-thirds of the States Parties shall constitute a quorum, the persons elected to the Committee shall be those nominees who obtain the largest number of votes and an absolute majority of the votes of the representatives of States Parties present and voting.

5. (a) The members of the Committee shall be elected for a term of four years. However, the terms of nine of the members elected at the first election shall expire at the end of two years; immediately after the first election the names of these nine members shall be chosen by lot by the Chairman of the Committee.

(b) For the filling of casual vacancies, the State Party whose expert has ceased to function as a member of the Committee shall appoint another expert from among its nationals, subject to the approval of the Committee.

6. States Parties shall be responsible for the expenses of the members of the Committee while they are in performance of Committee duties.

Art. 9. 1. States Parties undertake to submit to the Secretary-General of the United Nations, for consideration by the Committee, a report on the legislative, judicial, administrative or other measures which they have adopted and which give effect to the provisions of this Convention: (a) within one year after the entry into force of the Convention for the State concerned; and (b) thereafter every two years and whenever the Committee so requests. The Committee may request further information from the States Parties.

2. The Committee shall report annually, through the Secretary-General, to the General Assembly of the United Nations on its activities and may make suggestions and general recommendations based on the examination of the reports and information received from the States Parties. Such suggestions and general recommendations shall be reported to the General Assembly together with comments, if any, from States Parties.

Art. 10. 1. The Committee shall adopt its own rules of procedure.

2. The Committee shall elect its officers for a term of two years.

3. The secretariat of the Committee shall be provided by the Secretary-General of the United Nations.

4. The meetings of the Committee shall normally be held at United Nations Headquarters.

Para. 1. Provisional rules of procedure were adopted by the Committee at its First and Second Sessions (in 1970), and amended in 1971, 1972 and 1973.

Art. 11. 1. If a State Party considers that another State Party is not giving effect to the provisions of this Convention, it may bring the matter to the attention of the Committee. The Committee shall then transmit the communication to the State Party concerned. Within three months, the receiving State shall submit to the Committee written explanations or statements clarifying the matter and the remedy, if any, that may have been taken by that State.

2. If the matter is not adjusted to the satisfaction of both parties, either by bilateral negotiations or by any other procedure open to them, within six months after the receipt by the receiving State of the initial communication, either State shall have the right to refer the matter again to the Committee by notifying the Committee and also the other State.

3. The Committee shall deal with a matter referred to it in accordance with paragraph 2 of this article after it has ascertained that all available domestic remedies have been invoked and exhausted in the case, in conformity with the generally recognized principles of international law. This shall not be the rule where the application of the remedies is unreasonably prolonged.

4. In any matter referred to it, the Committee may call upon the States Parties concerned to supply any other relevant information.

5. When any matter arising out of this article is being considered by the Committee, the States Parties concerned shall be entitled to send a representative to take part in the proceedings of the Committee, without voting rights, while the matter is under consideration.

Art. 12. 1. (*a*) After the Committee has obtained and collated all the information it deems necessary, the Chairman shall appoint an *ad hoc* Conciliation Commission (hereinafter referred to as the Commission) comprising five persons who may or may not be members of the Committee. The members of the Commission shall be appointed with the unanimous consent of the parties to the dispute, and its good offices shall be made available to the States concerned with a view to an amicable solution of the matter on the basis of respect for this Convention.

(*b*) If the States Parties to the dispute fail to reach agreement within three months on all or part of the composition of the Commission, the members of the Commission not agreed upon by the States parties to the dispute shall be elected by secret ballot by a two-thirds majority vote of the Committee from among its own members.

2. The members of the Commission shall serve in their personal capacity. They shall not be nationals of the States parties to the dispute or of a State not Party to this Convention.

3. The Commission shall elect its own Chairman and adopt its own rules of procedure.

4. The meetings of the Commission shall normally be held at United Nations Headquarters or at any other convenient place as determined by the Commission.

5. The secretariat provided in accordance with article 10, paragraph 3, of this Convention shall also service the Commission whenever a dispute among States Parties brings the Commission into being.

6. The States Parties to the dispute shall share equally all the expenses of the members of the Commission in accordance with estimates to be provided by the Secretary-General of the United Nations.

7. The Secretary-General shall be empowered to pay the expenses of the members of the Commission, if necessary, before reimbursement by the States parties to the dispute in accordance with paragraph 6 of this article.

8. The information obtained and collated by the Committee shall be made available to the Commission, and the Commission may call upon the States concerned to supply any other relevant information.

Art. 13. 1. When the Commission has fully considered the matter, it shall prepare and submit to the Chairman of the Committee a report embodying its findings on all questions of fact relevant to the issue between the parties and containing such recommendations as it may think proper for the amicable solution of the dispute.

2. The Chairman of the Committee shall communicate the report of the Commission to each of the States Parties to the dispute. These States shall, within three months, inform the Chairman of the Committee whether or not they accept the recommendations contained in the report of the Commission.

3. After the period provided for in paragraph 2 of this article, the Chairman of the Committee shall communicate the report of the Commission and the declarations of the States Parties concerned to the other States Parties to this Convention.

Art. 14. 1. A State Party may at any time declare that it recognizes the competence of the Committee to receive and consider communications from individuals or groups of individuals within its jurisdiction claiming to be victims of a violation by that State Party of any of the rights set forth in this Convention. No communication shall be received by the Committee if it concerns a State Party which has not made such a declaration.

2. Any State Party which makes a declaration as provided for in paragraph 1 of this article may establish or indicate a body within its national legal order which shall be competent to receive and consider petitions from individuals and groups of individuals within its jurisdiction who claim to be victims of a violation of any of the rights set forth in this Convention and who have exhausted other available local remedies.

3. A declaration made in accordance with paragraph 1 of this article and the name of any body established or indicated in accordance with paragraph 2 of this article shall be deposited by the State Party concerned with the Secretary-General of the United Nations, who shall transmit copies thereof to the

other States Parties. A declaration may be withdrawn at any time by notification to the Secretary-General, but such a withdrawal shall not affect communications pending before the Committee.

4. A register of petitions shall be kept by the body established or indicated in accordance with paragraph 2 of this article, and certified copies of the register shall be filed annually through appropriate channels with the Secretary-General on the understanding that the contents shall not be publicly disclosed.

5. In the event of failure to obtain satisfaction from the body established or indicated in accordance with paragraph 2 of this article, the petitioner shall have the right to communicate the matter to the Committee within six months.

6. (a) The Committee shall confidentially bring any communication referred to it to the attention of the State Party alleged to be violating any provision of this Convention, but the identity of the individual or groups of individuals concerned shall not be revealed without his or their express consent. The Committee shall not receive anonymous communications.

(b) Within three months, the receiving State shall submit to the Committee written explanations or statements clarifying the matter and the remedy, if any, that may have been taken by that State.

7. (a) The Committee shall consider communications in the light of all information made available to it by the State Party concerned and by the petitioner. The Committee shall not consider any communication from a petitioner unless it has ascertained that the petitioner has exhausted all available domestic remedies. However, this shall not be the rule where the application of the remedies is unreasonably prolonged.

(b) The Committee shall forward its suggestions and recommendations, if any, to the State Party concerned and to the petitioner.

8. The Committee shall include in its annual report a summary of such communications and, where appropriate, a summary of the explanations and statements of the States Parties concerned and of its own suggestions and recommendations.

9. The Committee shall be competent to exercise the functions provided for in this article only when at least ten States Parties to this Convention are bound by declarations in accordance with paragraph 1 of this article.

> Para. 9. Only six States have made declarations in accordance with para. 1: Costa Rica, Ecuador, the Netherlands, Norway, Sweden and Uruguay.

Art. 15. 1. Pending the achievement of the objectives of the Declaration on the Granting of Independence to Colonial Countries and Peoples, contained in General Assembly resolution 1514 (XV) of 14 December 1960, the provisions of this Convention shall in no way limit the right of petition granted to these peoples by other international instruments or by the United Nations and its specialized agencies.

2. (a) The Committee established under article 8, paragraph 1, of this Convention shall receive copies of the petitions from, and submit expressions of opinion and recommendations on these petitions to, the bodies of the United Nations which deal with matters directly related to the principles and objectives of this Convention in their consideration of petitions from the inhabitants of Trust and Non-Self-Governing Territories and all other territories to which General Assembly resolution 1514 (XV) applies, relating to matters covered by this Convention which are before these bodies.

(b) The Committee shall receive from the competent bodies of the United Nations copies of the reports concerning the legislative, judicial, administrative or other measures directly related to the principles and objectives of this Convention applied by the administering Powers within the Territories mentioned in sub-paragraph (a) of this paragraph, and shall express opinions and make recommendations to these bodies.

3. The Committee shall include in its report to the General Assembly a summary of the petitions and reports it has received from United Nations bodies, and the expressions of opinion and recommendations of the Committee relating to the said petitions and reports.

4. The Committee shall request from the Secretary-General of the United

Nations all information relevant to the objectives of this Convention and available to him regarding the Territories mentioned in paragraph 2(*a*) of this article.

Art. 16. The provisions of this Convention concerning the settlement of disputes or complaints shall be applied without prejudice to other procedures for settling disputes or complaints in the field of discrimination laid down in the constituent instruments of, or in conventions adopted by, the United Nations and its specialized agencies, and shall not prevent the States Parties from having recourse to other procedures for settling a dispute in accordance with general or special international agreements in force between them.

Part III

Art. 17. 1. This Convention is open for signature by any State Member of the United Nations or member of any of its specialized agencies, by any State Party to the Statute of the International Court of Justice, and by any other State which has been invited by the General Assembly of the United Nations to become a Party to this Convention.

2. This Convention is subject to ratification. Instruments of ratification shall be deposited with the Secretary-General of the United Nations.

Art. 18. 1. This Convention shall be open to accession by any State referred to in article 17, paragraph 1, of the Convention.

2. Accession shall be effected by the deposit of an instrument of accession with the Secretary-General of the United Nations.

Art. 19. 1. This Convention shall enter into force on the thirtieth day after the date of the deposit with the Secretary-General of the United Nations of the twenty-seventh instrument of ratification or instrument of accession.

2. For each State ratifying this Convention or acceding to it after the deposit of the twenty-seventh instrument of ratification or instrument of accession, the Convention shall enter into force on the thirtieth day after the date of the deposit of its own instrument of ratification or instrument of accession.

Art. 20. 1. The Secretary-General of the United Nations shall receive and circulate to all States which are or may become Parties to this Convention reservations made by States at the time of ratification or accession. Any State which objects to the reservation shall, within a period of ninety days from the date of the said communication, notify the Secretary-General that it does not accept it.

2. A reservation incompatible with the object and purpose of this Convention shall not be permitted, nor shall a reservation the effect of which would inhibit the operation of any of the bodies established by this Convention be allowed. A reservation shall be considered incompatible or inhibitive if at least two-thirds of the States Parties to this Convention object to it.

3. Reservations may be withdrawn at any time by notification to this effect addressed to the Secretary-General. Such notification shall take effect on the date on which it is received.

Art. 21. A State Party may denounce this Convention by written notification to the Secretary-General of the United Nations. Denunciation shall take effect one year after the date of receipt of the notification by the Secretary-General.

Art. 22. Any dispute between two or more States Parties with respect to the interpretation or application of this Convention, which is not settled by negotiation or by the procedures expressly provided for in this Convention, shall, at the request of any of the parties to the dispute, be referred to the International Court of Justice for decision, unless the disputants agree to another mode of settlement.

Art. 23. 1. A request for the revision of this Convention may be made at any time by any State Party by means of a notification in writing addressed to the Secretary-General of the United Nations.

2. The General Assembly of the United Nations shall decide upon the steps, if any, to be taken in respect of such a request.

Art. 24. The Secretary-General of the United Nations shall inform all States referred to in article 17, paragraph 1, of this Convention of the following particulars:
   (a) Signatures, ratifications and accessions under articles 17 and 18;
   (b) The date of entry into force of this Convention under article 19;
   (c) Communications and declarations received under articles 14, 20 and 23;
   (d) Denunciations under article 21.

Art. 25. 1. This Convention, of which the Chinese, English, French, Russian and Spanish texts are equally authentic, shall be deposited in the archives of the United Nations.

2. The Secretary-General of the United Nations shall transmit certified copies of this Convention to all States belonging to any of the categories mentioned in article 17, paragraph 1, of the Convention.

29.

PROTOCOL RELATING TO THE STATUS OF REFUGEES

The Protocol was taken note of with approval by the Economic and Social Council in resolution 1186 (XLI) of 18 November 1966 and was taken note of by the General Assembly in resolution 2198 (XXI) of 16 December 1966. In the same resolution the General Assembly requested the Secretary-General to transmit the text of the Protocol to the States mentioned in article V thereof, with a view to enabling them to accede to the Protocol.

Entry into force: 4 October 1967, in accordance with article VIII.

The States Parties to the present Protocol,

Considering that the Convention relating to the Status of Refugees done at Geneva on 28 July 1951 (hereinafter referred to as the Convention) covers only those persons who have become refugees as a result of events occurring before 1 January 1951,

Considering that new refugee situations have arisen since the Convention was adopted and that the refugees concerned may therefore not fall within the scope of the Convention,

Considering that it is desirable that equal status should be enjoyed by all refugees covered by the definition in the Convention irrespective of the dateline 1 January 1951,

Have agreed as follows:

ARTICLE I
GENERAL PROVISION

1. The States Parties to the present Protocol undertake to apply articles 2 to 34 inclusive of the Convention to refugees as hereinafter defined.

2. For the purpose of the present Protocol, the term 'refugee' shall, except as

regards the application of paragraph 3 of this article, mean any person within the definition of article 1 of the Convention as if the words 'As a result of events occurring before 1 January 1951 and . . .' and the words '. . . as a result of such events', in article 1 A (2) were omitted.

3. The present Protocol shall be applied by the States Parties hereto without any geographic limitation, save that existing declarations made by States already Parties to the Convention in accordance with article 1 B (1) (a) of the Convention, shall, unless extended under article 1 B (2) thereof, apply also under the present Protocol.

ARTICLE II
CO-OPERATION OF THE NATIONAL AUTHORITIES WITH THE UNITED NATIONS

1. The States Parties to the present Protocol undertake to co-operate with the Office of the United Nations High Commissioner for Refugees, or any other agency of the United Nations which may succeed it, in the exercise of its functions, and shall in particular facilitate its duty of supervising the application of the provisions of the present Protocol.

2. In order to enable the Office of the High Commissioner or any other agency of the United Nations which may succeed it, to make reports to the competent organs of the United Nations, the States Parties to the present Protocol undertake to provide them with the information and statistical data requested, in the appropriate form, concerning:
(a) The condition of refugees;
(b) The implementation of the present Protocol;
(c) Laws, regulations and decrees which are, or may hereafter be, in force relating to refugees.

ARTICLE III
INFORMATION ON NATIONAL LEGISLATION

The States Parties to the present Protocol shall communicate to the Secretary-General of the United Nations the laws and regulations which they may adopt to ensure the application of the present Protocol.

ARTICLE IV
SETTLEMENT OF DISPUTES

Any dispute between States Parties to the present Protocol which relates to its interpretation or application and which cannot be settled by other means shall be referred to the International Court of Justice at the request of any one of the parties to the dispute.

ARTICLE V
ACCESSION

The present Protocol shall be open for accession on behalf of all States Parties to the Convention and of any other State Member of the United Nations or member of any of the specialized agencies or to which an invitation to accede may have been addressed by the General Assembly of the United Nations. Accession shall be effected by the deposit of an instrument of accession with the Secretary-General of the United Nations.

ARTICLE VI
FEDERAL CLAUSE

In the case of a Federal or non-unitary State, the following provisions shall apply:
(a) With respect to those articles of the Convention to be applied in accordance with article I, paragraph 1, of the present Protocol that come within the legislative jurisdiction of the federal legislative authority, the obligations of the Federal Government shall to this extent be the same as those of States Parties which are not Federal States;
(b) With respect to those articles of the Convention to be applied in accordance with article I, paragraph 1, of the present Protocol that come within the legislative jurisdiction of constituent states, provinces or cantons which are not, under the constitutional system of the Federation, bound to take legislative action, the Federal Government shall bring such articles with a favourable recommendation to the notice of the appropriate authorities of states, provinces or cantons at the earliest possible moment;
(c) A Federal State Party to the present Protocol shall, at the request of any other State Party hereto transmitted through the Secretary-General of the United Nations, supply a statement of the law and practice of the Federation and its constituent units in regard to any particular provision of the Convention to be applied in accordance with article I, paragraph 1, of the present Protocol, showing the extent to which effect has been given to that provision by legislative or other action.

ARTICLE VII
RESERVATIONS AND DECLARATIONS

1. At the time of accession, any State may make reservations in respect of article IV of the present Protocol and in respect of the application in accordance with article I of the present Protocol of any provisions of the Convention other than those contained in articles 1, 3, 4, 16 (1) and 33 thereof, provided that in the case of a State Party to the Convention reservations made under this article shall not extend to refugees in respect of whom the Convention applies.

2. Reservations made by States Parties to the Convention in accordance with article 42 thereof shall, unless withdrawn, be applicable in relation to their obligations under the present Protocol.

3. Any State making a reservation in accordance with paragraph 1 of this article may at any time withdraw such reservation by a communication to that effect addressed to the Secretary-General of the United Nations.

4. Declarations made under article 40, paragraphs 1 and 2, of the Convention by a State Party thereto which accedes to the present Protocol shall be deemed to apply in respect of the present Protocol, unless upon accession a notification to the contrary is addressed by the State Party concerned to the Secretary-General of the United Nations. The provisions of article 40, paragraphs 2 and 3, and of article 44, paragraph 3, of the Convention shall be deemed to apply *mutatis mutandis* to the present Protocol.

ARTICLE VIII
ENTRY INTO FORCE

1. The present Protocol shall come into force on the day of deposit of the sixth instrument of accession.

2. For each State acceding to the Protocol after the deposit of the sixth instrument of accession, the Protocol shall come into force on the date of deposit by such State of its instrument of accession.

ARTICLE IX
DENUNCIATION

1. Any State Party hereto may denounce this Protocol at any time by a notification addressed to the Secretary-General of the United Nations.

2. Such denunciation shall take effect for the State Party concerned one year from the date on which it is received by the Secretary-General of the United Nations.

ARTICLE X
NOTIFICATIONS BY THE SECRETARY-GENERAL OF THE UNITED NATIONS

The Secretary-General of the United Nations shall inform the States referred to in article V above of the date of entry into force, accessions, reservations and withdrawals of reservations to and denunciations of the present Protocol, and of declarations and notifications relating hereto.

ARTICLE XI
DEPOSIT IN THE ARCHIVES OF THE SECRETARIAT OF THE UNITED NATIONS

A copy of the present Protocol, of which the Chinese, English, French, Russian and Spanish texts are equally authentic, signed by the President of the General Assembly and by the Secretary-General of the United Nations, shall be deposited in the archives of the Secretariat of the United Nations. The Secretary-General will transmit certified copies thereof to all States Members of the United Nations and to the other States referred to in article V above.

30.

Convention on the Elimination of All Forms of Discrimination against Women

Annex to GA Res. 34/180 of 18 December 1979. 34 *G.A.O.R.*, Suppl. No. 46 (A/34/46) pp. 193 *et seq.*. Entered into force on 3 September 1981.

The States Parties to the present Convention,

Noting that the Charter of the United Nations reaffirms faith in fundamental human rights, in the dignity and worth of the human person and in the equal rights of men and women,

Noting that the Universal Declaration of Human Rights affirms the principle of the inadmissibility of discrimination and proclaims that all human beings are born free and equal in dignity and rights and that everyone is entitled to all the rights and freedoms set forth therein, without distinction of any kind, including distinction based on sex,

Noting that States Parties to the International Covenant on Human Rights have the obligation to secure the equal rights of men and women to enjoy all economic, social, cultural, civil and political rights,

Considering the international conventions concluded under the auspices of the United Nations and the specialized agencies promoting equality of rights of men and women,

Noting also the resolutions, declarations and recommendations adopted by the United Nations and the specialized agencies promoting equality of rights of men and women,

Concerned, however, that despite these various instruments extensive discrimination against women continues to exist,

Recalling that discrimination against women violates the principles of equality of rights and respect for human dignity, is an obstacle to the participation of women, on equal terms with men, in the political, social, economic and cultural life of their countries, hampers the growth of the prosperity of society and the family, and makes more difficult the full development of the potentialities of women in the service of their countries and of humanity,

Concerned that in situations of poverty women have the least access to food, health, education, training and opportunities for employment and other needs,

Convinced that the establishment of the new international economic order based on equity and justice will contribute significantly towards the promotion of equality between men and women,

Emphasizing that the eradication of apartheid, of all forms of racism, racial discrimination, colonialism, neo-colonialism, aggression, foreign occupation and domination and interference in the internal affairs of States is essential to the full enjoyment of the rights of men and women,

Affirming that the strengthening of international peace and security, relaxation of international tension, mutual co-operation among all States irrespective of their social and economic systems, general and complete disarmament and in particular nuclear disarmament under strict and effective international control, the affirmation of the principles of justice, equality and mutual benefit in relations among countries, and the realization of the right of peoples under alien and colonial domination and foreign occupation to self-determination and independence as well as respect for national sovereignty and territorial integrity will promote social progress and development and as a consequence will contribute to the attainment of full equality between men and women,

Convinced that the full and complete development of a country, the welfare of the world and the cause of peace require the maximum participation of women on equal terms with men in all fields,

Bearing in mind the great contribution of women to the welfare of the family and to the development of society, so far not fully recognized, the social significance of maternity and the role of both parents in the family and in the upbringing of children, and aware that the role of women in procreation should not be a basis for discrimination but that the upbringing of children requires a sharing of responsibility between men and women and society as a whole,

Aware that a change in the traditional role of men as well as the role of women in society and in the family is needed to achieve full equality between men and women,

Determined to implement the principles set forth in the Declaration on the Elimination of Discrimination against Women and, for that purpose, to adopt the measures required for the elimination of such discrimination in all its forms and manifestations,

Have agreed on the following:

PART I

Article 1

For the purposes of the present Convention, the term "discrimination against women" shall mean any distinction, exclusion or restriction made on the basis of sex which has the effect or purpose of impairing or nullifying the recognition, enjoyment or exercise by women, irrespective of their marital status, on a basis of equality of men and women, of human rights and fundamental freedoms in the political, economic, social, cultural, civil or any other field.

Article 2

States parties condemn discrimination against women in all its forms, agree to pursue, by all appropriate means and without delay, a policy of eliminating discrimination against women and, to this end, undertake:

(a) To embody the principle of the equality of men and women in their national Constitutions or other appropriate legislation if not yet incorporated therein, and to ensure, through law and other appropriate means, the practical realization of this principle;

(b) To adopt appropriate legislative and other measures, including sanctions where appropriate, prohibiting all discrimination against women;

(c) To establish legal protection of the rights of women on an equal basis with men and to ensure through competent national tribunals and other public institutions the effective protection of women against any act of discrimination;

(d) To refrain from engaging in any act or practice of discrimination against women and to ensure that public authorities and institutions shall act in conformity with this obligation;

(e) To take all appropriate measures to eliminate discrimination against women by any person, organization or enterprise;

(f) To take all appropriate measures, including legislation, to modify or abolish existing laws, regulations, customs and practices which constitute discrimination against women;

(g) To repeal all national penal provisions which constitute discrimination against women.

Article 3

States Parties shall take in all fields, in particular in the political, social, economic and cultural fields, all appropriate measures, including legislation, to ensure the full development and advancement of women, for the purpose of guaranteeing them the exercise and enjoyment of human rights and fundamental freedoms on a basis of equality with men.

Article 4

1. Adoption by States Parties of temporary special measures aimed at accelerating de facto equality between men and women shall not be considered discrimination as defined in this Convention, but shall in no way entail, as a consequence, the maintenance of unequal or separate standards; these measures shall be discontinued when the objectives of equality of opportunity and treatment have been achieved.

2. Adoption by States Parties of special measures, including those measures contained in the present Convention, aimed at protecting maternity, shall not be considered discriminatory

Article 5

States Parties shall take all appropriate measures:

(a) To modify the social and cultural patterns of conduct of men and women, with a view to achieving the elimination of prejudices and customary and all other practices which are based on the idea of the inferiority or the superiority of either of the sexes or on stereotyped roles for men and women;

(b) To ensure that family education includes a proper understanding of maternity as a social function and the recognition of the common responsibility of men and women in the upbringing and development of their children, it being understood that the interest of the children is the primordial consideration in all cases.

Article 6

States Parties shall take all appropriate measures, including legislation, to suppress all forms of traffic in women and exploitation of prostitution of women.

PART II

Article 7

States Parties shall take all appropriate measures to eliminate discrimination against women in the political and public life of the country and, in particular, shall ensure, on equal terms with men, the right:

(a) To vote in all elections and public referenda and to be eligible for election to all publicly elected bodies;

(b) To participate in the formulation of government policy and the implementation thereof and to hold public office and perform all public functions at all levels of government;

(c) To participate in non-governmental organizations and associations concerned with the public and political life of the country.

Article 8

States Parties shall take all appropriate measures to ensure to women on equal terms with men, and without any discrimination, the opportunity to represent their Governments at the international level and to participate in the work of international organizations.

Article 9

1. States Parties shall grant women equal rights with men to acquire, change or retain their nationality. They shall ensure in particular that neither marriage to an alien nor change of nationality by the husband during marriage shall automatically change the nationality of the wife, render her stateless or force upon her the nationality of the husband.

2. States Parties shall grant women equal rights with men with respect to the nationality of their children.

PART III

Article 10

States Parties shall take all appropriate measures to eliminate discrimination against women in order to ensure to them equal rights with men in the field of education and in particular to ensure, on a basis of equality of men and women:

(a) The same conditions for career and vocational guidance, for access to studies and for the achievement of diplomas in educational establishments of all categories in rural as well as in urban areas; this equality shall be ensured in pre-school, general, technical, professional and higher technical education, as well as in all types of vocational training;

(b) Access to the same curricula, the same examinations, teaching staff with qualifications of the same standard and school premises and equipment of the same quality;

(c) The elimination of any stereotyped concept of the roles of men and women at all levels and in all forms of education by encouraging coeducation and other types of education which will help to achieve this aim and, in particular, by the revision of textbooks and school programmes and the adaptation of teaching methods;

(d) The same opportunities to benefit from scholarships and other study grants;

(e) The same opportunities for access to programmes of continuing education, including adult and functional literacy programmes, particularly those aimed at reducing, at the earliest possible time, any gap in education existing between men and women;

(f) The reduction of female student drop-out rates and the organization of programmes for girls and women who have left school prematurely;

(g) The same opportunities to participate actively in sports and physical education;

(h) Access to specific educational information to help to ensure the health and well-being of families, including information and advice on family planning.

Article 11

1. States Parties shall take all appropriate measures to eliminate discrimination against women in the field of employment in order to ensure, on a basis of equality of men and women, the same rights, in particular:

(a) The right to work as an inalienable right of all human beings;

(b) The right to the same employment opportunities, including the application of the same criteria for selection in matters of employment;

(c) The right to free choice of profession and employment, the right to promotion, job security and all benefits and conditions of service and the right to receive vocational training and retraining, including apprenticeships, advanced vocational training and recurrent training;

(d) The right to equal remuneration, including benefits, and to equal treatment in respect of work of equal value, as well as equality of treatment in the evaluation of the quality of work;

(e) The right to social security, particularly in cases of retirement, unemployment, sickness, invalidity and old age and other incapacity to work, as well as the right to paid leave;

(f) The right to protection of health and to safety in working conditions, including the safeguarding of the function of reproduction.

2. In order to prevent discrimination against women on the grounds of marriage or maternity and to ensure their effective right to work, States Parties shall take appropriate measures:

(a) To prohibit, subject to the imposition of sanctions, dismissal on the grounds of pregnancy or of maternity leave and discrimination in dismissals on the basis of marital status;

(b) To introduce maternity leave with pay or with comparable social benefits without loss of former employment, seniority or social allowances;

(c) To encourage the provision of the necessary supporting social services to enable parents to combine family obligations with work responsibilities and participation in public life, in particular through promoting the establishment and development of a network of child-care facilities;

(d) To provide special protection to women during pregnancy in types of work proved to be harmful to them.

3. Protective legislation relating to matters covered in this article shall be reviewed periodically in the light of scientific and technological knowledge and shall be revised, repealed or extended as necessary.

Article 12

1. States Parties shall take all appropriate measures to eliminate discrimination against women in the field of health care in order to ensure, on a basis of equality of men and women, access to health care services, including those related to family planning.

2. Notwithstanding the provisions of paragraph 1 above, States Parties shall ensure to women appropriate services in connexion with pregnancy, confinement and the post-natal period, granting free services where necessary, as well as adequate nutrition during pregnancy and lactation.

Article 13

States Parties shall take all appropriate measures to eliminate discrimination against women in other areas of economic and social life in order to ensure, on a basis of equality of men and women, the same rights, in particular:

(a) The right to family benefits;

(b) The right to bank loans, mortgages and other forms of financial credit;

(c) The right to participate in recreational activities, sports and in all aspects of cultural life.

Article 14

1. States Parties shall take into account the particular problems faced by rural women and the significant roles which they play in the economic survival of their families, including their work in the non-monetized sectors of the economy, and shall take all appropriate measures to ensure the application of the provisions of this Convention to women in rural areas.

2. States Parties shall take all appropriate measures to eliminate discrimination against women in rural areas in order to ensure, on a basis of equality of men and women, that they participate in and benefit from rural development and, in particular, shall ensure to such women the right:

(a) To participate in the elaboration and implementation of development planning at all levels;

(b) To have access to adequate health care facilities, including information, counselling and services in family planning;

(c) To benefit directly from social security programmes;

(d) To obtain all types of training and education, formal and non-formal, including that relating to functional literacy, as well as the benefit of all community and extension services, *inter alia*, in order to increase their technical proficiency;

(e) To organize self-help groups and co-operatives in order to obtain equal access to economic opportunities through employment or self-employment;

(f) To participate in all community activities;

(g) To have access to agricultural credit and loans, marketing facilities, appropriate technology and equal treatment in land and agrarian reform as well as in land resettlement schemes;

(h) To enjoy adequate living conditions, particularly in relation to housing, sanitation, electricity and water supply, transport and communications.

PART IV

Article 15

1. States Parties shall accord to women equality with men before the law.

2. States Parties shall accord to women, in civil matters, a legal capacity identical to that of men and the same opportunities to exercise that capacity. They shall in particular give women equal rights to conclude contracts and to administer property and treat them equally in all stages of procedure in courts and tribunals.

3. States Parties agree that all contracts and all other private instruments of any kind with a legal effect which is directed at restricting the legal capacity of women shall be deemed null and void.

4. States Parties shall accord to men and women the same rights with regard to the law relating to the movement of persons and the freedom to choose their residence and domicile.

Article 16

1. States Parties shall take all appropriate measures to eliminate discrimination against women in all matters relating to marriage and family relations and in particular shall ensure, on a basis of equality of men and women:

(a) The same right to enter into marriage;

(b) The same right freely to choose a spouse and to enter into marriage only with their free and full consent;

(c) The same rights and responsibilities during marriage and at its dissolution;

(d) The same rights and responsibilities as parents, irrespective of their marital status, in matters relating to their children. In all cases the interests of the children shall be paramount;

(e) The same rights to decide freely and responsibly on the number and spacing of their children and to have access to the information, education and means to enable them to exercise these rights;

(f) The same rights and responsibilities with regard to guardianship, wardship, trusteeship and adoption of children, or similar institutions where these concepts exist in national legislation. In all cases the interest of the children shall be paramount;

(g) The same personal rights as husband and wife, including the right to choose a family name, a profession and an occupation;

(h) The same rights for both spouses in respect of the ownership, acquisition, management, administration, enjoyment and disposition of property, whether free of charge or for a valuable consideration.

2. The betrothal and the marriage of a child shall have no legal effect and all necessary action, including legislation, shall be taken to specify a minimum age for marriage and to make the registration of marriages in an official registry compulsory.

PART V

Article 17

1. For the purpose of considering the progress made in the implementation of the present Convention, there shall be established a Committee on the Elimination of Discrimination against Women (hereinafter referred to as the Committee) consisting, at the time of entry into force of the Convention, of 18 and, after its ratification or accession by the thirty-fifth State Party, of 23 experts of high moral standing and competence in the field covered by the Convention. The experts shall be elected by States Parties from among their nationals and shall serve in their personal capacity, consideration being given to equitable geographical distribution and to the representation of the different forms of civilization as well as the principal legal systems.

2. The members of the Committee shall be elected by secret ballot from a list of persons nominated by States Parties. Each State Party may nominate one person from among its own nationals.

3. The initial election shall be held six months after the date of the entry into force of the present Convention. At least three months before the date of each election the Secretary-General of the United Nations shall address a letter to the States Parties inviting them to submit their nominations within two months. The Secretary-General shall prepare a list in alphabetical order of all persons thus nominated, indicating the States Parties which have nominated them, and shall submit it to the States Parties.

4. Elections of the members of the Committee shall be held at a meeting of States Parties convened by the Secretary-General at United Nations Headquarters. At that meeting, for which two thirds of the States Parties shall constitute a quorum, the persons elected to the Committee shall be those nominees who obtain the largest number of votes and an absolute majority of the votes of the representatives of States Parties present and voting.

5. The members of the Committee shall be elected for a term of four years. However, the terms of nine of the members elected at the first election shall expire at the end of two years; immediately after the first election the names of these nine members shall be chosen by lot by the Chairman of the Committee.

6. The election of the five additional members of the Committee shall be held in accordance with the provisions of paragraphs 2, 3 and 4 of the present article following the thirty-fifth ratification or accession. The terms of two of the additional members elected on this occasion shall expire at the end of two years, the names of these two members having been chosen by lot by the Chairman of the Committee.

7. For the filling of casual vacancies, the State Party whose expert has ceased to function as a member of the Committee shall appoint another expert from among its nationals, subject to the approval of the Committee.

8. The members of the Committee shall, with the approval of the General Assembly, receive emoluments from United Nations resources on such terms and conditions as the General Assembly may decide, having regard to the importance of the Committee's responsibilities.

9. The Secretary-General of the United Nations shall provide the necessary staff and facilities for the effective performance of the functions of the Committee under the present Convention.

Article 18

1. States Parties undertake to submit to the Secretary-General of the United Nations, for consideration by the Committee, a report on the legislative, judicial, administrative or other measures which they have adopted to give effect to the provisions of the Convention and on the progress made in this respect:

   (a) Within one year after the entry into force for the State concerned;

   (b) Thereafter at least every four years and further whenever the Committee so requests.

2. Reports may indicate factors and difficulties affecting the degree of fulfilment of obligations under the present Convention.

Article 19

1. The Committee shall adopt its own rules of procedure.

2. The Committee shall elect its officers for a term of two years.

Article 20

1. The Committee shall normally meet for a period of not more than two weeks annually in order to consider the reports submitted in accordance with article 18 of the present Convention.

2. The meetings of the Committee shall normally be held at United Nations Headquarters or at any other convenient place as determined by the Committee.

Article 21

1. The Committee shall, through the Economic and Social Council, report annually to the General Assembly on its activities and may make suggestions and general recommendations based on the examination of reports and information received from the States Parties. Such suggestions and general recommendations shall be included in the report of the Committee together with comments, if any, from States Parties.

2. The Secretary-General shall transmit the reports of the Committee to the Commission on the Status of Women for its information.

Article 22

Specialized agencies shall be entitled to be represented at the consideration of the implementation of such provisions of the present Convention as fall within the scope of their activities. The Committee may invite the specialized agencies to submit reports on the implementation of the Convention in areas falling within the scope of their activities.

PART VI

Article 23

Nothing in this Convention shall affect any provisions that are more conducive to the achievement of equality between men and women which may be contained:

(a) In the legislation of a State Party; or

(b) In any other international convention, treaty or agreement in force for that State.

Article 24

States Parties undertake to adopt all necessary measures at the national level aimed at achieving the full realization of the rights recognized in the present Convention.

Article 25

1. The present Convention shall be open for signature by all States.

2. The Secretary-General of the United Nations is designated as the depositary of the present Convention.

3. The present Convention is subject to ratification. Instruments of ratification shall be deposited with the Secretary-General of the United Nations.

4. The present Convention shall be open to accession by all States. Accession shall be effected by the deposit of an instrument of accession with the Secretary-General of the United Nations.

Article 26

1. A request for the revision of the present Convention may be made at any time by any State Party by means of a notification in writing addressed to the Secretary-General of the United Nations.

2. The General Assembly of the United Nations shall decide upon the steps, if any, to be taken in respect of such a request.

Article 27

1. The present Convention shall enter into force on the thirtieth day after the date of deposit with the Secretary-General of the United Nations of the twentieth instrument of ratification or accession.

2. For each State ratifying the present Convention or acceding to it after the deposit of the twentieth instrument of ratification or accession, the Convention shall enter into force on the thirtieth day after the date of the deposit of its own instrument of ratification or accession.

Article 28

1. The Secretary-General of the United Nations shall receive and circulate to all States the text of reservations made by States at the time of ratification or accession.

2. A reservation incompatible with the object and purpose of the present Convention shall not be permitted.

3. Reservations may be withdrawn at any time by notification to this effect addressed to the Secretary-General of the United Nations, who shall then inform all States thereof. Such notification shall take effect on the date on which it is received.

Article 29

1. Any dispute between two or more States Parties concerning the interpretation or application of the present Convention which is not settled by negotiation shall, at the request of one of them, be submitted to arbitration. If within six months from the date of the request for arbitration the parties are unable to agree on the organization of the arbitration, any one of those parties may refer the dispute to the International Court of Justice by request in conformity with the Statute of the Court.

2. Each State Party may at the time of signature or ratification of this Convention or accession thereto declare that it does not consider itself bound by paragraph 1 of this article. The other States Parties shall not be bound by paragraph 1 of this article with respect to any State Party which has made such a reservation.

3. Any State Party which has made a reservation in accordance with paragraph 2 of this article may at any time withdraw that reservation by notification to the Secretary-General of the United Nations.

Article 30

The present Convention, the Arabic, Chinese, English, French, Russian and Spanish texts of which are equally authentic, shall be deposited with the Secretary-General of the United Nations.

IN WITNESS WHEREOF the undersigned, duly authorized, have signed the present Convention.

31.

Convention Against Torture and Other Cruel, Inhuman or Degrading Treatment or Punishment

Annex to GA Res. 39/46 of 10 December 1984.
Approved by consensus on 10 December 1984 and opened for signature on 4 February 1984.
Not yet entered into force.

The States Parties to this Convention,

Considering that, in accordance with the principles proclaimed in the Charter of the United Nations, recognition of the equal and inalienable rights of all members of the human family is the foundation of freedom, justice and peace in the world,

Recognizing that those rights derive from the inherent dignity of the human person,

Considering the obligation of States under the Charter, in particular Article 55, to promote universal respect for, and observance of, human rights and fundamental freedoms,

Having regard to article 5 of the Universal Declaration of Human Rights and article 7 of the International Covenant on Civil and Political Rights, both of which provide that no one shall be subjected to torture or to cruel, inhuman or degrading treatment or punishment,

Having regard also to the Declaration on the Protection of All Persons from Being Subjected to Torture and Other Cruel, Inhuman or Degrading Treatment or Punishment, adopted by the General Assembly on 9 December 1975,

Desiring to make more effective the struggle against torture and other cruel, inhuman or degrading treatment or punishment throughout the world,

Have agreed as follows:

PART I

Article 1

1. For the purposes of this Convention, the term "torture" means any act by which severe pain or suffering, whether physical or mental, is intentionally

inflicted on a person for such purposes as obtaining from him or a third person information or a confession, punishing him for an act he or a third person has committed or is suspected of having committed, or intimidating or coercing him or a third person, or for any reason based on discrimination of any kind, when such pain or suffering is inflicted by or at the instigation of or with the consent or acquiescence of a public official or other person acting in an official capacity. It does not include pain or suffering arising only from, inherent in or incidental to lawful sanctions.

2. This article is without prejudice to any international instrument or national legislation which does or may contain provisions of wider application.

Article 2

1. Each State Party shall take effective legislative, administrative, judicial or other measures to prevent acts of torture in any territory under its jurisdiction.

2. No exceptional circumstances whatsoever, whether a state of war or a threat of war, internal political instability or any other public emergency, may be invoked as a justification of torture.

3. An order from a superior officer or a public authority may not be invoked as a justification of torture.

Article 3

1. No State Party shall expel, return ("refouler") or extradite a person to another State where there are substantial grounds for believing that he would be in danger of being subjected to torture.

2. For the purpose of determining whether there are such grounds, the competent authorities shall take into account all relevant considerations including, where applicable, the existence in the State concerned of a consistent pattern of gross, flagrant or mass violations of human rights.

Article 4

1. Each State Party shall ensure that all acts of torture are offences under its criminal law. The same shall apply to an attempt to commit torture and to an act by any person which constitutes complicity or participation in torture.

2. Each State Party shall make these offences punishable by appropriate penalties which take into account their grave nature.

Article 5

1. Each State Party shall take such measures as may be necessary to establish its jurisdiction over the offences referred to in article 4 in the following cases:

(a) When the offences are committed in any territory under its jurisdiction or on board a ship or aircraft registered in that State;

(b) When the alleged offender is a national of that State;

(c) When the victim is a national of that State if that State considers it appropriate.

2. Each State Party shall likewise take such measures as may be necessary to establish its jurisdiction over such offences in cases where the alleged offender is present in any territory under its jurisdiction and it does not extradite him pursuant to article 8 to any of the States mentioned in paragraph 1 of this article.

3. This Convention does not exclude any criminal jurisdiction exercised in accordance with internal law.

Article 6

1. Upon being satisfied, after an examination of information available to it, that the circumstances so warrant, any State Party in whose territory a person alleged to have committed any offence referred to in article 4 is present shall take him into custody or take other legal measures to ensure his presence. The custody and other legal measures shall be as provided in the law of that State but may be continued only for such time as is necessary to enable any criminal or extradition proceedings to be instituted.

2. Such State shall immediately make a preliminary inquiry into the facts.

3. Any person in custody pursuant to paragraph 1 of this article shall be assisted in communicating immediately with the nearest appropriate representative of the State of which he is a national, or, if he is a stateless person, with the representative of the State where he usually resides.

4. When a State, pursuant to this article, has taken a person into custody, it shall immediately notify the States referred to in article 5, paragraph 1, of the fact that such person is in custody and of the circumstances which warrant his detention. The State which makes the preliminary inquiry contemplated in paragraph 2 of this article shall promptly report its findings to the said States and shall indicate whether it intends to exercise jurisdiction.

Article 7

1. The State Party in the territory under whose jurisdiction a person alleged to have committed any offence referred to in article 4 is found shall in the cases contemplated in article 5, if it does not extradite him, submit the case to its competent authorities for the purpose of prosecution.

2. These authorities shall take their decision in the same manner as in the case of any ordinary offence of a serious nature under the law of that State. In the cases referred to in article 5, paragraph 2, the standards of evidence required for prosecution and conviction shall in no way be less stringent than those which apply in the cases referred to in article 5, paragraph 1.

3. Any person regarding whom proceedings are brought in connection with any of the offences referred to in article 4 shall be guaranteed fair treatment at all stages of the proceedings.

Article 8

1. The offences referred to in article 4 shall be deemed to be included as extraditable offences in any extradition treaty existing between States Parties.

States Parties undertake to include such offences as extraditable offences in every extradition treaty to be concluded between them.

2. If a State Party which makes extradition conditional on the existence of a treaty receives a request for extradition from another State Party with which it has no extradition treaty, it may consider this Convention as the legal basis for extradition in respect of such offences. Extradition shall be subject to the other conditions provided by the law of the requested State.

3. States Parties which do not make extradition conditional on the existence of a treaty shall recognize such offences as extraditable offences between themselves subject to the conditions provided by the law of the requested State.

4. Such offences shall be treated, for the purpose of extradition between States Parties, as if they had been committed not only in the place in which they occurred but also in the territories of the States required to establish their jurisdiction in accordance with article 5, paragraph 1.

Article 9

1. States Parties shall afford one another the greatest measure of assistance in connection with criminal proceedings brought in respect of any of the offences referred to in article 4, including the supply of all evidence at their disposal necessary for the proceedings.

2. States Parties shall carry out their obligations under paragraph 1 of this article in conformity with any treaties on mutual judicial assistance that may exist between them.

Article 10

1. Each State Party shall ensure that education and information regarding the prohibition against torture are fully included in the training of law enforcement personnel, civil or military, medical personnel, public officials and other persons who may be involved in the custody, interrogation or treatment of any individual subjected to any form of arrest, detention or imprisonment.

2. Each State Party shall include this prohibition in the rules or instructions issued in regard to the duties and functions of any such persons.

Article 11

Each State Party shall keep under systematic review interrogation rules, instructions, methods and practices as well as arrangements for the custody and treatment of persons subjected to any form of arrest, detention or imprisonment in any territory under its jurisdiction, with a view to preventing any cases of torture.

Article 12

Each State Party shall ensure that its competent authorities proceed to a prompt and impartial investigation, wherever there is reasonable ground to believe that an act of torture has been committed in any territory under its jurisdiction.

Article 13

Each State Party shall ensure that any individual who alleges he has been subjected to torture in any territory under its jurisdiction has the right to complain to, and to have his case promptly and impartially examined by, its competent authorities. Steps shall be taken to ensure that the complainant and witnesses are protected against all ill-treatment or intimidation as a consequence of his complaint or any evidence given.

Article 14

1. Each State Party shall ensure in its legal system that the victim of an act of torture obtains redress and has an enforceable right to fair and adequate compensation, including the means for as full rehabilitation as possible. In the event of the death of the victim as a result of an act of torture, his dependants shall be entitled to compensation.

2. Nothing in this article shall affect any right of the victim or other persons to compensation which may exist under national law.

Article 15

Each State Party shall ensure that any statement which is established to have been made as a result of torture shall not be invoked as evidence in any proceedings, except against a person accused of torture as evidence that the statement was made.

Article 16

1. Each State Party shall undertake to prevent in any territory under its jurisdiction other acts of cruel, inhuman or degrading treatment or punishment which do not amount to torture as defined in article 1, when such acts are committed by or at the instigation of or with the consent or acquiescence of a public official or other person acting in an official capacity. In particular, the obligations contained in articles 10, 11, 12 and 13 shall apply with the substitution for references to torture of references to other forms of cruel, inhuman or degrading treatment or punishment.

2. The provisions of this Convention are without prejudice to the provisions of any other international instrument or national law which prohibits cruel, inhuman or degrading treatment or punishment or which relates to extradition or expulsion.

PART II

Article 17

1. There shall be established a Committee against Torture (hereinafter referred to as the Committee) which shall carry out the functions hereinafter provided. The Committee shall consist of ten experts of high moral standing and recognized competence in the field of human rights, who shall serve in their personal capacity. The experts shall be elected by the States Parties, consideration being given to equitable geographical distribution and to the usefulness of the participation of some persons having legal experience.

2.   The members of the Committee shall be elected by secret ballot from a list of persons nominated by States Parties. Each State Party may nominate one person from among its own nationals. States Parties shall bear in mind the usefulness of nominating persons who are also members of the Human Rights Committee established under the International Covenant on Civil and Political Rights and who are willing to serve on the Committee against Torture.

3.   Elections of the members of the Committee shall be held at biennial meetings of States Parties convened by the Secretary-General of the United Nations. At those meetings, for which two thirds of the States Parties shall constitute a quorum, the persons elected to the Committee shall be those who obtain the largest number of votes and an absolute majority of the votes of the representatives of States Parties present and voting.

4.   The initial election shall be held no later than six months after the date of the entry into force of this Convention. At least four months before the date of each election, the Secretary-General of the United Nations shall address a letter to the States Parties inviting them to submit their nominations within three months. The Secretary-General shall prepare a list in alphabetical order of all persons thus nominated, indicating the States Parties which have nominated them, and shall submit it to the States Parties.

5.   The members of the Committee shall be elected for a term of four years. They shall be eligible for re-election if renominated. However, the term of five of the members elected at the first election shall expire at the end of two years; immediately after the first election the names of these five members shall be chosen by lot by the chairman of the meeting referred to in paragraph 3 of this article.

6.   If a member of the Committee dies or resigns or for any other cause can no longer perform his Committee duties, the State Party which nominated him shall appoint another expert from among its nationals to serve for the remainder of his term, subject to the approval of the majority of the States Parties. The approval shall be considered given unless half or more of the States Parties respond negatively within six weeks after having been informed by the Secretary-General of the United Nations of the proposed appointment.

7.   States Parties shall be responsible for the expenses of the members of the Committee while they are in performance of Committee duties.

Article 18

1.   The Committee shall elect its officers for a term of two years. They may be re-elected.

2.   The Committee shall establish its own rules of procedure, but these rules shall provide, <u>inter alia</u>, that:

(<u>a</u>) Six members shall constitute a quorum;

(<u>b</u>) Decisions of the Committee shall be made by a majority vote of the members present.

3.   The Secretary-General of the United Nations shall provide the necessary staff and facilities for the effective performance of the functions of the Committee under this Convention.

4.   The Secretary-General of the United Nations shall convene the initial

meeting of the Committee. After its initial meeting, the Committee shall meet at such times as shall be provided in its rules of procedure.

5. The States Parties shall be responsible for expenses incurred in connection with the holding of meetings of the States Parties and of the Committee, including reimbursement to the United Nations for any expenses, such as the cost of staff and facilities, incurred by the United Nations pursuant to paragraph 3 of this article.

Article 19

1. The States Parties shall submit to the Committee, through the Secretary-General of the United Nations, reports on the measures they have taken to give effect to their undertakings under this Convention, within one year after the entry into force of the Convention for the State Party concerned. Thereafter the States Parties shall submit supplementary reports every four years on any new measures taken and such other reports as the Committee may request.

2. The Secretary-General of the United Nations shall transmit the reports to all States Parties.

3. Each report shall be considered by the Committee which may make such general comments on the report as it may consider appropriate and shall forward these to the State Party concerned. That State Party may respond with any observations it chooses to the Committee.

4. The Committee may, at its discretion, decide to include any comments made by it in accordance with paragraph 3 of this article, together with the observations thereon received from the State Party concerned, in its annual report made in accordance with article 24. If so requested by the State Party concerned, the Committee may also include a copy of the report submitted under paragraph 1 of this article.

Article 20

1. If the Committee receives reliable information which appears to it to contain well-founded indications that torture is being systematically practised in the territory of a State Party, the Committee shall invite that State Party to co-operate in the examination of the information and to this end to submit observations with regard to the information concerned.

2. Taking into account any observations which may have been submitted by the State Party concerned, as well as any other relevant information available to it, the Committee may, if it decides that this is warranted, designate one or more of its members to make a confidential inquiry and to report to the Committee urgently.

3. If an inquiry is made in accordance with paragraph 2 of this article, the Committee shall seek the co-operation of the State Party concerned. In agreement with that State Party, such an inquiry may include a visit to its territory.

4. After examining the findings of its member or members submitted in accordance with paragraph 2 of this article, the Committee shall transmit these findings to the State Party concerned together with any comments or suggestions which seem appropriate in view of the situation.

5. All the proceedings of the Committee referred to in paragraphs 1 to 4 of this article shall be confidential, and at all stages of the proceedings the

co-operation of the State Party shall be sought. After such proceedings have been completed with regard to an inquiry made in accordance with paragraph 2, the Committee may, after consultations with the State Party concerned, decide to include a summary account of the results of the proceedings in its annual report made in accordance with article 24.

Article 21

1. A State Party to this Convention may at any time declare under this article that it recognizes the competence of the Committee to receive and consider communications to the effect that a State Party claims that another State Party is not fulfilling its obligations under this Convention. Such communications may be received and considered according to the procedures laid down in this article only if submitted by a State Party which has made a declaration recognizing in regard to itself the competence of the Committee. No communication shall be dealt with by the Committee under this article if it concerns a State Party which has not made such a declaration. Communications received under this article shall be dealt with in accordance with the following procedure:

(a) If a State Party considers that another State Party is not giving effect to the provisions of this Convention, it may, by written communication, bring the matter to the attention of that State Party. Within three months after the receipt of the communication the receiving State shall afford the State which sent the communication an explanation or any other statement in writing clarifying the matter, which should include, to the extent possible and pertinent, reference to domestic procedures and remedies taken, pending or available in the matter;

(b) If the matter is not adjusted to the satisfaction of both States Parties concerned within six months after the receipt by the receiving State of the initial communication, either State shall have the right to refer the matter to the Committee, by notice given to the Committee and to the other State;

(c) The Committee shall deal with a matter referred to it under this article only after it has ascertained that all domestic remedies have been invoked and exhausted in the matter, in conformity with the generally recognized principles of international law. This shall not be the rule where the application of the remedies is unreasonably prolonged or is unlikely to bring effective relief to the person who is the victim of the violation of this Convention;

(d) The Committee shall hold closed meetings when examining communications under this article;

(e) Subject to the provisions of subparagraph (c), the Committee shall make available its good offices to the States Parties concerned with a view to a friendly solution of the matter on the basis of respect for the obligations provided for in this Convention. For this purpose, the Committee may, when appropriate, set up an ad hoc conciliation commission;

(f) In any matter referred to it under this article, the Committee may call upon the States Parties concerned, referred to in subparagraph (b), to supply any relevant information;

(g) The States Parties concerned, referred to in subparagraph (b), shall have the right to be represented when the matter is being considered by the Committee and to make submissions orally and/or in writing;

(h) The Committee shall, within twelve months after the date of receipt of notice under subparagraph (b), submit a report:

(i) If a solution within the terms of subparagraph (e) is reached, the Committee shall confine its report to a brief statement of the facts and of the solution reached;

(ii) If a solution within the terms of subparagraph (e) is not reached, the Committee shall confine its report to a brief statement of the facts; the written submissions and record of the oral submissions made by the States Parties concerned shall be attached to the report.

In every matter, the report shall be communicated to the States Parties concerned.

2. The provisions of this article shall come into force when five States Parties to this Convention have made declarations under paragraph 1 of this article. Such declarations shall be deposited by the States Parties with the Secretary-General of the United Nations, who shall transmit copies thereof to the other States Parties. A declaration may be withdrawn at any time by notification to the Secretary-General. Such a withdrawal shall not prejudice the consideration of any matter which is the subject of a communication already transmitted under this article; no further communication by any State Party shall be received under this article after the notification of withdrawal of the declaration has been received by the Secretary-General, unless the State Party concerned has made a new declaration.

Article 22

1. A State Party to this Convention may at any time declare under this article that it recognizes the competence of the Committee to receive and consider communications from or on behalf of individuals subject to its jurisdiction who claim to be victims of a violation by a State Party of the provisions of the Convention. No communication shall be received by the Committee if it concerns a State Party which has not made such a declaration.

2. The Committee shall consider inadmissible any communication under this article which is anonymous or which it considers to be an abuse of the right of submission of such communications or to be incompatible with the provisions of this Convention.

3. Subject to the provisions of paragraph 2, the Committee shall bring any communications submitted to it under this article to the attention of the State Party to this Convention which has made a declaration under paragraph 1 and is alleged to be violating any provisions of the Convention. Within six months, the receiving State shall submit to the Committee written explanations or statements clarifying the matter and the remedy, if any, that may have been taken by that State.

4. The Committee shall consider communications received under this article in the light of all information made available to it by or on behalf of the individual and by the State Party concerned.

5. The Committee shall not consider any communications from an individual under this article unless it has ascertained that:

(a) The same matter has not been, and is not being, examined under another procedure of international investigation or settlement;

(b) The individual has exhausted all available domestic remedies; this shall not be the rule where the application of the remedies is unreasonably prolonged or is unlikely to bring effective relief to the person who is the victim of the violation of this Convention.

6. The Committee shall hold closed meetings when examining communications under this article.

7. The Committee shall forward its views to the State Party concerned and to the individual.

8. The provisions of this article shall come into force when five States Parties to this Convention have made declarations under paragraph 1 of this article. Such declarations shall be deposited by the States Parties with the Secretary-General of the United Nations, who shall transmit copies thereof to the other States Parties. A declaration may be withdrawn at any time by notification to the Secretary-General. Such a withdrawal shall not prejudice the consideration of any matter which is the subject of a communication already transmitted under this article; no further communication by or on behalf of an individual shall be received under this article after the notification of withdrawal of the declaration has been received by the Secretary-General, unless the State Party has made a new declaration.

Article 23

The members of the Committee and of the <u>ad hoc</u> conciliation commissions which may be appointed under article 21, paragraph 1 (<u>e</u>), shall be entitled to the facilities, privileges and immunities of experts on mission for the United Nations as laid down in the relevant sections of the Convention on the Privileges and Immunities of the United Nations.

For the Convention on the Privileges and Immunities of the United Nations, see GA Res. 22A(I) of 13 February 1946, *I.O.I.*, I.A.3.4.c..

Article 24

The Committee shall submit an annual report on its activities under this Convention to the States Parties and to the General Assembly of the United Nations.

PART III

Article 25

1. This Convention is open for signature by all States.

2. This Convention is subject to ratification. Instruments of ratification shall be deposited with the Secretary-General of the United Nations.

Article 26

This Convention is open to accession by all States. Accession shall be effected by the deposit of an instrument of accession with the Secretary-General of the United Nations.

Article 27

1. This Convention shall enter into force on the thirtieth day after the date of the deposit with the Secretary-General of the United Nations of the twentieth instrument of ratification or accession.

2. For each State ratifying this Convention or acceding to it after the deposit of the twentieth instrument of ratification or accession, the Convention shall enter into force on the thirtieth day after the date of the deposit of its own instrument of ratification or accession.

Article 28

1. Each State may, at the time of signature or ratification of this Convention or accession thereto, declare that it does not recognize the competence of the Committee provided for in article 20.

2. Any State Party having made a reservation in accordance with paragraph 1 of this article may, at any time, withdraw this reservation by notification to the Secretary-General of the United Nations.

Article 29

1. Any State Party to this Convention may propose an amendment and file it with the Secretary-General of the United Nations. The Secretary-General shall thereupon communicate the proposed amendment to the States Parties with a request that they notify him whether they favour a conference of States Parties for the purpose of considering and voting upon the proposal. In the event that within four months from the date of such communication at least one third of the States Parties favours such a conference, the Secretary-General shall convene the conference under the auspices of the United Nations. Any amendment adopted by a majority of the States Parties present and voting at the conference shall be submitted by the Secretary-General to all the States Parties for acceptance.

2. An amendment adopted in accordance with paragraph 1 of this article shall enter into force when two thirds of the States Parties to this Convention have notified the Secretary-General of the United Nations that they have accepted it in accordance with their respective constitutional processes.

3. When amendments enter into force, they shall be binding on those States Parties which have accepted them, other States Parties still being bound by the provisions of this Convention and any earlier amendments which they have accepted.

Article 30

1. Any dispute between two or more States Parties concerning the interpretation or application of this Convention which cannot be settled through negotiation shall, at the request of one of them, be submitted to arbitration. If within six months from the date of the request for arbitration the Parties are unable to agree on the organization of the arbitration, any one of those Parties may refer the dispute to the International Court of Justice by request in conformity with the Statute of the Court.

2. Each State may, at the time of signature or ratification of this Convention or accession thereto, declare that it does not consider itself bound by paragraph 1 of this article. The other States Parties shall not be bound by paragraph 1 of this article with respect to any State Party having made such a reservation.

3. Any State Party having made a reservation in accordance with paragraph 2 of this article may at any time withdraw this reservation by notification to the Secretary-General of the United Nations.

Article 31

1. A State Party may denounce this Convention by written notification to the Secretary-General of the United Nations. Denunciation becomes effective one year after the date of receipt of the notification by the Secretary-General.

2. Such a denunciation shall not have the effect of releasing the State Party from its obligations under this Convention in regard to any act or omission which occurs prior to the date at which the denunciation becomes effective, nor shall denunciation prejudice in any way the continued consideration of any matter which is already under consideration by the Committee prior to the date at which the denunciation becomes effective.

3. Following the date at which the denunciation of a State Party becomes effective, the Committee shall not commence consideration of any new matter regarding that State.

Article 32

The Secretary-General of the United Nations shall inform all States Members of the United Nations and all States which have signed this Convention or acceded to it of the following:

(a) Signatures, ratifications and accessions under articles 25 and 26;

(b) The date of entry into force of this Convention under article 27 and the date of the entry into force of any amendments under article 29;

(c) Denunciations under article 31.

Article 33

1. This Convention, of which the Arabic, Chinese, English, French, Russian and Spanish texts are equally authentic, shall be deposited with the Secretary-General of the United Nations.

2. The Secretary-General of the United Nations shall transmit certified copies of this Convention to all States.

Other Instruments

32.

Statute of the Office of the United Nations High Commissioner for Refugees

Annex to GA Res. 428 (V) of 14 December 1950.

Chapter I. General Provisions

1. The High Commissioner, acting under the authority of the General Assembly, shall assume the function of providing international protection, under the auspices of the United Nations, to refugees who fall within the scope of this Statute and of seeking permanent solutions for the problem of refugees by assisting Governments and, subject to the approval of the Governments concerned, private organizations to facilitate the voluntary repatriation of such refugees, or their assimilation within new national communities.

In the exercise of his functions, more particularly when difficulties arise, and for instance with regard to any controversy concerning the international status of these persons, the High Commissioner shall request the opinion of the advisory committee if it is created.

2. The work of the High Commisioner shall be of an entirely non-political character; it shall be humanitarian and social and shall relate, as a rule, to groups and categories of refugees.

3. The High Commissioner shall follow policy directives given him by the General Assembly or the Economic and Social Council.

4. The Economic and Social Council may decide, after hearing the views of the High Commissioner on the subject, to establish an advisory committee on refugees, which shall consist of representatives of States Members and States non-members of the United Nations, to be selected by the Council on the basis of their demonstrated interest in and devotion to the solution of the refugee problem.

5. The General Assembly shall review, not later than at its Eighth regular Session, the arrangements for the High Commissioner's Office for Refugees with a view to determining whether the Office should be continued beyond 31 December 1953.

Chapter II. Functions of the High Commissioner

6. The competence of the High Commissioner shall extend to:
   a. (i) Any person who has been considered a refugee under the Arrangements of 12 May 1926 and 30 June 1928 or under the Conventions of 28 October 1933 and 10 February 1938, the Protocol of 14 September 1939 or the Constitution of the International Refugee Organization.
   (ii) Any person who, as a result of events occurring before 1 January 1951 and owing to well-founded fear of being persecuted for reasons of race, religion, nationality or political opinion, is outside the country of his nationality and is unable or, owing to such fear or for reasons other than personal convenience, is unwilling to avail himself of the protection of that country; or

who, not having a nationality and being outside the country of his former habitual residence, is unable or, owing to such fear or for reasons other than personal convenience, is unwilling to return to it. Decisions as to eligibility taken by the International Refugee Organization during the period of its activities shall not prevent the status of refugee being accorded to persons who fulfil the conditions of this paragraph.

The competence of the High Commissioner shall cease to apply to any person defined in section *a* above if:

(i) He has voluntarily reavailed himself of the protection of the country of his nationality; or

(ii) Having lost his nationality, he has voluntarily reacquired it; or

(iii) He has acquired a new nationality, and enjoys the protection of the country of his new nationality; or

(iv) He has voluntarily re-established himself in the country which he left or outside which he remained owing to fear of persecution; or

(v) He can no longer, because the circumstances in connection with which he has been recognized as a refugee have ceased to exist, claim grounds other than those of personal convenience for continuing to refuse to avail himself of the protection of the country of his nationality. Reasons of a purely economic character may not be invoked; or

(vi) Being a person who has no nationality, he can no longer, because the circumstances in connexion with which he has been recognized as a refugee have ceased to exist and he is able to return to the country of his former habitual residence, claim grounds other than those of personal convenience for continuing to refuse to return to that country.

b. Any other person, who is outside the country of his nationality or, if he has no nationality, the country of his former habitual residence, because he has or had well-founded fear of persecution by reason of his race, religion, nationality or political opinion and is unable or, because of such fear, is unwilling to avail himself of the protection of the Government of the country of his nationality, or, if he has no nationality, to return to the country of his former habitual residence.

7. Provided that the competence of the High Commissioner as defined in paragraph 6 above shall not extend to a person:

(i) Who is a national of more than one country unless he satisfies the provisions of the preceding paragraph in relation to each of the countries of which he is a national; or

(ii) Who is recognized by the competent authorities of the country in which he has taken residence as having the rights and obligations which are attached to the possession of the nationality of that country; or

(iii) Who continues to receive from other organs or agencies of the United Nations protection or assistance; or

(iv) In respect of whom there are serious reasons for considering that he has committed a crime covered by the provisions of treaties of extradition or a crime mentioned in Article VI of the London Charter of the International Military Tribunal or by the provisions of Article 14, paragraph 2, of the Universal Declaration of Human Rights.

8. The High Commissioner shall provide for the protection of refugees falling under the competence of his Office by:

a. Promoting the conclusion and ratification of international conventions for the protection of refugees, supervising their application and proposing amendments thereto;

b. Promoting through special agreements with Governments the execution of any measures calculated to improve the situation of refugees and to reduce the number requiring protection;

c. Assisting governmental and private efforts to promote voluntary repatriation or assimilation within new national communities;
d. Promoting the admission of refugees, not excluding those in the most destitute categories, to the territories of States;
e. Endeavouring to obtain permission for refugees to transfer their assets and especially those necessary for their resettlement;
f. Obtaining from Governments information concerning the number and conditions of refugees in their territories and the laws and regulations concerning them;
g. Keeping in close touch with the Governments and inter-governmental organizations concerned;
h. Establishing contact in such manner as he may think best with private organizations dealing with refugee questions;
i. Facilitating the co-ordination of the efforts of private organizations concerned with the welfare of refugees.

9. The High Commissioner shall engage in such additional activities, including repatriation and resettlement, as the General Assembly may determine, within the limits of the resources placed at his disposal.

10. The High Commissioner shall administer any funds, public or private, which he receives for assistance to refugees, and shall distribute them among the private and, as appropriate, public agencies which he deems best qualified to administer such assistance.

The High Commissioner may reject any offers which he does not consider appropriate or which cannot be utilized.

The High Commissioner shall not appeal to Governments for funds or make a general appeal, without the prior approval of the General Assembly.

The High Commissioner shall include in his annual report a statement of his activities in this field.

11. The High Commissioner shall be entitled to present his views before the General Assembly, the Economic and Social Council and their subsidiary bodies.

The High Commissioner shall report annually to the General Assembly through the Economic and Social Council; his report shall be considered as a separate item on the agenda of the General Assembly.

12. The High Commissioner may invite the co-operation of the various specialized agencies.

Chapter III. Organization and Finances

13. The High Commissioner shall be elected by the General Assembly on the nomination of the Secretary-General. The terms of appointment of the High Commissioner shall be proposed by the Secretary-General and approved by the General Assembly.

The High Commissioner shall be elected for a term of three years, from 1 January 1951.

14. The High Commissioner shall appoint, for the same term, a Deputy High Commissioner of a nationality other than his own.

15. *a.* Within the limits of the budgetary appropriations provided, the staff of the High Commissioner's Office shall be appointed by the High Commissioner and shall be responsible to him in the exercise of their functions.

b. Such staff shall be chosen from persons devoted to the purposes of the High Commissioner's Office.

c. Their conditions of employment shall be those provided under the staff regulations adopted by the General Assembly and the rules promulgated thereunder by the Secretary-General.

d. Provision may also be made to permit the employment of personnel without compensation.

16. The High Commissioner shall consult the Governments of the countries of residence of refugees as to the need for appointing representatives therein. In any country recognizing such need, there may be appointed a representative approved by the Government of that country. Subject to the foregoing, the same representative may serve in more than one country.

17. The High Commissioner and the Secretary-General shall make appropriate arrangements for liaison and consultation on màtters of mutual interest.

18. The Secretary-General shall provide the High Commissioner with all necessary facilities within budgetary limitations.

19. The High Commissioner's Office for Refugees shall be located in Geneva, Switzerland.

20. The High Commissioner's Office shall be financed under the budget of the United Nations. Unless the General Assembly subsequently decides otherwise, no expenditure other than administrative expenditures relating to the functioning of the High Commissioner's Office shall be borne on the budget of the United Nations and all other expenditures relating to the activities of the High Commissioner shall be financed by voluntary contributions.

21. The administration of the Office of the High Commissioner shall be subject to the Financial Regulations of the United Nations and to the financial rules promulgated thereunder by the Secretary-General.

22. Transactions relating to the High Commissioner's funds shall be subject to audit by the United Nations Boards of Auditors, provided that the Board may accept audited accounts from the agencies to which funds have been allocated. Administrative arrangements for the custody of such funds and their allocation shall be agreed between the High Commissioner and the Secretary-General in accordance with the Financial Regulations of the United Nations and rules promulgated thereunder by the Secretary-General.

33.

STANDARD MINIMUM RULES FOR THE TREATMENT OF PRISONERS

Adopted by the First United Nations Congress on the Prevention of Crime and the Treatment of Offenders, held at Geneva in 1955, and approved by the Economic and Social Council by its resolutions 663 C (XXIV) of 31 July 1957 and 2076 (LXII) of 13 May 1977

PRELIMINARY OBSERVATIONS

1. The following rules are not intended to describe detail a model system of penal institutions. They seek only, on the basis of the general consensus of contemporary thought and the essential elements of the most adequate systems of today, to set out what is generally accepted as being good principle and practice in the treatment of prisoners and the management of institutions.

2. In view of the great variety of legal, social, economic and geographical conditions of the world, it is evident that not all of the rules are capable of application in all places and at all times. They should, however, serve to stimulate a constant endeavour to overcome practical difficulties in the way of their application, in the knowledge that they represent, as a whole, the minimum conditions which are accepted as suitable by the United Nations.

3. On the other hand, the rules cover a field in which thought is constantly developing. They are not intended to preclude experiment and practices, provided these are in harmony with the principles and seek to further the purposes which derive from the text of the rules as a whole. It will always be justifiable for the central prison administration to authorize departures from the rules in this spirit.

4. (1) Part I of the rules covers the general management of institutions, and is applicable to all categories of prisoners, criminal or civil, untried or convicted, including prisoners subject to 'security measures' or corrective measures ordered by the judge.

(2) Part II contains rules applicable only to the special categories dealt with in each section. Nevertheless, the rules under section A, applicable to prisoners under sentence, shall be equally applicable to categories of prisoners dealt with in sections B, C and D, provided they do not conflict with the rules governing those categories and are for their benefit.

5. (1) The rules do not seek to regulate the management of institutions set aside for young persons such as borstal institutions or correctional schools, but in general part I would be equally applicable in such institutions.

(2) The category of young prisoners should include at least all young persons who come within the jurisdiction of juvenile courts. As a rule, such young persons should not be sentenced to imprisonment.

PART I
RULES OF GENERAL APPLICATION

Basic principle

6. (1) The following rules shall be applied impartially. There shall be no discrimination on grounds of race, colour, sex, language, religion, political or other opinion, national or social origin, property, birth or other status.

(2) On the other hand, it is necessary to respect the religious beliefs and moral precepts of the group to which a prisoner belongs.

Register

7. (1) In every place where persons are imprisoned there shall be kept a bound registration book with numbered pages in which shall be entered in respect of each prisoner received:
(a) Information concerning his identity;
(b) The reasons for his commitment and the authority therefor;
(c) The day and hour of his admission and release.

(2) No person shall be received in an institution without a valid commitment order of which the details shall have been previously entered in the register.

Separation of categories

8. The different categories of prisoners shall be kept in separate institutions or parts of institutions taking account of their sex, age, criminal record, the legal reason for their detention and the necessities of their treatment. Thus,

(a) Men and women shall so far as possible be detained in separate institutions; in an institution which receives both men and women the whole of the premises allocated to women shall be entirely separate;
(b) Untried prisoners shall be kept separate from convicted prisoners;
(c) Persons imprisoned for debt and other civil prisoners shall be kept separate from persons imprisoned by reason of a criminal offence;
(d) Young prisoners shall be kept separate from adults.

Accommodation

9. (1) Where sleeping accommodation is in individual cells or rooms, each prisoner shall occupy by night a cell or room by himself. If for special reasons, such as temporary overcrowding, it becomes necessary for the central prison administration to make an exception to this rule, it is not desirable to have two prisoners in a cell or room.

(2) Where dormitories are used, they shall be occupied by prisoners carefully selected as being suitable to associate with one another in those conditions. There shall be regular supervision by night, in keeping with the nature of the institution.

10. All accommodation provided for the use of prisoners and in particular all sleeping accommodation shall meet all requirements of health, due regard being paid to climatic conditions and particularly to cubic content of air, minimum floor space, lighting, heating and ventilation.

11. In all places where prisoners are required to live or work,
(a) The windows shall be large enough to enable the prisoners to read or work by natural light, and shall be so constructed that they can allow the entrance of fresh air whether or not there is artificial ventilation;
(b) Artificial light shall be provided sufficient for the prisoners to read or work without injury to eyesight.

12. The sanitary installations shall be adequate to enable every prisoner to comply with the needs of nature when necessary and in a clean and decent manner.

13. Adequate bathing and shower installations shall be provided so that every prisoner may be enabled and required to have a bath or shower, at a temperature suitable to the climate, as frequently as necessary for general hygiene according to season and geographical region, but at least once a week in a temperate climate.

14. All parts of an institution regularly used by prisoners shall be properly maintained and kept scrupulously clean at all times.

Personal hygiene

15. Prisoners shall be required to keep their persons clean, and to this end they shall be provided with water and with such toilet articles as are necessary for health and cleanliness.

16. In order that prisoners may maintain a good appearance compatible with their self-respect, facilities shall be provided for the proper care of the hair and beard, and men shall be enabled to shave regularly.

Clothing and bedding

17. (1) Every prisoner who is not allowed to wear his own clothing shall be provided with an outfit of clothing suitable for the climate and adequate to keep him in good health. Such clothing shall in no manner be degrading or humiliating.
   (2) All clothing shall be clean and kept in proper condition. Underclothing shall be changed and washed as often as necessary for the maintenance of hygiene.
   (3) In exceptional circumstances, whenever a prisoner is removed outside the institution for an authorized purpose, he shall be allowed to wear his own clothing or other inconspicuous clothing.

18. If prisoners are allowed to wear their own clothing, arrangements shall be made on their admission to the institution to ensure that it shall be clean and fit for use.

19. Every prisoner shall, in accordance with local or national standards, be provided with a separate bed, and with separate and sufficient bedding which shall be clean when issued, kept in good order and changed often enough to ensure its cleanliness.

Food

20. (1) Every prisoner shall be provided by the administration at the usual hours with food of nutritional value adequate for health and strength, of wholesome quality and well prepared and served.
   (2) Drinking water shall be available to every prisoner whenever he needs it.

Exercise and sport

21. (1) Every prisoner who is not employed in outdoor work shall have at

least one hour of suitable exercise in the open air daily if the weather permits.

(2) Young prisoners, and others of suitable age and physique, shall receive physical and recreational training during the period of exercise. To this end space, installations and equipment should be provided.

Medical services

22. (1) At every institution there shall be available the services of at least one qualified medical officer who should have some knowledge of psychiatry. The medical services should be organized in close relationship to the general health administration of the community or nation. They shall include a psychiatric service for the diagnosis and, in proper cases, the treatment of states of mental abnormality.

(2) Sick prisoners who require specialist treatment shall be transferred to specialized institutions or to civil hospitals. Where hospital facilities are provided in an institution, their equipment, furnishings and pharmoceutical supplies shall be proper for the medical care and treatment of sick prisoners, and there shall be a staff of suitably trained officers.

(3) The services of a qualified dental officer shall be available to every prisoner.

23. (1) In women's institutions there shall be special accommodation for all necessary pre-natal and post-natal care and treatment. Arrangements shall be made wherever practicable for children to be born in a hospital outside the institution. If a child is born in prison, this fact shall not be mentioned in the birth certificate.

(2) Where nursing infants are allowed to remain in the institution with their mothers, provision shall be made for a nursery staffed by qualified persons, where the infants shall be placed when they are not in the care of their mothers.

24. The medical officer shall see and examine every prisoner as soon as possible after his admission and thereafter as necessary, with a view particularly to the discovery of physical or mental illness and the taking of all necessary measures; the segregation of prisoners suspected of infectious or contagious conditions; the noting of physical or mental defects which might hamper rehabilitation, and the determination of the physical capacity of every prisoner for work.

25. (1) The medical officer shall have the care of the physical and mental health of the prisoners and should daily see all sick prisoners, all who complain of illness, and any prisoner to whom his attention is specially directed.

(2) The medical officer shall report to the director whenever he consid-

ers that a prisoner's physical or mental health has been or will be injuriously affected by continued imprisonment or by any condition of imprisonment.

26. (1) The medical officer shall regularly inspect and advise the director upon:
(a) The quantity, quality, preparation and service of food;
(b) The hygiene and cleanliness of the institution and the prisoners;
(c) The sanitation, heating, lighting and ventilation of the institution;
(d) The suitability and cleanliness of the prisoners' clothing and bedding;
(e) The observance of the rules concerning physical education and sports, in cases where there is no technical personnel in charge of these activities.

(2) The director shall take into consideration the reports and advice that the medical officer submits according to rules 25 (2) and 26 and, in case he concurs with the recommendations made, shall take immediate steps to give effect to those recommendations; if they are not within his competence or if he does not concur with them, he shall immediately submit his own report and the advice of the medical officer to higher authority.

Discipline and punishment

27. Discipline and order shall be maintained with firmness, but with no more restriction than is necessary for safe custody and well-ordered community life.

28. (1) No prisoner shall be employed, in the service of the institution, in any disciplinary capacity.

(2) This rule shall not, however, impede the proper functioning of systems based on self-government, under which specified social, educational or sports activities or reponsibilities are entrusted, under supervision, to prisoners who are formed into groups for the purposes of treatment.

29. The following shall always be determined by the law or by the regulation of the competent administrative authority:
(a) Conduct constituting a disciplinary offence;
(b) The types and duration of punishment which may be inflicted;
(c) The authority competent to impose such punishment.

30. (1) No prisoner shall be punished except in accordance with the terms of such law or regulation, and never twice for the same offence.

(2) No prisoner shall be punished unless he has been informed of the offence alleged against him and given a proper opportunity of presenting his defence. The competent authority shall conduct a thorough examination of the case.

(3) Where necessary and practicable the prisoner shall be allowed to make his defence through an interpreter.

31. Corporal punishment, punishment by placing in a dark cell, and all cruel, inhuman or degrading punishments shall be completely prohibited as punishments for disciplinary offences.

32. (1) Punishment by close confinement or reduction of diet shall never be inflicted unless the medical officer has examined the prisoner and certified in writing that he is fit to sustain it.
    (2) The same shall apply to any other punishment that may be prejudicial to the physical or mental health of a prisoner. In no case may such punishment be contrary to or depart from the principle states in rule 31.
    (3) The medical officer shall visit daily prisoners undergoing such punishments and shall advise the director if he considers the termination or alteration of the punishment necessary on grounds of physical or mental health.

Instruments of restraint

33. Instruments of restraint, such as handcuffs, chains, irons and straitjackets, shall never be applied as a punishment. Furthermore, chains or irons shall not be used as restraints. Other instruments of restraint shall not be used except in the following circumstances:
(a) As a precaution against escape during a transfer, provided that they shall be removed when the prisoner appears before a judicial or administrative authority;
(b) On medical grounds by direction of the medical officer;
(c) By order of the director, if other methods of control fail, in order to prevent a prisoner from injuring himself or others or from damaging property; in such instances the director shall at once consult the medical officer and report to the higher administrative authority.

34. The patterns and manner of use of instruments of restraint shall be decided by the central prison administration. Such instruments must not be applied for any longer time than is strictly necessary.

Information to and complaints by prisoners

35. (1) Every prisoner on admission shall be provided with written information about the regulations governing the treatment of prisoners of his category, the disciplinary requirements of the institution, the authorized methods of seeking information and making complaints, and all such other matters as are necessary to enable him to understand both his rights and his obligations and to adapt himself to the life of the institution.
    (2) If a prisoner is illiterate, the aforesaid information shall be conveyed to him orally.

36. (1) Every prisoner shall have the opportunity each week day of making requests or complaints to the director of the institution or the officer authorized to represent him.

(2) It shall be possible to make requests or complaints to the inspector of prisons during his inspection. The prisoner shall have the opportunity to talk to the inspector or to any other inspecting officer without the director or other members of the staff being present.

(3) Every prisoner shall be allowed to make a request or complaint, without censorship as to substance but in proper form, to the central prison administration, the judicial authority or other proper authorities through approved channels.

(4) Unless it is evidently frivolous or groundless, every request or complaint shall be promptly dealt with and replied to without undue delay.

Contact with the outside world

37. Prisoners shall be allowed under necessary supervision to communicate with their family and reputable friends at regular intervals, both by correspondence and by receiving visits.

38. (1) Prisoners who are foreign nationals shall be allowed reasonable facilities to communicate with the diplomatic and consular representatives of the State to which they belong.

(2) Prisoners who are nationals of States without diplomatic or consular representation in the country and refugees or stateless persons shall be allowed similar facilities to communicate with the diplomatic representative of the State which takes charge of their interests or any national or international authority whose task it is to protect such persons.

39. Prisoners shall be kept informed regularly of the more important items of news by the reading of newspapers, periodicals or special institutional publications, by hearing wireless transmissions, by lectures or by any similar means as authorized or controlled by the administration.

Books

40. Every institution shall have a library for the use of all categories of prisoners, adequately stocked with both recreational and instructional books, and prisoners shall be encouraged to make full use of it.

Religion

41. (1) If the institution contains a sufficient number of prisoners of the same

religion, a qualified representative of that religion shall be appointed or approved. If the number of prisoners justifies it and conditions permit, the arrangement should be on a full-time basis.

(2) A qualified representative appointed or approved under paragraph (1) shall be allowed to hold regular services and to pay pastoral visits in private to prisoners of his religion at proper times.

(3) Access to a qualified representative of any religion shall not be refused to any prisoner. On the other hand, if any prisoner should object to a visit of any religious representative, his attitude shall be fully respected.

42. So far as practicable, every prisoner shall be allowed to satisfy the needs of his religious life by attending the services provided in the institution and having in his possession the books of religious observance and instruction of his denomination.

Retention of prisoners' property

43. (1) All money, valuables, clothing and other effects belonging to a prisoner which under the regulations of the institution he is not allowed to retain shall on his admission to the institution be placed in safe custody. An inventory thereof shall be signed by the prisoner. Steps shall be taken to keep them in good condition.

(2) On the release of the prisoner all such articles and money shall be returned to him except in so far as he has been authorized to spend money or send any such property out of the institution, or it has been found necessary on hygienic grounds to destroy any article of clothing. The prisoner shall sign a receipt for the articles and money returned to him.

(3) Any money or effects received for a prisoner from outside shall be treated in the same way.

(4) If a prisoner brings in any drugs or medicine, the medical officer shall decide what use shall be made of them.

Notification of death, illness, transfer, etc.

44. (1) Upon the death or serious illness of, or serious injury to a prisoner, or his removal to an institution for the treatment of mental affections, the director shall at once inform the spouse, if the prisoner is married, or the nearest relative and shall in any event inform any other person previously designated by the prisoner.

(2) A prisoner shall be informed at once of the death or serious illness of any near relative. In case of the critical illness of a near relative, the prisoner should be authorized, whenever circumstances allow, to go to his bedside either under escort or alone.

(3) Every prisoner shall have the right to inform at once his family of his imprisonment or his transfer to another institution.

Removal of prisoners

45. (1) When prisoners are being removed to or from an institution, they shall be exposed to public view as little as possible, and proper safeguards shall be adopted to protect them from insult, curiosity and publicity in any form.

(2) The transport of prisoners in conveyances with inadequate ventilation or light, or in any way which would subject them to unnecessary physical hardship, shall be prohibited.

(3) The transport of prisoners shall be carried out at the expense of the administration and equal conditions shall obtain for all of them.

Institutional personnel

46. (1) The prison administration, shall provide for the careful selection of every grade of the personnel, since it is on their integrity, humanity, professional capacity and personal suitability for the work that the proper administration of the institutions depends.

(2) The prison administration shall constantly seek to awaken and maintain in the minds both of the personnel and of the public the conviction that this work is a social service of great importance, and to this end all appropriate means of informing the public should be used.

(3) To secure the foregoing ends, personnel shall be appointed on a full-time basis as professional prison officers and have civil service status with security of tenure subject only to good conduct, efficiency and physical fitness. Salaries shall be adequate to attract and retain suitable men and women; employment benefits and conditions of service shall be favourable in view of the exacting nature of the work.

47. (1) The personnel shall possess an adequate standard of education and intelligence.

(2) Before entering on duty, the personnel shall be given a course of training in their general and specific duties and be required to pass theoretical and practical tests.

(3) After entering on duty and during their career, the personnel shall maintain and improve their knowledge and professional capacity by attending courses of inservice training to be organized at suitable intervals.

48. All members of the personnel shall at all times so conduct themselves and perform their duties as to influence the prisoners for good by their example and to command their respect.

49. (1) So far as possible, the personnel shall include a sufficient number of specialists such as psychiatrists, psychologists, social workers, teachers and trade instructors.

(2) The services of social workers, teachers and trade instructors shall be secured on a permanent basis, without thereby excluding part-time or voluntary workers.

50. (1) The director of an institution should be adequately qualified for his task by character, administrative ability, suitable training and experience.

(2) He shall devote his entire time to his official duties and shall not be appointed on a part-time basis.

(3) He shall reside on the premises of the institution or in its immediate vicinity.

(4) When two or more institutions are under the authority of one director, he shall visit each of them at frequent intervals. A responsible resident official shall be in charge of each of these institutions.

51. (1) The director, his deputy, and the majority of the other personnel if the institution shall be able to speak the language of the greatest number of prisoners, or a language understood by the greatest number of them.

(2) Whenever necessary, the services of an interpreter shall be used.

52. (1) In institutions which are large enough to require the services of one or more full-time medical officers, at least once of them shall reside on the premises of the institution or in its immediate vicinity.

(2) In other institutions the medical officer shall visit daily and shall reside near enough to be able to attend without delay in cases of urgency.

53. (1) In an institution for both men and women, the part of the institution set aside for women shall be under the authority of a responsible woman officer who shall have the custody of the keys of all that part of the institution.

(2) No male member of the staff shall enter the part of the institution set aside for women unless accompanied by a woman officer.

(3) Women prisoners shall be attended and supervised only by women officers. This does not, however, preclude male members of the staff, particularly doctors and teachers, from carrying out their professional duties in institutions or parts of institutions set aside for women.

54. (1) Officers of the institutions shall not, in their relations with the prisoners, use force except in self-defence or in cases of attempted escape, or active or passive physical resistance to an order based on law or regulations. Officers who have recourse to force must use no more than is strictly necessary and must report the incident immediately to the director of the institution.

(2) Prison officers shall be given special physical training to enable them to restrain aggressive prisoners.

(3) Except in special circumstances, staff performing duties which bring them into direct contact with prisoners should not be armed. Furthermore, staff should in no circumstances be provided with arms unless they have been trained in their use.

Inspection

55. There shall be a regular inspection of penal institutions and services by qualified and experienced inspectors appointed by a competent authority. Their task shall be in particular to ensure that these institutions are administered in accordance with existing laws and regulations and with a view to bringing about the objectives of penal and correctional services.

PART II

RULES APPLICABLE TO SPECIAL CATEGORIES

A. PRISONERS UNDER SENTENCE

Guiding principles

56. The guiding principles hereafter are intended to show the spirit in which penal institutions should be administered and the purposes at which they should aim, in accordance with the declaration made under Preliminary Observation 1 of the present text.

57. Imprisonment and other measures which result in cutting off an offender from the outside world are afflictive by the very fact of taking from the person the right of self-determination by depriving him of his liberty. Therefore the prison system shall not, except as incidental to justifiable segregation or the maintenance of discipline, aggravate the suffering inherent in such a situation.

58. The purpose and justification of a sentence of imprisonment or a similar measure deprivative of liberty is ultimately to protect society against crime. This end can only be achieved if the period of imprisonment is used to ensure, so far as possible, that upon his return to society the offender is not only willing but able to lead a law-abiding and self-supporting life.

59. To this end, the institution should utilize all the remedial, educational, moral, spiritual and other forces and forms of assistance which are appropriate and available, and should seek to apply them according to the individual treatment needs of the prisoners.

60. (1) The régime of the institution should seek to minimize any differences

between prison life and life at liberty which tend to lessen the responsibility of the prisoners or the respect due to their dignity as human beings.

(2) Before the completion of the sentence, it is desirable that the necessary steps be taken to ensure for the prisoner a gradual return to life in society. This aim may be achieved, depending on the case, by a pre-release régime organized in the same institution or in another appropriate institution, or by release on trial under some kind of supervision which must not be entrusted to the police but should be combined with effective social aid.

61. The treatment of prisoners should emphasize not their exclusion from the community, but their continuing part in it. Community agencies should, therefore, be enlisted wherever possible to assist the staff of the institution in the task of social rehabilitation of the prisoners. There should be in connexion with every institution social workers charged with the duty of maintaining and improving all desirable relations of a prisoner with his family and with valuable social agencies. Steps should be taken to safeguard, to the maximum extent compatible with the law and the sentence, the rights relating to civil interests, social security rights and other social benefits of prisoners.

62. The medical services of the institution shall seek to detect and shall treat any physical or mental illnesses or defects which may hamper a prisoner's rehabilitation. All necessary medical, surgical and psychiatric services shall be provided to that end.

63. (1) The fulfilment of these principles requires individualization of treatment and for this purpose a flexible system of classifying prisoners in groups; it is therefore desirable that such groups should be distributed in separate institutions suitable for the treatment of each group.

(2) These institutions need not provide the same degree of security for every group. It is desirable to provide varying degrees of security according to the needs of different groups. Open institutions, by the very fact that they provide no physical security against escape but rely on the self-discipline of the inmates, provide the conditions most favourable to rehabilitation for carefully selected prisoners.

(3) It is desirable that the number of prisoners in closed institutions should not be so large that the individualization of treatment is hindered. In some countries it is considered that the population of such institutions should not exceed five hundred. In open institutions the population should be as small as possible.

(4) On the other hand, it is undesirable to maintain prisons which are so small that proper facilities cannot be provided.

64. The duty of society does not end with a prisoner's release. There should, therefore, be governmental or private agencies capable of lending the released

prisoner efficient after-care directed towards the lessening of prejudice against him and towards his social rehabilitation.

Treatment

65. The treatment of persons sentenced to imprisonment or a similar measure shall have as its purpose, so far as the length of the sentence permits, to establish in them the will to lead law-abiding and self-supporting lives after their release and to fit them to do so. The treatment shall be such as will encourage their self-respect and develop their sense of responsibility.

66. (1) To these ends, all appropriate means shall be used, including religious care in the countries where this is possible, education, vocational guidance and training, social casework, employment counselling, physical development and strengthening of moral character, in accordance with the individual needs of each prisoner, taking account of his social and criminal history, his physical and mental capacities and aptitudes, his personal temperament, the length of his sentence and his prospects after release.

(2) For every prisoner with a sentence of suitable length, the director shall receive, as soon as possible after his admission, full reports on all the matters referred to in the foregoing paragraph. Such reports shall always include a report by a medical officer, wherever possible qualified in psychiatry, on the physical and mental condition of the prisoner.

(3) The reports and other relevant documents shall be placed in an individual file. This file shall be kept up to date and classified in such a way that it can be consulted by the responsible personnel whenever the need arises.

Classification and individualization

67. The purposes of classification shall be:
(a) To separate from others those prisoners who, by reason of their criminal records or bad characters, are likely to exercise a bad influence;
(b) To divide the prisoners into classes in order to facilitate their treatment with a view to their social rehabilitation.

68. So far as possible separate institutions or separate sections of an institution shall be used for the treatment of the different classes of prisoners.

69. As soon as possible after admission and after a study of the personality of each prisoner with a sentence of suitable length, a programme of treatment shall be prepared for him in the light of the knowledge obtained about his individual needs, his capacities and dispositions.

Privileges

70. Systems of privileges appropriate for the different classes of prisoners and the different methods of treatment shall be established at every institution, in order to encourage good conduct, develop a sense of responsibility and secure the interest and co-operation of the prisoners in their treatment.

Work

71. (1) Prison labour must not be of an afflictive nature.

(2) All prisoners under sentence shall be required to work, subject to their physical and mental fitness as determined by the medical officer.

(3) Sufficient work of a useful nature shall be provided to keep prisoners actively employed for a normal working day.

(4) So far as possible the work provided shall be such as will maintain or increase the prisoners' ability to earn an honest living after release.

(5) Vocational training in useful trades shall be provided for prisoners able to profit thereby and especially for young prisoners.

(6) Within the limits compatible with proper vocational selection and with the requirements of institutional administration and discipline, the prisoners shall be able to choose the type of work they wish to perform.

72. (1) The organization and methods of work in the institutions shall resemble as closely as possible those of similar work outside institutions, so as to prepare prisoners for the conditions of normal occupational life.

(2) The interests of the prisoners and of their vocational training, however, must not be subordinated to the purpose of making a financial profit from an industry in the institution.

73. (1) Preferably institutional industries and farms should be operated directly by the administration and not by private contractors.

(2) Where prisoners are employed in work not controlled by the administration, they shall always be under the supervision of the institution's personnel. Unless the work is for other departments of the government the full normal wages for such work shall be paid to the administration by the persons to whom the labour is supplied, account being taken of the output of the prisoners.

74. (1) The precautions laid down to protect the safety and health of free workmen shall be equally observed in institutions.

(2) Provision shall be made to indemnify prisoners against industrial injury, including occupational disease, on terms not less favourable than those extended by law to free workmen.

75. (1) The maximum daily and weekly working hours of the prisoners shall be fixed by law or by administrative regulation, taking into account local rules or custom in regard to the employment of free workmen.

(2) The hours so fixed shall leave one rest day a week and sufficient time for education and other activities required as part of the treatment and rehabilitation of the prisoners.

76. (1) There shall be a system of equitable remuneration of the work of prisoners.

(2) Under the system prisoners shall be allowed to spend at least a part of their earnings on approved articles for their own use and to send a part of their earnings to their family.

(3) The system should also provide that a part of the earnings should be set aside by the administration so as to constitute a savings fund to be handed over to the prisoner on his release.

Education and recreation

77. (1) Provision shall be made for the further education of all prisoners capable of profiting thereby, including religious instruction in the countries where this is possible. The education of illiterates and young prisoners shall be compulsory and special attention shall be paid to it by the administration.

(2) So far as practicable, the education of prisoners shall be integrated with the educational system of the country so that after their release they may continue their education without difficulty.

78. Recreational and cultural activities shall be provided in all institutions for the benefit of the mental and physical health of prisoners.

Social relations and after-care

79. Special attention shall be paid to the maintenance and improvement of such relations between a prisoner and his family as are desirable in the best interests of both.

80. From the beginning of a prisoner's sentence consideration shall be given to his future after release and he shall be encouraged and assisted to maintain or establish such relations with persons or agencies outside the institution as may promote the best interests of his family and his own social rehabilitation.

81. (1) Services and agencies, governmental or otherwise, which assist released prisoners to re-establish themselves in society shall ensure, so far as is possible and necessary, that released prisoners be provided with appropriate documents and identification papers, have suitable homes and work to go to,

are suitably and adequately clothed having regard to the climate and season, and have sufficient means to reach their destination and maintain themselves in the period immediately following their release.

(2) The approved representatives of such agencies shall have all necessary access to the institution and to prisoners and shall be taken into consultation as to the future of a prisoner from the beginning of his sentence.

(3) It is desirable that the activities of such agencies shall be centralized or co-ordinated as far as possible in order to secure the best use of their efforts.

B. INSANE AND MENTALLY ABNORMAL PRISONERS

82. (1) Persons who are found to be insane shall not be detained in prisons and arrangements shall be made to remove them to mental institutions as soon as possible.

(2) Prisoners who suffer from other mental diseases or abnormalities shall be observed and treated in specialized institutions under medical management.

(3) During their stay in a prison, such prisoners shall be placed under the special supervision of a medical officer.

(4) The medical or psychiatric service of the penal institutions shall provide for the psychiatric treatment of all other prisoners who are in need of such treatment.

83. It is desirable that steps should be taken, by arrangement with the appropriate agencies, to ensure if necessary the continuation of psychiatric treatment after release and the provision of social-psychiatric after-care.

C. PRISONERS UNDER ARREST OR AWAITING TRIAL

84. (1) Persons arrested or imprisoned by reason of a criminal charge against them, who are detained either in police custody or in prison custody (jail) but have not yet been tried and sentenced, will be referred to as 'untried prisoners' hereinafter in these rules.

(2) Unconvicted prisoners are presumed to be innocent and shall be treated as such.

(3) Without prejudice to legal rules for the protection of individual liberty or prescribing the procedure to be observed in respect of untried prisoners, these prisoners shall benefit by a special régime which is described in the following rules in its essential requirements only.

85. (1) Untried prisoners shall be kept separate from convicted prisoners.

(2) Young untried prisoners shall be kept separate from adults and shall in principle be detained in separate institutions.

86. Untried prisoners shall sleep singly in separate rooms, with the reservation of different local custom in respect of the climate.

87. Within the limits compatible with the good order of the institution, untried prisoners may, if they so desire, have their food procured at their own expence from the outside, either through the administration or through their family or friends. Otherwise, the administration shall provide their food.

88. (1) An untried prisoner shall be allowed to wear his own clothing if it is clean and suitable.
(2) If he wears prison dress, it shall be different from that supplied to convicted prisoners.

89. An untried prisoner shall always be offered opportunity to work, but shall not be required to work. If he chooses to work, he shall be paid for it.

90. An untried prisoner shall be allowed to procure at his own expense or at the expense of a third party such books, newspapers, writing materials and other means of occupation as are compatible with the interests of the administration of justice and the security and good order of the institution.

91. An untried prisoner shall be allowed to be visited and treated by his own doctor or dentist if there is a reasonable ground for his application and he is able to pay any expenses incurred.

92. An untried prisoner shall be allowed to inform immediately his family of his detention and shall be given all reasonable facilities for communicating with his family and friends, and for receiving visits from them, subject only to such restrictions and supervision as are necessary in the interests of the administration of justice and of the security and good order of the institution.

93. For the purposes of his defence, an untried prisoner shall be allowed to apply for free legal aid where such aid is available, and to receive visits from his legal adviser with a view to his defence and to prepare and hand to him confidential instructions. For these purposes, he shall if he so desires be supplied with writing material. Interviews between the prisoner and his legal adviser may be within sight but not within the hearing of a police or institution official.

D. CIVIL PRISONERS

94. In countries where the law permits imprisonment for debt, or by order of a court under any other non-criminal process, persons so imprisoned shall not be subjected to any greater restriction or severity than is necessary to ensure safe custody and good order. Their treatment shall be not less favourable than

that of untried prisoners, with the reservation, however, that they may possibly be required to work.

E. PERSONS ARRESTED OR DETAINED WITHOUT CHARGE

95. Without prejudice to the provisions of article 9 of the International Covenant on Civil and Political Rights, persons arrested or imprisoned without charge shall be accorded the same protection as that accorded under part I and part II, section C. Relevant provisions of part II, section A, shall likewise be applicable where their application may be conducive to the benefit of this special group of persons in custody, provided that no measures shall be taken implying that re-education or rehabilitation is in any way appropriate to persons not convicted of any criminal offence.

34.

Declaration on the Granting of Independence to Colonial Countries and Peoples

GA Res. 1514 (XV) of 14 December 1960.
See also GA Res. 637 (VII) of 16 December 1952, GA Res. 2625 (XXV) of 24 October 1970, (for the text, see *I.O.I.*, I.A.6.6.b.   ), and Legal Consequences for States of the Continued Presence of South Africa in Namibia (South West Africa) notwithstanding Security Council Resolution 276 (1970), Advisory Opinion, *I.C.J. Reports*, 1971, p. 31; and Western Sahara, Advisory Opinion, *I.C.J. Reports*, 1975, pp. 31-37.
At its 102nd plenary meeting, on 13 December 1979, the GA by its Decision 34/125, increased the membership of the Special Committee from 24 to 25.

The General Assembly,
Mindful of the determination proclaimed by the peoples of the world in the Charter of the United Nations to reaffirm faith in fundamental human rights, in the dignity and worth of the human person, in the equal rights of men and women of nations large and small and to promote social progress and better standards of life in larger freedom,
Conscious of the need for the creation of conditions of stability and well-being and peaceful and friendly relations based on respect for the principles of equal rights and self-determination for all peoples, and of universal respect for, and observance of, human rights and fundamental freedoms for all without distinction as to race, sex, language or religion,
Recognizing the passionate yearning for freedom in all dependent peoples and the decisive role of such peoples in the attainment of their independence,
Aware of the increasing conflicts resulting from the denial of or impediments in the way of freedom of such peoples, which constitute a serious threat to world peace,
Considering the important role of the United Nations in assisting the movement for independence in Trust and Non-Self-Governing Territories,
Recognizing that the peoples of the world ardently desire the end of colonialism in all its manifestations,
Convinced that the continued existence of colonialism prevents the development of international economic co-operation, impedes the social, cultural and economic development of dependent peoples and militates against the United Nations ideal of universal peace,
Affirming that peoples may, for their own ends, freely dispose of their natural wealth and resources without prejudice to any obligations arising out of international economic co-operation, based upon the principle of mutual benefit, and international law,
Believing that the process of liberation is irresistible and irreversible and that, in order to avoid serious crisis, an end must be put to colonialism and all practices of segregation and discrimination associated therewith,
Welcoming the emergence in recent years of a large number of dependent territories into freedom and independence, and recognizing the increasingly powerful trends towards freedom in such territories which have not yet attained independence,

Convinced that all peoples have an inalienable right to complete freedom, the exercise of their sovereignty and the integrity of their national territory,

Solemnly proclaims the necessity of bringing to a speedy and unconditional end colonialism in all its forms and manifestations;

And to this end
Declares that:
1. The subjection of peoples to alien subjugation, domination and exploitation constitutes a denial of fundamental human rights, is contrary to the Charter of the United Nations and is an impediment to the promotion of world peace and co-operation.

2. All peoples have the right to self-determination; by virtue of that right they freely determine their political status and freely pursue their economic, social and cultural development.

3. Inadequacy of political, economic, social or educational preparedness should never serve as a pretext for delaying independence.

4. All armed action or repressive measures of all kinds directed against dependent peoples shall cease in order to enable them to exercise peacefully and freely their right to complete independence, and the integrity of their national territory shall be respected.

5. Immediate steps shall be taken, in Trust and Non-Self-Governing Territories or all other territories which have not yet attained independence, to transfer all powers to the peoples of those territories, without any conditions or reservations, in accordance with their freely expressed will and desire, without any distinction as to race, creed or colour, in order to enable them to enjoy complete independence and freedom.

6. Any attempt aimed at the partial or total disruption of the national unity and the territorial integrity of a country is incompatible with the purposes and principles of the Charter of the United Nations.

7. All States shall observe faithfully and strictly the provisions of the Charter of the United Nations, the Universal Declaration of Human Rights and the present Declaration on the basis of equality, non-interference in the internal affairs of all States, and respect for the sovereign rights of all peoples and their territorial integrity.

35.

GENERAL ASSEMBLY RESOLUTION 1803 (XVII) OF 14 DECEMBER 1962, 'PERMANENT SOVEREIGNTY OVER NATURAL RESOURCES'

The General Assembly,

Recalling its resolutions 523 (VI) of 12 January 1952 and 626 (VII) of 21 December 1952,

Bearing in mind its resolution 1314 (XIII) of 12 December 1958, by which it established the Commission on Permanent Sovereignty over Natural Resources and instructed it to conduct a full survey of the status of permanent sovereignty over natural wealth and resources as a basic constituent of the right to self-determination, with recommendations, where necessary, for its strengthening, and decided further that, in the conduct of the full survey of the status of the permanent sovereignty of peoples and nations over their natural wealth and resources, due regard should be paid to the rights and duties of States under international law and to the importance of encouraging international co-operation in the economic development of developing countries,

Bearing in mind its resolution 1515 (XV) of 15 December 1960, in which it recommended that the sovereign right of every State to dispose of its wealth and its natural resources should be respected,

Considering that any measure in this respect must be based on the recognition of the inalienable right of all States freely to dispose of their natural wealth and resources in accordance with their national interests, and on respect for the economic independence of States,

Considering that nothing in paragraph 4 below in any way prejudices the position of any Member State on any aspect of the question of the rights and obligations of successor States and Governments in respect of property acquired before the accession to complete sovereignty of countries formerly under colonial rule,

Noting that the subject of succession of States and Governments is being examined as a matter of priority by the International Law Commission,

Considering that it is desirable to promote international co-operation for the economic development of developing countries, and that economic and financial agreements between the developed and the developing countries must be based on the principles of equality and of the right of peoples and nations to self-determination,

Considering that the provision of economic and technical assistance, loans and increased foreign investment must not be subject to conditions which conflict with the interests of the recipient State,

Considering the benefits to be derived from exchanges of technical and scientific information likely to promote the development and use of such resources and wealth, and the important part which the United Nations and other international organizations are called upon to play in that connexion,

Attaching particular importance to the question of promoting the economic development of developing countries and securing their economic independence,

Noting that the creation and strengthening of the inalienable sovereignty of States over their natural wealth and resources reinforces their economic independence,

Desiring that there should be further consideration by the United Nations of the subject of permanent sovereignty over natural resources in the spirit of international co-operation in the field of economic development, particularly that of the developing countries,

I

Declares that:

1. The right of peoples and nations to permanent sovereignty over their natural wealth and resources must be exercised in the interest of their national development and of the well-being of the people of the State concerned.

2. The exploration, development and disposition of such resources, as well as the import of the foreign capital required for these purposes, should be in conformity with the rules and conditions which the peoples and nations freely consider to be necessary or desirable with regard to the authorization, restriction or prohibition of such activities.

3. In cases where authorization is granted, the capital imported and the earnings on that capital shall be governed by the terms thereof, by the national legislation in force, and by international law. The profits derived must be shared in the proportions freely agreed upon, in each case, between the investors and the recipient State, due care being taken to ensure that there is no impairment, for any reason, of that State's sovereignty over its natural wealth and resources.

4. Nationalization, expropriation or requisitioning shall be based on grounds or reasons of public utility, security or the national interest which are

recognized as overriding purely individual or private interests, both domestic and foreign. In such cases the owner shall be paid appropriate compensation, in accordance with the rules in force in the State taking such measures in the exercise of its sovereignty and in accordance with international law. In any case where the question of compensation gives rise to a controversy, the national jurisdiction of the State taking such measures shall be exhausted. However, upon agreement by sovereign States and other parties concerned, settlement of the dispute should be made through arbitration or international adjudication.

5. The free and beneficial exercise of the sovereignty of peoples and nations over their natural resources must be furthered by the mutual respect of States based on their sovereign equality.

6. International co-operation for the economic development of developing countries, whether in the form of public or private capital investments, exchange of goods and services, technical assistance, or exchange of scientific information, shall be such as to further their independent national development and shall be based upon respect for their sovereignty over their natural wealth and resources.

7. Violation of the rights of peoples and nations to sovereignty over their natural wealth and resources is contrary to the spirit and principles of the Charter of the United Nations and hinders the development of international co-operation and the maintenance of peace.

8. Foreign investment agreements freely entered into by or between sovereign States shall be observed in good faith; States and international organizations shall strictly and conscientiously respect the sovereignty of peoples and nations over their natural wealth and sources in accordance with the Charter and the principles set forth in the present resolution.

36.

Declaration on Territorial Asylum

GA Res. 2312 (XXII) of 14 December 1967. The General Assembly, in Res. 3456 (XXX) of 9 December 1975, called for a conference of plenipotentiaries to consider and adopt a Convention on Territorial Asylum. The Conference was duly held at Geneva from 10 January to 4 February 1977, but failed to adopt a Convention.

The General Assembly,
Recalling its resolutions 1839 (XVII) of 19 December 1962, 2100 (XX) of 20 December 1965 and 2203 (XXI) of 16 December 1966 concerning a declaration on the right of asylum,
Considering the work of codification to be undertaken by the International Law Commission in accordance with General Assembly resolution 1400 (XIV) of 21 November 1959,
Adopts the following *Declaration on Territorial Asylum:*
The General Assembly,
Noting that the purposes proclaimed in the Charter of the United Nations are to maintain international peace and security, to develop friendly relations among all nations and to achieve international co-operation in solving international problems of an economic, social, cultural or humanitarian character and in promoting and encouraging respect for human rights and for fundamental freedoms for all without distinction as to race, sex, language or religion,
Mindful of the Universal Declaration of Human Rights, which declares in article 14 that:
"1. Everyone has the right to seek and to enjoy in other countries asylum from persecution,
"2. This right may not be invoked in the case of prosecutions genuinely arising from non-political crimes or from acts contrary to the purposes and principles of the United Nations",
Recalling also article 13, paragraph 2, of the Universal Declaration of Human Rights, which states:
"Everyone has the right to leave any country, including his own, and to return to his country",
Recognizing that the grant of asylum by a State to persons entitled to invoke article 14 of the Universal Declaration of Human Rights is a peaceful and humanitarian act and that, as such, it cannot be regarded as unfriendly by any other State,
Recommends that, without prejudice to existing instruments dealing with asylum and the status of refugees and stateless persons, States should base themselves in their practices relating to territorial asylum on the following principles:

Article 1

1. Asylum granted by a State, in the exercise of its sovereignty, to persons entitled to invoke article 14 of the Universal Declaration of Human Rights, including persons struggling against colonialism, shall be respected by all other States.

2. The right to seek and to enjoy asylum may not be invoked by any person with respect to whom there are serious reasons for considering that he has committed a crime against peace, a war crime or a crime against humanity, as defined in the international instruments drawn up to make provision in respect of such crimes.
3. It shall rest with the State granting asylum to evaluate the gronds for the grant of asylum.

Article 2

1. The situation of persons referred to in article 1, paragraph 1, is, without prejudice to the sovereignty of States and the purposes and principles of the United Nations, of concern to the international community.
2. Where a State finds difficulty in granting or continuing to grant asylum, States individually or jointly or through the United Nations shall consider, in a spirit of international solidarity, appropriate measures to lighten the burden on that State.

Article 3

1. No person referred to in article 1, paragraph 1, shall be subjected to measures such as rejection at the frontier or, if he has already entered the territory in which he seeks asylum, expulsion or compulsory return to any State where he may be subjected to persecution.
2. Exception may be made to the foregoing principle only for overriding reasons of national security or in order to safeguard the population, as in the case of a mass influx of persons.
3. Should a State decide in any case that exception to the principle stated in paragraph 1 of this article would be justified, it shall consider the possibility of granting to the person concerned, under such conditions as it may deem appropriate, an opportunity, whether by way of provisional asylum or otherwise, of going to another State.

Article 4

States granting asylum shall not permit persons who have received asylum to engage in activities contrary to the purposes and principles of the United Nations.

37.

PROCLAMATION OF TEHERAN

Proclaimed by the International Conference on Human Rights at Teheran on 13 May 1968

The International Conference on Human Rights,

Having met at Teheran from April 22 to May 13, 1968 to review the progress made in the twenty years since the adoption of the Universal Declaration of Human Rights and to formulate a programme for the future,

Having considered the problems relating to the activities of the United Nations for the promotion and encouragement of respect for human rights and fundamental freedoms,

Bearing in mind the resolutions adopted by the Conference,

Noting that the observance of the International Year for Human Rights takes place at a time when the world is undergoing a process of unprecedented change,

Having regard to the new opportunities made available by the rapid progress of science and technology,

Believing that, in an age when conflict and violence prevail in many parts of the world, the fact of human interdependence and the need for human solidarity are more evident than ever before,

Recognizing that peace is the universal aspiration of mankind and that peace and justice are indispensable to the full realization of human rights and fundamental freedoms,

Solemnly proclaims that:

1. It is imperative that the members of the international community fulfill their solemn obligations to promote and encourage respect for human rights and fundamental freedoms for all without distinctions of any kind such as race, colour, sex, language, religion, political or other opinions;

2. The Universal Declaration of Human Rights states a common understanding of the peoples of the world concerning the inalienable and inviolable rights of all members of the human family and constitutes an obligation for the members of the international community;

3. The International Covenant on Civil and Political Rights, the International Covenant on Economic, Social and Cultural Rights, the Declaration on the Granting of Independence to Colonial Countries and Peoples, the International Convention on the Elimination of All Forms of Racial Discrimination as well as other conventions and declarations in the field of human rights adopted under the auspices of the United Nations, the specialized agencies and the regional intergovernmental organizations, have created new standards and obligations to which States should conform;

4. Since the adoption of the Universal Declaration of Human Rights the United Nations has made substantial progress in defining standards for the enjoyment and protection of human rights and fundamental freedoms. During this period many important international instruments were adopted but much remains to be done in regard to the implementation of those rights and freedoms;

5. The primary aim of the United Nations in the sphere of human rights is the achievement by each individual of the maximum freedom and dignity. For the realization of this objective, the laws of every country should grant each individual, irrespective of race, language, religion or political belief, freedom of expression, of information, of conscience and of religion, as well as the right to participate in the political, economic, cultural and social life of his country;

6. States should reaffirm their determination effectively to enforce the principles enshrined in the Charter of the United Nations and in other international instruments that concern human rights and fundamental freedoms;

7. Gross denials of human rights under the repugnant policy of *apartheid* is a matter of the gravest concern to the international community. This policy of *apartheid* condemned as a crime against humanity, continues seriously to disturb international peace and security. It is therefore imperative for the international community to use every possible means to eradicate this evil. The struggle against *apartheid* is recognized as legitimate;

8. The peoples of the world must be made fully aware of the evils of racial discrimination and must join in combating them. The implementation of this principle of non-discrimination, embodied in the Charter of the United Nations, the Universal Declaration of Human Rights, and other international instruments in the field of human rights, constitutes a most urgent task of mankind at the international as well as at the national level. All ideologies based on racial superiority and intolerance must be condemned and resisted;

9. Eight years after the General Assembly's Declaration on the Granting of Independence to Colonial Countries and Peoples the problems of colonialism

continue to preoccupy the international community. It is a matter of urgency that all Member States should co-operate with the appropriate organs of the United Nations so that effective measures can be taken to ensure that the Declaration is fully implemented;

10. Massive denials of human rights, arising out of aggression or any armed conflict with their tragic consequences, and resulting in untold human misery, engender reactions which could engulf the world in ever growing hostilities. It is the obligation of the international community to co-operate in eradicating such scourges;

11. Gross denials of human rights arising from discrimination on grounds of race, religion, belief or expressions of opinion outrage the conscience of mankind and endanger the foundations of freedom, justice and peace in the world;

12. The widening gap between the economically developed and developing countries impedes the realization of human rights in the international community. The failure of the Development Decade to reach its modest objectives makes it all the more imperative for every nation, according to its capacities, to make the maximum possible effort to close this gap;

13. Since human rights and fundamental freedoms are indivisible, the full realization of civil and political rights without the enjoyment of economic, social and cultural rights is impossible. The achievement of lasting progress in the implementation of human rights is dependent upon sound and effective national and international policies of economic and social development;

14. The existence of over seven hundred million illiterates throughout the world is an enormous obstacle to all efforts at realizing the aims and purposes of the Charter of the United Nations and the provisions of the Universal Declaration of Human rights. International action aimed at eradicating illiteracy from the face of the earth and promoting education at all levels requires urgent attention;

15. The discrimination of which women are still victims in various regions of the world must be eliminated. An inferior status for women is contrary to the Charter of the United Nations as well as the provisions of the Universal Declaration of Human Rights. The full implementation of the Declaration on the Elimination of Discrimination against Women is a necessity for the progress of mankind;

16. The protection of the family and of the child remains the concern of the international community. Parents have a basic human right to determine freely and responsibly the number and the spacing of their children;

17. The aspirations of the younger generation for a better world, in which human rights and fundamental freedoms are fully implemented, must be given the highest encouragement. It is imperative that youth participate in shaping the future of mankind;

18. While recent scientific discoveries and technological advances have opened vast prospects for economic, social and cultural progress, such developments may nevertheless endanger the rights and freedoms of individuals and will require continuing attention;

19. Disarmament would release immense human and material resources now devoted to military purposes. These resources should be used for the promotion of human rights and fundamental freedoms. General and complete disarmament is one of the highest aspirations of all peoples;

Therefore,

The International Conference on Human Rights,

1. *Affirming* its faith in the principles of the Universal Declaration of Human Rights and other international instruments in this field,

2. *Urges* all peoples and governments to dedicate themselves to the principles enshrined in the Universal Declaration of Human Rights and to redouble their efforts to provide for all human beings a life consonant with freedom and dignity and conducive to physical, mental, social and spiritual welfare.

38.

DECLARATION ON SOCIAL PROGRESS AND DEVELOPMENT

Proclaimed by the General Assembly of the United Nations on 11 December 1969 (resolution 2542 (XXIV))

The General Assembly,

Mindful of the pledge of Members of the United Nations under the Charter to take joint and separate action in co-operation with the Organization to promote higher standards of living, full employment and conditions of economic and social progress and development,

Reaffirming faith in human rights and fundamental freedoms and in the principles of peace, of the dignity and worth of the human person, and of social justice proclaimed in the Charter,

Recalling the principles of the Universal Declaration of Human Rights, the International Covenants on Human Rights, the Declaration of the Rights of the Child, the Declaration on the Granting of Independence to Colonial Countries and Peoples, the International Convention on the Elimination of All Forms of Racial Discrimination, the United Nations Declaration on the Elimination of All Forms of Racial Discrimination, the Declaration on the Promotion among Youth of the Ideals of Peace, Mutual Respect and Understanding between Peoples, the Declaration on the Elimination of Discrimination against Women and of resolutions of the United Nations,

Bearing in mind the standards already set for social progress in the constitutions, conventions, recommendations and resolutions of the International Labour Organisation, the Food and Agriculture Organization of the United Nations, the United Nations Educational, Scientific and Cultural Organization, the World Health Organization, the United Nations Children's Fund and of other organizations concerned,

Convinced that man can achieve complete fulfilment of his aspirations only within a just social order and that it is consequently of cardinal importance to accelerate social and economic progress everywhere, thus contributing to international peace and solidarity,

Convinced that international peace and security on the one hand, and social progress and economic development on the other, are closely interdependent and influence each other,

Persuaded that social development can be promoted by peaceful coexistence, friendly relations and co-operation among States with different social, economic or political systems,

Emphasizing the interdependence of economic and social development in the wider process of growth and change, as well as the importance of a strategy of integrated development which takes full account at all stages of its social aspects,

Regretting the inadequate progress achieved in the world social situation despite the efforts of States and the international community,

Recognizing that the primary responsibility for the development of the developing countries rests on those countries themselves and acknowledging the pressing need to narrow and eventually close the gap in the standards of living between economically more advanced and developing countries and, to that end, that Member States shall have the responsibility to pursue internal and external policies designed to promote social development throughout the world, and in particular to assist developing countries to accelerate their economic growth,

Recognizing the urgency of devoting to works of peace and social progress resources being expended on armaments and wasted on conflict and destruction,

Conscious of the contribution that science and technology can render towards meeting the needs common to all humanity,

Believing that the primary task of all States and international organizations is to eliminate from the life of society all evils and obstacles to social progress, particularly such evils as inequality, exploitation, war, colonialism and racism,

Desirous of promoting the progress of all mankind towards these goals and of overcoming all obstacles to their realization,

Solemnly proclaims this Declaration on Social Progress and Development and calls for national and international action for its use as a common basis for social development policies:

PART I - PRINCIPLES

Article 1

All peoples and all human beings, without distinction as to race, colour, sex, language, religion, nationality, ethnic origin, family or social status, or political or other conviction, shall have the right to live in dignity and freedom and to enjoy the fruits of social progress and should, on their part, contribute to it.

Article 2

Social progress and development shall be founded on respect for the dignity and value of the human person and shall ensure the promotion of human rights and social justice, which requires:
(a) The immediate and final elimination of all forms of inequality, exploitation of peoples and individuals, colonialism and racism, including nazism and *apartheid*, and all other policies and ideologies opposed to the purposes and principles of the United Nations;
(b) The recognition and effective implementation of civil and political rights as well as of economic, social and cultural rights without any discrimination.

Article 3

The following are considered primary conditions of social progress and development:
(a) National independence based on the right of peoples to self-determination;
(b) The principle of non-interference in the internal affairs of States;
(c) Respect for the sovereignty and territorial integrity of States;
(d) Permanent sovereignty of each nation over its natural wealth and resources;
(e) The right and responsibility of each State and, as far as they are concerned, each nation and people to determine freely its own objectives of social development, to set its own priorities and to decide in conformity with the principles of the Charter of the United Nations the means and methods of their achievement without any external interference;
(f) Peaceful coexistence, peace, friendly relations and co-operation among States irrespective of differences in their social, economic or political systems.

Article 4

The family as a basic unit of society and the natural environment for the growth and well-being of all its members, particularly children and youth, should be assisted and protected so that it may fully assume its responsibilities within the community. Parents have the exclusive right to determine freely and responsibly the number and spacing of their children.

Article 5

Social progress and development require the full utilization of human resources, including, in particular:
(a) The encouragement of creative initiative under conditions of enlightened public opinion;
(b) The dissemination of national and international information for the purpose of making individuals aware of changes occurring in society as a whole;
(c) The active participation of all elements of society, individually or through associations, in defining and in achieving the common goals of development with full respect for the fundamental freedoms embodied in the Universal Declaration of Human Rights;
(d) The assurance to disadvantaged or marginal sectors of the population of equal opportunities for social and economic advancement in order to achieve an effectively integrated society.

Article 6

Social development requires the assurance to everyone of the right to work and the free choice of employment.

Social progress and development require the participation of all members of society in productive and socially useful labour and the establishment, in conformity with human rights and fundamental freedoms and with the principles of justice and the social function of property, of forms of ownership of land and of the means of production which preclude any kind of exploitation of man, ensure equal rights to property for all and create conditions leading to genuine equality among people.

Article 7

The rapid expansion of national income and wealth and their equitable distribution among all members of society are fundamental to all social progress, and they should therefore be in the forefront of the preoccupations of every State and Government.

The improvement in the position of the developing countries in international trade resulting among other things from the achievement of favourable terms of trade and of equitable and remunerative prices at which developing countries market their products is necessary in order to make it possible to increase national income and in order to advance social development.

Article 8

Each Government has the primary role and ultimate responsibility of ensuring the social progress and well-being of its people, of planning social development measures as part of comprehensive development plans, of encouraging and co-ordinating or integrating all national efforts towards this end and of introducing necessary changes in the social structure. In planning social development measures, the diversity of the needs of developing and developed areas, and of urban and rural areas, within each country, shall be taken into due account.

Article 9

Social progress and development are the common concerns of the international community, which shall supplement, by concerted international action, national efforts to raise the living standards of peoples.

Social progress and economic growth require recognition of the common interest of all nations in the exploration, conservation, use and exploitation, exclusively for peaceful purposes and in the interests of all mankind, of those areas of the environment such as outer space and the sea-bed and ocean floor and the subsoil thereof, beyond the limits of national jurisdiction, in accordance with the Purposes and Principles of the Charter of the United Nations.

PART II - OBJECTIVES

Social progress and development shall aim at the continuous raising of the material and spiritual standards of living of all members of society, with respect for and in compliance with human rights and fundamental freedoms, through the attainment of the following main goals:

Article 10

(a) The assurance at all levels of the right to work and the right of everyone to form trade unions and workers' associations and to bargain collectively; promotion of full productive employment and elimination of unemployment and under-employment; establishment of equitable and favourable conditions of work for all, including the improvement of health and safety conditions; assurance of just remuneration for labour without any discrimination as well as a sufficiently high minimum wage to ensure a decent standard of living; the protection of the consumer;

(b) The elimination of hunger and malnutrition and the guarantee of the right to proper nutrition;

(c) The elimination of poverty; the assurance of a steady improvement in levels of living and of a just and equitable distribution of income;

(d) The achievement of the highest standards of health and the provision of health protection for the entire population, if possible free of charge;

(e) The eradication of illiteracy and the assurance of the right to universal access to culture, to free compulsory education at the elementary level and to free education at all levels; the raising of the general level of life-long education;

(f) The provision for all, particularly persons in low income groups and large families, of adequate housing and community services.

Social progress and development shall aim equally at the progressive attainment of the following main goals:

Article 11

(a) The provision of comprehensive social security schemes and social welfare services; the establishment and improvement of social security and insurance schemes for all persons who, because of illness, disability or old age, are temporarily or permanently unable to earn a living, with a view to ensuring a proper standard of living for such persons and for their families and dependants;

(b) The protection of the rights of the mother and child; concern for the upbringing and health of children; the provision of measures to safeguard the health and welfare of women and particularly of working mothers during pregnancy and the infancy of their children, as well as of mothers whose earnings are the sole source of livelihood for the family; the granting to women of pregnancy and maternity leave and allowances without loss of employment or wages;

(c) The protection of the rights and the assuring of the welfare of children, the aged and the disabled; the provision of protection for the physically or mentally disadvantaged;

(d) The education of youth in, and promotion among them of, the ideals of justice and peace, mutual respect and understanding among peoples; the promotion of full participation of youth in the process of national development;

(e) The provision of social defence measures and the elimination of conditions leading to crime and delinquency, especially juvenile delinquency;

(f) The guarantee that all individuals, without discrimination of any kind, are made aware of their rights and obligations and receive the necessary aid in the exercise and safeguarding of their rights.

Social progress and development shall further aim at achieving the following main objectives:

Article 12

(a) The creation of conditions for rapid and sustained social and economic development, particularly in the developing countries; change in international economic relations, new and effective methods of international co-operation in which equality of opportunity should be as much a prerogative of nations as of individuals within a nation;
(b) The elimination of all forms of discrimination and exploitation and all other practices and ideologies contrary to the purposes and principles of the Charter of the United Nations;
(c) The elimination of all forms of foreign economic exploitation, particularly that practised by international monopolies, in order to enable the people of every country to enjoy in full the benefits of their national resources.

Social progress and development shall finally aim at the attainment of the following main goals:

Article 13

(a) Equitable sharing of scientific and technological advances by developed and developing countries, and a steady increase in the use of science and technology for the benefit of the social development of society;
(b) The establishment of a harmonious balance between scientific, technological and material progress and the intellectual, spiritual, cultural and moral advancement of humanity;
(c) The protection and improvement of the human environment.

PART III - MEANS AND METHODS

On the basis of the principles set forth in this Declaration, the achievement of the objectives of social progress and development requires the mobilization of the necessary resources by national and international action, with particular attention to such means and methods as:

Article 14

(a) Planning for social progress and development, as an integrated part of balanced over-all development planning;

(b) The establishment, where necessary, of national systems for framing and carrying out social policies and programmes, and the promotion by the countries concerned of planned regional development, taking into account differing regional conditions and needs, particularly the development of regions which are less favoured or under-developed by comparison with the rest of the country;

(c) The promotion of basic and applied social research, particularly comparative international research applied to the planning and execution of social development programmes.

Article 15

(a) The adoption of measures to ensure the effective participation, as appropriate, of all the elements of society in the preparation and execution of national plans and programmes of economic and social development;

(b) The adoption of measures for an increasing rate of popular participation in the economic, social, cultural and political life of countries through national governmental bodies, non-governmental organizations, co-operatives, rural associations, workers' and employers' organizations and women's and youth organizations, by such methods as national and regional plans for social and economic progress and community development, with a view to achieving a fully integrated national society, accelerating the process of social mobility and consolidating the democratic system;

(c) Mobilization of public opinion, at both national and international levels, in support of the principles and objectives of social progress and development;

(d) The dissemination of social information, at the national and the international level, to make people aware of changing circumstances in society as a whole, and to educate the consumer.

Article 16

(a) Maximum mobilization of all national resources and their rational and efficient utilization; promotion of increased and accelerated productive investment in social and economic fields and of employment; orientation of society towards the development process;

(b) Progressively increasing provision of the necessary budgetary and other resources required for financing the social aspects of development;

(c) Achievement of equitable distribution of national income, utilizing, *inter alia*, the fiscal system and government spending as an instrument for the equitable distribution and redistribution of income in order to promote social progress;

(d) The adoption of measures aimed at prevention of such an outflow of

capital from developing countries as would be detrimental to their economic and social development.

Article 17

(a) The adoption of measures to accelerate the process of industrialization, especially in developing countries, with due regard for its social aspects, in the interests of the entire population; development of an adequate organizational and legal framework conducive to an uninterrupted and diversified growth of the industrial sector; measures to overcome the adverse social effects which may result from urban development and industrialization, including automation; maintenance of a proper balance between rural and urban development, and in particular, measures designed to ensure healthier living conditions, especially in large industrial centres;

(b) Integrated planning to meet the problems of urbanization and urban development;

(c) Comprehensive rural development schemes to raise the levels of living of the rural populations and to facilitate such urban-rural relationships and population distribution as will promote balanced national development and social progress;

(d) Measures for appropriate supervision of the utilization of land in the interests of society.

The achievement of the objectives of social progress and development equally requires the implementation of the following means and methods:

Article 18

(a) The adoption of appropriate legislative, administrative and other measures ensuring to everyone not only political and civil rights, but also the full realization of economic, social and cultural rights without any discrimination;

(b) The promotion of democratically based social and institutional reforms and motivation for change basic to the elimination of all forms of discrimination and exploitation and conducive to high rates of economic and social progress, to include land reform, in which the ownership and use of land will be made to serve best the objectives of social justice and economic development;

(c) The adoption of measures to boost and diversify agricultural production through, *inter alia,* the implementation of democratic agrarian reforms, to ensure an adequate and well-balanced supply of food, its equitable distribution among the whole population and the improvement of nutritional standards;

(d) The adoption of measures to introduce, with the participation of the Government, low-cost housing programmes in both rural and urban areas;

(e) Development and expansion of the system of transportation and communications, particularly in developing countries.

Article 19

(a) The provision of free health services to the whole population and of adequate preventive and curative facilities and welfare medical services accessible to all;

(b) The enactment and establishment of legislative measures and administrative regulations with a view to the implementation of comprehensive programmes of social security schemes and social welfare services and to the improvement and co-ordination of existing services;

(c) The adoption of measures and the provision of social welfare services to migrant workers and their families, in conformity with the provisions of Convention No. 97 of the International Labour Organisation* and other international instruments relating to migrant workers;

(d) The institution of appropriate measures for the rehabilitation of mentally or physically disabled persons, especially children and youth, so as to enable them to the fullest possible extent to be useful members of society – these measures shall include the provision of treatment and technical appliances, education, vocational and social guidance, training and selective placement, and other assistance required – and the creation of social conditions in which the handicapped are not discriminated against because of their disabilities.

Article 20

(a) The provision of full democratic freedoms to trade unions; freedom of association for all workers, including the right to bargain collectively and to strike; recognition of the right to form other organizations of working people; the provision for the growing participation of trade unions in economic and social development; effective participation of all members of trade unions in the deciding of economic and social issues which affect their interests;

(b) The improvement of health and safety conditions for workers, by means of appropriate technological and legislative measures and the provision of the material prerequisites for the implementation of those measures, including the limitation of working hours;

(c) The adoption of appropriate measures for the development of harmonious industrial relations.

* Convention concerning Migration for Employment (Revised 1949), International Labour Office, *Conventions and Recommendations, 1919–1966* (Geneva, 1966), p. 743.

Article 21

(a) The training of national personnel and cadres, including administrative, executive, professional and technical personnel needed for social development and for over-all development plans and policies;

(b) The adoption of measures to accelerate the extension and improvement of general, vocational and technical education and of training and retraining, which should be provided free at all levels;

(c) Raising the general level of education; development and expansion of national information media, and their rational and full use towards continuing education of the whole population and towards encouraging its participation in social development activities; the constructive use of leisure, particularly that of children and adolescents;

(d) The formulation of national and international policies and measures to avoid the 'brain drain' and obviate its adverse effects.

Article 22

(a) The development and co-ordination of policies and measures designed to strengthen the essential functions of the family as a basic unit of society;

(b) The formulation and establishment, as needed, of programmes in the field of population, within the framework of national demographic policies and as part of the welfare medical services, including education, training of personnel and the provision to families of the knowledge and means necessary to enable them to exercise their right to determine freely and responsibly the number and spacing of their children;

(c) The establishment of appropriate child-care facilities in the interest of children and working parents.

The achievement of the objectives of social progress and development finally requires the implementation of the following means and methods:

Article 23

(a) The laying down of economic growth rate targets for the developing countries within the United Nations policy for development, high enough to lead to a substantial acceleration of their rates of growth;

(b) The provision of greater assistance on better terms; the implementation of the aid volume target of a minimum of 1 per cent of the gross national product at market prices of economically advanced countries; the general easing of the terms of lending to the developing countries through low interest rates on loans and long grace periods for the repayment of loans, and the

assurance that the allocation of such loans will be based strictly on socio-economic criteria free of any political considerations;

(c) The provision of technical, financial and material assistance, both bilateral and multilateral, to the fullest possible extent and on favourable terms, and improved co-ordination of international assistance for the achievement of the social objectives of national development plans;

(d) The provision to the developing countries of technical, financial and material assistance and of favourable conditions to facilitate the direct exploitation of their national resources and natural wealth by those countries with a view to enabling the peoples of those countries to benefit fully from their national resources;

(e) The expansion of international trade based on principles of equality and non-discrimination, the rectification of the position of developing countries in international trade by equitable terms of trade, a general, non-reciprocal and non-discriminatory system of preferences for the exports of developing countries to the developed countries, the establishment and implementation of general and comprehensive commodity agreements, and the financing of reasonable buffer stocks by international institutions.

Article 24

(a) Intensification of international co-operation with a view to ensuring the international exchange of information, knowledge and experience concerning social progress and development;

(b) The broadest possible international technical, scientific and cultural co-operation and reciprocal utilization of the experience of countries with different economic and social systems and different levels of development, on the basis of mutual advantage and strict observance of and respect for national sovereignty;

(c) Increased utilization of science and technology for social and economic development; arrangements for the transfer and exchange of technology, including know-how and patents, to the developing countries.

Article 25

(a) The establishment of legal and administrative measures for the protection and improvement of the human environment, at both national and international level;

(b) The use and exploitation, in accordance with the appropriate international régimes, of the resources of areas of the environment such as outer space and the sea-bed and ocean floor and the subsoil thereof, beyond the limits of national jurisdiction, in order to supplement national resources available for the achievement of economic and social progress and development in every country, irrespective of its geographical location, special consideration being given to the interests and needs of the developing countries.

Article 26

Compensation for damages, be they social or economic in nature – including restitution and reparations – caused as a result of aggression and of illegal occupation of territory by the aggressor.

Article 27

(a) The achievement of general and complete disarmament and the channelling of the progressively released resources to be used for economic and social progress for the welfare of people everywhere and, in particular, for the benefit of developing countries;
(b) The adoption of measures contributing to disarmament, including, *inter alia,* the complete prohibition of tests of nuclear weapons, the prohibition of the development, production and stockpiling of chemical and bacteriological (biological) weapons and the prevention of the pollution of oceans and inland waters by nuclear wastes.

39.

Declaration on Principles of International Law Concerning Friendly Relations and Cooperation Among States in Accordance with the Charter of the United Nations

The seven principles elaborated in this declaration were enunciated by the General Assembly in 1962, which at the same time decided that they should be further studied (GA Res. 1815 (XVII) of 18 December 1962). With this object, a "Special Committee on Principles of International Law Concerning Friendly Relations among States" was established by GA Res. 1966 (XVIII) of 16 December 1963, instructing the Special Committee to study and report on four of the principles. GA Res. 2103 (XX) of 20 December 1965 requested the Special Committee to complete the elaboration of all seven principles. The Special Committee held several sessions and completed its work at the session held in Geneva from 31 March to 1 May 1970, adopting a Draft Declaration of Principles on 1 May.

On 24 October 1970 the General Assembly adopted without vote the Declaration on Principles of International Law Concerning Friendly Relations and Co-operation among States in Accordance with the Charter of the United Nations, which was annexed to GA Res. 2625 (XXV).

Preamble

The General Assembly,

Reaffirming in the terms of the Charter of the United Nations that the maintenance of international peace and security and the development of friendly relations and co-operation between nations are among the fundamental purposes of the United Nations,

Recalling that the peoples of the United Nations are determined to practise tolerance and live together in peace with one another as good neighbours,

Bearing in mind the importance of maintaining and strengthening international peace founded upon freedom, equality, justice and respect for fundamental human rights and of developing friendly relations among nations irrespective of their political, economic and social systems or the levels of their development,

Bearing in mind also the paramount importance of the Charter of the United Nations in the promotion of the rule of law among nations,

Considering that the faithful observance of the principles of international law concerning friendly relations and co-operation among States and the fulfilment in good faith of the obligations assumed by States, in accordance with the Charter, is of the greatest importance for the maintenance of international peace and security and for the implementation of the other purposes of the United Nations,

Noting that the great political, economic and social changes in scientific progress which have taken place in the world since the adoption of the Charter give increased importance to these principles and to the need for their more effective application in the conduct of States wherever carried on,

Recalling the established principle that outer space, including the Moon and other celestial bodies, is not subject to national appropriation by claim of sovereignty, by means of use or occupation, or by any other means, and mindful of the fact that consideration is being given in the United Nations to the question of establishing other appropriate provisions similarly inspired,

Convinced that the strict observance by States of the obligation not to intervene in the affairs of any other State is an essential condition to ensure that nations live together in peace with one another, since the practice of any form of intervention not only violates the spirit and letter of the Charter, but also leads to the creation of situations which threaten international peace and security,

Recalling the duty of States to refrain in their international relations from military, political, economic or any other form of coercion aimed against the political independence or territorial integrity of any State,

Considering it essential that all States shall refrain in their international relations from the threat or use of force against the territorial integrity or political independence of any State, or in any other manner inconsistent with the purposes of the United Nations,

Considering it equally essential that all States shall settle their international disputes by peaceful means in accordance with the Charter,

Reaffirming, in accordance with the Charter, the basic importance of sovereign equality and stressing that the purposes of the United Nations can be implemented only if States enjoy sovereign equality and comply fully with the requirements of this principle in their international relations,

Convinced that the subjection of peoples to alien subjugation, domination and exploitation constitutes a major obstacle to the promotion of international peace and security,

Convinced that the principle of equal rights and self-determination of peoples constitutes a significant contribution to contemporary international law, and that its effective application is of paramount importance for the promotion of friendly relations among States, based on respect for the principle of sovereign equality,

Convinced in consequence that any attempt aimed at the partial or total disruption of the national unity and territorial integrity of a State or country or at its political independence is incompatible with the purposes and principles of the Charter,

Considering the provisions of the Charter as a whole and taking into account the role of relevant resolutions adopted by the competent organs of the United Nations relating to the content of the principles,

Considering that the progressive development and codification of the following principles:
(a) The principles that States shall refrain in their international relations from the threat or use of force against the territorial integrity or political independence of any State, or in any other manner inconsistent with the purposes of the United Nations,
(b) The principle that States shall settle their international disputes by peaceful means in such a manner that international peace and security and justice are not endangered,
(c) The duty not to intervene in matters within the domestic jurisdiction of any State, in accordance with the Charter,
(d) The duty of States to co-operate with one another in accordance with the Charter,
(e) The principle of equal rights and self-determination of peoples,
(f) The principle of sovereign equality of States,
(g) The principle that States shall fulfil in good faith the obligations assumed by them in accordance with the Charter,
so as to secure their more effective application within the international community, would promote the realization of the purposes of the United Nations,

Having considered the principles of international law relating to friendly relations and co-operation among States,

1. *Solemnly proclaims* the following principles:

The principle that States shall refrain in their international relations from the threat or use of force against the territorial integrity or political independence of any State, or in any other manner inconsistent with the purposes of the United Nations

Every State has the duty to refrain in its international relations from the threat or use of force against the territorial integrity or political independence of any State, or in any other manner inconsistent with the purposes of the United Nations. Such a threat or use of force constitutes a violation of international law and the Charter of the United Nations and shall never be employed as a means of settling international issues.

A war of aggression constitutes a crime against the peace, for which there is responsibility under international law.

In accordance with the purposes and principles of the United Nations, States have the duty to refrain from propaganda for wars of aggression.

Every State has the duty to refrain from the threat or use of force to violate the existing international boundaries of another State or as a means of solving international disputes, including territorial disputes and problems concerning frontiers of States.

Every State likewise has the duty to refrain from the threat or use of force to violate international lines of demarcation, such as armistice lines, established by or pursuant to an international agreement to which it is a party or which it is otherwise bound to respect. Nothing in the foregoing shall be construed as prejudicing the positions of the parties concerned with regard to the status and effects of such lines under their special régimes or as affecting their temporary character.

States have a duty to refrain from acts of reprisal involving the use of force.

Every State has the duty to refrain from any forcible action which deprives peoples referred to in the elaboration of the principle of equal rights and self-determination of their right to self-determination and freedom and independence.

Every State has the duty to refrain from organizing or encouraging the organization of irregular forces or armed bands, including mercenaries, for incursion into the territory of another State.

Every State has the duty to refrain from organizing, instigating, assisting or participating in acts of civil strife or terrorist acts in another State or acquiescing in organized activities within its territory directed towards the commission of such acts, when the acts referred to in the present paragraph involve a threat or use of force.

The territory of a State shall not be the object of military occupation resulting from the use of force in contravention of the provisions of the Charter. The territory of a State shall not be the object of acquisition by another State resulting from the threat or use of force. No territorial acquisition resulting from the threat or use of force shall be recognized as legal. Nothing in the foregoing shall be construed as affecting:

(*a*) Provisions of the Charter or any international agreement prior to the Charter régime and valid under international law; or

(*b*) The powers of the Security Council under the Charter.

All States shall pursue in good faith negotiations for the early conclusion of a universal treaty on general and complete disarmament under effective international control and strive to adopt appropriate measures to reduce international tensions and strengthen confidence among States.

All States shall comply in good faith with their obligations under the generally recognized principles and rules of international law with respect to the maintenance of international peace and security, and shall endeavour to make the United Nations security system based on the Charter more effective.

Nothing in the foregoing paragraphs shall be construed as enlarging or diminishing in any way the scope of the provisions of the Charter concerning cases in which the use of force is lawful.

The principle that States shall settle their international disputes by peaceful means in such a manner that international peace and security and justice are not endangered

Every State shall settle its international disputes with other States by peaceful means, in such a manner that international peace and security and justice are not endangered.

States shall accordingly seek early and just settlement of their international disputes by negotiation, inquiry, mediation, conciliation, arbitration, judicial settlement, resort to regional agencies or arrangements or other peaceful means of their choice. In seeking such a settlement the parties shall agree upon such peaceful means as many be appropriate to the circumstances and nature of the dispute.

The parties to a dispute have the duty, in the event of failure to reach a solution by any one of the above peaceful means, to continue to seek a settlement of the dispute by other peaceful means agreed upon by them.

States parties to an international dispute, as well as other States, shall refrain from any action which may aggravate the situation so as to endanger the maintenance of international peace and security, and shall act in accordance with the purposes and principles of the United Nations.

International disputes shall be settled on the basis of the sovereign equality of States and in accordance with the principle of free choice of means. Recourse to, or acceptance of, a settlement procedure freely agreed to by States with regard to existing or future disputes to which they are parties shall not be regarded as incompatible with sovereign equality.

Nothing in the foregoing paragraphs prejudices or derogates from the applicable provisions of the Charter, in particular those relating to the pacific settlement of international disputes.

The principle concerning the duty not to intervene in matters within the domestic jurisdiction of any State, in accordance with the Charter

No State or group of States has the right to intervene, directly or indirectly, for any reason whatever, in the internal or external affairs of any other State. Consequently, armed intervention and all other forms of interference or attempted threats against the personality of the State or against its political, economic and cultural elements, are in violation of international law.

No State may use or encourage the use of economic, political or any other type of measures to coerce another State in order to obtain from it the subordination of the exercise of its sovereign rights and to secure from it advantages of any kind. Also, no State shall organize, assist, foment, finance, incite or tolerate subversive, terrorist or armed activities directed towards the violent overthrow of the régime of another State, or interfere in civil strife in another State.

The use of force to deprive peoples of their national identity constitutes a violation of their inalienable rights and of the principle of non-intervention.

Every State has an inalienable right to choose its political, economic, social and cultural systems, without interference in any form by another State.

Nothing in the foregoing paragraphs shall be construed as affecting the relevant provisions of the Charter relating to the maintenance of international peace and security.

The duty of States to co-operate with one another in accordance with the Charter

States have the duty to co-operate with one another, irrespective of the differences in their political, economic and social systems, in the various spheres of international relations, in order to maintain international peace and security and to promote international economic stability and progress, the general welfare of nations and international co-operation free from discrimination based on such differences.

To this end:

(*a*) States shall co-operate with other States in the maintenance of international peace and security;

(*b*) States shall co-operate in the promotion of universal respect for, and observance of, human rights and fundamental freedoms for all, and in the elimination of all forms of racial discrimination and all forms of religious intolerance;

(*c*) States shall conduct their international relations in the economic, social, cultural, technical and trade fields in accordance with the principles of sovereign equality and non-intervention;

(*d*) States Members of the United Nations have the duty to take joint and separate action in co-operation with the United Nations in accordance with the relevant provisions of the Charter.

States should co-operate in the economic, social and cultural fields as well as in the field of science and technology and for the promotion of international cultural and educational progress. States should co-operate in the promotion of economic growth throughout the world, especially that of the developing countries.

The principle of equal rights and self-determination of peoples

By virtue of the principle of equal rights and self-determination of peoples enshrined in the Charter of the United Nations, all peoples have the right freely to determine, without external interference, their political status and to pursue their economic, social and cultural development, and every State has the duty to respect this right in accordance with the provisions of the Charter.

Every State has the duty to promote, through joint and separate action, realization of the principle of equal rights and self-determination of peoples, in accordance with the provisions of the Charter, and to render assistance to the United Nations in carrying out the responsibilities entrusted to it by the Charter regarding the implementation of the principle, in order:

(a) To promote friendly relations and co-operation among States; and
(b) To bring a speedy end to colonialism, having due regard to the freely expressed will of the peoples concerned;

and bearing in mind that subjection of peoples to alien subjugation, domination and exploitation constitutes a violation of the principle, as well as a denial of fundamental human rights, and is contrary to the Charter.

Every State has the duty to promote through joint and separate action universal respect for and observance of human rights and fundamental freedoms in accordance with the Charter.

The establishment of a sovereign and independent State, the free association or integration with an independent State or the emergence into any other political status freely determined by a people constitute modes of implementing the right of self-determination by that people.

Every State has the duty to refrain from any forcible action which deprives peoples referred to above in the elaboration of the present principle of their right to self-determination and freedom and independence. In their actions against, and resistance to, such forcible action in pursuit of the exercise of their right to self-determination, such peoples are entitled to seek and to receive support in accordance with the purposes and principles of the Charter.

The territory of a colony or other Non-Self-Governing Territory has, under the Charter, a status separate and distinct from the territory of the State administering it; and such separate and distinct status under the Charter shall exist until the people of the colony or Non-Self-Governing Territory have exercised their right of self-determination in accordance with the Charter, and particularly its purposes and principles.

Nothing in the foregoing paragraphs shall be construed as authorizing or encouraging any action which would dismember or impair, totally or in part, the territorial integrity or political unity of sovereign and independent States conducting themselves in compliance with the principle of equal rights and self-determination of peoples as described above and thus possessed of a government representing the whole people belonging to the territory without distinction as to race, creed or colour.

Every State shall refrain from any action aimed at the partial or total disruption of the national unity and territorial integrity of any other State or country.

The principle of sovereign equality of States

All States enjoy sovereign equality. They have equal rights and duties and are equal members of the international community, notwithstanding differences of an economic, social, political or other nature.

In particular, sovereign equality includes the following elements:
(a) States are juridically equal;
(b) Each State enjoys the rights inherent in full sovereignty;
(c) Each State has the duty to respect the personality of other States;

(*d*) The territorial integrity and political independence of the State are inviolable;
(*e*) Each State has the right freely to choose and develop its political, social, economic and cultural systems;
(*f*) Each State has the duty to comply fully and in good faith with its international obligations and to live in peace with other States.

The principle that States shall fulfil in good faith the obligations assumed by them in accordance with the Charter

Every State has the duty to fulfil in good faith the obligations assumed by it in accordance with the Charter of the United Nations.

Every State has the duty to fulfil in good faith its obligations under the generally recognized principles and rules of international law.

Every State has the duty to fulfil in good faith its obligations under international agreements valid under the generally recognized principles and rules of international law.

Where obligations arising under international agreements are in conflict with the obligations of Members of the United Nations under the Charter of the United Nations, the obligations under the Charter shall prevail.

General part

2. *Declares* that:

In their interpretation and application the above principles are interrelated and each principle should be construed in the context of the other principles.

Nothing in this Declaration shall be construed as prejudicing in any manner the provisions of the Charter or the rights and duties of Member States under the Charter or the rights of peoples under the Charter, taking into account the elaboration of these rights in this Declaration.

3. *Declares further* that:

The principles of the Charter which are embodied in this Declaration constitute basic principles of international law, and consequently appeals to all States to be guided by these principles in their international conduct and to develop their mutual relations on the basis of the strict observance of these principles.

40.

UNIVERSAL DECLARATION ON THE ERADICATION OF HUNGER AND MALNUTRITION

Adopted on 16 November 1974 by the World Food Conference convened under General Assembly resolution 3180 (XXVIII) of 17 December 1973; and endorsed by the General Assembly in its resolution 3348 (XXIX) of 17 December 1974

The World Food Conference,

Convened by the General Assembly of the United Nations and entrusted with developing ways and means whereby the international community, as a whole, could take specific action to resolve the world food problem within the broader context of development and international economic co-operation,
Adopts the following Declaration:

UNIVERSAL DECLARATION ON THE ERADICATION OF HUNGER AND MALNUTRITION

Recognizing that:

(a) The grave food crisis that is afflicting the peoples of the developing countries where most of the world's hungry and ill-nourished live and where more than two thirds of the world's population produce about one third of the world's food – an imbalance which threatens to increase in the next 10 years – is not only fraught with grave economic and social implications, but also acutely jeopardizes the most fundamental principles and values associated with the right to life and human dignity as enshrined in the Universal Declaration of Human Rights;

(b) The elimination of hunger and malnutrition, included as one of the objectives in the United Nations Declaration on Social Progress and Development, and the elimination of the causes that determine this situation are the common objectives of all nations;

(c) The situation of the peoples afflicted by hunger and malnutrition arises from their historical circumstances, especially social inequalities, including in many cases alien and colonial domination, foreign occupation, racial discrimination, *apartheid* and neo-colonialism in all its forms, which continue to be among the greatest obstacles to the full emancipation and progress of the developing countries and all the peoples involved;

(d) This situation has been aggravated in recent years by a series of crises to which the world economy has been subjected, such as the deterioration in the international monetary system, the inflationary increase in import costs, the heavy burdens imposed by external debt on the balance of payments of many developing countries, a rising food demand partly due to demographic pressure, speculation, and a shortage of, and increased costs for, essential agricultural inputs;

(e) These phenomena should be considered within the framework of the on-going negotiations on the Charter of Economic Rights and Duties of States, and the General Assembly of the United Nations should be urged unanimously to agree upon, and to adopt, a Charter that will be an effective instrument for the establishment of new international economic relations based on principles of equity and justice;

(f) All countries, big or small, rich or poor, are equal. All countries have the full right to participate in the decisions on the food problem;

(g) The well-being of the peoples of the world largely depends on the adequate production and distribution of food as well as the establishment of a world food security system which would ensure adequate availability of, and reasonable prices for, food at all times, irrespective of periodic fluctuations and vagaries of weather and free of political and economic pressures, and should thus facilitate, amongst other things, the development process of developing countries;

(h) Peace and justice encompass an economic dimension helping the solution of the world economic problems, the liquidation of under-development, offering a lasting and definitive solution of the food problem for all peoples and guaranteeing to all countries the right to implement freely and effectively their development programmes. To this effect, it is necessary to eliminate threats and resort to force and to promote peaceful co-operation between States to the fullest extent possible, to apply the principles of non-interference in the internal affairs of other States, full equality of rights and respect of national independence and sovereignty, as well as to encourage the peaceful co-operation between all States, irrespective of their political, social and economic systems. The further improvement of international relations will create better conditions for international co-operation in all fields which should make possible large financial and material resources to be used, *inter alia*, for developing agricultural production and substantially improving world food security;

(i) For a lasting solution of the food problem all efforts should be made to eliminate the widening gaps which today separate developed and developing countries and to bring about a new international economic order. It should be possible for all countries to participate actively and effectively in the new international economic relations by the establishment of suitable international systems, where appropriate, capable of producing adequate action in order to establish just and equitable relations in international economic co-operation;

(j) Developing countries reaffirm their belief that the primary responsibility for ensuring their own rapid development rests with themselves. They declare, therefore, their readiness to continue to intensify their individual and collective efforts with a view to expanding their mutual co-operation in the field of agricultural development and food production, including the eradication of hunger and malnutrition;

(k) Since, for various reasons, many developing countries are not yet always able to meet their own food needs, urgent and effective international action should be taken to assist them, free of political pressures,

Consistent with the aims and objectives of the Declaration* on the Establishment of a New International Economic Order and the Programme of Action adopted by the General Assembly at its sixth special session,

The Conference consequently solemnly proclaims:

1. Every man, woman and child has the inalienable right to be free from hunger and malnutrition in order to develop fully and maintain their physical and mental faculties. Society today already possesses sufficient resources, organizational ability and technology and hence the competence to achieve this objective. Accordingly, the eradication of hunger is a common objective of all the countries of the international community, especially of the developed countries and others in a position to help.

2. It is a fundamental responsibility of Governments to work together for higher food production and a more equitable and efficient distribution of food between countries and within countries. Governments should initiate immediately a greater concerted attack on chronic malnutrition and deficiency diseases among the vulnerable and lower income groups. In order to ensure adequate nutrition for all, Governments should formulate appropriate food and nutrition policies integrated in over-all socio-economic and agricultural development plans based on adequate knowledge of available as well as potential food resources. The importance of human milk in this connexion should be stressed on nutritional grounds.

---

* General Assembly resolutions 3201 (S-VI) and 3202 (S-VI) of 1 May 1974.

3. Food problems must be tackled during the preparation and implementation of national plans and programmes for economic and social development, with emphasis on their humanitarian aspects.

4. It is a responsibility of each State concerned, in accordance with its sovereign judgement and internal legislation, to remove the obstacles to food production and to provide proper incentives to agricultural producers. Of prime importance for the attainment of these objectives are effective measures of socio-economic transformation by agrarian, tax, credit and investment policy reform and the reorganization of rural structures, such as the reform of the conditions of ownership, the encouragement of producer and consumer co-operatives, the mobilization of the full potential of human resources, both male and female, in the developing countries for an integrated rural development and the involvement of small farmers, fishermen and landless workers in attaining the required food production and employment targets. Moreover, it is necessary to recognize the key role of women in agricultural production and rural economy in many countries, and to ensure that appropriate education, extension programmes and financial facilities are made available to women on equal terms with men.

5. Marine and inland water resources are today becoming more important than ever as a source of food and economic prosperity. Accordingly, action should be taken to promote a rational exploitation of these resources, preferably for direct human consumption, in order to contribute to meeting the food requirements of all peoples.

6. The efforts to increase food production should be complemented by every endeavour to prevent wastage of food in all its forms.

7. To give impetus to food production in developing countries and in particular in the least developed and most seriously affected among them, urgent and effective international action should be taken, by the developed countries and other countries in a position to do so, to provide them with sustained additional technical and financial assistance on favourable terms and in a volume sufficient to their needs on the basis of bilateral and multilateral arrangements. This asssistance must be free of conditions inconsistent with the sovereignty of the receiving States.

8. All countries, and primarily the highly industrialized countries, should promote the advancement of food production technology and should make all efforts to promote the transfer, adaptation and dissemination of appropriate food production technology for the benefit of the developing countries and, to that end, they should *inter alia* make all efforts to disseminate the results of their research work to Governments and scientific institutions of developing

countries in order to enable them to promote a sustained agricultural development.

9. To assure the proper conservation of natural resources being utilized, or which might be utilized, for food production, all countries must collaborate in order to facilitate the preservation of the environment, including the marine environment.

10. All developed countries and other able to do so should collaborate technically and financially with the developing countries in their efforts to expand land and water resources for agricultural production and to assure a rapid increase in the availability, at fair costs, of agricultural inputs such as fertilizers and other chemicals, high-quality seeds, credit and technology. Co-operation among developing countries, in this connexion, is also important.

11. All States should strive to the utmost to readjust, where appropriate, their agricultural policies to give priority to food production, recognizing, in this connexion the interrelationship between the world food problem and international trade. In the determination of attitudes towards farm support programmes for domestic food production, developed countries should take into account, as far as possible, the interest of the food-exporting developing countries, in order to avoid detrimental effect on their exports. Moreover, all countries should co-operate to devise effective steps to deal with the problem of stabilizing world markets and promoting equitable and remunerative prices, where appropriate through international arrangements, to improve access to markets through reduction or elimination of tariff and non-tariff barriers on the products of interest to the developing countries, to substantially increase the export earnings of these countries, to contribute to the diversification of their exports, and apply to them in the multilateral trade negotiations, the principles as agreed upon in the Tokyo Declaration, including the concept of non-reciprocity and more favourable treatment.

12. As it is the common responsibility of the entire international community to ensure the availability at all times of adequate world supplies of basic food-stuffs by way of appropriate reserves, including emergency reserves, all countries should co-operate in the establishment of an effective system of world food security by:
- Participating in and supporting the operation of the Global Information and Early Warning System on Food and Agriculture;
- Adhering to the objectives, policies and guidelines of the proposed International Undertaking on World Food Security as endorsed by the World Food Conference;
- Earmarking, where possible, stocks or funds for meeting international

emergency food requirements as envisaged in the proposed International Undertaking on World Food Security and developing international guidelines to provide for the co-ordination and the utilization of such stocks;
– Co-operating in the provision of food aid for meeting emergency and nutritional needs as well as for stimulating rural employment through development projects.

All donor countries should accept and implement the concept of forward planning of food aid and make all efforts to provide commodities and/or financial assistance that will ensure adequate quantities of grains and other food commodities.

Time is short. Urgent and sustained action is vital. The Conference, therefore, calls upon all peoples expressing their will as individuals, and through their Governments, and non-governmental organizations, to work together to bring about the end of the age-old scourge of hunger.

The Conference affirms:

The determination of the participating States to make full use of the United Nations system in the implementation of this Declaration and the other decisions adopted by the Conference.

41.

Declaration on the Establishment of a New International Economic Order

GA Res. 3201 (S-VI) of 1 May 1974.

We, the Members of the United Nations,
Having convened a special session of the General Assembly to study for the first time the problems of raw materials and development, devoted to the consideration of the most important economic problems facing the world community,
Bearing in mind the spirit, purposes and principles of the Charter of the United Nations to promote the economic advancement and social progress of all peoples,
Solemnly proclaim our united determination to work urgently for

THE ESTABLISHMENT OF A NEW INTERNATIONAL ECONOMIC ORDER

based on equity, sovereign equality, interdependence, common interest and co-operation among all States, irrespective of their economic and social systems, which shall correct inequalities and redress existing injustices, make it possible to eliminate the widening gap between the developed and the developing countries and ensure steadily accelerating economic and social development in peace and justice for present and future generations, and, to that end, declare:

1. The greatest and most significant achievement during the last decades has been the indepedence from colonial and alien domination of a large number of peoples and nations which has enabled them to become members of the community of free peoples. Technological progress has also been made in all spheres of economic activities in the last three decades, thus providing a solid potential for improving the well-being of all peoples. However, the remaining vestiges of alien and colonial domination, foreign occupation, racial discrimination, *apartheid* and neo-colonialism in all its forms continue to be among the greatest obstacles to the full emancipation and progress of the developing countries and all the peoples involved. The benefits of technological progress are not shared equitably by all members of the international community. The developing countries, which constitute 70 per cent of the world population, account for only 30 per cent of the world's income. It has proved impossible to achieve an even and balanced development of the international community under the existing international economic order. The gap between the developed and the developing countries continues to widen in a system which was established at a time when most of the developing countries did not even exist as indepent States and which perpetuates inequality.

2. The present international economic order is in direct conflict with current developments in international political and economic relations. Since 1970, the world economy has experienced a series of grave crises which have had severe repercussions, especially on the developing countries because of their generally greater vulnerability to external economic impulses. The developing world has become a powerful factor that makes its influence felt in all fields of international activity. These irreversible

changes in the relationship of forces in the world necessitate the active, full and equal participation of the developing countries in the formulation and application of all decisions that concern the international community.

3. All these changes have thrust into prominence the reality of interdependence of all the members of the world community. Current events have brought into sharp focus the realization that the interests of the developed countries and the interests of the developing countries can no longer be isolated from each other; that there is close interrelationship between the prosperity of the developed countries and the growth and development of the developing countries, and that the prosperity of the international community as a whole depends upon the prosperity of its constituent parts. International co-operation for development is the shared goal and common duty of all countries. Thus the political, economic and social well-being of present and future generations depends more than ever on co-operation between all members of the international community on the basis of sovereign equality and the removal of the disequilibrium that exists between them.

4. The new international economic order should be founded on full respect for the following principles:

(a) Sovereign equality of States, self-determination of all peoples, inadmissibility of the acquisition of territories by force, territorial integrity and non-interference in the internal affairs of other States;

(b) Broadest co-operation of all the States members of the International community, based on equity, whereby the prevailing disparities in the world may be banished and prosperity secured for all;

(c) Full and effective participation on the basis of equality of all countries in the solving of world economic problems in the common interest of all countries, bearing in mind the necessity to ensure the accelerated development of all the developing countries, while devoting particular attention to the adoption of special measures in favour of the least developed, land-locked and island developing countries as well as those developing countries most seriously affected by economic crises and natural calamities, without losing sight of the interests of other developing countries;

(d) Every country has the right to adopt the economic and social system that it deems to be the most appropriate for its own development and not to be subjected to discrimination of any kind as a result;

(e) Full permanent sovereignty of every State over its natural resources and all economic activities. In order to safeguard these resources, each State is entitled to exercise effective control over them and their exploitation with means suitable to its own situation, including the right to nationalization or transfer of ownership to its nationals, this right being an expression of the full sovereignty of the State. No State may be subjected to economic, political or any other type of coercion to prevent the free and full exercise of this inalienable right;

(f) All States, territories and peoples under foreign occupation, alien and colonial domination or *apartheid* have the right to restitution and full compensation for the exploitation and depletion of, and damages to, the natural and all other resources of those States, territories and peoples;

(g) Regulation and supervision of the activities of transnational corporations by taking measures in the interest of the national economies of the countries where such transnational corporations operate on the basis of the full sovereignty of those countries;

(h) Right of the developing countries and the peoples of territories under colonial and racial domination and foreign occupation to achieve their liberation and to regain effective control over their natural resources and economic activities;

(i) Extending of assistance to developing countries, peoples and territories under colonial and alien domination, foreign occupation, racial discrimination or *apartheid* or which are subjected to economic, political or any other type of coercive measures to obtain from them the subordination of the exercise of their sovereign rights and to secure from them advantages of any kind, and to neo-colonialism in all its forms and which have established or are endeavouring to establish effective control over their natural resources and economic activities that have been or are still under foreign control;

(j) Just and equitable relationship between the prices of raw materials, primary products, manufactured and semi-manufactured goods exported by developing countries and the prices of raw materials, primary commodities, manufactures, capital goods and equipment imported by them with the aim of bringing about sustained improvement in their unsatisfactory terms of trade and the expansion of the world economy;

(k) Extension of active assistance to developing countries by the whole international community, free of any political or military conditions;

(l) Ensuring that one of the main aims of the reformed international monetary system shall be the promotion of the development of the developing countries and the adequate flow of real resources to them;

(m) Improving the competitiveness of natural materials facing competition from synthetic substitutes;

(n) Preferential and non-reciprocal treatment for developing countries wherever feasible, in all fields of international economic co-operation, whenever possible;

(o) Securing favourable conditions for the transfer of financial resources to developing countries;

(p) To give to the developing countries access to the achievements of modern science and technology, to promote the transfer of technology and the creation of indigenous technology for the benefit of the developing countries in forms and in accordance with procedures which are suited to their economies;

(q) The need for all States to put an end to the waste of natural resources, including food products;

(r) The need for developing countries to concentrate all their resources for the cause of development;

(s) Strengthening — through individual and collective actions — of mutual economic, trade, financial and technical co-operation among the developing countries mainly on a preferential basis;

(t) Facilitating the role which producers' associations may play, within the framework of international co-operation, and in pursuance of their aims, *inter alia*, assisting in promotion of sustained growth of world economy and accelerating development of developing countries.

5. The unanimous adoption of the International Development Strategy for the Second Development Decade was an important step in the promotion of international economic co-operation on a just and equitable basis. The accelerated implementation of obligations and commitments assumed by the international community within the framework of the Strategy, particularly those concerning imperative development needs of developing countries, would contribute significantly to the fulfilment of the aims and objectives of the present Declaration.

6. The United Nations as a universal organization should be capable of dealing with problems of international economic co-operation in a comprehensive manner and ensuring equally the interests of all countries. It must have an even greater role in the establishment of a new international economic order. The Charter of Economic Rights and Duties of States, for the preparation of which this Declaration will provide an additional source of inspiration, will constitute a significant contribution in this respect. All the States Members of the United Nations are therefore called upon to exert maximum efforts with a view to securing the implementation of this Declaration, which is one of the principal guarantees for the creation of better conditions for all peoples to reach a life worthy of human dignity.

7. This Declaration on the Establishment of a New International Economic Order shall be one of the most important bases of economic relations between all peoples and all nations.

42.

Programme of Action for the Establishment of a New International Economic Order

GA Res. 3202 (S-VI) of 1 May 1974.

The General Assembly
Adopts the following Programme of Action:

PROGRAMME OF ACTION ON THE ESTABLISHMENT OF A NEW INTERNATIONAL ECONOMIC ORDER

In view of the continuing severe economic imbalance in the relations between developed and developing countries, and in the context of the constant and continuing aggravation of the imbalance of the economies of the developing countries and the consequent need for the mitigation of their current economic difficulties, urgent and effective measures need to be taken by the international community to assist the developing countries, while devoting particular attention to the least developed, land-locked and island developing countries and those developing countries most seriously affected by economic crises and natural calamities leading to serious retardation of development processes.

With a view to ensuring the application of the Declaration on the Establishment of a New International Economic Order it will be necessary to adopt and implement within a specified period a programme of action of unprecedented scope and to bring about maximum economic co-operation and understanding among all States, particularly between developed and developing countries based on the principles of dignity and sovereign equality.

PROGRAMME OF ACTION

I. *Fundamental problems of raw materials and primary commodities a related to trade and development*

1. *Raw materials*

All efforts should be made:

(a) To put an end to all forms of foreign occupation, racial discrimination, *apartheid*, colonial, neo-colonial and alien domination and the exploitation through the exercise of permanent sovereignty over natural resources.

(b) To take measures for the recovery, exploitation, development, marketing and distribution of natural resources, particularly of developing countries, to serve their national interests, to promote collective self-reliance among them, and to strengthen mutually beneficial international economic co-operation with a view to bringing about the accelerated development of developing countries.

(c) To facilitate the functioning, and to further the aims, of producers' associations, including their joint marketing arrangements, orderly commodity trading, improvement in export income of producing developing countries and in their terms of trade, and sustained growth of world economy for the benefit of all.

(d) To evolve a just and equitable relationship between prices of raw materials, primary commodities, semi-manufactured and manufactured goods exported by developing countries and the prices of raw materials, primary commodities, food, manufactured and semi-maufactured goods and capital equipment imported by them and to work for a link between the prices of exports of developing countries and the prices of their imports from developed countries.

(e) To take measures to reverse the continued trend of stagnation or decline in the real price of several commodities exported by developing countries, despite a general rise in commodity prices, resulting in a decline in the export earnings of these developing countries.

(f) To take measures to expand the markets for natural products in relation to synthetics, taking into account the interests of the developing countries, and to utilize fully the ecological advantages of these products.

(g) To take measures to promote the processing of raw materials in the producer developing countries.

2. *Food*

All efforts should be made:
(a) To take full account of specific problems of developing countries, particularly in times of food shortages, in the international efforts connected with the food problem.

(b) To take into account that, owing to lack of means, some developing countries have vast potentialities of unexploited or underexploited land which, if reclaimed and put into practical use, would contribute considerably to the solution of the food crisis.

(c) By the international community to undertake concrete and speedy measures with a view to arresting desertification, salination, and damage by locusts or any other similar phenomenon involving several developing countries, particularly in Africa, and gravely affecting the capacity of agricultural production of these countries. Furthermore, the international community should assist the developing countries affected by any such phenomenon to develop the affected zones with a view to contributing to the solution of their food problems.

(d) To refrain from damaging or deteriorating natural resources and food resources, especially those derived from the sea, by preventing pollution and taking appropriate steps to protect and reconstitute those resources.

(e) By developed countries in evolving their policies relating to production, stocks, imports and exports of food, to take full account of the interests of:
   (i) Developing importing countries which cannot afford high prices for their imports, and
   (ii) Developing exporting countries which need increased market opportunities for their exports.

(f) To ensure that developing countries can import the necessary quantity of food without undue strain on their foreign exchange resources and without unpredictable deterioration in their balance of payments. In this context, special measures should be taken in respect of the least developed, the land-locked and island developing countries as well as those developing countries most seriously affected by economic crises and natural calamities.

(g) To ensure that concrete measures to increase food production and storage facilities in developing countries should be introduced, *inter alia,* by ensuring an increase in all available essential inputs, including fertilizers, from developed countries on favourable terms.

(h) To promote exports of food products of developing countries through just and equitable arrangements, *inter alia,* by the progressive elimination of such protective and other measures as constitute unfair competition.

3. *General trade*

All efforts should be made:
(a) To take the following measures for the amelioration of terms of trade of developing countries and concrete steps to eliminate chronic trade deficits of developing countries:
- (i) Fulfilment of relevant commitments already undertaken in the United Nations Conference on Trade and Development and in the International Development Strategy for the Second United Nations Development Decade.
- (ii) Improved access to markets in developed countries through the progressive removal of tariff and non-tariff barriers and of restrictive business practices.
- (iii) Expeditious formulation of commodity agreements where appropriate, in order to regulate as necessary and to stabilize the world markets for raw materials and primary commodities.
- (iv) Preparation of an over-all integrated programme, setting out guidelines and taking into account the current work in this field, for a comprehensive range of commodities of export interest to developing countries.
- (v) Where products of developing countries compete with the domestic production in developed countries, each developed country should facilitate the expansion of imports from developing countries and provide a fair and reasonable opportunity to the developing countries to share in the growth of the market.
- (vi) When the importing developed countries derive receipts from customs duties, taxes and other protective measures applied to imports of these products, consideration should be given to the claim of the developing countries that these receipts should be reimbursed in full to the exporting developing countries or devoted to providing additional resources to meet their development needs.
- (vii) Developed countries should make appropriate adjustments in their economies so as to facilitate the expansion and diversification of imports from developing countries and thereby permit a rational, just and equitable international division of labour.
- (viii) Setting up general principles for pricing policy for exports of commodities of developing countries, with a view to rectifying and achieving satisfactory terms of trade for them.
- (ix) Until satisfactory terms of trade are achieved for all developing countries, consideration should be given to alternative means, including improved compensatory financing schemes for meeting the development needs of developing countries concerned.
- (x) Implementation, improvement and enlargement of the Generalized System of Preferences for exports of agricultural primary commodities, manufactures and semi-manufactures from developing to developed countries and consideration of its extension to commodities, including those which are processed or semi-processed. Developing countries which are or will be sharing their existing tariff advantages in some developed countries as the result of the introduction and eventual enlargement of the Generalized System of Preferences should, as a matter of urgency, be granted new openings in the markets of other developed countries which should offer them export opportunities that at least compensate for the sharing of those advantages.
- (xi) Setting up of buffer stocks within the framework of commodity arrangements and their financing by international financial institutions, wherever necessary, the developed countries and — when they are able to do so — by the developing countries, the aim being to favour the producing and consuming developing countries and to contribute to the expansion of world trade as a whole.
- (xii) In cases where natural materials can satisfy the requirements of the market, new investment for the expansion of capacity to produce synthetic materials and substitutes should not be made.

(b) To be guided by the principles of non-reciprocity and preferential treatment of developing countries in multilateral trade negotiations between developed and developing countries, and to seek sustained and additional benefits for the international trade of developing countries, so as to achieve a substantial increase in their foreign exchange earnings, diversification of their exports and acceleration of the rate of their economic growth.

Transportation and insurance:

All efforts should be made:
  (i) To promote an increasing and equitable participation of developing countries in the world shipping tonnage;
  (ii) To arrest and reduce the ever-increasing freight rates in order to reduce the cost of imports to, and exports from, the developing countries;
  (iii) To minimize cost of insurance and reinsurance for developing countries and to assist the growth of domestic insurance and reinsurance markets in developing countries and the establishment to this end, where appropriate, of institutions in in these countries or at the regional level;
  (iv) To ensure the early implementation of the code of conduct for liner conferences.
  (v) To take urgent measures to increase the import and export capability of the least developed countries and to offset the disadvantages of the adverse geographic situation of land-locked countries, particularly with regard to their transportation and transit costs, as well as developing island countries in order to increase their trading ability.
  (vi) By the developed countries to refrain from imposing measures or implementing policies designed to prevent the importation, at equitable prices, of commodities from the developing countries or from frustrating the implementation of legitimate measures and policies adopted by the developing countries in order to improve prices and encourage the export of such commodities.

II. *International monetary system and financing of development of developing countries*

All efforts should be made:

1. To reform the international monetary system with, *inter alia,* the following objectives:

(a) Measures to check the inflation already experienced by the developed countries, to prevent it from being transferred to developing countries and to study and devise possible arrangements within the International Monetary Fund to mitigate the effects of inflation in developed countries on the economies of developing countries;

(b) Measures to eliminate the instability of the international monetary system, in particular the uncertainty of the exchange rates especially as it affects adversely the trade in commodities;

(c) Maintenance of the real value of the currency reserves of the developing countries by preventing their erosion from inflation and exchange rate depreciation of reserve currencies;

(d) Full and effective participation of developing countries in all phases of decision-making for the formulation of an equitable and durable monetary system and adequate participation of developing countries in all bodies entrusted with this reform and, particularly, in the proposed Council of Governors of the International Monetary Fund;

(e) Adequate and orderly creation of additional liquidity with particular regard to the needs of the developing countries through the additional allocation of Special Drawing Rights based on the concept of world liquidity needs to be appropriately revised in the light of the new international environment. Any creation of international liquidity should be made through international multilateral mechanisms;

(f) Early establishment of a link between Special Drawing Rights and additional development financing in the interest of developing countries, consistent with the monetary characteristics of Special Drawing Rights;

(g) The International Monetary Fund should review the relevant provisions in order to ensure effective participation by developing countries in the decision-making process;

(h) Arrangements to promote an increasing net transfer of real resources from the developed to the developing countries;

(i) Review the methods of operation of the International Monetary Fund, in particular the terms for both credit repayments and "standby" arrangements, the system of compensatory financing, and the terms of the financing of commodity buffer stocks, so as to enable the developing countries to make more effective use of them.

2. To take the following urgent measures to finance the development of developing countries and to meet the balance-of-payment crises in the developing world:

(a) Implementation at an accelerated pace by the developed countries of the time-bound programme, as already laid down in the International Development Strategy for the Second United Nations Development Decade, for the net amount of financial resource transfers to developing countries. Increase in the official component of the net amount of financial resource transfers to developing countries so as to meet and even to exceed the target of the International Development Strategy;

(b) International financing institutions to effectively play their role as development financing banks without discrimination on account of the political or economic system of any member country, assistance being untied;

(c) More effective participation by developing countries, whether recipients or contributors, in the decision-making process in the competent organs of the International Bank for Reconstruction and Development and the International Development Association through the establishment of a more equitable pattern of voting rights;

(d) Exemption, wherever possible, of the developing countries from all import and capital outflow controls imposed by the developed countries;

(e) Promotion of foreign investment both public and private from developed to developing countries in accordance with the needs and requirements in sectors of their economies as determined by the recipient countries;

(f) Appropriate urgent measures, including international action, to be taken to mitigate adverse consequences for the current and future development of developing countries arising from the burden of external debt contracted on hard terms;

(g) Debt renegotiation on a case-by-case with a view to concluding agreements on debt cancellation, moratorium, rescheduling, or interest subsidization;

(h) International financial institutions to take into account the special situation of each developing country in reorienting their lending policies to suit these urgent needs. There is also need for improvement in practices of international financial institutions in regard to, *inter alia,* development financing and international monetary problems;

(i) Appropriate steps to be taken to give priority to the least developed, land-locked and island developing countries and to the countries most seriously affected by economic crises and natural calamities, in the availability of loans for development purposes which should include more favourable terms and conditions.

III. *Industrialization*

All efforts should be made by the international community to take measures to encourage the industrialization of the developing countries.

To this end:

(a) The developed countries should respond favourably, within the framework of their official aid as well as international financial institutions, to the requests of developing countries for the financing of industrial projects;

(b) The developed countries should encourage investors to finance industrial production projects, particularly export-oriented production, in developing countries, in agreement with the latter and within the contex of their laws and regulations;

(c) With a view to bringing about a new international economic structure which should increase the share of the developing countries in world industrial production, the developed countries and the agencies of the United Nations system, in co-operation with the developing countries, should contribute to setting up new industrial capacities including raw material and commodity transforming facilities as a matter of priority in the developing countries that produce those raw materials and commodities;

(d) Continue and expand, with the aid of the developed countries and the international institutions, the operational and instruction-oriented technical assistance programmes including vocational training and management development of national personnel of the developing countries in the light of their special development requirements.

IV. *Transfer of technology*

All efforts should be made:

(a) To formulate an international code of conduct for the transfer of technology corresponding to needs and conditions prevalent in developing countries;

(b) To give access on improved terms to modern technology and the adaptation of that technology, as appropriate, to specific economic, social and ecological conditions and varying stages of development in developing countries;

(c) To expand significantly the assistance from developed to developing countries in programmes of research and development and in the creation of suitable indigenous technology;

(d) To adapt commercial practices governing transfer of technology to the requirements of the developing countries, and to prevent abuse of the rights of sellers;

(e) To promote international co-operation in research and development in exploration and exploitation, conservation and legitimate utilization of natural resources and all sources of energy;

In taking the above measures, the special needs of the least developed and land-locked countries should be borne in mind.

V. *Regulation and control over the activities of transnational corporations*

All efforts should be made to formulate, adopt and implement an international code of conduct for transnational corporations to:

(a) Prevent interference in the internal affairs of the countries where they operate and their collaboration with racist régimes and colonial administrations;

(b) Regulate their activities in host countries, to eliminate restrictive business practices and to conform to the national development plans and objevtives of developing countries, and in this context facilitate, as necessary, review and revision of previously concluded arrangements;

(c) Bring about assistance, transfer of technology and management skills to developing countries on equitable and favourable terms;

(d) Regulate the repatriation of the profits accruing from their operations, taking into account the legitimate interests of all parties concerned;

(e) Promote reinvestment of their profits in developing countries.

VI. *Charter of Economic Rights and Duties of States*

The Charter of Economic Rights and Duties of States, the draft of which is being prepared by a working group of the United Nations and which the General Assembly has already expressed the intention of adopting at its twenty-ninth regular session, shall constitute an effective instrument towards the establishment of a new system of international economic relations based on equity, sovereign equality, and interdependence of the interests of developed and developing countries. It is therefore of vital importance that the Charter be adopted by the General Assembly at its twenty-ninth session.

VII. *Promotion of co-operation among developing countries*

1. Collective self-reliance and growing co-operation among developing countries will further strengthen their role in the new international economic order. Developing countries, with a view to expanding co-operation at the regional, subregional and inter-

regional levels, should take further steps *inter alia:*

(a) To support the establishment and/or improvement of appropriate mechanism to defend the prices of their exportable commodities and to improve access to and to stabilize markets for them. In this context the increasingly effective mobilization by the whole group of oil exporting countries of their natural resources for the benefit of their economic development is to be welcomed. At the same time there is the paramount need for co-operation among the developing countries in evolving urgently and in a spirit of solidarity all possible means to assist developing countries to cope with the immediate problems resulting from this legitimate and perfectly justified action. The measures already taken in this regard are a positive indication of the evolving co-operation between developing countries.

(b) To protect their inalienable right to permanent sovereignty over their natural resources.

(c) To promote, establish or strengthen economic integration at the regional and subregional levels.

(d) To increase considerably their imports from other developing countries.

(e) No developing country should accord to imports from developed countries more favourable treatment than that accorded to imports from developing countries. Taking into account the existing international agreements, current limitations and possibilities and also their future evolution, preferential treatment should be given to the procurement of import requirements from other developing countries. Wherever possible, preferential treatment should be given to imports from developing countries and the exports of those countries.

(f) To promote close co-operation in the fields of finance, credit relations and monetary issues, including the development of credit relations on a preferential basis and on favourable terms.

(g) To strengthen efforts which are already being made by developing countries to utilize available financial resources for financing development in the developing countries through investment, financing of export-oriented and emergency projects and other long-term assistance.

(h) To promote and establish effective instruments of co-operation in the fields of industry, science and technology, transport, shipping and mass communication media.

2. Developed countries should support initiatives in the regional, subregional and interregional co-operation of developing countries through the extension of financial and technical assistance through more effective and concrete actions, particularly in the field of commercial policy.

VIII. *Assistance in the exercise of permanent sovereignty of States over natural resources*

All efforts should be made:

(a) To defeat attempts to prevent the free and effective exercise of the rights of every State to full and permanent sovereignty over its natural resources.

(b) By competent agencies of the United Nations system to meet requests for assistance from developing countries in connexion with the operation of nationalized means of production.

IX. *Strengthening the role of the United Nations system in the field of international economic co-operation*

1. In furtherance of the objectives of the International Development Strategy and in accordance with the aims and objectives of the Declaration on the Establishment of a New International Economic Order, all Member States pledge to make full use of the United Nations system in the implementation of this Programme of Action they have jointly adopted in working for the establishment of a new international economic order and thereby strengthening the role of the United Nations in the field of world-wide co-operation for economic and social development.

2. The General Assembly of the United Nations shall conduct an over-all review of the implementation of the Programma of Action as a priority item. All the activities of the United Nations system to be undertaken under the Programme of Action as well as those already planned, such as the World Population Conference, the World Food Conference, the Second General Conference of the United Nations Industrial Development Organization and the mid-term review and appraisal of the International Development Strategy, should be so directed as to enable the special session of the General Assembly on development, called for under General Assembly resolution 3172 (XXVIIII), to make its full contribution to the establishment of the new international economic order. All Member States are urged jointly and individually to direct their efforts and policies towards the success of that special session.

3. The Economic and Social Council shall define the policy framework and co-ordinate the activities of all organizations, institutions and susbidiary bodies within the United Nations system which shall be entrusted with the task of implementing this Programme. In order to enable the Economic and Social Council to carry out its tasks effectively:

(a) All organizations, institutions and subsidiary bodies concerned within the United Nations system shall submit to the Economic and Social Council progress reports on the implementation of this Programme within their respective fields of competence as often as necessary, but not less than once a year.

(b) The Economic and Social Council shall examine the progress reports as a matter of urgency, to which end it may be convened as necessary, in special sessions or, if need be, may function continuously. It shall draw the attention of the General Assembly to the problems and difficulties arising in connexion with the implementation of this Programme.

4. All organizations, institutions, subsidiary bodies and conferences of the United Nations system are entrusted with the implementation of this Programme of Action. The activities of the United Nations Conference on Trade and Development as set forth in General Assembly resolution 1995 (XIX) should be strengthened for the purpose of following in collaboration with other competent organizations the development of international trade in raw materials throughout the world.

5. Urgent and effective measures should be taken to review the lending policies of international financial institutions, taking into account the special situation of each developing country, to suit urgent needs, to improve the practices of these institutions in regard to, *inter alia,* development financing and international monetary problems, and to ensure more effective participation by developing countries — whether recipients or contributors — in the decision-making process through appropriate revision of the pattern of voting rights.

6. The developed countries and others in a position to do so should contribute substantially to the various organizations, programmes and funds established within the United Nations system for the purpose of accelerating economic and social development in developing countries.

7. This Programme of Action complements and strengthens the goals and objectives embodied in the International Development Strategy as well as the new measures formulated by the General Assembly at its twenty-eighth session to offset the short-falls in achieving those goals and objectives.

8. The implementation of the Programme of Action should be taken into account at the time of the mid-term review and appraisal of the International Development Strategy for the Second United Nations Development Decade. New commitments, changes, additions and adaptations in the International Development Strategy should be made, as appropriate, taking into account the Declaration on the Establishment of a New International Economic Order and this Programme of Action.

X. *Special Programme*

The General Assembly adopts the following Special Programme, including particularly emergency measures to mitigate the difficulties of the developing countries most seriously affected by economic crisis bearing in mind the particular problem of the least developed and land-locked countries:

The General Assembly,
Considering that:

(a) The sharp increase in the prices of their essential imports such as food, fertilizers, energy products, capital goods, equipment and services, including transportation and transit costs, has gravely exacerbated the increasingly adverse terms of trade of a number of developing countries, added to the burden of their foreign debt and, cumulatively, created a situation which, if left untended, will make it impossible for them to finance their essential imports and development and result in a further deterioration in the levels and conditions of life in these countries. The present crisis is the outcome of all the problems that have accumulated over the years: in the field of trade, in monetary reform, the world-wide inflationary situation, inadequacy and delay in provision of financial assistance and many other similar problems in the economic and developmental fields. In facing the crisis, this complex situation must be borne in mind so as to ensure that the special programme adopted by the international community provides emergency relief and timely assistance to the most seriously affected countries. Simultaneously, steps are taken to resolve these outstanding problems through a fundamental restructuring of the world economic system, in order to allow these countries while solving the present difficulties to reach an acceptable level of development.

(b) The special measures adopted to assist the most seriously affected countries must encompass not only the relief which they require on an emergency basis to maintain their import requirements but also, beyond that, steps to consciously promote the capacity of these countries to produce and earn more. Unless such a comprehensive approach is adopted there is every likelihood that the difficulties of the most seriously affected countries may be perpetuated. Nevertheless, the first and most pressing task of the international community is to enable these countries to meet the shortfall in their balance of payments positions. But this must be simultaneoulsy supplemented by additional development assistance to maintain and thereafter accelerate their rate of economic development.

(c) The countries which have been most seriously affected are precisely those which are at the greatest disadvantage in the world economy: the least developed, the land-locked and other low-income developing countries as well as other developing countries whose economies have been seriously dislocated as a result of the present economic crisis, natural calamities, and foreign aggression and occupation. An indication of the countries thus affected, the level of the impact on their economies and the kind of relief and assistance they require can be assessed on the basis, *inter alia,* of the following criteria:
  (i) Low *per capita* income as a reflection of relative poverty, low productivity, low level of technology and development.
  (ii) Sharp increase in their import cost of essentials relative to export earnings.
  (iii) High ration of debt servicing to export earnings.
  (iv) Insufficiency in export earnings, comparative inelasticity of export incomes and unavailability of exportable surplus.
  (v) Low level of foreign exchange reserves or their inadequacy for requirements.
  (vi) Adverse impact of higher transportation and transit costs.
  (vii) Relative importance of foreign trade in the development process.

(d) The assessment of the extent and nature of the impact on the economies of the most seriously affected countries must be made flexible keeping in mind the present uncertainty in the world economy, the adjustment policies that may be adopted by the developed countries, the flow of capital and investment. Estimates of the payments situation and needs of these countries can be assessed and projected reliably only on the basis of their average performance over a number of years. Long-term projections, at this time, cannot but be uncertain.

(e) It is important that in the special measures to mitigate the difficulties of the most seriously affected countries, all the developed countries as well as developing countries should contribute according to their level of development and the capacity and strength of their economies. It is notable that some developing countries, despite their own difficulties and development needs, have shown a willingness to play a concrete and helpful role in ameliorating the difficulties faced by the poorer developing countries. The various initiatives and measures taken recently by certain developing countries with adequate resources on a bilateral and multilateral basis to contribute to alleviating the difficulties of other developing countries are a reflection of their commitment to the principle of effective economic co-operation among developing countries.

(f) The response of the developed countries which have by far the greater capacity to assist the affected countries in overcoming their present difficulties must be commensurate with their responsibilites. Their assistance should be in addition to the presently available levels of aid. They should fulfill and if possible exceed the targets of the International Development Strategy on financial assistance to the developing countries, especially that relating to official development assistance. They should also give serious consideration to the cancellation of the external debts of the most seriously affected countries. This would provide the simplest and quickest relief to the affected countries. Favourable consideration should also be given to debt moratorium and rescheduling. The current situation should not lead the industrialized countries to adopt what will ultimately prove to be a self-defeating policy aggravating the present crisis.

Recalling the constructive proposals made by His Imperial Majesty the Shahanshah of Iran and His Excellency President Boumediène of Algeria,

1. *Decides* to launch a Special Programme to provide emergency relief and development assistance to the developing countries most seriously affected, as a matter of urgency, and for the period of time necessary, at least until the end of the Second United Nations Development Decade, to help them overcome their present difficulties and to achieve self-sustaining economic development;

2. *Decides* as a first step in the Special Programme to request the Secretary-General to launch an emergency operation to provide timely relief to the most seriously affected developing countries as defined in subparagraph (c) above, with the aim of maintaining unimpaired essential imports for the duration of the coming 12 months and to invite the industrialized countries and other potential contributors to announce their contributions for emergency assistance or intimate their intention to do so by 15 June 1974 to be provided through bilateral or multilateral channels, taking into account commitments and measures of assistance announced or already taken by some countries and *further requests the* Secretary-General to report the progress of the emergency operation to the twenty-ninth session of the General Assembly through the Economic and Social Council at its fifty-seventh session;

3. *Calls upon* the industrialized countries and other potential contributors to extend immediate relief and assistance to the most seriously affected countries which must be of an order of magnitude that is commensurate with the needs of these countries. Such assistance should be in addition to the existing level of aid and provided at a very early date to the maximum possible extent on grant basis and where not possible on soft terms. The disbursement and relevant operational procedures and terms must reflect this exceptional situation. The assistance could be provided either through bilateral or multilateral channels, including such new institutions and facilities that have been or are to be set up. The special measures may include the following:

(a) Special arrangements on particularly favourable terms and conditions including possible subsidies for and assured supplies of essential commodities and goods;
(b) Deferred payments for all or part of imports of essential commodities and goods;
(c) Commodity assistance, including food aid, on grant basis or deferred payments in local currencies, bearing in mind that this should not adversely affect the exports of developing countries;
(d) Long-term suppliers' credits on easy terms;

(e) Long-term financial assistance on concessionary terms;
(f) Drawings from special International Monetary Fund facilities on concessional terms;
(g) Establishment of a link between the creation of Special Drawing Rights and development assistance, taking into account the additional financial requirement of the most seriously affected countries;
(h) Subsidies, provided bilaterally or multilaterally, for interest on funds available on commercial terms borrowed by most seriously affected countries;
(i) Debt renegotiation on a case-by-case basis with a view to concluding agreements on debt cancellation, moratorium or rescheduling;
(j) Provision on more favourable terms of capital goods and technical assistance to accelerate the industrialization of the affected countries;
(k) Investment in industrial and development projects on favourable terms;
(l) Subsidizing the additional transit and transport costs, especially of the landlocked countries;

4. *Appeals* to the developed countries to consider favourably the cancellation, moratorium or rescheduling of the debts of the most seriously affected developing countries on their request, as an important contribution to mitigating the grave and urgent difficulties of these countries;

5. *Decides* to establish a Special Fund under the auspices of the United Nations, through voluntary contributions from industrialized countries and other potential contributors, as a part of the Special Programme, to provide emergency relief and development assistance, which will commence its operations at the latest by 1 January 1975;

6. *Establishes* an *Ad Hoc* Committee on the Special Programme, composed of thirty-six Member States appointed by the President of the General Assembly after appropriate consultations, bearing in mind the purposes of the Special Fund and its terms of reference, to:

(a) Make recommendations on the scope, machinery, modes of operation etc. of the Special Fund, taking into account the need for:
   (i) Equitable representation on its governing body;
   (ii) Equitable distribution of its resources;
   (iii) Full utilization of the services and facilities of existing international organizations;
   (iv) The possibility of merging the United Nations Capital Development Fund with operations of the Special Fund;
   (v) A central monitoring body to oversee the various measures being taken both bilaterally and multilaterally;

and, to this end, bearing in mind the different ideas and proposals made at the sixth special session, including those contained in document A/AC.166/L.15 and A/PV.2208 and comments thereon and the possibility of utilizing the Special Fund to provide an alternative channel for normal development assistance after the emergency period;

(b) Monitor, pending commencement of the operations of the Special Fund, the various measures being taken both bilaterally and multilaterally to assist the most seriously affected countries;

(c) Prepare, on the basis of information provided by the countries concerned and by appropriate agencies of the United Nations system, a broad assessment of:
   (i) The magnitude of the difficulties facing the most seriously affected countries;
   (ii) The kind and quantities of the commodities and goods essentially required by them;
   (iii) Their need for financial assistance;
   (iv) Their technical assistance requirements, including especially access to technology;

7. *Requests* the Secretary-General of the United Nations, the Secretary-General of the United Nations Conference on Trade and Development, the President of the International Bank for Reconstruction and Development, the Managing Director of the International Monetary Fund, the Administrator of the United Nations Development

Programme and the heads of the other competent international organizations to assist the *Ad Hoc* Committee in performing the functions assigned to it under operative paragraph 6, and help, as appropriate, in the operations of the Special Fund;

8. *Requests* the International Monetary Fund to expedite decisions on:

(a) The establishment of an extended special facility with a view to enabling the most seriously affected developing countries to participate in it on favourable terms;

(b) The creation of Special Drawing Rights and the early establishment of the link between the allocation of Special Drawing Rights and development financing; and

(c) The establishment and operation of the proposed new special facility to extend credits and subsidize interest charges on commercial funds borrowed by Member States bearing in mind the interest of the developing countries and especially the additional financial requirements of the most seriously affected countries;

9. *Requests* the World Bank Group and the International Monetary Fund to place their managerial, financial and technical services at the disposal of Governments contributing to emergency financial relief so as to enable them to assist without delay in channelling funds to the recipients, making such institutional and procedural changes as may be required;

10. *Invites* the United Nations Development Programme to take the necessary steps, particularly at the country level, to respond on an emergency basis to requests for additional assistance which it may be called upon to render within the framework of the Special Programme;

11. *Requests* the *Ad Hoc* Committee to submit its report and recommendations to the Economic and Social Council at its fifty-seventh session and invites the Council, on the basis of its consideration of that report, to submit suitable recommendations to the General Assembly at its twenty-ninth session;

12. *Decides* to consider, within the framework of a new international economic order, as a matter of high priority at the twenty-ninth session of the General Assembly, the question of special measures for the most seriously affected countries.

43.

Charter of Economic Rights and Duties of States

GA Res. 3281 (XXIX) of 12 December 1974.
At the third Conference of UNCTAD, held at Santiago, Chile, in May 1972, a working group was established to draw up a Charter of Economic Rights and Duties of States. After three inconclusive meetings of this Working Group, GA Res. 3201 (S-VI) and GA Res. 3202 (S-VI) of 1 May 1974, stressed the importance of the adoption of such a Charter. At the next meeting of the Working Group it appeared that the developing countries did not want to continue negotiations in the Working Group and in September 1974 the Trade and Development Board referred the matter to the General Assembly, which adopted the Charter by Res. 3281 (XXIX) of 12 December 1974.

The General Assembly,
Recalling that the United Nations Conference on Trade and Development, in its resolution 45 (III) of 18 May 1972, stressed the urgency to establish generally accepted norms to govern international economic relations systematically and recognized that it is not feasible to establish a just order and a stable world as long as a Charter to protect the rights of all countries, and in particular the developing States, is not formulated,
Recalling further that in the same resolution it was decided to establish a Working Group of governmental representatives to draw up a draft Charter of Economic Rights and Duties of States, which the General Assembly, in its resolution 3037 (XXVII) of 19 December 1972, decided should be composed of forty Member States,
Noting that, in its resolution 3082 (XXVIII) of 6 December 1973, it reaffirmed its conviction of the urgent need to establish or improve norms of universal application for the development of international economic relations on a just and equitable basis and urged the Working Group on the Charter of Economic Rights and Duties of States to complete, as the first step in the codification and development of the matter, the elaboration of a final draft Charter of Economic Rights and Duties of States, to be considered and approved by the General Assembly at its twenty-ninth session,
Bearing in mind the spirit and terms of its resolutions 3201 (S-VI) and 3202 (S-VI) of 1 May 1974, containing the Declaration and the Programme of Action on the Establishment of a New International Economic Order, which underlined the vital importance of the Charter to be adopted by the General Assembly at its twenty-ninth session and stressed the fact that the Charter shall constitute an effective instrument towards the establishment of a new system of international economic relations based on equity, sovereign equality, and interdependence of the interests of developed and developing countries,
Having examined the report of the Working Group on the Charter of Economic Rights and Duties of States on its fourth session, transmitted to the General Assembly by the Trade and Development Board at its fourteenth session.
Expressing its appreciation to the Working Group on the Charter of Economic Rights

and Duties of States which, as a result of the task performed in its four sessions held between February 1973 and June 1974, assembled the elements required for the completion and adoption of the Charter of Economic Rights and Duties of States at the twenty-ninth session of the General Assembly, as previously recommended,

Adopts and solemnly proclaims the following Charter:

CHARTER OF ECONOMIC RIGHTS AND DUTIES OF STATES

PREAMBLE

The General Assembly,

Reaffirming the fundamental purposes of the United Nations, in particular the maintenance of international peace and security, the development of friendly relations among nations and the achievement of international co-operation in solving international problems in the economic and social fields,

Affirming the need for strengthening international co-operation in these fields,

Reaffirming further the need for strengthening international co-operation for development,

Declaring that it is a fundamental purpose of the present Charter to promote the establishment of the new international economic order, based on equity, sovereign equality, interdependence, common interest and co-operation among all States, irrespective of their economic and social systems,

Desirous of contributing to the creation of conditions for:

(*a*) The attainment of wider prosperity among all countries and of higher standards of living for all peoples,

(*b*) The promotion by the entire international community of the economic and social progress of all countries, especially developing countries,

(*c*) The encouragement of co-operation, on the basis of mutal advantage and equitable benefits for all peace-loving States which are willing to carry out the provisions of the present Charter, in the economic, trade, scientific and technical fields, regardless of political, economic or social systems,

(*d*) The overcoming of main obstacles in the way of the economic development of the developing countries,

(*e*) The acceleration of the economic growth of developing countries with a view to bridging the economic gap between developing and developed countries,

(*f*) The protection, preservation and enhancement of the environment,

Mindful of the need to establish and maintain a just and equitable economic and social order through:

(*a*) The achievement of more rational and equitable international economic relations and the encouragement of structural changes in the world economy,

(*b*) The creation of conditions which permit the further expansion of trade and intensification of economic co-operation among all nations,

(*c*) The strengthening of the economic independence of developing countries,

(*d*) The establishment and promotion of international economic relations taking into account the agreed differences in development of the developing countries and their specific needs,

Determined to promote collective economic security for development, in particular of the developing countries, with strict respect for the sovereign equality of each State and through the co-operation of the entire international community,

Considering that genuine co-operation among States, based on joint consideration of and concerted action regarding international economic problems, is essential for fulfilling the international community's common desire to achieve a just and rational development of all parts of the world,

Stressing the importance of ensuring appropriate conditions for the conduct of normal economic relations among all States, irrespective of differences in social and economic systems, and for the full respect of the rights of all peoples, as well as strengthening instruments of international economic co-operation as a means for the consolidation of peace for the benefit of all,

Convinced of the need to develop a system of international economic relations on the basis of sovereign equality, mutual and equitable benefit and the close interrelationship of the interests of all States,

Reiterating that the responsibility for the development of every country rests primarily upon itself but that concomitant and effective international co-operation is an essential factor for the full achievement of its own development goals,

Firmly convinced of the urgent need to evolve a substantially improved system of international economic relations,

Solemnly adopts the present Charter of Economic Rights and Duties of States.

CHAPTER I

Fundamentals of international economic relations

Economic as well as political and other relations among States shall be governed, *inter alia*, by the following principles:
(a) Sovereignty, territorial integrity and political independence of States;
(b) Sovereign equality of all States;
(c) Non-aggression;
(d) Non-intervention;
(e) Mutual and equitable benefit;
(f) Peaceful coexistence;
(g) Equal rights and self-determination of peoples;
(h) Peaceful settlement of disputes;
(i) Remedying of injustices which have been brought about by force and which deprive a nation of the natural means necessary for its normal development;
(j) Fulfilment in good faith of international obligations;
(k) Respect for human rights and fundamental freedoms;
(l) No attempt to seek hegemony and spheres of influence;
(m) Promotion of international social justice;
(n) International co-operation for development;
(o) Free access to and from the sea by land-locked countries within the framework of the above principles.

CHAPTER II

Economic rights and duties of States

Article 1

Every State has the sovereign and inalienable right to choose its economic system as well as its political, social and cultural systems in accordance with the will of its people, without outside interference, coercion or threat in any form whatsoever.

Article 2

1. Every State has and shall freely exercise full permanent sovereignty, including possession, use and disposal, over all its wealth, natural resources and economic activities.
2. Each State has the right:
(a) To regulate and exercise authority over foreign investment within its national

jurisdiction in accordance with its laws and regulations and in conformity with its national objectives and priorities. No State shall be compelled to grant preferential treatment to foreign investment;
(b) To regulate and supervise the activities of transnational corporations within its national jurisdiction and take measures to ensure that such activities comply with its laws, rules and regulations and conform with its economic and social policies. Transnational corporations shall not intervene in the internal affairs of a host State. Every State should, with full regard for its sovereign rights, co-operate with other States in the exercise of the right set forth in this subparagraph;
(c) To nationalize, expropriate or transfer ownership of foreign property, in which case appropriate compensation should be paid by the State adopting such measures, taking into account its relevant laws and regulations and all circumstances that the State considers pertinent. In any case where the question of compensation gives rise to a controversy, it shall be settled under the domestic law of the nationalizing State and by its tribunals, unless it is freely and mutually agreed by all States concerned that other peaceful means be sought on the basis of the sovereign equality of States and in accordance with the principle of free choice of means.

Article 3

In the exploitation of natural resources shared by two or more countries each State must co-operate on the basis of a system of information and prior consultations in order to achieve optimum use of such resources without causing damage to the legitimate interest of others.

Article 4

Every State has the right to engage in international trade and other forms of economic co-operation irrespective of any differences in political, economic and social systems. No State shall be subjected to discrimination of any kind based solely on such differences. In the pursuit of international trade and other forms of economic co-operation, every State is free to choose the forms of organization of its foreign economic relations and to enter into bilateral and multilateral arrangements consistent with its international obligations and with the needs of international economic co-operation.

Article 5

All States have the right to associate in organizations of primary commodity producers in order to develop their national economies, to achieve stable financing for their development and, in pursuance of their aims, to assist in the promotion of sustained growth of the world economy, in particular accelerating the development of developing countries. Correspondingly, all States have the duty to respect that right by refraining from applying economic and political measures that would limit it.

Article 6

It is the duty of States to contribute to the development of international trade of goods, particularly by means of arrangements and by the conclusion of long-term multilateral commodity agreements, where appropriate, and taking into account the interests of producers and consumers. All States share the responsibility to promote the regular flow and access of all commercial goods traded at stable, remunerative and equitable prices, thus contributing to the equitable development of the world economy, taking into account, in particular, the interests of developing countries.

Article 7

Every State has the primary responsibility to promote the economic, social and cultural development of its people. To this end, each State has the right and the responsibility to choose its means and goals of development, fully to mobilize and use its resources, to implement progressive economic and social reforms and to ensure the full participation of its people in the process and benefits of development. All States have the duty, individually and collectively, to co-operate in order to eliminate obstacles that hinder such mobilization and use.

Article 8

States should co-operate in facilitating more rational and equitable international economic relations and in encouraging structural changes in the context of a balanced world economy in harmony with the needs and interests of all countries, especially developing countries, and should take appropriate measures to this end.

Article 9

All States have the responsibility to co-operate in the economic, social, cultural, scientific and technological fields for the promotion of economic and social progress throughout the world, especially that of the developing countries.

Article 10

All States are juridically equal and, as equal members of the international community, have the right to participate fully and effectively in the international decision-making process in the solution of world economic, financial and monetary problems, *inter alia*, through the appropriate international organizations in accordance with their existing and evolving rules, and to share equitably in the benefits resulting therefrom.

Article 11

All States should co-operate to strengthen and continuously improve the efficiency of international organizations in implementing measures to stimulate the general economic progress of all countries, particularly of developing countries, and therefore should co-operate to adapt them, when appropriate, to the changing needs of international economic co-operation.

Article 12

1. States have the right, in agreement with the parties concerned, to participate in sub-regional, regional and interregional co-operation in the pursuit of their economic and social development. All States engaged in such co-operation have the duty to ensure that the policies of those groupings to which they belong correspond to the provisions of the present Charter and are outward-looking, consistent with their international obligations and with the needs of international economic co-operation, and have full regard for the legitimate interests of third countries, especially developing countries.
2. In the case of groupings to which the States concerned have transferred or may transfer certain competences as regards matters that come within the scope of the present Charter, its provisions shall also apply to those groupings, in regard to such matters, consistent with the responsibilities of such States as members of such groupings. Those States shall co-operate in the observance by the groupings of the provisions of this Charter.

Article 13

1. Every State has the right to benefit from the advances and developments in science and technology for the acceleration of its economic and social development.
2. All States should promote international scientific and technological co-operation and the transfer of technology, with proper regard for all legitimate interests including, *inter alia*, the rights and duties of holders, suppliers and recipients of technology. In particular, all States should facilitate the access of developing countries to the achievements of modern science and technology, the transfer of technology and the creation of indigenous technology for the benefit of the developing countries in forms and in accordance with procedures which are suited to their economies and their needs.
3. Accordingly, developed countries should co-operate with the developing countries

in the establishment, strengthening and development of their scientific and technological infrastructures and their scientific research and technological activities so as to help to expand and transform the economies of developing countries.

4. All States should co-operate in research with a view to evolving further internationally accepted guidelines or regulations for the transfer of technology, taking fully into account the interests of developing countries.

Article 14

Every State has the duty to co-operate in promoting a steady and increasing expansion and liberalization of world trade and an improvement in the welfare and living standards of all peoples, in particular those of developing countries. Accordingly, all States should co-operate, *inter alia,* towards the progressive dismantling of obstacles to trade and the improvement of the international framework for the conduct of world trade and, to these ends, co-ordinated efforts shall be made to solve in an equitable way the trade problems of all countries, taking into account the specific trade problems of the developing countries. In this connexion, States shall take measures aimed at securing additional benefits for the international trade of developing countries so as to achieve a substantial increase in their foreign exchange earnings, the diversification of their exports, the acceleration of the rate of growth of their trade, taking into account their development needs, an improvement in the possibilities for these countries to participate in the expansion of world trade and a balance more favourable to developing countries in the sharing of the advantages resulting from this expansion, through, in the largest possible measure, a substantial improvement in the conditions of access for the products of interest to the developing countries and, wherever appropriate, measures designed to attain stable, equitable and remunerative prices for primary products.

Article 15

All States have the duty to promote the achievement of general and complete disarmament under effective international control and to utilize the resources released by effective disarmament measures for the economic and social development of countries, allocating a substantial portion of such resources as additional means for the development needs of developing countries.

Article 16

1. It is the right and duty of all States, individually and collectively, to eliminate colonialism, *apartheid,* racial discrimination, neo-colonialism and all forms of foreign aggression, occupation and domination, and the economic and social consequences thereof, as a prerequisite for development. States which practise such coercive policies are economically responsible to the countries, territories and peoples affected for the restitution and full compensation for the exploitation and depletion of, and damages to, the natural and all other resources of those countries, territories and peoples. It is the duty of all States to extend assistance to them.

2. No State has the right to promote or encourage investments that may constitute an obstacle to the liberation of a territory occupied by force.

Article 17

International co-operation for development is the shared goal and common duty of all States. Every State should co-operate with the efforts of developing countries to accelerate their economic and social development by providing favourable external conditions and by extending active assistance to them, consistent with their development needs and objectives, with strict respect for the sovereign equality of States and free of any conditions derogating from their sovereignty.

Article 18

Developed countries should extend, improve and enlarge the system of generalized non-reciprocal and non-discriminatory tariff preferences to the developing countries consistent with the relevant agreed conclusions and relevant decisions as adopted on this subject, in the framework of the competent international organizations. Developed countries should also give serious consideration to the adoption of other differential measures, in areas where this is feasible and appropriate and in ways which will provide special and more favourable treatment, in order to meet the trade and development needs of the developing countries. In the conduct of international economic relations the developed countries should endeavour to avoid measures having a negative effect on the development of the national economies of the developing countries, as promoted by generalized tariff preferences and other generally agreed differential measures in their favour.

Article 19

With a view to accelerating the economic growth of developing countries and bridging the economic gap between developed and developing countries, developed countries should grant generalized preferential, non-reciprocal and non-discriminatory treatment to developing countries in those fields of international economic co-operation where it may be feasible.

Article 20

Developing countries should, in their efforts to increase their over-all trade, give due attention to the possibility of expanding their trade with socialist countries, by granting to these countries conditions for trade not inferior to those granted normally to the developed market economy countries.

Article 21

Developing countries should endeavour to promote the expansion of their mutual trade and to this end may, in accordance with the existing and evolving provisions and procedures of international agreements where applicable, grant trade preferences to other developing countries without being obliged to extend such preferences to developed countries, provided these arrangements do not constitute an impediment to general trade liberalization and expansion.

Article 22

1. All States should respond to the generally recognized or mutually agreed development needs and objectives of developing countries by promoting increased net flows of real resources to the developing countries from all sources, taking into account any obligations and commitments undertaken by the States concerned, in order to reinforce the efforts of developing countries to accelerate their economic and social development.
2. In this context, consistent with the aims and objectives mentioned above and taking into account any obligations and commitments undertaken in this regard, it should be their endeavour to increase the net amount of financial flows from official sources to developing countries and to improve the terms and conditions thereof.
3. The flow of development assistance resources should include economic and technical assistance.

Article 23

To enhance the effective mobilization of their own resources, the developing countries should strengthen their economic co-operation and expand their mutual trade so as to accelerate their economic and social development. All countries, especially developed countries, individually as well as through the competent international organizations of which they are members, should provide appropriate and effective support and co-operation.

Article 24

All States have the duty to conduct their mutual economic relations in a manner which takes into account the interests of other countries. In particular, all States should avoid prejudicing the interests of developing countries.

Article 25

In furtherance of world economic development, the international community, especially its developed members, shall pay special attention to the particular needs and problems of the least developed among the developing countries, of land-locked developing countries and also island developing countries, with a view to helping them to overcome their particular difficulties and thus contribute to their economic and social development.

Article 26

All States have the duty to coexist in tolerance and live together in peace, irrespective of differences in political, economic, social and cultural systems, and to facilitate trade between States having different economic and social systems. International trade should be conducted without prejudice to generalized non-discriminatory and non-reciprocal preferences in favour of developing countries, on the basis of mutual advantage, equitable benefits and the exchange of most-favoured-nation treatment.

Article 27

1. Every State has the right to enjoy fully the benefits of world invisible trade and to engage in the expansion of such trade.
2. World invisible trade, based on efficiency and mutual and equitable benefit, furthering the expansion of the world economy, is the common goal of all States. The role of developing countries in world invisible trade should be enhanced and strengthened consistent with the above objectives, particular attention being paid to the special needs of developing countries.
3. All States should co-operate with developing countries in their endeavours to increase their capacity to earn foreign exchange from invisible transactions, in accordance with the potential and needs of each developing country and consistent with the objectives mentioned above.

Article 28

All States have the duty to co-operate in achieving adjustments in the prices of exports of developing countries in relation to prices of their imports so as to promote just and equitable terms of trade for them, in a manner which is remunerative for producers and equitable for producers and consumers.

CHAPTER III

Common responsibilities towards the international community

Article 29

The sea-bed and ocean floor and the subsoil thereof, beyond the limits of national jurisdiction, as well as the resources of the area, are the common heritage of mankind. On the basis of the principles adopted by the General Assembly in resolution 2749 (XXV) of 17 December 1970, all States shall ensure that the exploration of the area and exploitation of its resources are carried out exclusively for peaceful purposes and that the benefits derived therefrom are shared equitable by all States, taking into account the particular interests and needs of developing countries; an international régime applying to the area and its resources and including appropriate international machinery to give effect to its provisions shall be established by an international treaty of a universal character, generally agreed upon.

Article 30

The protection, preservation and enhancement of the environment for the present and future generations is the responsibility of all States. All States shall endeavour to establish their own environmental and developmental policies in conformity with such responsibility. The environmental policies of all States should enhance and not adversely affect the present and future development potential of developing countries. All States have the responsibility to ensure that activities within their jurisdiction or control do not cause damage to the environment of other States or of areas beyond the limits of national jurisdiction. All States should co-operate in evolving international norms and regulations in the field of the environment.

CHAPTER IV

Final provisions

Article 31

All States have the duty to contribute to the balanced expansion of the world economy, taking duly into account the close interrelationship between the well-being of the developed countries and the growth and development of the developing countries, and the fact that the prosperity of the international community as a whole depends upon the prosperity of its constituent parts.

Article 32

No State may use or encourage the use of economic, political or any other type of measures to coerce another State in order to obtain from it the subordination of the exercise of its sovereign rights.

Article 33

1. Nothing in the present Charter shall be construed as impairing or derogating from the provisions of the Charter of the United Nations or actions taken in pursuance thereof.
2. In their interpretation and application, the provisions of the present Charter are interrelated and each provision should be construed in the context of the other provisions.

Article 34

An item on the Charter of Economic Rights and Duties of States shall be included in the agenda of the General Assembly at its thirtieth session, and thereafter on the agenda of every fifth session. In this way a systematic and comprehensive consideration of the implementation of the Charter, covering both progress achieved and any improvements and additions which might become necessary, would be carried out and appropriate measures recommended. Such consideration should take into account the evolution of all the economic, social, legal and other factors related to the principles upon which the present Charter is based and on its purpose.

44.

CODE OF CONDUCT FOR LAW ENFORCEMENT OFFICIALS

Adopted by the General Assembly of the United Nations on 17 December 1979 (resolution 34/169)

The General Assembly

Considering that the purposes proclaimed in the Charter of the United Nations include the achievement of international co-operation in promoting and encouraging respect for human rights and for fundamental freedoms for all without distinction as to race, sex, language or religion,

Recalling, in particular, the Universal Declaration of Human Rights and the International Covenants on Human Rights,

Recalling also the Declaration on the Protection of All Persons from Being Subjected to Torture and Other Cruel, Inhuman or Degrading Treatment or Punishment, adopted by the General Assembly in its resolution 3452 (XXX) of 9 December 1975,

Mindful that the nature of the functions of law enforcement in the defence of public order and the manner in which those functions are exercised have a direct impact on the quality of life of individuals as well as of society as a whole,

Conscious of the important task which law enforcement officials are performing diligently and with dignity, in compliance with the principles of human rights,

Aware, nevertheless, of the potential for abuse which the exercise of such duties entails,

Recognizing that the establishment of a code of conduct for law enforcement officials is only one of several important measures for providing the citizenry served by law enforcement officials with protection of all their rights and interests,

Aware that there are additional important principles and prerequisites for the humane performance of law enforcement functions, namely:

(*a*) That, like all agencies of the criminal justice system, every law enforcement agency should be representative of and responsive and accountable to the community as a whole,

(*b*) That the effective maintenance of ethical standards among law enforcement officials depends on the existence of a well-conceived, popularly accepted and humane system of laws,

(c) That every law enforcement official is part of the criminal justice system, the aim of which is to prevent and control crime, and that the conduct of every functionary within the system has an impact on the entire system,

(d) That every law enforcement agency, in fulfilment of the first premise of every profession, should be held to the duty of disciplining itself in complete conformity with the principles and standards herein provided and that the actions of law enforcement officials should be responsive to public scrutiny, whether exercised by a review board, a ministry, a procuracy, the judiciary, an ombudsman, a citizens' committee or any combination thereof, or any other reviewing agency,

(e) That standards as such lack practical value unless their content and meaning, through education and training and through monitoring, become part of the creed of every law enforcement official,

Adopts the Code of Conduct for Law Enforcement Officials set forth in the annex to the present resolution and decides to transmit it to Governments with the recommendation that favourable consideration should be given to its use within the framework of national legislation or practice as a body of principles for observance by law enforcement officials.

CODE OF CONDUCT FOR LAW ENFORCEMENT OFFICIALS

Article 1

Law enforcement officials shall at all times fulfil the duty imposed upon them by law, by serving the community and by protecting all persons against illegal acts, consistent with the high degree of responsibility required by their profession.

Commentary:

(a) The term 'law enforcement officials' includes all officers of the law, whether appointed or elected, who exercise police powers, especially the powers of arrest or detention.

(b) In countries where police powers are exercised by military authorities, whether uniformed or not, or by state security forces, the definition of law enforcement officials shall be regarded as including officers of such services.

(c) Service to the community is intended to include particularly the rendition of services of assistance to those members of the community who by reason of personal, economic, social or other emergencies are in need of immediate aid.

(d) This provision is intended to cover not only all violent, predatory and harmful acts, but extends to the full range of prohibitions under penal statutes. It extends to conduct by persons not capable of incurring criminal liability.

Article 2

In the performance of their duty, law enforcement officials shall respect and protect human dignity and maintain and uphold the human rights of all persons.

Commentary:

(*a*) The human rights in question are identified and protected by national and international law. Among the relevant international instruments are the Universal Declaration of Human Rights, the International Covenant on Civil and Political Rights, the Declaration on the Protection of All Persons from Being Subjected to Torture and Other Cruel, Inhuman or Degrading Treatment or Punishment, the United Nations Declaration on the Elimination of All Forms of Racial Discrimination, the International Convention on the Elimination of All Forms of Racial Discrimination, the International Convention on the Suppression and Punishment of the Crime of *Apartheid*, the Convention on the Prevention and Punishment of the Crime of Genocide, the Standard Minimum Rules for the Treatment of Prisoners and the Vienna Convention on Consular Relations.

(*b*) National commentaries to this provision should indicate regional or national provisions identifying and protecting these rights.

Article 3

Law Enforcement officials may use force only when strictly necessary and to the extent required for the performance of their duty.

Commentary:

(*a*) This provision emphasizes that the use of force by law enforcement officials should be exceptional; while it implies that law enforcement officials may be authorized to use force as is reasonably necessary under the circumstances for the prevention of crime or in effecting or assisting in the lawful arrest of offenders or suspected offenders, no force going beyond that may be used.

(*b*) National law ordinarily restricts the use of force by law enforcement officials in accordance with a principle of proportionality. It is to be understood that such national principles of proportionality are to be respected in the interpretation of this provision. In no case should this provision be interpreted to authorize the use of force which is disproportionate to the legitimate objective to be achieved.

(*c*) The use of firearms is considered an extreme measure. Every effort should be made to exclude the use of firearms, especially against children. In general, firearms should not be used except when a suspected offender offers armed resistance or otherwise jeopardizes the lives of others and less extreme measures are not sufficient to restrain or apprehend the suspected offender. In every instance in which a firearm is discharged, a report should be made promptly to the competent authorities.

Article 4

Matters of a confidential nature in the possession of law enforcement officials shall be kept confidential, unless the performance of duty or the needs of justice strictly require otherwise.

Commentary:

By the nature of their duties, law enforcement officials obtain information which may relate to private lives or be potentially harmful to the interests, and especially the reputation, of others. Great care should be exercised in safeguarding and using such information, which should be disclosed only in the performance of duty or to serve the needs of justice. Any disclosure of such information for other purposes is wholly improper.

Article 5

No law enforcement official may inflict, instigate or tolerate any act of torture or other cruel, inhuman or degrading treatment or punishment, nor may any law enforcement official invoke superior orders or exceptional circumstances such as a state of war or a threat of war, a threat to national security, internal political instability or any other public emergency as a justification of torture or other cruel, inhuman or degrading treatment or punishment.

Commentary:

(*a*) This prohibition derives from the Declaration on the Protection of All Persons from Being Subjected to Torture and Other Cruel, Inhuman or Degrading Treatment or Punishment, adopted by the General Assembly, according to which:

'[Such an act is] an offence to human dignity and shall be condemned as a denial of the purposes of the Charter of the United Nations and as a violation of the human rights and fundamental freedoms proclaimed in the Universal Declaration of Human Rights [and other international human rights instruments].'

(*b*) The Declaration defines torture as follows:

'... torture means any act by which severe pain or suffering, whether physical or mental, is intentionally inflicted by or at the instigation of a public official on a person for such purposes as obtaining from him or a third person information or confession, punishing him for an act he has committed or is suspected of having committed, or intimidating him or other persons. It does not include pain or suffering arising only from, inherent in or incidental to, lawful sanctions to the extent consistent with the Standard Minimum Rules for the Treatment of Prisoners.'

(*c*) The term 'cruel, inhuman or degrading treatment or punishment' has not been defined by the General Assembly but should be interpreted so as to extend the widest possible protection against abuses, whether physical or mental.

Article 6

Law enforcement officials shall ensure the full protection of the health of persons in their custody and, in particular, shall take immediate action to secure medical attention whenever required.

Commentary:

(*a*) 'Medical attention', which refers to services rendered by any medical personnel, including certified medical practitioners and paramedics, shall be secured when needed or requested.

(*b*) While the medical personnel are likely to be attached to the law enforcement operation, law enforcement officials must take into account the judgement of such personnel when they recommend providing the person in custody with appropriate treatment through, or in consultation with, medical personnel from outside the law enforcement operation.

(*c*) It is understood that law enforcement officials shall also secure medical attention for victims of violations of law or of accidents occurring in the course of violations of law.

Article 7

Law enforcement officials shall not commit any act of corruption. They shall also rigorously oppose and combat all such acts.

Commentary:

(*a*) Any act of corruption, in the same way as any other abuse of authority, is incompatible with the profession of law enforcement officials. The law must be enforced fully with respect to any law enforcement official who commits an act of corruption, as Governments cannot expect to enforce the law among their citizens if they cannot, or will not, enforce the law against their own agents and within their own agencies.

(*b*) While the definition of corruption must be subject to national law, it should be understood to encompass the commission or omission of an act in the performance of or in connexion with one's duties, in response to gifts, promises or incentives demanded or accepted, or the wrongful receipt of these once the act has been committed or omitted.

(*c*) The expression 'act of corruption' referred to above should be understood to encompass attempted corruption.

Article 8

Law enforcement officials shall respect the law and the present Code. They shall also, to the best of their capability, prevent and rigorously oppose any violations of them.

Law enforcement officials who have reason to believe that a violation of the present Code has occurred or is about to occur shall report the matter to their superior authorities and, where necessary, to other appropriate authorities or organs vested with reviewing or remedial power.

Commentary:

(*a*) This code shall be observed whenever it has been incorporated into national legislation or practice. If legislation or practice contains stricter provisions than those of the present Code, those stricter provisions shall be observed.

(*b*) The article seeks to preserve the balance between the need for internal discipline of the agency on which public safety is largely dependent, on the one hand, and the need for dealing with violations of basic human rights, on the other. Law enforcement officials shall report violations within the chain of command and take other lawful action outside the chain of command only when no other remedies are available or effective. It is understood that law enforcement officials shall not suffer administrative or other penalties because they have reported that a violation of this Code has occurred or is about to occur.

(*c*) The term 'appropriate authorities or organs vested with reviewing or remedial power' refers to any authority or organ existing under national law, whether internal to the law enforcement agency or independent thereof, with statutory, customary or other power to review grievances and complaints arising out of violations within the purview of this Code.

(*d*) In some countries, the mass media may be regarded as performing complaint review functions similar to those described in sub-paragraph (*c*) above. Law enforcement officials may, therefore, be justified if, as a last resort and in accordance with the laws and customs of their own countries and with the provisions of article 4 of the present Code, they bring violations to the attention of public opinion through the mass media.

(*e*) Law enforcement officials who comply with the provisions of this Code deserve the respect, the full support and the co-operation of the community and of the law enforcement agency in which they serve, as well as the law enforcement profession.

45.

Declaration on the Elimination of All Forms of Intolerance and of Discrimination Based on Religion or Belief

GA Res. 36/55 of 25 November 1981.
36 *G.A.O.R.*, Suppl. No. 51 (A/36/51), pp. 171 *et seq.*.

The General Assembly,

Considering that one of the basic principles of the Charter of the United Nations is that of the dignity and equality inherent in all human beings, and that all Member States have pledged themselves to take joint and separate action in co-operation with the Organization to promote and encourage universal respect for and observance of human rights and fundamental freedoms for all, without distinction as to race, sex, language or religion,

Considering that the Universal Declaration of Human Rights and the International Covenants on Human Rights proclaim the principles of non-discrimination and equality before the law and the right to freedom of thought, conscience, religion and belief,

Considering that the disregard and infringement of human rights and fundamental freedoms, in particular of the right to freedom of thought, conscience, religion or whatever belief, have brought, directly or indirectly, wars and great suffering to mankind, especially where they serve as a means of foreign interference in the internal affairs of other States and amount to kindling hatred between peoples and nations,

Considering that religion or belief, for anyone who professes either, is one of the fundamental elements in his conception of life and that freedom of religion or belief should be fully respected and guaranteed,

Considering that it is essential to promote understanding, tolerance and respect in matters relating to freedom of religion and belief and to ensure that the use of religion or belief for ends inconsistent with the Charter of the United Nations, other relevant instruments of the United Nations and the purposes and principles of the present Declaration is inadmissible,

Convinced that freedom of religion and belief should also contribute to the attainment of the goals of world peace, social justice and friendship among peoples and to the elimination of ideologies or practices of colonialism and racial discrimination,

Noting with satisfaction the adoption of several, and the coming into force of some, conventions, under the aegis of the United Nations and of the specialized agencies, for the elimination of various forms of discrimination,

Concerned by manifestations of intolerance and by the existence of discrimination in matters of religion or belief still in evidence in some areas of the world,

Resolved to adopt all necessary measures for the speedy elimination of such intolerance in all its forms and manifestations and to prevent and combat discrimination on the ground of religion or belief,

Proclaims this Declaration on the Elimination of All Forms of Intolerance and of Discrimination Based on Religion or Belief:

Article 1

1. Everyone shall have the right to freedom of thought, conscience and religion. This right shall include freedom to have a religion or whatever belief of his choice, and freedom, either individually or in community with others and in public or private, to manifest his religion or belief in worship, observance, practice and teaching.

2. No one shall be subject to coercion which would impair his freedom to have a religion or belief of his choice.

3. Freedom to manifest one's religion or beliefs may be subject only to such limitations as are prescribed by law and are necessary to protect public safety, order, health or morals or the fundamental rights and freedoms of others.

Article 2

1. No one shall be subject to discrimination by any State, institution, group of persons, or person on grounds of religion or other beliefs.

2. For the purposes of the present Declaration, the expression "intolerance and discrimination based on religion or belief" means any distinction, exclusion, restriction or preference based on religion or belief and having as its purpose or as its effect nullification or impairment of the recognition, enjoyment or exercise of human rights and fundamental freedoms on an equal basis.

Article 3

Discrimination between human beings on grounds of religion or belief constitutes an affront to human dignity and a disavowal of the principles of the Charter of the United Nations, and shall be condemned as a violation of the human rights and fundamental freedoms proclaimed in the Universal Declaration of Human Rights and enunciated in detail in the International Covenants on Human Rights, and as an obstacle to friendly and peaceful relations between nations.

Article 4

1. All States shall take effective measures to prevent and eliminate discrimination on the grounds of religion or belief in the recognition, exercise and enjoyment of human rights and fundamental freedoms in all fields of civil, economic, political, social and cultural life.

2. All States shall make all efforts to enact or rescind legislation where necessary to prohibit any such discrimination, and to take all appropriate measures to combat intolerance on the grounds of religion or other beliefs in this matter.

Article 5

1. The parents or, as the case may be, the legal guardians of the child have the right to organize the life within the family in accordance with their religion or belief and bearing in mind the moral education in which they believe the child should be brought up.

2. Every child shall enjoy the right to have access to education in the matter of religion or belief in accordance with the wishes of his parents or, as the case may be, legal guardians, and shall not be compelled to receive teaching on religion or belief against the wishes of his parents or legal guardians, the best interests of the child being the guiding principle.

3. The child shall be protected from any form of discrimination on the ground of religion or belief. He shall be brought up in a spirit of understanding, tolerance, friendship among peoples, peace and universal brotherhood, respect for freedom of religion or belief of others, and in full consciousness that his energy and talents should be devoted to the service of his fellow men.

4. In the case of a child who is not under the care either of his parents or of legal guardians, due account shall be taken of their expressed wishes or of any other proof of their wishes in the matter of religion or belief, the best interests of the child being the guiding principle.

5. Practices of a religion or beliefs in which a child is brought up must not be injurious to his physical or mental health or to his full development, taking into account article 1, paragraph 3, of the present Declaration.

Article 6

In accordance with article 1 of the present Declaration, and subject to the provisions of article 1, paragraph 3, the right to freedom of thought, conscience, religion or belief shall include, <u>inter alia</u>, the following freedoms:

(<u>a</u>) To worship or assemble in connexion with a religion or belief, and to establish and maintain places for these purposes;

(<u>b</u>) To establish and maintain appropriate charitable or humanitarian institutions;

(<u>c</u>) To make, acquire and use to an adequate extent the necessary articles and materials related to the rites or customs of a religion or belief;

(<u>d</u>) To write, issue and disseminate relevant publications in these areas;

(<u>e</u>) To teach a religion or belief in places suitable for these purposes;

(<u>f</u>) To solicit and receive voluntary financial and other contributions from individuals and institutions;

(<u>g</u>) To train, appoint, elect or designate by succession appropriate leaders called for by the requirements and standards of any religion or belief;

(<u>h</u>) To observe days of rest and to celebrate holidays and ceremonies in accordance with the precepts of one's religion or belief;

(<u>i</u>) To establish and maintain communications with individuals and communities in matters of religion and belief at the national and international levels.

Article 7

The rights and freedoms set forth in the present Declaration shall be accorded in national legislation in such a manner that everyone shall be able to avail himself of such rights and freedoms in practice.

Article 8

Nothing in the present Declaration shall be construed as restricting or derogating from any right defined in the Universal Declaration of Human Rights and the International Covenants on Human Rights.

46.

DECLARATION ON THE HUMAN RIGHTS OF INDIVIDUALS WHO ARE NOT NATIONALS OF THE COUNTRY IN WHICH THEY LIVE

Report of the Economic and Social Council, Third Committee (Fortieth Session), Agenda item 12: Draft Resolution of Morocco

The General Assembly,

Having considered the question of the human rights of individuals who are not nationals of the country in which they live,

Decides to adopt the Declaration on the human rights of individuals who are not nationals of the country in which they live, the text of which is annexed to this resolution.

Annex

DECLARATION ON THE HUMAN RIGHTS OF INDIVIDUALS WHO ARE NOT NATIONALS OF THE COUNTRY IN WHICH THEY LIVE

The General Assembly,

Considering that the Charter of the United Nations encourages the promotion of universal respect for and observance of the human rights and fundamental freedoms of all human beings, without distinction as to race, sex, language or religion,

Considering that the Universal Declaration of Human Rights* proclaims that all human beings are born free and equal in dignity and rights and that everyone is entitled to all the rights and freedoms set forth in the Declaration,

_____
* Resolution 217 A (III).

without distinction of any kind, such as race, colour, sex, language, religion, political or other opinion, national or social origin, property, birth or other status,

Considering that the Universal Declaration of Human Rights proclaims further that everyone has the right to recognition everywhere as a person before the law, that all are equal before the law, are entitled without any discrimination to equal protection of the law, and that all are entitled to equal protection against any discrimination in violation of the aforementioned Declaration and against any incitement to such discrimination,

Being aware that the States parties to the International Covenants on human rights now in force undertake to guarantee that the rights enunciated in these Covenants will be exercised without discrimination of any kind as to race, colour, sex, language, religion, political or other opinion, national or social origin, property, birth or other status,

Conscious that, with improving communications and the development of peaceful and friendly relations among countries, individuals increasingly live in countries of which they are not nationals,

Reaffirming the purposes and principles of the Charter of the United Nations,

Recognizing that the protection of human rights and fundamental freedoms provided for in international instruments should also be ensured for individuals who are not nationals of the country in which they live,

Proclaims this Declaration:

Article 1

For the purposes of this Declaration, the term 'alien' shall apply, with due regard to qualifications made in subsequent articles, to any individual who is not a national of the State in which he or she is present.

Article 2

1. Nothing in this Declaration shall be interpreted as legitimizing any alien's illegal entry into and presence in a State, nor shall any provision be interpreted as restricting the right of any State to promulgate laws and regulations concerning the entry of aliens and the terms and conditions of their stay or to establish differences between nationals and aliens. However, such laws and regulations shall not be incompatible with the international legal obligations of that State, including those in the field of human rights.

2. This Declaration shall not prejudice the enjoyment of the rights accorded by domestic law and of the rights which under international law a State is obliged to accord to aliens, even where the present Declaration does not recognize such rights or recognizes them to a lesser extent.

Article 3

Every State shall make public its national legislation or regulations affecting aliens.

Article 4

Aliens shall observe the laws of the State in which they reside or are present and regard with respect the customs and traditions of the people of that State.

Article 5

1. Aliens shall enjoy in accordance with domestic law in particular the following rights:
(a) The right to life and security of person; no alien shall be subjected to arbitrary arrest or detention; no alien shall be deprived of his liberty except on such grounds and in accordance with such procedures as are established by law;
(b) The right to protection against arbitrary or unlawful interference with privacy, family, home or correspondence;
(c) The right to be equal before the courts, tribunals and all other organs and authorities administering justice and, when necessary, to free assistance of an interpreter in criminal proceedings and, when prescribed by law, other proceedings;
(d) The right to choose a spouse, to marry, to found a family;
(e) The right to freedom of though, opinion, conscience and religion; the right to manifest one's religion or beliefs subject only to such limitations as are prescribed by law and are necessary to protect public safety, order, health or morals or the fundamental rights and freedoms of others;
(f) The right to retain their own language, culture and tradition;
(g) The right to transfer abroad earnings, savings or other personal monetary assets, subject to domestic currency regulations.
2. Subject to such restrictions as are prescribed by law and which are necessary in a democratic society to protect national security, public safety, public order (ordre public), public health or morals or the rights and freedoms of others, and which are consistent with the other rights recognized in the relevant international instruments and those set forth in the present Declaration, aliens shall enjoy the following rights:
(a) The right to leave the country;
(b) The right to freedom of expression;
(c) The right to peaceful assembly;
(d) The right to own property alone as well as in association with others, subject to domestic law.

3. Subject to the provisions referred to in paragraph 2, aliens lawfully in the territory of a State shall enjoy the right to liberty of movement and freedom to choose their residence within the borders of the State.

4. Subject to national legislation and due authorization, the spouse and minor or dependent children of an alien lawfully residing in the territory of a State shall be admitted to accompany, join and stay with the alien.

Article 6

No alien shall be subjected to torture or to cruel, inhuman or degrading treatment or punishment and, in particular, no alien shall be subjected without his free consent to medical or scientific experimentation.

Article 7

An alien lawfully in the territory of a State may be expelled therefrom only in pursuance of a decision reached in accordance with law and shall, except where compelling reasons of national security otherwise require, be allowed to submit the reasons against his expulsion and to have his case reviewed by, and be represented for the purpose before, the competent authority or a person or persons specially designated by the competent authority. Individual or collective expulsion of such aliens on grounds of race, colour, religion, culture, descent or national or ethnic origin is prohibited.

Article 8

1. Aliens lawfully residing in the territory of a State shall also enjoy, in accordance with the national laws, the following rights, subject to their obligations referred to in article 4:
(a) The right to safe and healthy working conditions, to fair wages and equal remuneration for work of equal value without distinction of any kind, in particular, women being guaranteed conditions of work not inferior to those enjoyed by men, with equal pay for equal work;
(b) The right to join trade unions and other organizations or associations of their choice and to participate in their activities. No restrictions may be placed on the exercise of this right other than those prescribed by law and which are necessary in a democratic society in the interests of national security or public order or for the protection of the rights and freedoms of others;
(c) The right to health protection, medical care, social security, social service, education, rest and leisure, provided that they fulfil the requirements under the relevant regulations for participation and that undue strain is not placed on the resources of the State.

2. With a view to protecting the rights of aliens carrying on lawful paid activities in the country in which they find themselves, such rights may be specified by the Governments concerned in multilateral or bilateral conventions.

Article 9

No alien shall be arbitrarily deprived of his lawfully acquired assets.

Article 10

Any alien shall be free at any time to communicate with the consulate or diplomatic mission of the State of which he is a national or, in their absence, with the consulate or diplomatic mission of any other State entrusted with the protection of the interests of the State of which he is a national in the State where he resides.

47.

List of other Global Instruments*

CHILDHOOD AND YOUTH

Declaration of the Rights of the Child, 1959
Declaration on the Protection of Women and Children in Emergency and Armed Conflict, 1974
Declaration on the Promotion among Youth of the Ideals of Peace, Mutual Respect and understanding between Peoples, 1965

CULTURE

Declaration of the Principles of International Cultural Co-operation, 1966

DISCRIMINATION

Equal Remuneration Convention, 1951
Discrimination (Employment and Occupation) Convention, 1958
Convention against Discrimination in Education, 1960
Protocol Instituting a Conciliation and Good Offices
   Commission to be responsible for seeking a settlement of any disputes which may arise between States Parties to the Convention against Discrimination in Education, 1962
Declaration on the Elimination of All Forms of Racial Discrimination, 1963
Declaration on the Elimination of Discrimination against Women, 1967

---

*For other global human rights instruments, see *Human Rights: A Compilation of International Instruments*. New York: United Nations, 1983. St./HR/Rev. 2.

EMPLOYMENT POLICY

Employment Policy Convention, 1964

FREEDOM OF INFORMATION

Convention on the International Rights of Correction, 1952

FREEDOM OF ASSICIATION

ILO Convention (n° 135) concerning protection and facilities to be afforded to workers' representatives in the undertaking
ILO Convention (n° 141) concerning organisations of rural workers and their role in economic and social development
ILO Convention (n° 151) concerning protection of the right to organise and procedures for determining conditions of employment in the public service

FREEDOM OF ASSOCIATION

INTERNATIONAL HUMANITARIAN LAWS

The Hague Convention of 1899
The Hague Convention of 1907
1949 Geneva Conventions:
    I Wounded and sick in the field
    II Wounded and sick at sea
    III Treatment of prisoners of war
    IV Protection of civilians in war
The 1977 Protocols:
    I Protocol on victims of international armed conflict
    II Protocol on victims of non-international armed conflict

NATIONALITY AND STATELESSNESS

Convention on the Nationality of Married Women, 1957
Convention relating to the Status of Stateless Persons, 1954
Convention on the Reduction of Statelessness, 1961

SLAVERY, FORCED LABOUR AND PROSTITUTION

Slavery Convention, 1926
Protocol amending the Slavery Convention, 1953
Supplementary Convention on the Abolition of Slavery, the Slave Trade, and Institutions and Practices Similar to Slavery, 1956
Convention for the Suppression of the Traffic in Persons and of the Exploitation of the Prostitution of Others, 1949
Forced Labour Convention, 1957

SOCIAL WELFARE AND PROGRESS

Declaration on the Use of Scientific and Technological Progress in the Interests of Peace and for the Benefit of Mankind, 1975
Declaration on the Rights of Mentally Retarded Persons, 1971
Declaration on the Rights of Disabled Persons, 1975

TREATMENT OF OFFENDERS

Declaration on the Protection of All Persons from Being Subjected to Torture and Other Cruel, Inhuman or Degrading Treatment or Punishment, 1975
Caracas Declaration on the Prevention of Crime and Treatment of Offenders, 1980
Principles of Medical Ethics Relevant to the Role of Health Personnel, 1982

WAR CRIMES

Convention on the Non-Applicability of Statutory Limitations to War Crimes, 1968
Principles of International Cooperation in the Detection, Arrest, Extradition and Punishment of Persons Guilty of War Crimes and Crimes Against Humanity, 1973

WOMEN

Convention on Nationality of Married Women, 1957
Recommendation on Consent to Marriage, Minimum Age for Marriage and Registration of Marriages, 1965
Declaration on the Participation of Women in Promoting International Peace and Cooperation, 1982

PART IV

Human Rights Communications

48.

RESOLUTION 728 F (XXVIII) OF THE ECONOMIC AND SOCIAL COUNCIL

ECOSOC Res. 728 F (XXVIII) of 30 July 1959. See also ECOSOC Res. 75 (V) of 5 August 1947, amended by ECOSOC Res. 275 (X) of 17 February 1950, and ECOSOC Res. 76 (V) (communications concerning the status of women) of 5 August 1947, amended by ECOSOC Res. 304 I (XI) of 17 July 1950.

The Economic and Social Council,

Having considered chapter V of the report of the Commission on Human Rights on its first session, concerning communications, and chapter IX of the report of the Commission on its fifteenth session;

1. Approves the statement that the Commission on Human Rights recognizes that it has no power to take any action in regard to any complaints concerning human rights;

2. Requests the Secretary-General:

a. To compile and distribute to members of the Commission on Human Rights before each session a non-confidential list containing a brief indication of the substance of each communication, however addressed, which deals with the principles involved in the promotion of universal respect for, and observance of, human rights and to divulge the identity of the authors of such communications unless they indicate that they wish their names to remain confidential;

b. To compile before each session of the Commission a confidential list containing a brief indication of the substance of other communications concerning human rights, however addressed, and to furnish this list to members of the Commission, in private meeting, without divulging the identity of the authors of communications except in cases where the authors state that they have already divulged or intend to divulge their names or that they have no objection to their names being divulged;

c. To enable the members of the Commission, upon request, to consult the originals of communications dealing with the principles involved in the promotion of universal respect for, and observance of, human rights;

d. To inform the writers of all communications concerning human rights, however addressed, that their communications will be handled in accordance with this resolution, indicating that the Commission has no power to take any action in regard to any complaint concerning human rights;

e. To furnish each Member State concerned with a copy of any communication concerning human rights which refers explicitly to that State or to territories under its jurisdiction, without divulging the identity of the author, except as provided for in sub-paragraph (b) above;

f. To ask Governments sending replies to communications brought to their attention in accordance with sub-paragraph (c) whether they wish their replies to be presented to the Commission in summary form or in full;

3. Resolves to give members of the Sub-Commission on Prevention of Discrimination and Protection of Minorities, with respect to communications dealing with discrimination and minorities, the same facilities as are enjoyed by members of the Commission on Human Rights under the present resolution;

4. Suggests to the Commission on Human Rights that it should at each session appoint an ad hoc committee to meet shortly before its next session for the purpose of reviewing the list of communications prepared by the Secretary-General under paragraph 2 (a) above and of recommending which of these communications in original, should, in accordance with paragraph 2 (c) above, be made available to members of the Commission on request.

49.

RESOLUTION 1235 (XLII) OF THE ECONOMIC AND SOCIAL COUNCIL

[1] VIOLATIONS OF HUMAN RIGHTS AND FUNDAMENTAL FREEDOMS, INCLUDING POLICIES OF RACIAL DISCRIMINATION AND SEGREGATION AND OF *APARTHEID* IN ALL COUNTRIES, WITH PARTICULAR REFERENCE TO COLONIAL AND OTHER DEPENDENT COUNTRIES AND TERRITORIES

| ECOSOC Res. 1235 (XLII) of 6 June 1967.

The Economic and Social Council,

Noting resolutions 8 (XXIII) and 9 (XXIII) of the Commission on Human Rights,

1. *Welcomes* the decision of the Commission on Human Rights to give annual consideration to the item entitled "Question of the violation of human rights and fundamental freedoms, including policies of racial discrimination and segregation and of apartheid, in all countries, with particular reference to colonial and other dependent countries and territories," without prejudice to the functions and powers of organs already in existence or which may be established within the framework of measures of implementation included in international covenants and conventions on the protection of human rights and fundamental freedoms; and concurs with the requests for assistance addressed to the Sub-Commission on Prevention of Discrimination and Protection of Minorities and to the Secretary-General;

2. *Authorizes* the Commission on Human Rights and the Sub-Commission on Prevention of Discrimination and Protection of Minorities, in conformity with the provisions of paragraph 1 of the Commission's resolution 8 (XXIII), to examine information relevant to gross violations of human rights and fundamental freedoms, as exemplified by the policy of apartheid as practised in the Republic of South Africa and in the Territory of South West Africa under the direct responsibility of the United Nations and now illegally

occupied by the Government of the Republic of South Africa, and to racial discrimination as practised notably in Southern Rhodesia, contained in the communications listed by the Secretary-General pursuant to Economic and Social Council resolution 728 F (XXVIII) of 30 July 1959;

3. *Decides* that the Commission on Human Rights may, in appropriate cases, and after careful consideration of the information thus made available to it, in conformity with the provisions of paragraph 1 above, make a thorough study of situations which reveal a consistent pattern of violations of human rights, as exemplified by the policy of apartheid as practised in the Republic of South Africa and in the Territory of South West Africa under the direct responsibility of the United Nations and now illegally occupied by the Government of the Republic of South Africa, and racial discrimination as practised notably in Southern Rhodesia, and report, with recommendations thereon, to the Economic and Social Council;

4. *Decides* to review the provisions of paragraphs 2 and 3 of the present resolution after the entry into force of the International Covenants on Human Rights;

5. *Takes note* of the fact that the Commission on Human Rights, in its resolution 6 (XXIII), has instructed an *ad hoc* study group to study in all its aspects the question of the ways and means by which the Commission might be enabled or assisted to discharge functions in relation to violations of human rights and fundamental freedoms, whilst maintaining and fulfilling its other functions;

6. *Requests* the Commission on Human Rights to report to it on the result of this study after having given consideration to the conclusions of the *ad hoc* study group referred to in paragraph 5 above.

50.

RESOLUTION 1503 (XLVIII) OF THE ECONOMIC AND SOCIAL COUNCIL

PROCEDURE FOR DEALING WITH COMMUNICATIONS RELATING TO VIOLATIONS OF HUMAN RIGHTS AND FUNDAMENTAL FREEDOMS

ECOSOC Res. 1503 (XLVIII) of 27 May 1970.

Noting resolutions 7 (XXVI) and 17 (XXV) of the Commission on Human Rights and resolution 2 (XXI) of the Sub-Commission on Prevention of Discrimination and Protection of Minorities,

1. *Authorizes* the Sub-Commission on Prevention of Discrimination and Protection of Minorities to appoint a working group consisting of not more than five of its members, with due regard to geographical distribution, to meet once a year in private meetings for a period not exceeding ten days immediately before the sessions of the Sub-Commission to consider all communications, including replies of Governments thereon, received by the Secretary-General under Council resolution 728 F (XXVIII) of 30 July 1959 with a view to bringing to the attention of the Sub-Commission those communications, together with replies of Governments, if any, which appear to reveal a consistent pattern of gross and reliably attested violations of human rights and fundamental freedoms within the terms of reference of the Sub-Commission;

2. *Decides* that the Sub-Commission on Prevention of Discrimination and Protection of Minorities should, as the first stage in the implementation of the present resolution, devise at its twenty-third session appropriate procedures for dealing with the question of admissibility of communications received by the Secretary-General under Council resolution 728 F (XXVIII) and in accordance with Council resolution 1235 (XLII) of 6 June 1967;

3. *Requests* the Secretary-General to prepare a

document on the question of admissibility of communications for the Sub-Commission's consideration at its twenty-third session;

4. *Further requests* the Secretary-General:

(a) To furnish to the members of the Sub-Commission every month a list of communications prepared by him in accordance with Council resolution 728 F (XXVIII) and a brief description of them, together with the text of any replies received from Governments;

(b) To make available to the members of the working group at their meetings the originals of such communications listed as they may request, having due regard to the provisions of paragraph 2 (b) of Council resolution 728 F (XXVIII) concerning the divulging of the identity of the authors of communications;

(c) To circulate to the members of the Sub-Commission, in the working languages, the originals of such communications as are referred to the Sub-Commission by the working group;

5. *Requests* the Sub-Commission on Prevention of Discrimination and Protection of Minorities to consider in private meetings, in accordance with paragraph 1 above, the communications brought before it in accordance with the decision of a majority of the members of the working group and any replies of Governments relating thereto and other relevant information, with a view to determining whether to refer to the Commission on Human Rights particular situations which appear to reveal a consistent pattern of gross and reliably attested violations of human rights requiring consideration by the Commission;

6. *Requests* the Commission on Human Rights after it has examined any situation referred to it by the Sub-Commission to determine:

(a) Whether it requires a thorough study by the Commission and a report and recommendations thereon to the Council in accordance with paragraph 3 of Council resolution 1235 (XLII);

(b) Whether it may be a subject of an investigation by an *ad hoc* committee to be appointed by the Commission which shall be undertaken only with the express consent of the State concerned and shall be conducted in constant co-operation with that State and under conditions determined by agreement with it. In any event, the investigation may be undertaken only if:

(i) All available means at the national level have been resorted to and exhausted;

(ii) The situation does not relate to a matter which is being dealt with under other procedures prescribed in the constituent instruments of, or conventions adopted by, the United Nations and the specialized agencies, or in regional conventions, or which the State concerned wishes to submit to other procedures in accordance with general or special international agreements to which it is a party.

7. *Decides* that if the Commission on Human Rights appoints an *ad hoc* committee to carry on an investigation with the consent of the State concerned:

(*a*) The composition of the committee shall be determined by the Commission. The members of the committee shall be independent persons whose competence and impartiality is beyond question. Their appointment shall be subject to the consent of the Government concerned;

(*b*) The committee shall establish its own rules of procedure. It shall be subject to the quorum rule. It shall have authority to receive communications and hear witnesses, as necessary. The investigation shall be conducted in co-operation with the Government concerned;

(*c*) The committee's procedure shall be confidential, its proceedings shall be conducted in private meetings and its communications shall not be publicized in any way;

(*d*) The committee shall strive for friendly solutions before, during and even after the investigation;

(*e*) The committee shall report to the Commission on Human Rights with such observations and suggestions as it may deem appropriate;

8. *Decides* that all actions envisaged in the implementation of the present resolution by the Sub-Commission on Prevention of Discrimination and Protection of Minorities or the Commission on Human Rights shall remain confidential until such time as the Commission may decide to make recommendations to the Economic and Social Council;

9. *Decides* to authorize the Secretary-General to provide all facilities which may be required to carry out the present resolution, making use of the existing staff of the Division of Human Rights of the United Nations Secretariat;

10. *Decides* that the procedure set out in the present resolution for dealing with communications relating to violations of human rights and fundamental freedoms should be reviewed if any new organ entitled to deal with such communications should be established within the United Nations or by international agreement.

51.

RESOLUTION 1 (XXIV) OF THE SUB-COMMISSION ON PREVENTION OF DISCRIMINATION AND PROTECTION OF MINORITIES

> Res. 1 (XXIV) of 14 August 1971, entitled "Question of the Violation of Human Rights and Fundamental Freedoms including Policies of Racial Discrimination and Segregation and of *Apartheid*, in all Countries, with Particular Reference to Colonial and Other Dependent Countries and Territories".
> (*U.N. Doc.* E/CN.4/1070/Corr. 1, E/CN.4/Sub. 2/323/Corr. 1)
> As published in 66 *A.J.I.L.* (1972), pp. 240 *et seq.*.

The Sub-Commission on Prevention of Discrimination and Protection of Minorities,

Considering that the Economic and Social Council, by its Resolution 1503 (XLVIII), decided that the Sub-Commission should devise appropriate procedures for dealing with the question of admissibility of communications received by the Secretary-General under Council Resolution 728 F (XXVIII) of 30 July 1959 and in accordance with Council Resolution 1235 (XLII) of 6 June 1967,

Adopts the following provisional procedures for dealing with the question of admissibility of communications referred to above:

(1) *Standards and criteria*

(a) The object of the communication must not be inconsistent with the relevant principles of the Charter, of the Universal Declaration of Human Rights and of the other applicable instruments in the field of human rights.

(b) Communications shall be admissible only if, after consideration thereof, together with the replies, if any, of the governments concerned, there are reasonable grounds to believe that they may reveal a consistent pattern of gross and reliably attested violations of human rights and fundamental freedoms, including policies of racial discrimination and segregation and of *apartheid*, in any country, including colonial and other dependent countries and peoples.

(2) *Source of communications*

(a) Admissible communications may originate from a person or group of persons who, it can be reasonably presumed, are victims of the violations referred to in subparagraph (1) (b) above, any person or group of persons who have direct and reliable knowledge of those violations, or non-governmental organizations acting in good faith in accordance with recognized principles of human rights, not resorting to politically motivated stands contrary to the provisions of the Charter of the United Nations and having direct and reliable knowledge of such violations.

(b) Anonymous communications shall be inadmissible; subject to the requirements of subparagraph 2 (b) of Resolution 728 F (XXVIII) of the Economic and Social Council, the author of a communication, whether an individual, a group of individuals or an organization, must be clearly identified.

(c) Communications shall not be inadmissible solely because the knowledge of the individual authors is second hand provided that they are accompanied by clear evidence.

(3) *Contents of communications and nature of allegations*

(a) The communication must contain a description of the facts and must indicate the purpose of the petition and the rights that have been violated.

(b) Communications shall be inadmissible if their language is essentially abusive and in particular if they contain insulting references to the State against which the complaint is directed. Such communications may be considered if they meet the other criteria for admissibility after deletion of the abusive language.

(c) A communication shall be inadmissible if it has manifestly political motivations and its subject is contrary to the provisions of the Charter of the United Nations.

(d) A communication shall be inadmissible if it appears that it is based exclusively on reports disseminated by mass media.

(4) *Existence of other remedies*

(a) Communications shall be inadmissible if their admission would prejudice the functions of the specialized agencies of the United Nations system.

(b) Communications shall be inadmissible if domestic remedies have not been exhausted, unless it appears that such remedies would be ineffective or unreasonably prolonged. Any failure to exhaust remedies should be satisfactorily established.

(c) Communications relating to cases which have been settled by the State concerned in accordance with the principles set forth in the Universal Declaration of Human Rights and other applicable documents in the field of human rights will not be considered.

(5) *Timeliness*

A communication shall be inadmissible if it is not submitted to the United Nations within a reasonable time after the exhaustion of the domestic remedies as provided above.

PART V

Bibliography

A bibliography is provided here in the belief that the reader will thirst after materials beyond what has been assembled in this collection.

The varied topics covered by writers from almost all parts of the world attest to the growing interest in universal human rights in general and in particular human rights in Africa. Much of the work on human rights in Africa, as on other subjects relating to Africa, has been undertaken by non-Africans. Some of the constraints on potential writers in Africa are well-known: poorly equipped libraries, limited financial resources to undertake studies, social and other pressure on time, and, in the case of human rights, real or imaginary danger of the consequences of any objective work. But as participant-observers Africans have both the burden and privilege to present their perspective of the issues and problems involved in the effective promotion and observance of human rights in Africa as well as a direction towards those goals. We hope that the bibliography will both stimulate and challenge potential writers, especially those in Africa, to contribute to the discussion and analysis of human rights in Africa as a first stage in the protection and promotion of human rights.

As stated in the Preface, the bibliography in both English and French are divided into two parts: a general part covers work on human rights with a universal perspective and the other part is devoted to commentaries and other materials on human rights in Africa. We have included in the second part of the bibliography in English a few writings on third world or developing countries as well as military regimes. We also have mentioned some fact-finding reports by Non-Governmental Organisations. An analysis of fact-finding reports by such bodies covering the period 1970–85 can be found in a book which was published recently.* The extensive work in Human Rights (The Netherlands Institute of Human Rights, Utrecht alone has over 3000 titles in English and more than 500 in French) prevents us from providing an exhaustive bibliography.

---

*Hans Thoolen and Berth Verstappen (1986) A Study of The Fact-Finding Practice, Dordrecht, The Netherlands: Kluwer Academic Publishers.

GENERAL

1. Adamantia Pollis and Peter Schwab, editors (1979) Human Rights: Cultural and Ideological Perspectives. New York: Praeger.
2. Alston, Philip (1979) 'United Nations' Specialized Agencies and Implementation of the International Covenant on Economic, Social and Cultural Rights'. Columbia Journal of Transnational Law 18, pp. 79–118.
3. Asbjorn Eide and August Schou (1980) International Protection of Human Rights. Uppsala: Almqvist and Wiksells.
4. Bossuyt, Marc (1975) 'La Distinction Juridique Entre les Droits Civils et Politiques et Les Droits Economiques, Sociaux et Culturels'. Human Rights Journal VIII, pp. 783–813.
5. Bossuyt, Marc (1976) L'Interdiction de la Discrimination dans le Droit International des Droits de l'Homme. (Brussels), pp. 184–217.
6. Bilder, Richard B. (1969) 'Rethinking International Human Rights: Some Basic Questions'. Human Rights Journal 2, no. 4, pp. 186–213.
7. Braham, Randolf L. editor (1980) Human Rights: Contemporary Domestic and International Issues and Conflicts. New York: Invington Publishers.
8. Brownlie I. (1981) Basic Documents on Human Rights. 2nd ed. Oxford: Clarendon Press.
9. Brownlie I. (1971) Basic Documents on African Affairs. Oxford: Clarendon Press.
10. Buergenthal, Thomas (1977) 'International and Regional Human Rights Law and Institutions: Some Examples of Their Interaction'. Texas International Law Journal 12, nos. 2–3, pp. 312–330.
11. Carey, J. (1968) International Protection of Human Rights. Dobbs Ferry, New York: Oceana Publications.
12. Garey, J. (1970) United Nations Protection of Civil and Political Rights. Syracuse: Syracuse University Press.
13. Chossudovsky, Michel (1979) 'The Political Economy of Human Rights'. Bulletin of Peace Proposals 10, no. 2, pp. 172–178.
14. Claude, Richard P., editor (1976) Comparative Human Rights. Baltimore: John Hopkins University Press.
15. Del Russo, A.L. (1971) International Protection of Human Rights. Washington D.C. Lerner Law Book.
16. Del Russo, A.L. (1977) La protection internationale des droits de l'Homme, Bruxelles, Edition l'Université de Bruxelles (Publications, Centre de droit internationale, 8).
17. Domiguez, Jorge I. Rodley, Nigel S. Wood, Bryce: and Falk, Richard (1979) Enhancing Global Human Rights. New York: McGraw-Hill.
18. International Commission of Jurists (1983) States of Emergency: Their Impact on Human Rights. Geneva.
19. Donnelly, Jack (1982) 'Human Rights and Human Dignity: An Analytic Critique of Non-Western Conceptions of Human Rights'. American Political Science Review 76, no. 2, pp. 303–316.
20. Donnelly, Jack (1981) 'Recent Trends in United Nations Human Rights Activity: Description and Polemic'. International Organization 35, no. 4, pp. 633–655.
21. Franck, Thomas M. (1982) Human Rights in Third World Perspective Dobbs Ferry, N.Y.: Oceana Publications.
22. Henkin, Louis, editor (1978) The International Bill of Rights: The Covenant on Civil and Political Rights. New York: Columbia University Press.
23. Henkin, Louis (1978) The Rights of Man Today. Boulder, Colorado: Westview Press.
24. Jack L. Nelson and Vera M. Green, editors (1980) International Human Rights: Contemporary Issues. Standfordville, N.Y.: Human Rights Publishing Group.

25. Joyce, J.A. (1978) Human Rights, International documents (3 vols). Alphen a.d. Rijn.
26. Joyce, J.A. (1979) The New Politics of Human Rights. New York: St. Martin's Press.
27. Lauterpacht, Hersh (1968) International Law and Human Rights. Hamden, Conn.: Shoestring Press.
28. Lillich, Richard B. and Newman, Frank C. (1979) International Human Rights: Problems of Law and Policy. Boston: Little, Brown & Co.
29. Nayar, M.G.K. (1980) 'Human Rights and Economic Development: the Legal Foundations'. Universal Human Rights 2, pp. 55–81.
30. Luard, Evan, editor (1967) International Protection of Human Rights. New York: Praeger.
31. Marks, Stephen P. (1977) 'Development and Human Rights: Some Reflections on the Study of Development, Human Rights, and Peace'. Bulletin of Peace Proposals 8, no. 3, pp. 236–246.
32. McDougal, Myers S. (1974) 'Human Rights and World Public Order: Principles of Content and Procedures for Clarifying General Community Policies'. Virginia Journal of International Law 14, no. 3, pp. 387–421.
33. Newberg, Paula R., editor (1980) The Politics of Human Rights. New York: New York University Press.
34. Ramcharan, B.G. (1979) Human Rights, Thirty Years after the Universal Declaration: Martinus Nijhoff.
35. Ramcharan, B.G. (1976) 'Implementation of the International Covenant on Economic, Social and Cultural Rights'. Netherlands International Law Review 23, pp. 151–161.
36. Ramcharan, B.G. (1976) 'Implementation of Economic, Social and Cultural Rights After the Entry Into Force of the International Covenant on Economic, Social and Cultural Rights'. Eastern Africa Law Review 9, pp. 27–49.
37. Robertson, A.H. (1968) Human Rights in National and International Law. Dobbs Ferry, New York: Oceana Publications.
38. Robertson, A.H. (1972) Human Rights in the World. Manchester: Manchester University Press.
39. Schwelb, Egon (1964) Human Rights and the International Community: The Roots and Growth of the Universal Declaration of Human Rights, 1948–1963, Chicago: Quadrangle Books.
40. Schwelb, Egon (1972) 'The International Court of Justice and the Human Rights Clauses of the Charter', American Journal of International Law 66, pp. 337–51.
41. Schwelb, Egon (1966) 'The International Convention on the Elimination of All Forms of Racial Discrimination'. International and Comparative Law Quarterly 15, pp. 996–1068.
42. Schwelb, Egon (1986) 'Some Aspects of the Measures of Implementation of the International Covenant on Economic, Social and Cultural Rights'. Human Rights Journal 1, p. 363.
43. Sohn, L.B. (1972) Basic documents of African regional organizations, (Vols 1–4) Dobbs Ferry, N.Y.: Oceana Publications.
    Vol. 1. Documents relating to the Organization of African Unity, the African Development Bank and some of the organizations of French-speaking Africa.
    Vol. 2. Documents relating to French-speaking Africa.
    Vol. 3. Documents of regional organizations in West, North and East-Africa.
44. Sohn, L.B. and Buergenthal, T. (1973) International Protection of Human Rights, Indianapolis: Bobbs-Merrill.
45. Sohn, L.B. and Buergenthal, T. (1973) Basic Documents on International Protection of Human Rights (Companion volume to International Protection of Human Rights). Indianapolis: Bobbs-Merrill.
46. The Rule of Law and Human Rights: Principles and Definitions, (1966) International Commission of Jurists: Geneva.

47. United Nations: Human Rights, A Compilation of International Instruments. New York, (1978), Sales No. E. 78 XIV.
48. Van Boven, Theo C. (1977) 'The United Nations and Human Rights: A Critical Appraisal'. Bulletin of Peace Proposals 8, no. 3 (1977), pp. 198–208.
49. Van Dijke, Vernon (1980) 'The Cultural Rights of Peoples'. Universal Human Rights 2, no. 1, pp. 1–20.
50. Vasak, Karel editor (1982), The International Dimensions of Human Rights. 2 vols. Westport, Connecticut: Greenwood Press and Paris: UNESCO.
51. Vierdag, E.W. (1978) 'Legal Nature of the Rights Granted by the International Covenant on Economic, Social and Cultural Rights'. Netherlands Yearbook of International Law 9, pp. 69–105.
52. Weissbrodt, David (1977) 'The Role of International Non-governmental Organizations in the Implementation of Human Rights'. Texas International Law Journal 12, nos. 2–3, pp. 293–320.
53. Weston, B.H. 1984) Human Rights, Human Rights Quarterly 6 (1984), pp. 257–283.

HUMAN RIGHTS IN AFRICA

54. Adegbite, L.O. (1980) 'African Attitudes to Human Rights' in Eide, A. and Shou, A., eds. International Protection of Human Rights. Uppsala: Almqvist and Wiksells.
55. Adegbite, L.O. (1972) 'Human Rights in Nigeria'. In Law and Social Change in Nigeria, edited by T.O. Elias, 223–253. Ibadan and London: University of Lagos and Evans Bros.
56. Adelman, K.L. (1977) 'The Black Man's Burden'. Foreign Affairs 28, pp. 86–109.
57. Aiboni, S.A. (1978) Protection of Refugees in Africa. Uppsala: Scandinavian Institute of African Studies.
58. Akinyemi, A.B. (1972–1973) 'The O.A.U. and the Concept of Non-interference in Internal Affairs of Member States'. British Yearbook of International Law 46, pp. 393–400.
59. Akpan Moses E. (1980) 'The 1979 Nigerian Constitution and Human Rights'. Human Rights Quarterly Vol. 2, No. 2.
60. All African Council of Churches (1976) 'Factors Responsible for the Violation of Human Rights in Africa'. Issue Vol. 1.
61. Aluko, O. (1981) 'The Organization of African Unity and Human Rights'. Round Table 283, pp. 234–242.
62. Amachree Godfrey (1965) 'Fundamental Rights in Nigeria'. Howard Law Journal Vol. II, No. 2. pp. 463–500.
63. Amnesty International (1978) Human Rights Violations in Ethiopia. London: Amnesty International, 1978.
64. Amnesty International. Annual Reports. London: Amnesty International.
65. Amnesty International (1984) Torture in the Eighties. London: Amnesty International.
66. Amnesty International (1983) Political Killings By Governments. London: Amnesty International.
67. Amnesty International (1983) Uganda: Memorandum to the Government. London: Amnesty International.
68. Amnesty International (1980) Human Rights Violations in Zaire. London: Amnesty International.
69. Amnesty International (1979) Recent Human Rights Violations in the Central African Empire. London: Amnesty International.
70. Amnesty International (1979) Guinea. London: Amnesty International.

71. Amnesty International (1978) Human Rights in Uganda. London: Amnesty International.
72. Amnesty International (1987) Political Imprisonment in South Africa. London: Amnesty International.
73. Amnesty International (1977) Human Rights Violations in Ethiopia. London: Amnesty International.
74. Amnesty International (1977) Namibia. London: Amnesty International.
75. Amnesty International (1973) Terrorism in South Africa. London: Amnesty International.
76. Amnesty International (1981) Disappearances: A Workbook. New York: Amnesty International, U.S.A.
77. Amoah, P. (1982) 'The African Charter on Human and People's Rights: Implementation Machinery'. Gaborone Conference on Human Rights in Africa, May 24–29.
78. Anifowose, R. (1977) 'The Military and Human Rights in Nigeria'. Paper presented to the African Association of Political Science, Rabat.
79. Ankrah, E. Maxine (1975) 'Has the African Woman Settled for Tokens?' Lutheran World 22, no. 1, pp. 22–31.
80. Archarya, S. (1982) 'Development Priorities and Constraints in Sub-Saharan Africa', Buffalo Conference on Human Rights in Africa, May 7–9.
81. Arnold, M. (1982) 'Urban Relocation: An Example of Current Dilemmas in South Africa', Buffalo Conference on Human Rights in Africa, May 7–9.
82. Asante, S.K.B. (1969) 'Nation Building and Human Rights in Emergent African Nations'. Cornell International Law Journal. 2. pp. 72–107.
83. Ault, D.E., and Rutman, G.L. (1979) 'The Development of Individual Rights to Property in Tribal Africa'. Journal of Law and Economics 23, no. 1. pp. 163–182.
84. Awori, T. (1975) 'For African Women Equal Rights are Not Enough'. UNESCO Courier, 28, pp. 21–25.
85. Babu, A.M. (1979) 'African and Human Rights'. New African, No. 139 (March), pp. 83–85.
86. Baker John, T. (1965) 'Human Rights in South Africa'. Howard Law Journal, Vol. II, No. 2. pp. 549–583.
87. Ballinger, R.B. (1967) 'U.N. and Human Rights in South Africa' in Luard, ed. International Protection of Human Rights. London: Thames and Hudson.
88. Bello, Emmanuel, G. (1980) African Customary Humanitarian Law, Geneva: Oyez Publishing Ltd.
89. Bello, Emmanuel G. (1981) 'Human Rights: The Rule of Law in Arica'. International and Comparative Law Quarterly 30, pp. 628–637.
90. Berger, I. (1982) 'The Myth of Reform: Labor Laws in South Africa', Buffalo Conference on Human Rights in Africa, May 7–9.
91. Bernstein, H. (1978) For Their Triumphs and for Their Tears: Conditions and Resistance of Women in Apartheid South Africa. London: International Defence and Aid Fund.
92. Booysen Hercules (1978) Convention on the Crime of Apartheid, Human Rights and Self-Determination. No other publication data available.
93. Bozeman, A.B. (1976) Conflict in Africa: Concepts and Realities. Princeton, N.J.: Princeton University Press.
94. Brain, J.L. (1976) 'Less than Second Class'. In Women in Africa: Studies in Social and Economic Change, edited by Nancy J. Hafkin and Edna C. Bay, pp. 275–279. Stanford, California: Stanford University Press.
95. Brietzke, P.H. (1982) Law, Development, and the Ethiopian Revolution. Lewisburg, Pa.: Bucknell University Press.
96. Brock, A. (1975) 'A UNESCO Inquiry on Women's Status in Five Countries'. UNESCO Courier 28, pp. 39–42.
97. Bukh, J. (1979) The Village Woman in Ghana. Uppsala: Scandinavian Institute of African Studies.

98. Buthelezi Gatsha (1976) Human Rights and Constitutional Developments in South Africa. Other publication data unavailable.
99. Cariglia, A. (1983) 'Human Rights in the World: Countries Which Have Close Ties with the Community and South Africa'. Human Rights Law Journal 4, Part 1, pp. 22–33.
100. Carter Marshall and Otwin Marenin (1979) 'Human Rights in the Nigerian Context: A case Study and Discussion of the Nigerian Police'. Universal Human Rights, Vol. 1, No. 2, pp. 43–61.
101. Chand, Hari (1980) Fundamental Rights in Nigeria, JOS. Nigeria. Discusses Human Rights in Nigeria in the context of the 1979 Constitution and the return of the civilian government to power in 1979.
102. Chihana, C. (1982) 'African Charter on Human and People's Rights: The Question of Enforcement of Rights and Freedoms – A Critrique and/or Commentary Plus Suggestions'. Gaborone Conference on Human Rights in Africa, May 24–29.
103. Chihana, C. (1982) 'Human Rights and Development in Africa'. Gaborone Conference on Human Rights in Africa, May 24–29.
104. Clark, R.S. (1981) 'The International League for Human Rights and South West Africa, 1947–1957: The Human Rights NGO as Catalyst in the International Legal Process'. Human Rights Quarterly 3, no. 4, pp. 101–136.
105. Collier G.B.O. (1965) 'Human Rights in Sierra Leone'. Howard Law Journal Vol. 11. No. 2, pp. 500–508.
106. Collins Daisy (1969) 'American Companies in South Africa and Human Rights'. Howard Law Journal Vol. 15, No. 4, pp. 625–673.
107. Commission to Study the Organization of Peace (1980): Regional Protection and Promotion of Human Rights in Africa, New York.
108. Conboy, K. (1978) 'Detention Without Trial in Kenya'. Georgia Journal of International and Comparative Law, No. 8.
109. Cone B. and Harris, J. (1982) Human Rights in Africa. Wellington, New Zealand: African Information Centre, 1982.
110. Deffenbaugh, Ralston (1981) 'The South African Project for Lawyers' Committee for Civil Rights Under Law'. In Global Human Rights, Public Policies, Comparative Measures, and NGO Strategies, edited by Ved P. Nanda et al, 289–303. Boulder, Colorado: Westview Press.
111. De Villiers, Casper F. (1978) Human Rights and Homelands, Other publication data unavailable.
112. Diallo, Y. (1976) African Traditions and Humanitarian Law. Geneva: International Committee of the Red Cross.
113. Dieng, A. (1982) 'The Dakar Seminar on Development and Human Rights: A Synopsis'. Gaborone Conference on Human Rights in Africa, May 24–29.
114. Dimitrijevic, V. (1982) 'Development as a Right'. Gaborone Conference on Human Rights in Africa, May 24–29.
115. Don Nanjira, Daniel D. (1976) The Status of Asians in East Africa: Asians and Europeans in Tanzania, Uganda, and Kenya. New York: Praeger.
116. Dryden, P.K. (1972) 'Annotated Bibliography of Political Rights of African Women'. African Law Studies 7, pp. 27–61.
117. Dugard, J. (1978) Human Rights and the South African Legal Order. Princeton: Princeton University Press.
118. Dugard, J. (1976) Namibia and Human Rights. Braamfontein: South African Institute of International Affairs.
119. Dunstan, M. (1979) 'Human Rights in Sub-Saharan Africa'. In A. Pollis and P. Schwab, eds. Human Rights: Cultural and Ideological Perspectives, New York: Praeger, pp. 115–144.

120. Ebiasah John (1979) 'Protecting the Human Rights of Political Detainees: The Contradictions and Paradoxes in the African Experience'. Howard Law Journal Vol. 22, No. 3, pp. 249–283.
121. El-Ayouty, Y. (1982) 'Thinking About the Future of Human Rights in Africa'. Buffalo Conference on Human Rights in Africa, May 7–9.
122. Elnaiem, A. (1982) 'Human Rights in Islam'. Buffalo Conference on Human Rights in Africa, May 7–9.
123. Emerson, Rupert (1975) 'The Fate of Human Rights in the Third World'. World Politics 27, no. 2, pp. 201–26.
124. Esiemokhai, E.O. (1980) 'Towards Adequate Defense of Human Rights in Africa'. Quarterly Journal of Administration 14, no. 4, pp. 451–461.
125. Eze, Osita C. (1984) Human Rights in Africa: Some Selected Problems. New York: St. Martin's Press and Nigeria Institute of International Affairs.
126. Eze, Osita C. (1979) 'Rights to Health as Human Right in Africa' in Rene-Jean Dupuy, Le Droit à la Santé en tant que Droit de l'Homme. The Netherlands: Sijthoff and Noordhoff.
127. Eze Osita C. (1974) 'Prospects for International Protection of Human Rights in Africa'. African Review Vol. 4, no. 1.
128. Eze Osita C. (1980) 'Prospects for International Protection of Human Rights in Africa'. Quarterly Journal of Administration 24, no. 4, pp. 451–461.
129. Falk, Richard A. (1977) 'Militarization and Human Rights in the Third World'. Bulletin of Peace Proposals 8, no. 3, pp. 220–32.
130. Fegley Randall (1981) 'The U.N. Human Rights Commission: The Equatorial Guinea Case'. Human Rights Quarterly Vol. 3, no. 1, pp. 34–47.
131. Finley, T. (1976) 'The Permanent Settlement of African Refugees'. International Migration Review Vol. 14.
132. Flinterman, C. (1984) Human Rights in Ghana, International Commission of Jurists, Geneva.
133. Forsyth, C.F. and Schiller, J.E. eds. (1979) Human Rights: The Cape Town Conference. Cape Town: Juta and Co. Ltd.
134. Franck, Thomas (1982) 'Preventive Detention and Other Emergency Powers in Africa and Asia' in Franck, Human Rights in Third World Perspective, New York: Oceana Publications Vol. II, pp. 49–253.
135. Franck, T.M.; Padgett, A.; Mitchell, J.; Kaanan, L.; Bonbright, D. and Moelis, R. (1982) 'An Investment Boycott by the Developing Countries Against South Africa: A Rationale and Preliminary Assessment of Feasibility'. Human Rights Quarterly 4, no. 3, pp. 309–332.
136. Carnick, Laura and Twitchett, Carol Cosgrove (1979) 'Human Rights and Successor to the Lomé Convention'. International Relations 6, no. 3, pp. 540–557.
137. Gittleman, R. (1982) 'Ambiguities and Opportunities in the Banjul Charter', Buffalo Conference on Human Rights in Africa, May 7–9.
138. Gittleman, R. (1982) 'The African Charter on Human and Peoples' Rights: A. Legal Analysis'. Virginia Journal of International Law, Vol. 22: 4, pp. 667–714.
139. Goody, Jack and Buckley, J. (1983) 'Inheritance and Women's Labor in Africa'. Africa 43, no. 2, pp. 108–121.
140. Government of Gambia (1981) The Gambia's Stand on Human Rights. Banjul: Government Printer.
141. Gower, L. and Bartlett, C. (1967) Independent Africa: The Challenge to the Legal profession. Cambridge, Mass.: Harvard University Press.
142. Gutto, S.B.O. (1980) 'Kenya's Petit-bourgeois State, the Public, and the Rule/Misrule of Law'. International Journal of the Sociology of Law 9, pp. 341–363.
143. Gutto, S.B.O. (1976) 'The Legal Status of Women in Kenya: Paternalism and Inequality'. Fletcher Forum 1, pp. 62–82.

144. Hamalengwa Munyonzwe (1983) 'The Political Economy of Human Rights in Africa: Historical and Contemporary Perspectives'. Philosophy and Social Action Vol. IX, no. 3, pp. 15–26.
145. Hamrell, S. (1967) Refugee Problems in Africa. Uppsala: Scandinavian Institute of African Studies.
146. Hannum Hurst (1979) 'The Butare Colloquium on Human Rights and Economic Development in Francophone Africa: A Summary and Analysis'. Universal Human Rights Vol. 1, no. 2, pp. 63–87.
147. Harshe, Rajen (1983) 'France Francophone African States and South Africa: The Complex Triangle and Apartheid'. Alternatives 9, no. 1, pp. 51–72.
148. Hayson Nicholas (1983) Ruling with the Whip: A Report on the Violation of Human Rights in the Ciskei. Johannesburg: Center for Applied Legal Studies, University of the Witwatersrand.
149. Hodges, Tony. Jehovah Witnesses in Central Africa, London: Minority Rights Group Report, no. 29.
150. Howard, Rhoda (1984) 'Evaluating Human Rights in Africa: Some Problems of Implicit Comparisons'. Human Rights Quarterly, Vol. 6, no. 2, pp. 160–179.
151. Howard, Rhoda (1984) 'Human Rights in Commonwealth Africa: Security, Subsistence and Participation'. Paper presented to the Annual Conference of the Canadian Association of African Studies, Antigonish, May 9–12.
152. Howard, Rhoda (1984) 'Women's Rights in English-Speaking Sub-Saharan Africa' in Claude E. Welch and Ron. I. Meltzer, eds. Human Rights and Development in Africa. Albany, New York: Suny Press. pp. 46–74.
153. Howard, Rhoda (1983) 'The Full-Belly Thesis: Should Economic Rights take Priority over Civil and Political Rights? Evidence from Sub-Saharan Africa'. Human Rights Quarterly, Vol. 5, no. 4, pp. 467–490.
154. Howard, Rhoda (1983) 'Is There an African Concept of Human Rights'. Working Paper no. a. 8, Development Studies Programme, University of Toronto.
155. Howard, Rhoda (1980) 'The Dilemma of Human Rights in Sub-Saharan Africa'. International Journal, Vol. 35, no. 4, pp. 724–747.
156. Howard, Rhoda (1981) 'The Canadian Government Response to Africa's Refugee Problem'. Canadian Journal of African Studies 15, pp. 95–116.
157. Howard, Rhoda, (1978) Colonialism and Underdevelopment in Ghana (London: Croom Helm).
158. Howard, Rhoda (1982) 'Human Rights and Personal Law: Women in Sub-Saharan Africa'. Issue 12, pp. 45–52.
159. International Commission of Jurists (1983) States of Emergency: Their Impact on Human Rights. Geneva.
160. International Commission of Jurists (1978) Human Rights in a One-Party State. London: Search Press.
161. International Commission of Jurists (1977) Uganda and Human Rights: Reports of the ICJ to the U.N., Geneva.
162. International Commission of Jurists (1973) 'Infringements of the Universal Declaration of Human Rights in South Africa'. Objective Justice, Vol. 4, pp. 9–20.
163. International Commission of Jurists (1969) 'Human Rights in Southern Africa'. The Review, September.
164. International Commission of Jurists (1961) African Conference on the Rule of Law. Geneva.
165. International Commission of Jurists (1960) South Africa and the Rule of Law. Geneva: ICJ.
166. International Commission of Jurists (1981) Development, Human Rights and the Rule of Law. New York: Pergamon Press.

167. International League for Human Rights (1983) Guinea's Human Rights Record. New York.
168. Jespersen, Rob Rand (1977) 'The Jurisprudential Problem of Apartheid'. Texas Southern University Law Review 4, pp. 323–341.
169. Jimenez Fernando, V. (1980) 'Study of the Human Rights Situation in Equatorial Guinea'. New York: United Nations Doc. E/CN.4/1371.
170. Jinadu, L. Adele (1980) Human Rights and OAU-African Policy under President Carter. Lagos: Nigerian Institute of International Affairs.
171. Jose, Alhaji Babatunde (1975) 'Press Freedom in Africa'. African Affairs 74, no. 296 pp. 255–262.
172. Kaba, Lansine (1976) 'The Cultural Revolution, Artistic Creativity and Freedom of Expression in Guinea'. Journal of Modern African Studies 14, no. 2, pp. 201–218.
173. Kannyo, Edward (1982) 'The African Commission on Human Rights: Origins and Regional Parallels', Buffalo Conference on Human Rights in Africa, May 7–9.
174. Kannyo, Edward (1982) Defending Civil and Political Rights in Africa: The Case of Ghana, 1976–1979. New York: The Jacob Blanstein Institute for the Advancement of Human Rights.
175. Kannyo, Edward (1980) Human Rights in Africa: Problems and Prospects. New York: International League for Human Rights.
176. Kannyo, Edward (1981) 'Human Rights in Africa'. Bulletin of the Atomic Scientists 37 pp. 14–19.
177. Khalifa Ahmed, M. (1979) Assistance to Racist Regimes in Southern Africa: Impact on the Enjoyment of Human Rights. Geneva: United Nations.
178. Khusalani, Yongindra (1983) 'Human Rights in Asia and Africa'. Human Rights Law Journal 4, Part 4, pp. 403–442.
179. Kibola, H. (1982) 'Some Conceptual Aspects of Human Rights: The Basis for the Right to Development in Africa', Gaborone Conference on Human Rights in Africa, May 24–29.
180. Kibola, H.S. (no date) 'Human Rights in Africa During the Colonial Period'. (Mimeo).
181. Kiwanuka, R. (1982) 'Wither Human Rights Education in Africa', Gaborone Conference on Human Rights in Africa, May 24–29.
182. Kunig Philip (1983) 'The Protection of Human Rights by International Law in Africa'. Law and State, Vol. 27, pp. 7–31.
183. Kunnert, Dirk (1977) 'Carter, the Tradition of American Foreign Policy, and Africa'. South Africa International 8, no. 2, pp. 65–78 and 99–105.
184. Lawyers Committee for International Human Rights (1978) Violations of Human Rights in Uganda, New York.
185. Legesse, Asmarom (1980) 'Human Rights in African Political Culture'. In The Moral Imperatives of Human Rights: A World Survey, edited by Kenneth W. Thompson, 81–108 Washington, D.C.: University Press of America for the Council on Religion and International Affairs.
186. Lens, Marlene (1983) 'Human Rights in the World: States of the Near East and African States Not Signatories to the Lome Agreement'. Human Rights Law Journal 4, Part 2, pp. 60–82.
187. Lockwood, Bert B. (1983) 'A Study in Black and White: The South Africa of James McClure'. Human Rights Quarterly 5, no. 4, pp. 440–446.
188. Luckham, Yaa. 'Law and the Status of Women in Ghana'. Columbia Human Rights Law Review 8, no. 1 (Spring-Summer 1976): 69–94.
189. Magapatona, P. (1982) 'The Struggle for Human Rights and Development'. Gaborone Conference on Human Rights in Africa, May 24–29.
190. Maina, Rose; Machai, V.W. and Gatto, S.B.O. (1976) 'Law and the Status of Women in Kenya'. Columbia Human Rights Law Review 8, no. 1, pp. 185–206.

191. Makoti, E. (1982) 'Law and Human Rights in National Development', Gaborone Conference on Human Rights in Africa, May 24–29.
192. Maope, K. (1982) 'Development and Legitimacy of Government in Lesotho', Gaborone Conference on Human Rights in Africa, May 24–29.
193. Marasinghe, M. (1982) 'Traditional Concepts of Human Rights in Africa', Buffalo Conference on Human Rights in Africa, May 7–9.
194. Martin, Robert (1974) Personal Freedom and the Law in Tanzania: A Study of Socialist State Administration. Nairobi: Oxford University Press.
195. Mason, J. (1977) 'Human Rights in Africa'. Intellect, Vol. 105.
196. Mathews, Anthony S. (1971) Law, Order and Liberty in South Africa Cape Town: Juta.
197. Mazrui, Ali A. (1975) 'Academic Freedom in Africa: The Dual Tyranny'. African Affairs 74, no. 297, pp. 393–400.
198. Mazrui Ali A. (1983) 'Zionism and Apartheid: Strange Bedfollows or Natural Allies?' Alternatives 9, no. 1, pp. 73–79.
199. M'baye Ke'ba (1982) 'Human Rights in Africa' in Karel Vasak, ed. The International Dimensions of Human Rights, Vol. 2 Westport: Greenwood Press. pp. 583–601.
200. Mbaya, R. (1982) 'Sovereign Equality and the Right to Development', Gaborone Conference on Human Rights in Africa, May 24–29.
201. Mboukoy, Alexandre (1981) 'The Forgotten Refugees of Africa'. New Directions (1981) pp. 24–29.
202. McChesney, R.A. (1980) The Promotion of Economic and Political Rights: 2 African Approaches 24 Journal of African Law, pp. 163–205.
203. Mcfadden, P. (1982) 'The Status of Women and Human Rights: A Brief Assessment', Gaborone Conference on Human Rights in Africa, May 24–29.
204. McLean, Scilla, Female Circumcision, Excision and Infubulation. London: Minority Rights Group Report no. 47.
205. Melander, Goran, and Nobel, Peter (1978) African Refugees and the Law Uppsala: Scandinavian Institute of African Studies.
206. Meltzer, R. (1982) 'International Human Rights and the North-South Dialogue', Buffalo Conference on Human Rights in Africa, May 7–9.
207. Meltzer, R. (1982) 'Themes of the Conference', Paper read at the Buffalo Conference on Human Rights in Africa, May 7–9.
208. Menkiti, Ifeanyi A. (1979) 'Person and Community in African Traditional Thought'. In African Philosophy: An Introduction, edited by Richard A. Wright, 2nd ed., 157–168 Washington, D.C.: University Press of America.
209. Mettelman, J. (1982) 'International Human Rights and Socialist Development', Buffalo Conference on Human Rights in Africa, May 7–9.
210. Miers, Suzanne, and Kopytoff, Igor, eds. (1977) Slavery in Africa: Historical and Anthropological Perspectives. Madison: University of Wisconsin Press.
211. Mojekwu, Chris C. (1980) 'International Human Rights: The African Perspective'. In International Human Rights: Contemporary Issues, edited by Jack L. Nelson and Vera M. Green, 85–95. Standfordville, N.Y.: Human Rights Publishing Group.
212. Montsi, M. (1982) 'The Organization of Human Rights Information, Research and Education in Lesotho', Gaborone Conference on Human Rights in Africa, May 24–29.
213. Mower, A.G. (1976) 'Human Rights in Black Africa: A Double Standard?' Human Rights Journal 9, no. 1, pp. 39–70.
214. Murungi Kiraitu (1982) 'A Contribution to the Critique of Human Rights Scholarship in Africa', Mineo.
215. Murungi Kiraitu (1982) 'The Implementation of the International Covenant on Civil and Political Rights in Kenya', LLM Thesis. University of Nairobi.

216. Nahum, F. (1982) 'African Contribution to Human Rights', Gaborone Conference on Human Rights in Africa, May 24–29.
217. Ndiaye Birane (1982) 'The Place of Human Rights in the Charter of the Organization of African Unity' in Karel Vasak, ed., The International Dimensions of Human Rights, Vol. 2 UNESCO and Westport: Greenwood Press. pp. 601–616.
218. Nengwekhulu, R. (1982) 'The Meaning and Character of Development', Gaborone Conference on Human Rights in Africa, May 24–29.
219. Ngugi wa Thiong'o (1983) Barrel of A Pen: Resistance to Repression in Neo-Colonial Kenya. London: New Beacon Press.
220. Ngugi wa Thiong'o (1981) Detained: A Writer's Prison Diary, London: Heinemann.
221. Nhlapo, R. (1982) 'Limitations on Human Rights: The Cultural Argument', Gaborone Conference on Human Rights in Africa, May 24–29.
222. Nwabueze, B.O. (1977) Judicialism in Commonwealth Africa: The Role of the Courts in Government, New York: St Martin's Press.
223. Nwosu, Humphrey N. (1976) 'The Concepts of Nationalism and Right to Self Determination: Cameroon as a Case Study', Africa Quarterly 16, no. 2 pp. 1–26.
224. Obbo, Christine (1980) African Women: Their Struggle for Economic Independence. London: Zed Press.
225. Ojo, Michael Adeleye (1976) 'U.N. and Freedom for Portuguese Colonies', Africa Quarterly 16, no. 1, pp. 5–28.
226. Okere, Obinna B. (1983) 'Freedom of the Press in Nigeria', Human Rights Law Journal 4, Part 2, pp. 149–166.
227. Okere, Obinna B. (1984) 'The Protection of Human Rights in Africa and the African Charter on People's Rights: A Comparative Analysis with the European and American Systems', Human Rights Quarterly 6, no. 2, pp. 141–159.
228. Okeyo, Achola Pala (1980) 'Daughters of the Lakes and Rivers: Colonization and the Land Rights of Luo Women', In Women and Colonization, edited by Mona Etienne and Eleanor Leacock, pp. 186–213. New York Review: Praeger.
229. Okolie, Charles C. (1977) International Law Perspectives of the Developing Countries: The Relationship of Law and Economic Development to Basic Human Rights, New York: NOK Publishers.
230. Okolie, Charles C. (1978) 'Human Rights in Southern Africa in the Context of Public International Law', Glendale Law Review 2, no. 3, pp. 219–272.
231. Okonkwo, R. Chude (1978) 'The Legal Basis of Freedom of Expression in Nigeria', California Western International Law Journal 8, no. 2, pp. 256–273.
232. Okoth-Ogendo, H. (1982) 'National Implementation of International Responsibility: Some Thoughts on Human Rights in Africa', Gaborone Conference on Human Rights in Africa, May 24–29.
232a. Okoth-Ogendo, H.W.O. (1974) 'National Implementation of International Responsibility: Some Thoughts on Human Rights in Africa', East African Law Journal, vol. 10, no 1, p. 1–16.
233. Olson, D. (1982) 'Protection of Individual Rights in Emergent African States: Luxury or Necessity?' Gaborone Conference on Human Rights in Africa, May 24–29.
234. Osiemokhai, E.O. (1981) 'Towards Adequate Defence of Human Rights in Africa', Indian Journal of International Law 21 (1).
235. Parpart, J. (1982) 'African Labor and Human Rights: Champions or Saboteurs? The Case of Zambian Copper Miners', Buffalo Conference on Human Rights in Africa, May 7–9.
236. Paul James C.N. (1982) 'Basic Needs and Emerging Human Rights in Africa', Buffalo Conference on Human Rights in Africa, May 7–9.
236a. Paul James C.N. (1981) 'Law, Socialism and the Human Right to Development in Third World Countries', Review of Socialist Law Vol. 7, no. 3, pp. 235–242.

237. Paul, James C.N. (1978) 'Human Rights and Legal Development: The African Model to Date' in J.C. Tuttle, ed. International Human Rights Law and Practice.
238. Paul, James C.N. (1974) 'Some observations on Constitutionalism, Judicial Review, and the Rule of Law in Africa', Ohio State Law Journal 35, no. 4, pp. 851–869.
239. Peil, Margaret (1971) 'The Expulsion of West African Aliens', Journal of Modern Africa Studies 9, pp. 205–229.
240. Perlman, M.L. (1975–1976) 'Children Born out of Wedlock and the Status of Women in Toro, Uganda', Rural Africana 29, pp. 95–119.
241. Pfeiffer, Steven B. (1978) 'The Judiciary in the Constitutional Systems of East Africa', Journal of Modern African Studies 16, no. 1, pp. 33–66.
242. Plender, Richard (1971) 'The Exodus of Asians from East and Central Africa: Some Comparative and International Law Aspects', American Journal of Comparative Law 19, no. 2, pp. 287–324.
243. Pollock, A.J. (1969) 'The South West Africa Cases and the Jurisprudence of International Law', International Organization 23, no. 4, pp. 767–787.
244. Ramcharan, B.G. (1982) 'Regional versus Global Approaches to International Human Rights', Buffalo Conference on Human Rights in Africa, May 7–9.
245. Ramcharan, B.G. (1975) 'Human Rights in Africa: Whitter Now? U. Ghana Law Journal Vol. 12, no. 2.
246. Richardson, Henry J. (1978) 'Self-Determination, International Law, and the South African Bantustan Policy', Columbia Journal of Transnational Law 2, pp. 185–219.
247. Ringera, A. (1982) 'Human Rights and Limitations Imposed Upon Their Enjoyment in Kenya', Gaborone Conference on Human Rights in Africa, May 24–29.
248. Robertson, A.H. (1979) 'African Legal Process and the Individual', Human Rights Journal 5, nos. 2–3, pp. 465–478.
249. Rubin Leslie (1978) Universal Declaration of Human Rights in South Africa: The Anatomy of a Racist Society. No other publication data available.
250. Samson, K.T. (1982) 'Human Rights and Development: ILO Approaches', Gaborone Conference on Human Rights in Africa, May 24–29.
251. Scarritt, James R. (1978) 'The External Pressures on Human Rights in South Africa: Problems of Research and Design', Paper presented at the Annual Meeting of the African Studies Association, Baltimore.
252. Schwab, Peter (1982) 'The Response of the Left to Violence and Human Rights 'Abuses' in the Ethiopian Revolution' in Peter Schwab and Adamantia Pollis, eds. Toward a Human Rights Framework. New York: Praeger.
253. Schwab, Peter (1980/81) 'Rethinking of Human Rights in Ethiopia', Horn of Africa Vol. 3, no. 4.
254. Schwab, Peter (1976) 'Human Rights in Ethiopia', Journal of Modern African Studies. 14, pp. 155–160.
255. Scoble, H. and Wiseberg, L. (1983) 'Non-Governmental Human Rights Organizations in Africa', Buffalo Conference on Human Rights in Africa, May 7–9.
256. Seck M.M. (1982) 'Relation Between Development and Human Rights', Gaborone Conference on Human Rights in Africa, May 24–29.
257. Seidman, A. (1982) 'Human Rights, Law and Development', Gaborone Conference on Human Rights in Africa, May 24–29.
258. Seideman, Robert B. (1974) 'Judicial Review and Fundamental Freedoms in Anglophonic Independent Africa', Ohio State Law Journal 35, pp. 820–850.
259. Sesay Amadu and Sola Ojo (1984) 'The OAU and Human Rights: Prospects for the 1980s and Beyond', paper presented to the 14th Annual Conference of the Canadian Association of African Studies, Antigonish, May 9–12; and published in Human Rights Quarterly 8, no. 1 (1986), pp. 89–103.

260. Sharma, K. (1982) 'Compatibility of a Conciliatory Federal Political Framework and Development Planning: Some Tentative Formulations Towards the Development of "Conflict Model" and "Harmony Model"', Gaborone Conference on Human Rights in Africa, May 24–29.
261. Sharma, Vishnu D., and Wooridge F. (1974) 'Some Legal Questions Arising from the Expulsion of the Ugandan Asians'. International and Comparative Law Quarterly 34, no. 2, pp. 397–425.
262. Shaw, T. (1982) 'The Political Economy of Self-Determination: From Decolonization to Self-Reliance', Buffalo Conference on Human Rights in Africa, May 7–9.
263. Shepherd, George W. Jr. (1982) 'The Constitutional Proposal in Namibia: Group Rights Versus Majority Rule', Buffalo Conference on Human Rights in Africa, May 7–9.
264. Shepherd, George W. Jr. (1974) 'Humanitarian Assistance to Liberation Movements', Africa Today 21, no. 4, pp. 75–87.
265. Shepherd, George W. Jr. (1977) Anti-Apartheid: Transnational Conflict and Western Policy in the Liberation of South Africa, Westport, Conn: Greenwood Press.
266. Slabbert Fredrik van Zyl (1982) Change and Human Rights in South Africa. No other publication data available.
267. Stokke O., and Widstrand, C. eds. (1973) The UN-OAU Conference on Southern Africa. Uppsala: Scandinavian Institute of African Studies.
268. Taubenfeld R.R., and Taubenfeld, Howard J. Race (1968), Peace, Law and Southern Africa Dobbs Ferry, N.Y.: The Association of the Bar of the City of New York/Oceana Publications, Inc.
269. Thomashausen, Andre (1983) 'Forfeiture of Enemy Property in Zimbabwe'. Human Rights Law Journal 4, Part 2, pp. 167–178.
270. Tsie, B. (1982) 'The Impact of Foreign Private Investment on Human Rights and Development', Gaborone Conference on Human Rights in Africa, May 24–29.
271. Tucker Carol M. Regional Human Rights Models in Europe and Africa: A Comparison, Syracuse Journal of International and Comparative Law Vol. 10: 135.
272. Turkin Grigory, ed. (1969) Contemporary International Law, Moscow: Progress Publishers.
273. Ullman Richard H. (1978) 'Human Rights and Economic Power: The United States versus Idi Amin'. Foreign Affairs 56, pp. 529–543.
274. Umozurike, U.O. (1982) 'The African Charter of Human and People's Rights and the Right to Development'. Gaborone Conference on Human Rights in Africa, May 24–29.
275. Umozurike U.O. (1971) 'The Geneva Conventions and Africa'. East African Journal Vol. VIII, no. 3, pp. 275–289.
276. Umozurike U.O. (1979) 'The Domestic Jurisdiction Clause in the OAU Charter'. African Affairs 78, no. 311, pp. 167–209.
277. United Nations (1979) 'Seminar on the Establishment of Regional Commissions on Human Rights with Special Reference to Africa'. U.N. DOC. ST/HR/Ser. A/4.
278. U.S. Congress (Annual Reports). Country Reports on Rights Practices. Washington, D.C. Government Printing Office.
279. United States Congress, House Committee on Foreign Affairs (1980) Human Rights in Africa, Washington, D.C.: Government Printers.
280. United States Congress, House Committee on Foreign Affairs, Sub-committee on International Organizations and Movements (1974) Human Rights in Africa, Washington, D.C.: Government Printer. Report by the International Commission of Jurists.
281. Van der Linden, Jacques (1971) 'African Legal Process and the Individual: African Source Materials, Including Background Papers, a Bibliography, and Selected Legislation, edited by Thierry G. Verhelst, pp. 376–381. Addis Ababa: Centre for African Legal Development.
282. Van der Vyver J.D. (1976) Seven Lectures on Human Rights. Cape Town: Juta.

283. Vasak Karel (1967) 'Les droits de l'Homme et l'Afrique'. Revue belge de droit international, no. 2, pp. 459–478.
284. Weinstein Warren (1983) 'Human Rights and Development in Africa: Dilemmas and Options'. Deadalus, pp. 171–196.
285. Weinstein Warren (1980) 'Human Rights in Africa: A Long-Awaited Voice'. Current History pp. 78, 455, 97–101, 130–132.
286. Weinstein Warren (1977) 'Human Rights and Economic Development: An Overview for Latin America and Africa'. Paper presented to the Latin American Studies Association/African Studies Association Joint Meeting, Houston, November 1977.
287. Weinstein Warren (1976) 'Africa's Approach to Human Rights at the United Nations'. Issue VI. pp. 14–21.
288. Weinstein Warren (no date) 'African Perspectives on Human Rights'. Washington, D.C. Council for Policy and Social Research.
289. Weis Paul (1982) 'The Convention of the Organization of African Unity Governing the Specific Aspects of Refugee Problems in Africa'. Human Rights Journal 3, no. 2, pp. 449–464.
290. Weisfelder, R. (1982) 'The Impact on Other African States of South African Human Rights Policies', Buffalo Conference on Human Rights in Africa, May 7–9.
291. Weisfelder R.F.(1976) 'The Decline of Human Rights in Lesotho: An Evaluation of Domestic and External Determination', Issue 6, no. 4, pp. 22–23.
292. Welch Claude E. Jr. (1982) 'Agenda for Human Rights Research', Buffalo Conference on Human Rights in Africa, May 7–9.
293. Welch Claude E. Jr. (1978) 'The Right of Association in Ghana and Tanzania'. Journal of Modern African Studies 16, no. 4, pp. 639–656.
294. Welch Claude E. Jr. and Meltzer Ronald, eds. (1984) Human Rights and Development in Africa. Albany, New York: State University of New York Press.
295. Williamson L. (1980) 'Dilemmas and Opportunities for United States Encouragement of Human Rights in Africa', Buffalo Conference on Human Rights in Africa, May 7–9.
295a. Zvobgo Eddison (1979) 'A Third World View of Human Rights'. In Kommers and Loescher, eds. Human Rights and American Foreign Policy, Notre Dame, Indiana: University of Notre Dame Press.
296. Wiseberg, L.S. (1976) 'Human Rights in Africa: Toward a Definition of the Problem of a Double Standard'. Issue: A Quarterly Journal of Africanist Opinion, Vol. 6, no. 4.
297. Wiseberg Laurie (1974) 'Humanitarian Intervention: Lessons from the Nigerian Civil War'. Human Rights Journal, Vol. 7, no. 1, pp. 61–98.
298. Young-Anawaty Amy (1980) 'Human Rights and the ACP-EEC Lomé II Convention: Business as usual at the EEC'. New York University Journal of International Law Politics, Vol. 3, no. 1, pp. 63–100.
299. Zimmerli C.H. (1971) 'Human Rights and the Rule of Law in Southern Rhodesia'. International and Comparative Law Quarterly, Vol. 20, no. 2, pp. 239–300.

GÉNÉRAL

1. Abu-Sahlieh, S.A.A. (1985) La définition internationale des droits de l'homme et l'Isalam. Revue générale de droit international public. Tomé 89, pp. 691–703.
2. Ahmedou Puld Adballah (1983), Dialogue Nord-Sud et libertés démocratiques Politique Internationale no. 21, pp. 281–295.
3. Amnesty International, (section française) (1984) La Torture, instrument de pouvoir, fléau à combattre. Paris: Seuil.
4. Battati, M.M.; (1986) Etrangers, réfugiés: la Précarité du droit d'asile. Seventeenth Study session: Strasbourg. 7 July-1 August 1986: collection of lectures: texts and summaries. Strasbourg: International Institute of Human Rights.
5. Bossuyt, Marc (1975) La distinction juridique entre les droits civils et politiques et les droits économiques, sociaux et culturels. Human Rights Journal 8, pp. 783–781.
6. Bossuyt, Marc (1976) L'interdiction de la discrimination droit internationale des droits de l'homme, pp. 184–217 (Bruxelles).
7. Cassin, R. (1951) La déclaration universelle et la mise en oeuvre des droits de l'homme. Recueil des Cours de l'académie de droit international de la Haye, pp. 241–365.
8. Chaliand, Gérard (ed) (1986) Les Minorités a l'age de l'Etat Nation. Un Ouvrage collectif du groupement pour les droits minoritées. Edition Fagard (Collection Géopolitiques et Stratégies) 324 pp.
9. Comité suisse contre la torture (CSCT) (1983) Combattre la torture. Genève: CSCT.
10. Droits de l'homme et relations Nord-Sud (1985) Actes du Congrès de la Fédération internationale des droits de l'homme (FIDH) Paris: UNESCO (Ed. L'Hamattan).
11. Del Russo, A.L. (1971) La protection internationale des droits de l'homme. Bruxelles: Edition l'Université de Bruxelles (Publications, Centre de droit international, 8).
12. Delmas-Marty (1986), Droits de l'homme et droit pénal. Seventeenth study session: Strasbourg. 7 July–1 August 1986: Collection of lectures: texts and summaries, Strasbourg, International Institute of Human Rights.
13. Drai, Raphael; Cao-Huy Thuan; Tran-Van Minh (et al) (1984) Multinationales et droits de l'homme. Amiens Franceij: Presse Universitaires de France 220 pp.
14. El Kouhene, Mohamed (1984) Droit de la guerre-droits de l'homme. Study Informatica v. 37 (2), pp. 207–228.
15. Ferrero, R. (1985) Le nouvel ordre économique international et la protection des droits de l'homme. Geneva: ONU.
16. Haquani, Z. (1986) La Convention des Nations Unies contre la torture. Revue Générale de Droit International Public, pp. 127–170.
17. Hirsch, E. (1984) Christianisme et droits de l'homme. Recueil de textes présentés par E. Hirsch Paris: Librairie des Libertés.
18. Humana, C. (1985) Guide mondial des droits de l'homme traduit par D. Lemoine (Ed. Buchet/Chastel, Paris).
19. Kayser, P. (1984) La protection de la vie privée (Ed Economica, Paris).
20. Kiss, A.C. (1973) La protection internationale du droit de l'enfant à l'éducation. Revue des droits de l'homme/Human Rights Journal (Paris) Vol. vl. No. 3–4, pp. 467–487.
21. Léaud, A., (1983) Amnesty International: un combat de l'homme pour l'homme (Livre) (Ed. Librairie des Libertés, Paris).
22. Liniger-Goumaz, Max (1984) ONU et dictatures: de la démocratie et des droits de l'homme. (Paris: l'Harmattan) 285 pp.
23. M'baye, Keba (1969), La réalité du monde noir et les droits de l'homme, in Revue des droits de l'homme. Paris Vol. III, no. 3, pp. 382–394.*
24. M'baye, Keba (1972), Le droit au développement comme un droit de l'homme, in Revue des droits de l'homme, Paris Vol. V. no. 2–3, pp. 503–534.*

25. Martens, P. (1968) L'application de la Convention de la Recommendation de l'Unesco Concernant la lutte entre la discrimination dans le domaine de l'enseignement: un bilan provisoire. Human rights Journal/Revue Droits de l'homme Vol. 1 no. 1, pp. 9–108.
26. N'diaye, Birame (1978) La place des droits de l'homme dans la Charte de l'Organisation de l'Unité africaine in Vasak, K. Dimension internationales de droits de l'homme. Paris: UNESCO ,pp. 664–679.*
27. Orianne, Paul (1974) De la juridicité des droits économiques et sociaux reconnus dans les déclarations internationales. Annales de droit: Revue trimestrielle de droit belge, pp. 147–163.
28. Pictet, J. (1983) Dévelopment et principes du droits international humanitaire Genève: Institut Henry-Dunant.
29. ONU (1985) Exécutions Sommaires ou arbitraires: Rapport de S.A. Wako, Rapporteur Spécial de la Commission des droits de l'homme de l'ONU, E/CN 4/1985/17 12-2-85.
30. Rybak, B. (1982) La formalisation du droit avec application aux droits de l'homme. Human Rights Quarterly 4, pp. 261–274.
31. Université de Fribourg (1985) Indivisibilité des droits de l'homme: Actes du II-ème colloque interuniversitaire (1983).
32. UNESCO (1983) Violation des droits de l'homme: quel recours, quelle résistance? Paris UNESCO.
33. Université de Fribourg (1984) Universalité des droits de l'homme et diversité des cultures: Actes du 1er colloque interuniversitaire (1982).
34. l'Université Catholique de Louvain, 2e Colloque du Département des Droits de l'homme à l'Université Catholique de Louvain, Le 10 Novembre 1972. Title: Vers une protection efficace des droits économiques et sociaux. Bruxelles Braylant, 1973, 209 pp.
35. Valtiers, N. (1969) Universalité des droits de l'homme et diversité de conditions nationales, dans René Cassin, Amicorum Discipulorumque Liber. Vol. 1. Paris: Pedone, pp. 394.
36. Vasak, K. (1974) Le droit international des droits de l'homme dans Recueil des Cours de l'Académie de Droit International de Haye IV Vol. 140, pp. 333–416.
37. Vasak K. (1967) Les droits de l'homme et l'Afrique, in Revue Belge de droit international. Bruxelles Vol. 3, pp. 459–478.
38. Verdoodt, A. (1964) Naissance et Signification de la Déclaration Universelle de droits de l'homme, pp. 241–252. Edition Nauwelaerts Louvain-Paris.
39. White, Helen C., Cazamian, Madeleine L. (ed.) (1951) Les droits de l'homme: notre tache. London: International Federation of University Women, 110 pp.

LES DROITS DE L'HOMME EN L'AFRIQUE

40. Amnesty International (1982) La mission d'Amnesty International en République Populaire et Revolutionnaire de Guinée (décembre 1981). London: Amnesty International, p. 23.
41. Ait-Ahmed, H. (1977) Les droits de l'homme dans la Charte et la Pratique de l'Organisation de l'Unité Africaine. Thèse: Université de Nancy, pp. 437.
42. Bandelot, Y. et Pognon A., (1984) Procès de M. Ahidjo et ses deux aides de camp. (Rapport de mission d'observation judicaire). Paris: FIDH.
43. Bentoumi, Amar: Winter Timo (1977) Rapport sur la mission d'information de l'IDAL en Egypte du 16 au 23 avril 1977. Bruxelles: Association Internationale des Juristes Démocrates.
44. CETIM (Centre Europe-Tiers-Monde), Département missionnaires des églises protestantes de Suisse romande (DM), Entraide protestante Suisse (EPER), Mouvement anti-apartheid de Suisse (MAAS) (1984) Afrique du Sud, du discours à la réalité. Genève: CETIM.

45. Cissoko, Mody S. (1982) Droits de l'homme et des peuples dans les traditions historiques africaines; Niang, M., Place des droits de l'homme dans les traditions culturels africains. Papers submitted to the International Symposium on the Charter of Human and People's Rights, Dakar 25–30 October 1982.
46. Diallo, A. (1983) La mort de Diallo Telli (Ed. Karthala).
47. El-Tinay, H.M. (1985) Pour les libertés démocratiques et la défense des droits élémentaires de l'homme au Soudan.
48. Fall, Ibrahima, (1977) 'Des structures possibles à l'échelon régional africain pour la promotion des droits de l'homme, in Revue Sénégalaise de droit (Dakar) Vol. 11, No. 22. décembre 1977, pp. 69–80.
49. Fédération internationale des droits de l'homme (FIDH) 1984. Situation des droits de l'homme au Matabeland, Rapport d'enquête, par L. Laurin. Paris; FIDH.
50. Gonidec, P.F. (1983) Un espoir pour l'homme et les peuples africains?: La Charte Africaine des Droits de l'homme et des droits des peuples. Le Mois en Afrique v. 18 (209–210), pp. 22–40.
51. Henny, P. (1980) Rapport de mission effectuée en République Fédérale et Islamique des Comores du 21 au 28 juin 1980. Paris: FIDH.
52. Laurin, Y. (1984) Situation des droits de l'homme au Matabeland. FIDH.
53. Laurin, Y. (1983) La situation des réfugiés Sud-africains au Lesotho et au Botswana: mission d'enquête effectuée au mois de Juin 1983. Paris: FIDH.
54. Martens, G. (1984) L'Afrique a-t-elle besoin de syndicats? Le Mois en Afrique vl. 0 (219–220), pp. 51–66.
55. Masseron, Jean-Paul (1966) Le Pouvoir et la Justice en Afrique noire francophone et à Madagascar. Paris: Col. Perdone.*
56. M'baye Keba (1978) Les droits de l'homme en Afrique in Vasak, K. Dimension internationale des droits de l'homme. Paris: UNESCO, pp. 645–663.
57. Menga, R.J. (1984), Geneva La Charte africaine des droits de l'homme et des peuples et l'ordre juridique concolais.
58. Mignon, T. (1974) Mission concernant la Guinée Equatoriale: août 1974 Paris: FIDH.
59. Muteba, T. (1985) Dossier: mes 395 jours dans les caves de l'Oua II au Zaire.
60. Ngom, B.S. (1984) Les droits de l'homme et l'Afrique. Paris: Silex.
61. ONU (1982) Un crime contre l'humanité (l'apartheid) E/CN. 4/1983/25 (1983); E/CN. 4/1984/48.
62. ONU (1985) Rapport de M. Marc Bossuyt (expert de la Belgique) sur les pratiques esclavagistes en Mauritanie, E/CN. 4/Sub.2/1985.
63. ONU (1983/1984). Rapport du Groupe des Trois créé conformément à la Convention internationale du Crime apartheid. E/CN.4/1983/25; E/CN.4/1984/48.
64. Paime-Ololo, Nono Lutula (1985) Le maréchal Mobutu du Zaire à l'an vingt de son pouvoir: démocratie, légalisme, opposition Le Mois en Afrique no. 229–230, pp. 47–56.
65. Puylagarde, B. (1983) Mission en République Arabe Egyptienne 30 Avril – 1er mai 1983. Bruxelles: Association Internationale des juristes Démocrates.
66. Raoul, M. (1983) Déclaration universelle des droits de l'homme et réalités africaines. Paris: UNESCO.
67. Rapport du Groupe des Trois créé conformément à la Convention internationale sur l'élimination et la repression du crime apartheid 1983 E/CN.4/1983/25.; E/CN.4/1984/48.
68. Weber, A. (1984) Procès de Bahai (Maroc) Rapport de mission d'observation judicaire. FIDH.

* We are grateful to Mr. S.C. Konaté of Mission du Sénégal, Genève for drawing our attention to these works.

PART VI

Appendices

APPENDIX I

Status of Ratification of Some of the Instruments as at 31 December 1986

The particulars below were compiled from the United Nations publication, Multilateral Treaties Deposited With The Secretary-General (ST/LEG/SER. E/5).

Key

1. International Covenant on Economic, Social and Cultural Rights.
2. International Covenant on Civil and Political Rights.
3. Optional Protocol to the International Covenant on Civil and Political Rights.
4. Convention on the Prevention and Punishment of the Crime of Genocide.
5. Convention Relating to the Status of Refugees.
6. Convention on the Political Rights of Women.
7. Convention on Consent to Marriage, Minimum Age for Marriage and Registration of Marriages.
8. International Convention on the Elimination of All Forms of Racial Discrimination.
9. Protocol Relating to the Status of Refugees.
10. Convention on the Elimination of All Forms of Discrimination against Women.
11. International Convention on the Suppression and Punishment of the Crime of Apartheid.
12. Convention Against Torture and other Cruel, Inhuman or Degrading Treatment or Punishment.
13. African Charter on Human and Peoples' Rights.

X. Accession/Ratification
S. Signature

	1	2	3	4	5	6	7	8	9	10	11	12	13
Algeria	S	S		X	X			X	X		X	S	
Angola					X	X			X	X			
Benin					X		X	S	X	S	X		X
Botswana					X			X	X				X
Burundi					X			X	X	S	X		
Burkina Faso				X	X		X	X	X		X		X
Cape Verde								X		X	X		
Central African Republic	X	X	X		X	X		X	X		X		X
Chad					X			X	X		X		X
Comoros													X
Congo	X	X	X		X	X			X	X	X		X
Djibouti					X				X				
Egypt	X	X		X	X	X		X	X	X	X	X	X
Equatorial Guinea										X			X
Ethiopia				X	X	X		X	X	X			
Gabon	X	X		X	X	X		X	X	X	X	S	X
Gambia	X	X		X	X			X	X	S	X	S	X
Ghana				X	X	X		X	X	X			
Guinea	X	X	S		X	X	X	X	X	X	X	S	X
Guinea-Bissau					X				X	X			X
Ivory Coast					X			X	X				
Kenya	X	X			X				X	X	S		
Lesotho				X	X	X		X	X	S	X		X
Liberia	S	S		X	X	S		X	X	X	X		
Libyan Arab Jamahiriya	X	X						X			X		
Madagascar	X	X	X		X	X		X		S	X		
Malawi					X								
Mali	X	X		X	X	X	X	X	X	X	X		X
Mauritania					X			S					X
Mauritius	X	X	X		X			X		X			
Morocco	X	X		X	X	X		X	X		S		
Mozambique					X	X		X		X			
Namibia (U.N. Council for Namibia)								X		X			
Niger	X	X	X		X	X	X	X	X		X		X
Nigeria					X	X		X	X	X	X		X
Rwanda	X	X		X	X			X	X	X	X		X
Sao Tome and Principe					X			X		X			X
Senegal	X	X	X	X	X	X		X	X	X	X	X	X
Seychelles					X			X	X	X			
Sierra Leone					X	X		X	X			S	X
Somalia					X			X	X		X		X
Sudan	X	X			X			X	X		X	S	X
Swaziland						X		X	X				
Togo	X	X		X	X			X	X	X	X		X
Tunisia	X	X		X	X	X	X	X	X	X	X		X
Uganda					X			X	X	X	X	X	X
United Republic of Cameroon	X	X	X	X	X			X	X	S	X	X	

	1	2	3	4	5	6	7	8	9	10	11	12	13
United Republic of Tanzania	X	X		X	X	X		X	X	X	X		X
Zaire	X	X	X	X	X	X		X	X	X	X		
Zambia	X	X	X		X	X		X	X	X	X		X
Zimbabwe					X				X				X

APPENDIX II

Declarations, Reservations and Objections*

1. INTERNATIONAL COVENANT ON ECONOMIC, SOCIAL AND CULTURAL RIGHTS

Congo

The Government of the People's Republic of the Congo declares that it does not consider itself bound by the provisions of article 13, paragraphs 3 and 4 . . .

Paragraphs 3 and 4 of article 13 of the International Covenant on Economic, Social and Cultural Rights embody the principle of freedom of education by allowing parents the liberty to choose for their children schools other than those established by the public authorities. Those provisions also authorize individuals to establish and direct educational institutions.

In our country, such provisions are inconsistent with the principle of nationalization of education and with the monopoly granted to the State in that area.

Guinea

In accordance with the principle whereby all States whose policies are guided by the purposes and principles of the Charter of the United Nations are entitled to become parties to covenants affecting the interests of the international community, the Government of the Republic of Guinea considers that the provisions of article 26, paragraph 1, of the International Covenant on Economic, Social and Cultural Rights are contrary to the principle of the universality of international treaties and the democratization of international relations.

The Government of the Republic of Guinea likewise considers that article 1,

---

* The dates of receipt by the Secretary-General of the communications notifying the objections, other than those formulated at the time of ratification or accession, are shown in brackets after their texts.

paragraph 3, and the provisions of article 14 of that instrument are contrary to the provisions of the Charter of the United Nations, in general, and United Nations resolutions on the granting of independence to colonial countries and peoples, in particular.

The above provisions are contrary to the Declaration on Principles of International Law Concerning Friendly Relations and Co-operation among States contained in General Assembly resolution 2625 (XXV), pursuant to which every State has the duty to promote realization of the principle of equal rights and self-determination of peoples in order to put an end to colonialism.

Kenya

While the Kenya Government recognizes and endorses the principles laid down in paragraph 2 of article 10 of the Covenant, the present circumstances obtaining in Kenya do not render necessary or expedient the imposition of those principles by legislation.

Libyan Arab Jamahiriya

The acceptance and the accession to this Covenant by the Libyan Arab Republic shall in no way signify a recognition of Israel or be conducive to entry by the Libyan Arab Republic into such dealings with Israel as are regulated by the Covenant.

Madagascar

The Government of Madagascar states that it reserves the right to postpone the application of article 13, paragraph 2, of the Covenant, more particularly in so far as relates to primary education, since, while the Malagasy Government fully accepts the principles embodied in the said paragraph and undertakes to take the necessary steps to apply them in their entirety at the earliest possible date, the problems of implementation, and particularly the financial implications, are such that full application of the principles in question cannot be guaranteed at this stage.

Rwanda

The Rwandese Republic [is] bound, however, in respect of education, only by the provisions of its Constitution.

Zambia

The Government of the Republic of Zambia states that it reserves the right to postpone the application of article 13 (2) (a) of the Covenant, in so far as it relates to primary education; since, while the Government of the Republic of Zambia fully accepts the principles embodied in the same article and undertakes to take the necessary steps to apply them in their entirety, the problems of implementation, and particularly the financial implications, are such that full application of the principles in question cannot be guaranteed at this stage.

2. INTERNATIONAL COVENANT ON CIVIL AND POLITICAL RIGHTS

Congo

The Government of the People's Republic of Congo declares that it does not consider itself bound by the provisions of article 11 . . .

Article 11 of the International Covenant on Civil and Political Rights is quite incompatible with articles 386 *et seq.* of the Congolese Code of Civil, Commercial, Administrative and Financial Procedure, derived from Act 51/83 of 21 April 1983. Under those provisions, in matters of private law, decisions or orders emanating from conciliation proceedings may be enforced through imprisonment for debt when other means of enforcement have failed, when the amount due exceeds 20,000 CFA francs and when the debtor, between 18 and 60 years of age, makes himself insolvent in bad faith.

Gambia

For financial reasons free legal assistance for accused persons is limited in our constitution to persons charged with capital offences only. The Government of the Gambia therefore wishes to enter a reservation in respect of article 14 (3) d of the Covenant in question.

Libyan Arab Jamahiriya

The acceptance and the accession to this Covenant by the Libyan Arab Republic shall in no way signify a recognition of Israel or be conducive to entry by the Libyan Arab Republic into such dealings with Israel as are regulated by the Covenant.

Senegal

The Goverment of Senegal declares, under article 41 of the International Covenant on Civil and Political Rights, that it recognizes the competence of the Human Rights Committee referred to in article 28 of the Said Covenant to receive and consider communications submitted by another State Party, provided that such State Party has, not less than twelve months prior to the submission by it of a communication relating to Senegal, made a declaration under article 41 recognizing the competence of the Committee to receive and consider communications relating to itself.

4. CONVENTION ON THE PREVENTION AND PUNISHMENT OF THE CRIME OF GENOCIDE

Algeria

The Democratic and Popular Republic of Algeria does not consider itself bound by article IX of the Convention, which confers on the International Court of Justice jurisdiction in all disputes relating to the said Convention.

The Democratic and Popular Republic of Algeria declares that no provision of article VI of the said Convention shall be interpreted as depriving its tribunals of jurisdiction in cases of genocide or other acts enumerated in article III which have been committed in its territory or as conferring such jurisdiction on foreign tribunals.

International tribunals may, as an exceptional measure, be recognized as having jurisdiction, in cases in which the Algerian Government has given its express approval.

The Democratic and Popular Republic of Algeria declares that it does not accept the terms of article XII of the Convention and considers that all the provisions of the said Convention should apply to Non-Self-Governing Territories, including Trust Territories.

Morocco

With reference to article VI, the Government of His Majesty the King considers that Moroccan courts and tribunals alone have jurisdiction with respect to acts of genocide committed within the territory of the Kingdom of Morocco.

The competence of international courts may be admitted exceptionally in cases with respect to which the Moroccan Government has given its specific agreement.

With reference to article IX, the Moroccan Government states that no dispute relating to the interpretation, application or fulfilment of the present

Convention can be brought before the International Court of Justice, without the prior agreement of the parties to the dispute.

Rwanda

The Rwandese Republic does not consider itself as bound by article IX of the Convention.

5. CONVENTION RELATING TO THE STATUS OF REFUGEES

Angola

Declarations.

The Government of the People's Republic of Angola also declares that the provisions of the Convention shall be applicable in Angola provided that they are not contrary to or incompatible with the constitutional and legal provisions in force in the People's Republic of Angola, especially as regards articles 7, 13, 15, 18 and 24 of the Convention. Those provisions shall not be construed so as to accord to any category of aliens resident in Angola more extensive rights than are enjoyed by Angolan citizens.

The Government of the People's Republic of Angola also considers that the provisions of articles 8 and 9 of the Convention cannot be construed so as to limit its right to adopt in respect of a refugee or group of refugees such measures as it deems necessary to safeguard national interests and to ensure respect for its sovereignty, whenever circumstances so require.

Reservations.

Ad article 17: The Government of the People's Republic of Angola accepts the obligations set forth in article 17, provided that:
(a) Paragraph 1 of this article shall not be interpreted to mean that refugees must enjoy the same privileges as may be accorded to nationals of countries with which the People's Republic of Angola has signed special cooperation agreements;
(b) Paragraph 2 of this article shall be construed as a recommendation and not as an obligation.

Ad article 26: The Government of the People's Republic of Angola reserves the right to prescribe, transfer or circumscribe the place of residence of certain refugees or groups of refugees, and to restrict their freedom of movement, whenever considerations of national or international order make it advisable to do so.

Botswana

'Subject to the reservation of articles 7, 17, 26, 31, 32 and 34 and paragraph 1 of article 12 of the Convention.'

Egypt

The Government of Egypt accedes to the Convention with reservations in respect of article 12 (1), articles 20 and 22 (1), and articles 23 and 24.

Nature of the reservations made by the Arab Republic of Egypt on some articles of the Convention relating to the status of refugees signed at Geneva on 28 July 1951 and to the Protocol relating to the status of refugees signed at New York on 31 January 1967

1. Egypt formulated a reservation to article 12 (1) because it is in contradiction with the internal laws of Egypt. This article provides that the personal status of a refugee shall be governed by the law of the country of his domicile or, failing this, of his residence. This formula contradicts article 25 of the Egyptian civil code, which reads as follows:

'The judge declares the applicable law in the case of persons without nationality or with more than one nationality at the same time. In the case of persons where there is proof, in accordance with Egypt, of Egyptian nationality, and at the same time in accordance with one or more foreign countries, of nationality of that country, the Egyptian law must be applied.'

The competent Egyptian authorities are not in a position to amend this article (25) of the civil code.

2. Concerning articles 20, 22 (paragraph 1), 23 and 24 of the Convention of 1951, the competent Egyptian authorities had reservations because these articles consider the refugee as equal to the national.

We made this general reservation to avoid any obstacle which might affect the discretionary authority of Egypt in granting privileges to refugees on a case-by-case basis. (24 September 1981)

Ethiopia

'The provisions of articles 8, 9, 17 (2) and 22 (1) of the Convention are recognized only as recommendations and not as legally binding obligations.'

Objection.
'The Provisional Military Government of Socialist Ethiopia wishes to place on record its objection to the declaration (made by Somalia upon accession) and that it does not recognize it as valid on the ground that there are no Somali territories under alien domination.' (10 January 1979).

Mozambique

Reservations.

In respect of articles 13 and 22:

The Government of Mozambique will take these provisions as simple recommendation not binding it to accord to refugees the same treatment as is accorded to Mozambicans with respect to elementary education and property.

In respect of articles 17 and 19:

The Government of Mozambique will interpret [these provisions] to the effect that it is not required to grant privileges from obligation to obtain a work permit.

As regards article 15:

The Government of Mozambique will not be bound to accord to refugees or group of refugees resident in its territory more extensive rights than those enjoyed by nationals with respect to the right of association and it reserves the right to restrict them in the interest of national security.

As regards article 26:

The Government of Mozambique reserves its right to designate place or places for principal residence for refugees or to restrict their freedom of movement whenever considerations of national security make it advisable.

As regards article 34:

The Government of Mozambique does not consider itself bound to grant to refugees facilities greater than those granted to other categories of aliens in general, with respect to naturalization laws.

Madagascar

The provisions of article 7 (1) shall not be interpreted as requiring the same treatment as is accorded to nationals of countries with which the Malagasy Republic has concluded conventions of establishment or agreements on cooperation;

The provisions of articles 8 and 9 shall not be interpreted as forbidding the Malagasy Government to take, in time of war or other grave and exceptional circumstances, measures with regard to a refugee because of his nationality in the interests of national security.

The provisions of article 17 cannot be interpreted as preventing the application of the laws and regulations establishing the proportion of alien workers that employers are authorized to employ in Madagascar or affecting the obligations of such employers in connection with the employment of alien workers.

Rwanda

Reservation to article 26.
For reasons of public policy (ordre public), the Rwandese Republic reserves the right to determine the place of residence of refugees and to establish limits to their freedom of movement.

Sierra Leone

'The Government of Sierra Leone wishes to state with regard to article 17 (2) that Sierra Leone does not consider itself bound to grant to refugees the rights stipulated therein.'

'Further, with regard to article 17 as a whole, the Government of Sierra Leone wishes to state that it considers the article to be a recommendation only and not a binding obligation.'

'The Government of Sierra Leone wishes to state that it does not consider itself bound by the provisions of article 29, and it reserves the right to impose special taxes on aliens as provided for in the Constitution.'

Somalia

'The Government of the Somali Democratic Republic acceded to the Convention and Protocol on the understanding that nothing in the said Convention or Protocol will be construed to prejudice or adversely affect the national status, or political aspiration of displaced people from Somali Territories under alien domination.'

'It is in this spirit, that the Somali Democratic Republic will commit itself to respect the terms and provisions of the said Convention and Protocol.'

Sudan

With reservation as to article 26.

Uganda

(1) *In respect of article 7:* 'The Government of the Republic of Uganda understands this provision as not conferring any legal, political or other enforceable right upon refugees who, at any given time may be in Uganda. On the basis of this understanding the Government of the Republic of Uganda shall accord refugees such facilities and treatment as the Government of the Republic of Uganda shall in her absolute discretion, deem fit having regard to her own security, economic and social needs.'

(2) *In respect of articles 8 and 9:* 'The Government of the Republic of Uganda declares that the provisions of articles 8 and 9 are recognized by it as recommendations only.'

(3) *In respect of article 13:* 'The Government of the Republic of Uganda reserves to itself the right to abridge this provision without recourse to courts of law or abitral tribunals, national or international, if the Government of the Republic of Uganda deems such abridgement to be in the public interest.'

(4) *In respect of article 15:* The Government of the Republic of Uganda shall in the public interest have the full freedom to withhold any or all rights conferred by this article from any refugees as a class of residents within her territory.'

(5) *In respect of article 16:* 'The Government of the Republic of Uganda understands article 16 paragraphs 2 and 3 thereof as not requiring the Government of the Republic of Uganda to accord to a refugee in need of legal assistance, treatment more favourable than that extended to aliens generally in similar circumstances.'

(6) *In respect of article 17:* 'The obligation specified in article 17 to accord to refugees lawfully staying in the country in the same circumstances shall not be construed as extending to refugees the benefit of preferential treatment granted to nationals of the States who enjoy special privileges on account of existing or future treaties between Uganda and those countries, particularly States of the East African Community and the Organization of African Unity, in accordance with the provisions which govern such charters in this respect.'

(7) *In respect of article 25:* 'The Government of the Republic of Uganda understands that this article shall not require the Government of the Republic of Uganda to incur expenses on behalf of the refugees in connection with the granting of such assistance except in so far as such assistance is requested by and the resulting expense is reimbursed to the Government of the Republic of Uganda by the United Nations High Commissioner for Refugees or any other agency of the United Nations which may succeed it.'

(8) *In respect of article 32:* 'Without recourse to legal process the Government of the Republic of Uganda shall, in the public interest, have the unfettered right to expel any refugee in her territory and may at any time apply such internal measures as the Government may deem necessary in the circumstances; so however that, any action taken by the Government of the Republic of Uganda in this regard shall not operate to the prejudice of the provisions of article 33 of this Convention.'

Zambia

'Subject to the following reservations made pursuant to article 42 (1) of the Convention:

Article 17 (2)

'The Government of the Republic of Zambia wishes to state with regard to article 17, paragraph 2, that Zambia does not consider itself bound to grant to a refugee who fulfils any one of the conditions set out in subparagraphs (a) to (c) automatic exemption from the obligation to obtain a work permit.'

'Further, with regard to article 17 as a whole, Zambia does not wish to undertake to grant to refugees rights of wage-earning employment more favourable than those granted to aliens generally.'

Article 22 (1)

'The Government of the Republic of Zambia wishes to state that it considers article 22 (1) to be a recommendation only and not a binding obligation to accord to refugees the same treatment as is accorded to nationals with respect to elementary education.'

Article 26

'The Government of the Republic of Zambia wishes to state with regard to article 26 that it reserves the right to designate a place or places of residence for refugees.'

Article 28

'The Government of the Republic of Zambia wishes to state with regard to article 28 that Zambia considers itself not bound to issue a travel document with a return clause in cases where a country of second asylum has accepted or indicated its willingness to accept a refugee from Zambia.'

Zimbabwe

'1. The Government of the Republic of Zimbabwe declares that it is not bound by any of the reservations to the Convention relating to the Status of Refugees, the application of which had been extended by the Government of the United Kingdom to its territory before the attainment of independence.'

'2. The Government of the Republic of Zimbabwe wishes to state with regard to article 17, paragraph 2, that it does not consider itself bound to grant a refugee who fulfils any of the conditions set out in subparagraphs *(a)* to (c) automatic exemption from the obligation to obtain a work permit. In addition, with regard to article 17 as a whole, the Republic of Zimbabwe does not undertake to grant to refugees rights of wage-earning employment more favourable than those granted to aliens generally.'

'3. The Government of the Republic of Zimbabwe wishes to state that it considers article 22 (1) as being a recommendation only and not an obligation to accord to refugees the same treatment as it accords to nationals with respect to elementary education.'

'4. The Government of the Republic of Zimbabwe considers articles 23 and 24 as being recommendations only.'

'5. The Government of the Republic of Zimbabwe wishes to state with regard to article 26 that it reserves the right to designate a place or places of residence for refugees.'

Objections

Ethiopia

The Provisional Military Government of Socialist Ethiopia wishes to place on record its objection to the declaration [made by Somalia upon accession] and that is does not recognize it as valid on the ground that there are no Somali territories under alien domination.

6. CONVENTION ON THE POLITICAL RIGHTS OF WOMEN

Lesotho

'Article III is accepted subject to reservation, pending notification of withdrawal in any case, so far as it relates to: Matters regulated by Basotho Law and Custom.'

Mauritius

'The Government of Mauritius hereby declares that it does not consider itself bound by article III of the Convention in so far as that Article applies to recruitment to and conditions of service in the armed forces or to jury service.'

Morocco

The consent of all the parties concerned is required for the referral of any dispute to the International Court of Justice.

Sierra Leone

'In acceding to this Convention, the Government of Sierra Leone hereby declares that it does not consider itself bound by article III in so far as that article applies to recruitment to and conditions of service in the Armed Forces or to jury service.'

Swaziland

'(a) Article III of the Convention shall have no application as regards remuneration for women in certain posts in the Civil Service of the Kingdom of Swaziland;

'(b) The Convention shall have no application to matters which are regulated by Swaziland Law and Custom in accordance with Section 62 (2) of the Constitution of the Kingdom of Swaziland.'

Tunisia

[Article IX] For any dispute to be referred to the International Court of Justice, the agreement of all the parties to the dispute shall be necessary in every case.

Objections

Ethiopia

Objection to the reservations in respect of articles VII and IX by the Governments of Albania, Bulgaria, the Byelorussian Socialist Soviet Republic, Czechoslovakia, Hungary, Poland, Romania, Ukrainian Soviet Socialist Republic and Union of Soviet Socialist Republics.

8. INTERNATIONAL CONVENTION ON THE ELIMINATION OF ALL FORMS OF RACIAL DISCRIMINATION

Egypt

'The United Arab Republic does not consider itself bound by the provisions of article 22 of the Convention, under which any dispute between two or more States Parties with respect to the interpretation or application of the Convention is, at the request of any of the parties to the dispute, to be referred to the International Court of Justice for decision, and it states that, in each individual case, the consent of all parties to such a dispute is necessary for referring the dispute to the International Court of Justice.

Libyan Arab Jamahiriya

'(a) The Kingdom of Libya does not consider itself bound by the provisions of article 22 of the Convention, under which any dispute between two or more States Parties with respect to the interpretation or application of the Convention is, at the request of any of the parties to the dispute, to be referred to the International Court of Justice for decision, and it states that, in each individual case, the consent of all parties to such a dispute is necessary for referring the dispute to the International Court of Justice.

(b) It is understood that the accession to this Convention does not mean in any way a recognition of Israel by the Government of the Kingdom of Libya. Furthermore, no treaty relations will arise between the Kingdom of Libya and Israel.'

Madagascar

The Government of the Malagasy Republic does not consider itself bound by the provisions of article 22 of the Convention, under which any dispute between two or more States Parties with respect to the interpretation or application of the Convention is, at the request of any of the parties to the dispute, to be referred to the International Court of Justice for decision, and states that, in each individual case, the consent of all parties to such a dispute is necessary for referral of the dispute to the International Court.

Morocco

The Kingdom of Morocco does not consider itself bound by the provisions of article 22 of the Convention, under which any dispute between two or more States Parties with respect to the interpretation or application of the Convention is, at the request of any of the parties to the dispute, to be referred to the International Court of Justice for decision. The Kingdom of Morocco states that, in each individual case, the consent of all parties to such a dispute is necessary for referring the dispute to the International Court of Justice.

Mozambique

Reservation.
The People's Republic of Mozambique does not consider to be bound by the provision of article 22 and wishes to restate that for the submission of any dispute to the International Court of Justice for decision in terms of the said article, the consent of all parties to such a dispute is necessary in each individual case.

Rwanda

The Rwandese Republic does not consider itself as bound by article 22 of the Convention.

Senegal

In accordance with [article 14], The Government of Senegal declares that it recognizes the competence of the Committee (on the Elimination of Racial Discrimination) to receive and consider communications from individuals within its jurisdiction claiming to be victims of a violation by Senegal of any of the rights set forth in the Convention on the Elimination of All Forms of Racial Discrimination.

Objections

Ethiopia

The Provisional Military Government of Socialist Ethiopia should like to reiterate that the Government of the People's Republic of Kampuchea is the sole legitimate representative of the People of Kampuchea and as such it alone has the authority to act on behalf of Kampuchea.

The Provisional Military Government of Socialist Ethiopia, therefore, considers the ratification of the so-called 'Government of Democratic Kampuchea' to be null and void. (25 January 1984)

9. PROTOCOL RELATING TO THE STATUS OF REFUGEES

Angola

The Government of Angola, in accordance with article VII, paragraph 1, declares that it does not consider itself bound by article IV of the Protocol, concerning settlement of disputes relating to the interpretation of the Protocol.

Botswana

'Subject to the reservation in respect of article IV of the said Protocol and in respect of the application in accordance with article I thereof of the provisions of articles 7, 17, 26, 31, 32 and 34 and paragraph 1 of article 12 of the

Convention relating to the Status of Refugees, done at Geneva on 28 July 1951.'

Burundi

In acceding to this Protocol, the Government of the Republic of Burundi enters the following reservations:

1. The provisions of article 22 are accepted, in respect of elementary education, only
(a) In so far as they apply to public education, and not to private education;
(b) On the understanding that the treatment applicable to refugees shall be the most favourable accorded to nationals of other States.

2. The provisions of article 17 (1) and (2) are accepted as mere recommendations and, in any event, shall not be interpreted as necessarily involving the régime accorded to nationals of countries with which the Republic of Burundi may have concluded regional, customs, economic or political agreements.

3. The provisions of article 26 are accepted only subject to the reservation that refugees:
(a) Do not choose their place of residence in a region bordering on their country of origin;
(b) Refrain, in any event, when exercising their right to move freely, from any activity or incursion of a subversive nature with respect to the country of which they are nationals.

Congo

The Protocol is accepted with the exception of article IV.

Ethiopia

Subject to the following reservation in respect of the application, under article I of the Protocol, of the Convention relating to the Status of Refugees, done at Geneva on 28 July 1951:

'The provisions of articles 8, 9, 17 (2) and 22 (1) of the Convention are recognized only as recommendations and not as legally binding obligations.'

Ghana

'The government of Ghana does not consider itself bound by article IV of the Protocol regarding the settlement of disputes.'

Rwanda

Reservation to article IV:
For the settlement of any dispute between States Parties, recourse may be had to the International Court of Justice only with the prior agreement of the Rwandese Republic.

Somalia

(For the text of the declaration, see under the Convention relating to the Status of Refugees, supra p. 417.)

Swaziland

Subject to the following reservations in respect of the application of the Convention relating to the Status of Refugees, done at Geneva on 28 July 1951, under article I of the Protocol:

'(1) The Government of the Kingdom of Swaziland is not in a position to assume obligations as contained in article 22 of the said Convention, and therefore will not consider itself bound by the provisions therein;

'(2) Similarly, the Government of the Kingdom of Swaziland is not in a position to assume the obligations of article 34 of the said Convention, and must expressly reserve the right not to apply the provisions therein.'

and with the following declaration:

'The Government of the Kingdom of Swaziland deems it essential to draw attention to the accession herewith as a Member of the United Nations, and not as a party to the said Convention by reason of succession or otherwise.'

Uganda

(Same reservations as for the Convention relating to the Status of Refugees: see p. 417.)

United Republic of Tanzania

'... Subject to the reservation, hereby made, that the provisions of Article IV of the Protocol shall not be applicable to the United Republic of Tanzania except within the explicit consent of the Government of the United Republic of Tanzania.'

Objections

Ethiopia

For the text of the objection, see under the Convention relating to the Status of Regugees, supra p. 423.

10. CONVENTION ON THE ELIMINATION OF ALL FORMS OF DISCRIMINATION AGAINST WOMEN

Egypt

Reservations made upon signature and confirmed upon ratification:

In respect of article 9.

Reservation to the text of article 9, paragraph 2, concerning the granting to women of equal rights with men with respect to the nationality of their children, without prejudice to the acquisition by a child born of a marriage of the nationality of his father. This is in order to prevent a child's acquisition of two nationalities where his parents are of different nationalities, since this may be prejudicial to his future. It is clear that the child's acquisition of his father's nationality is the procedure most suitable for the child and that this does not infringe upon the principle of equality between men and women, since it is customary for a woman to agree, upon marrying an alien, that her children shall be of the father's nationality.

In respect of article 16.

Reservation to the text of article 16 concerning the equality of men and women in all matters relating to marriage and family relations during the marriage and upon its dissolution, without prejudice to the Islamic Sharia's provisions whereby women are accorded rights equivalent to those of their spouses so as to ensure a just balance between them. This is out of respect for the sacrosanct nature of the firm religious beliefs which govern marital relations in Egypt and which may not be called in question and in view of the fact that one of the most important bases of these relations is an equivalency of rights and duties so as to ensure complementarity which guarantees true equality between the spouses. The provisions of the Sharia lay down that the husband shall pay bridal money to the wife and maintain her fully and shall also make a payment to her upon divorce, whereas the wife retains full rights over her property and is not obliged to spend anything on her keep. The Sharia therefore restricts the wife's rights to divorce by making it contingent on a judge's ruling, whereas no such restriction is laid down in the case of the husband.

In respect of article 29.
The Egyptian delegation also maintains the reservation contained in article 29, paragraph 2, concerning the right of a State signatory to the Convention to declare that it does not consider itself bound by paragraph 1 of that article concerning the submission to an arbitral body of any dispute which may arise between States concerning the interpretation or application of the Convention. This is in order to avoid being bound by the system of arbitration in this field.

Reservation made upon ratification:

General reservation on article 2.
The Arab Republic of Egypt is willing to comply with the content of this article, provided that such compliance does not run counter to the Islamic Sharia.

Mauritius

The Government of Mauritius does not consider itself bound by sub-paragraph (b) and (d) of paragraph 1 of article 11 and subparagraph (g) of paragraph 1 of article 16.
The Government of Mauritius does not consider itself bound by paragraph 1 of article 29 of the Convention, in pursuance of paragraph 2 of article 29.

11. INTERNATIONAL CONVENTION ON THE SUPPRESSION AND PUNISHMENT OF THE CRIME OF APARTHEID

Mozambique

The People's Republic of Mozambique interprets article 12 of the Convention as to mean that the submission of any dispute concerning the interpretation and application of the Convention to the International Court of Justice shall be at the previous consent and request of all the parties to the dispute.